BREXITLAND

Long-term social and demographic changes – and the conflicts they create – continue to transform British politics. In this accessible and authoritative book Sobolewska and Ford show how deep the roots of this polarisation and volatility run, drawing out decades of educational expansion and rising ethnic diversity as key drivers in the emergence of new divides within the British electorate over immigration, identity and diversity. They argue that choices made by political parties from the 1960s onwards have mobilised these divisions into politics, first through conflicts over immigration, then through conflicts over the European Union, culminating in the 2016 EU Referendum. Providing a comprehensive and far-reaching view of a country in turmoil, *Brexitland* explains how and why this happened, for students, researchers and anyone who wants to better understand the remarkable political times in which we live.

Maria Sobolewska FRSA is a Professor of Political Science, and Deputy Director of the Cathie Marsh Institute for Social Research, at the University of Manchester. She writes about race and ethnicity in British politics, from elections to political representation. She is co-author of *The Political Integration of Ethnic Minorities in Britain* (2013).

Robert Ford FRSA is a Professor of Political Science at the University of Manchester. He is an expert on immigration, public opinion and party politics in Britain. His first book, *Revolt on the Right* (2013), was named Political Book of the Year in 2015. He writes regularly on British electoral politics for national and international media outlets.

'A sharp, accessible investigation of the key fault lines of modern British politics: education, immigration, age and identity.'

Adam Boulton, Sky News

'Maria Sobolewska and Robert Ford have produced the best account I have read of our cultural civil wars. The work is not just an explanation of the way we live now, but of how we reached a state of institutionalised rage and why peace will be so hard to find.'

Nick Cohen, The Spectator and The Observer

'Brexitland brilliantly unpicks the old and new forces that shaped our brittle political age. Who is exploiting the anger? And is it with us for good? A fascinating and convincing study: essential reading for anyone wanting to understand why tolerance of the other side in British politics seems to have disappeared. How did our political background turn so ugly and intolerant? Brexitland delves deep into decades of history and attitudes to race and ethnic identity to answer that question and does it with style. Sobolewska and Ford have written the new political bible of our times: how did we stop debating and start shouting? Can normal service resume? Brexitland is a razor sharp and compelling answer to those questions.'

Gary Gibbon, Channel 4 News

'A brilliant, original, powerful book. For Remainers, Brexiters or indeed anyone interested in why divided Britain cut itself adrift from the EU, this is unmissable. It is also totally riveting.'

Toby Helm, The Observer

'Whether we like it or not, we are all living in Brexitland. In the forensic detail Sobolewska and Ford plot the long road of social change which led us here. En route they look ahead to where the UK's explosive culture wars would take us next. Essential reading for those not wearing blinkers.'

Helen Lewis, author of Difficult Women

Brexitland

Identity, Diversity and the Reshaping of British Politics

MARIA SOBOLEWSKA
University of Manchester

ROBERT FORD
University of Manchester

CAMBRIDGE
UNIVERSITY PRESS

University Printing House, Cambridge CB2 8BS, United Kingdom

One Liberty Plaza, 20th Floor, New York, NY 10006, USA

477 Williamstown Road, Port Melbourne, VIC 3207, Australia

314–321, 3rd Floor, Plot 3, Splendor Forum, Jasola District Centre, New Delhi – 110025, India

79 Anson Road, #06-04/06, Singapore 079906

Cambridge University Press is part of the University of Cambridge.

It furthers the University's mission by disseminating knowledge in the pursuit of education, learning, and research at the highest international levels of excellence.

www.cambridge.org
Information on this title: www.cambridge.org/9781108473576
DOI: 10.1017/9781108562485

First published 2020

Printed in the United Kingdom by TJ Books Limited, Padstow Cornwall

A catalogue record for this publication is available from the British Library.

ISBN 978-1-108-47357-6 Hardback
ISBN 978-1-108-46190-0 Paperback

CONTENTS

FIGURES AND TABLES

Figures

Tables

ACKNOWLEDGEMENTS

They say it takes a village to raise a child. It takes a village to write a book too. There are many people to thank, but, first and foremost, we would like to thank all of the survey respondents who have, over decades, sacrificed their precious time so that we can understand better what people think, and how people decide what to do when they arrive in the polling stations. Second, we would like to thank our children for their immense patience through many months of the book-writing process. Zofia and Adam: we promise we can now make our dinner-table conversations a Brexit-free zone. We would also like to thank the ESRC for their generous grant funding (ES/R000522/122/1), and UK in a Changing Europe for their support of our research (in particular, Anand Menon). We also want to thank Matthew Goodwin, who was our co-investigator on the grant. Thanks are owed to our many colleagues who have listened and offered feedback over almost two years of presentations, including the audiences at various conferences, and seminars at the Universities of Montreal, Toronto, Durham, RHUL, QMUL, UCL, Oxford and, of course, Manchester University. In particular, we would like to thank Ron Johnston, who very kindly allowed us to use his graph on party campaign spending, and whose recent death has saddened us immensely towards the very end of this project. He has been one of the smartest, loveliest and most generous colleagues. We feel very lucky to have known him. Special mention also goes to the current British Election Study (BES) team – Geoff Evans, Ed Fieldhouse, Jane Green, Jon Mellon, Chris Prosser, Herman Schmitt and Cees Van Der Eijk – for allowing us to ask questions of the sub-sample of BES online panel respondents for our survey, and for providing the rich and detailed survey data without which this book would not be possible. Thanks also go to YouGov for their diligent efforts fielding many academic surveys, including the BES online panel and our own more modest surveys. Other colleagues who also have our thanks for their collaboration, comments and thoughts on the various aspects of the work that went into this book are Ben Ansell, Tim Bale, Steve Ballinger, Andrew Barclay, Neema Begum, Matthew Bevington, Sara Binzer-Hobolt, Scott Blinder, Rosie Campbell, Leonardo Carella, Nick Cohen, Phil Cowley, Sir John Curtice, Chris Curtis, Rafaela Dancygier, Eldad Davidov, John Denham, Peter Thisted Dinesen, Michael Donnelley, Bobby Duffy, Patrick English, Justin Fisher, Steve Fisher, Peter Geohagen, Justin Gest, Eva Green, Ruth Grove-White, Armen Hakhverdian, Alison Harrell, John Harris, Anthony Heath, Marc Helbling, Toby Helm, Ailsa Henderson, Frederik Hjorth, Dan Hopkins, Jennifer Hudson, Elisabeth Ivarsflaten, Laurence Janta-Lipinski, Will Jennings, Sunder Katwala, Gavin Kelly, Michael Kenny, Omar Khan, Anouk Kootstra, Laurence Lessard-Phillips, Nick Lowles, Kitty Lymperopoulou, Nicole Martin, Rahsaan Maxwell, Adam McDonnell, Rebecca McKee, Iain McLean, Alison Park, Akash Paun, Nick Pearce, Jonathan Portes, Alice Ramos, Carolin Rapp, Harvey Redgrave, Jill Rutter, Shamit Saggar, Peter Schmidt, Paul Sniderman, Will Somerville, Ingrid Storm, Paula Surridge, Joe Twyman, Menno Van Setten, Alan Wager, Ian Warren, Paul Webster, Anthony Wells, Stuart Wilks-Heeg, Jennifer Williams and Robert Yates. Your ideas, questions and praise have been inspirational, as has all your own work, from which we learnt so much. We are sorry for the delays this book has produced on the projects we have with some of you – these will be our priority now! We also owe a huge debt to the vibrant and exciting intellectual community in the Democracy and Elections research cluster, with its ever-growing body of talented young people. We are so proud to be part of such a lively and talented group. We would like to thank, in particular, James Griffith for his help with the book's index.

We also want to thank the immensely patient, meticulous and supportive staff at Cambridge University Press – in particular, John Haslam, Tobias Ginsberg, Robert Judkins and our copy-editor Lyn Flight. We also thank our anonymous reviewers and the reader for their positive comments and helpful advice on improving the manuscript. Obviously, any remaining errors are our sole responsibility.

One needs to remain sane to be able to complete a long project such as a book, and especially so if the book is about the ever-shifting sands of British politics. For keeping us sane and happy throughout, no matter how many elections we had thrown at us and needed to add to the book, we would like to thank our friends and family, who, much like our children, had to put up with many arguments about Brexit, and a fair amount of moaning. You know who you are – we thank you for your friendship, help with school runs, fun holidays and all the wine and beer. In particular, we'd like to thank Vikki and Malcolm, especially for looking after our kids at a crucial book-writing moment – without you, this book would have never seen the light of day – and Rachel for volunteering to be the 'general-audience guinea pig'. Malcolm, you are also thanked in footnote 73. Maria's mum is also to be thanked for all her help, and we are hoping her book will come out not long after ours! Rob's mum and brothers have our gratitude for patiently enduring many long evenings of political discussion over the years.

We would like to dedicate this book to the memory of both of our late fathers, Joe Ford and Marek Sobolewski, in whose long shadows we labour, and on whose shoulders we stand.

1 INTRODUCTION: HOW BRITAIN BECAME BREXITLAND

> One temptation should be avoided – to seek, month after month, to prove that membership of the Community has created all Britain's ills ... Above all we should avoid creating a new, semi-permanent rift in British society, between pro- and anti-Europeans.
>
> *The Guardian*, 1 January 1973 (the day Britain joined the EEC)

Brexit is not Year Zero

As dawn broke on Friday, 24 June 2016, a nation struggled to make sense of the dramatic events which had unfolded overnight. From welcoming the 'Birth of New Britain' in the *Telegraph*, to the *Daily Mail*'s praise for the 'quiet people of Britain [who] rose up against an arrogant out of touch political class', to the panicky 'What the hell happens now?' question posed on the front of the *Daily Mirror*,[1] the media were as divided in their reactions to Brexit as they were in their pre-referendum allegiances. *The Times* called it an earthquake and warned that it threatened the break-up of the Union, and as the markets took a tumble in response, foreign newspapers painted Britain as an international laughing stock.[2]

---

[1] Available at: www.theguardian.com/media/gallery/2016/jun/25/brexit-front-pages-in-pictures, last accessed 28 October 2019.

[2] The *New York Times* used a picture of a John Cleese lookalike stepping off the edge of a cliff in his famous Ministry of Silly Walks suit, and *Libération* found a particularly ridiculous picture of Boris Johnson to accompany their sarcastic

Plenty of more sober and reflective analysis has appeared in the years since those breathless first reactions, as the nation's journalists, politicians and academics have wrestled with the causes and consequences of the most dramatic and disruptive exercise in direct democracy Britain has ever seen. While these accounts offer a rich tapestry of different perspectives, most take a narrow view of the referendum, starting their analysis in the run-up to the campaign, and finishing it soon after the votes were cast. The longer-term social changes and political conflicts that brought us to this point are left in the background. This book moves them to centre stage. What happened on 23 June was not solely a product of the referendum campaign, and the deep divisions laid bare by the vote will not be healed by Britain's exit from the European Union (EU).[3] Brexit is the expression of conflicts which have been building in the electorate for decades, not their cause. 'Brexitland' is the name we give to our divided nation, but while Brexit gives a name and a voice to these divides, they are not new. They have their roots in trends which have been running for generations – educational expansion, mass immigration and ethnic change.

The EU Referendum itself was not so much a moment of creation, but rather a moment of awakening: a moment when the social and political processes long underway finally became obvious, and the different groups of voters finally recognised themselves as two distinct and opposed camps. We cannot understand this moment without understanding what forces it awakened, so much of this book focuses on the decades before the referendum. We show how demographic change and rising conflicts over identity put mounting pressures on the mainstream parties, but we also seek to explain why they proved able, for a while, to respond to these pressures. We want to

---

'Good Luck' heading, available at: www.theguardian.com/media/gallery/2016/jun/25/brexit-front-pages-in-pictures, last accessed 2 April 2020.

[3] Nor would returning to the EU heal these divides.

understand why the dam eventually burst, but we also want to know why it did not burst earlier.

In looking both to the long term and the short term, we go beyond explaining how Britain arrived at the decision to leave the EU and show how the changes which drove Brexit will continue to generate volatility and political change for many years to come. We map out how the referendum made voters acutely aware of new identity divisions and helped to forge new partisan identities rooted in these divisions. These identities are already having major effects on how British voters think of themselves, how they judge political parties and the 'other side'. These divides may continue to exert a disruptive influence for many years to come.

Our argument is presented in three parts. The first focuses on the long-term drivers of identity conflict: demographic change and its political consequences, in particular, educational expansion and ethnic change. We show how a tendency to divide the world into groups – ethnocentrism – shapes the views of different groups of voters and is structured in particular by voters' education levels and socialisation experiences. We then show how conflicts rooted in ethnocentrism had a profoundly disruptive impact in an earlier period of post-Second World War politics, as ethnocentric voters mobilised in opposition to the first wave of non-white migration.

The second part builds on this picture by discussing the political and social changes of the past twenty years, which have again mobilised these demographic divides into political competition. These include the gradual erosion of links between the traditional political parties and the electorate, the return of conflicts over immigration to the top of the political agenda, the emergence of a new party (UKIP) mobilising one pole of the identity divide, and the consolidation of voters at the other pole of the identity divide behind Labour.

The third part focuses on the EU Referendum and its aftermath. Brexit has proved to be a moment of awakening, revealing identity conflicts and forging new political identities rooted in divides over education, age and ethnicity which cut across the traditional dividing lines of class, income and ideology. We also compare the disruptive impact of the EU Referendum in England and Wales with the very different patterns of political change in Scotland, where the impact of Brexit was layered on top of the disruptions generated by the 2014 Independence Referendum. The mobilisation of Scottish voters in the Independence Referendum itself also highlights the power of campaigns and political parties to channel similar social and identity divisions into very different outcomes. Parties do not just passively respond to social and demographic change – they help to shape its political meaning and electoral effects. We then consider the disruptive and volatile voter shifts seen in the two general elections since Brexit and contemplate some of the paths political change may take in the years to come. Finally, in the conclusion we reflect on the implications of the Brexitland story for our broader understanding of political change, showing that while the mobilisation of identity conflicts around the question of EU membership is unique to Britain, the divisions over education, ethnocentrism and identity which it has laid bare are also visible in other countries, and have growing potential to drive electoral disruptions elsewhere too. The triggering events which mobilise identity conflicts are particular to each country, but the underlying demographic trends creating such conflicts are common across many societies. We also reflect on the broader implications of Brexitland identity conflicts for British politics beyond elections, considering how the mobilisation of identity divides may impact on areas such as policy making and social cohesion.

Part I Demographic change and the emergence of new political divides over identity

Part I tells the story of how long-term social and political changes have generated new groups in the electorate with conflicting interests. Such changes have relatively minor effects from one election to the next and are next to invisible in the hurly-burly of day-to-day politics, but as they build over decades, they accumulate the potential to fundamentally shift the balance of electoral power. In Chapter 2, we trace three developments that have driven both the rise of new 'identity liberal' electorates and the decline of the formerly dominant 'identity conservative' group. First, educational expansion has opened universities, formerly the preserve of a small elite, to the masses. In two generations, this has shifted British voters' educational experience from one where the typical voter left school in their mid-teens with few or no qualifications to one where the majority remain in school to at least eighteen, and nearly half go on to attend university. Secondly, mass migration and rising ethnic diversity have transformed the typical experience of a young person growing up in Britain. A pensioner born in the 1940s grew up in a far more ethnically and culturally homogeneous society, and most likely had little or no contact with people of different ethnic or religious backgrounds. Her granddaughter growing up in the 2010s had a dramatically different experience, growing up in a society where ethnic and religious diversity is a normal part of everyday life for most young people. The generational structure of both these changes and, hence, of the identities and values associated with them, drives the third demographic trend we identify: the opening up of a major generational divide in the electorate.

Three distinct groups have emerged in British society as a cumulative result of these changes. University expansion has driven the emergence of *conviction liberals*. University graduates have distinctive identities and values: they value individual freedoms very highly, have little attachment to traditional majority identities or values, and, crucially for our arguments, they are cosmopolitan, pro-migration and embrace diversity. They not only see diversity as a social good in itself, but also see defending diversity and minorities as an important part of their social and political identity. These anti-racism social norms align graduate conviction liberals with our second identity liberal group: ethnic minorities, whose motivations are somewhat different. For ethnic minorities, anti-racist and pro-diversity stances are not a matter of personal values but of necessity. Hostility from the majority group fundamentally impacts on their interests and social prospects, and the experience of such hostility is a fundamental part of ethnic minorities' social experiences and group identities. Ethnic minority voters are not consistently supportive of liberal stances on issues such as gender equality or LGBTQ rights, but they do favour strong political action to defend diversity and prohibit expressions of prejudice and discrimination as this is a matter of basic self-interest for ethnic minority voters. We therefore call them *necessity liberals*.

The third group structuring the identity politics divide is the antagonist to these two rising identity liberal groups. The growth of graduates and ethnic minorities is mirrored by the demographic decline in white voters who leave school with few or no educational qualifications. Until just a few decades ago these white school leavers formed a dominant majority of the electorate, and hence set the tone of politics. Their decline since has been dramatic, and the experience of this decline has been disorienting and disillusioning for them. White school leavers sense that they are rapidly losing cultural and political influence, becoming a marginalised 'new minority'[4] whose concerns politicians no longer listen to or represent. This perception is not irrational – as this group shrinks, so the political incentive to respond to it also declines, particularly when its concerns conflict with the concerns of rapidly rising identity liberal groups. This experience of change as decline is not just a reaction to individual and local circumstances. It is also a reflection of the worldview of identity conservative voters, a worldview known to academics as ethnocentrism. This is a technical term for a persistent tendency to see the social and political world as a battle between groups, pitting the familiar 'us' against the unfamiliar 'them'. This tendency makes this group experience demographic and social change as a threat, and as they want to slow or reverse this change, we refer to this group as *identity conservatives*.

In Chapter 3 we take a more in-depth look at the differences in the attitudes and values of identity conservatives and identity

---

[4] Gest (2016).

liberals, which are key to understanding the political conflicts emerging between them. We draw on a range of survey data to paint a portrait of each group, highlighting their distinctive values and concerns. The ethnocentric worldview of *identity conservatives* has two aspects: attachment to in-groups and hostility towards out-groups. They have clear ideas about who belongs to 'us', and strong suspicions of groups deemed to fall outside the tribe. *Conviction identity liberals* see this worldview, and the political stances which flow from it, as morally wrong, and regard combatting ethnocentrism and the hostility to outsiders associated with it as a core political value. This conviction is reflected in a commitment to entrenching anti-prejudice social norms. Ethnic minority *necessity identity liberals* also strongly oppose ethnocentrism and its effects, because those effects are often visited upon them. They ally strongly with conviction liberals on identity conflicts, but do not share their broader socially liberal agenda.

The conflicts between these groups focus on group identities and group attachments, and such arguments become polarised because the stakes are high. There is wide agreement that racism is unacceptable, and strong sanctions are applied to those perceived to have violated this anti-racism social norm. But there is deep and enduring dispute about which attitudes and behaviours should be sanctioned as racism. Even among identity conservatives social identities are not fixed: the sense of who is 'us' and who is 'them', and what expressions of loyalty to 'us' and suspicion of 'them' are acceptable, is constantly evolving in response to social change. Younger generations of identity conservatives are much more comfortable with diversity than their parents or grandparents. They often resent accusations of racism and xenophobia from their identity liberal peers, as they feel they have moved away from the prejudices of their parents, but this inclusive shift is not acknowledged by identity liberal voters whose attitudes have moved further and faster. With no universally agreed rules available, the politics of identity is in part a tug-of-war over social norms, with identity liberals seeking stronger and more expansive definitions of racism sanctioning a wider range of attitudes and behaviour, while identity conservatives push back against this process, attacking it as the unjust imposition of excessively stringent rules, which stigmatise the legitimate expression of group attachments and anxieties about change.

Having laid out the social and psychological foundations of the new identity conflicts, in Chapter 4 we tell the story of how such conflicts were first mobilised into electoral politics during the first wave of migration to Britain after the Second World War. This period of British history is rarely mentioned in conjunction with our decision to leave the EU in 2016, but it is critical for understanding the more recent identity conflicts. The first wave of sustained mass migration was the first demonstration of the disruptive power of identity conflicts, producing a wave of voter mobilisation which upended political competition and continued to reverberate in debates over multiculturalism, discrimination and identity. The new political conflicts generated more recently by another surge in immigration have interacted with, and sometimes reinforced, these older divisions. The legacy of parties' choices and rhetoric in this period has informed how voters see Labour and the Conservatives on identity issues ever since. We cannot understand the identity conflicts mobilised by Cameron, May and Farage without first understanding the forces unleashed in the era of Heath, Thatcher and Powell.

Part II Identity conflicts from New Labour to the Coalition

Part II turns to the story of how identity conflicts have become politically mobilised over the past two decades, showing how developments set in train during the New Labour governments of 1997–2010 culminated in the dramatic political shifts of the Coalition government of 2010–15, when conflicts over immigration organised identity divides into the heart of political competition. We start in Chapter 5 with a discussion of the 'long divorce' of the New Labour years, as voters and parties steadily drifted apart. Both Labour and the Conservatives changed in ways which alienated voters and eroded traditional partisan political identities. The two governing parties converged ideologically, and their elites became dominated by identity liberal politicians recruited from a limited number of professions, reducing the differences between parties and narrowing the sections of society they represented. Voters responded to these changes with growing disaffection and disinterest, reflecting a growing belief that they were being denied a meaningful choice. This feeling was exacerbated by changes in campaign strategies – with a growing focus of resources on 'target seats' and 'swing voters', eroding contact between political parties and voters, particularly in the safe seats deemed unlikely to change hands at elections.

By the mid-2000s the consequences of these changes were already becoming clear: growing apathy and disenchantment, and a steady decline in partisan attachments. It is not a simple or inevitable process for latent discontent to shift into active antagonism, but these changes in the relationship between parties and the voters created the potential for a later, more dramatic re-alignment of voter preferences. Then, in the second half of the period of New Labour governments, an issue emerged with the ability to realise this potential, by mobilising latent discontents and identity conflicts. The issue was the very same issue that had disrupted politics decades earlier: immigration. We show how and why it rose up the agenda, and why it was such a powerful lightning rod for discontent among identity conservatives.

In Chapter 6, we examine the emergence of a new party, UKIP, which exploited the opening of political opportunity, mobilising identity conservatives to secure the strongest electoral performance by a new British party since the 1920s. We also unravel the puzzling timing of UKIP's surge. Though both the British National Party (BNP) and UK Independence Party (UKIP) grew through the 2000s, it was not until the Coalition years that the radical right revolt went mainstream. If immigration rose to the top of the political agenda in the mid-2000s, why did it take nearly a decade for a radical right party to fully capitalise on public discontent? This delay was the consequence of an older reputational legacy from the first wave of immigration. Ever since Enoch Powell and Margaret Thatcher, the Conservatives had been seen as the party of immigration control. The Conservatives used this reputation to win over the anxious identity conservatives in 2010. But doing so required the setting up of expectations of radical cuts to immigration that the party was unable to meet in government. The Conservatives' reputation therefore collapsed at the start of the Coalition, and as their inability to control migration became clear, identity conservative voters turned to the radical right. UKIP surged in this period not because of their stance on Europe, which was an issue of marginal interest to most of their new voters, but because their anti-immigration stance positioned them to profit from the Conservatives' failure. The 'revolt on the right' which UKIP mobilised was a revolt of identity conservative voters fundamentally threatened by immigration, which UKIP could also link to EU free movement rights, thus tying their core political concern to the very different core concern of their new electorate.

However, although surging support for UKIP was the most dramatic electoral development of the Coalition period, it was not the only important change. There was also a 'reshuffle on the left', with identity liberals switching their votes to parties better aligned with their preferences. We examine this in Chapter 7. Coalition with the Conservatives unravelled the Liberal Democrats' electoral alliance of identity liberals, protest voters and tactical anti-Tory voters. More than one voter in eight in England and Wales switched from the Liberal Democrats to someone else during the Coalition. Protest-motivated Liberal Democrat supporters switched in large numbers to UKIP, but the biggest shift was the migration of identity liberals to Labour, tipping the balance of the Labour electoral coalition in a liberal direction.[5] At the same time, the traditional alliance of ethnic minority voters with Labour, strained by New Labour's foreign

[5] Many identity liberals also switched from the Liberal Democrats to the Greens, who secured a record election result in 2015.

policy in the mid-2000s, was restored during the Coalition as formerly alienated Muslim voters re-aligned themselves with the party. The strengthening of liberal and ethnic minority voices within the Labour coalition was also accelerated by the departure of many identity conservative white school leavers from Labour to UKIP. As a result, the 2015 Labour electorate, though similar in size to that of 2010, was radically transformed in ways that very few commentators noticed at the time. In 2015, for the first time, the new identity liberal groups outnumbered the core identity conservative demographic of white school leavers within the Labour electorate.

Part III Brexitland

Nearly all the critical ingredients for Brexitland were already in place before 2016: new groups had risen in the electorate, divided over new issues and disenchanted with the old parties, with old loyalties withering away. Yet one vital thing was missing, which appeared as if from nowhere on the morning of 24 June 2016: self-consciousness. Before Brexit, the groups who form the building blocks of the identity politics conflict of Brexitland had no sense of themselves as political tribes with distinct and conflicting interests. Brexit changed that overnight. Britain woke up to a referendum result which demonstrated to everyone that they lived in a country evenly divided into two opposing tribes: 'Leave' and 'Remain'. These new tribes swiftly became more meaningful political identities to voters than waning loyalties to the traditional political parties. The story of how the EU Referendum and its aftermath transformed identity conflicts into a battle between two politically conscious opposing tribes forms the focus of Chapter 8.

The 2016 referendum was the first national political choice to be structured primarily around identity divides. Traditional conflicts over class, income, economic ideology and economic competence were pushed into the background. Instead, it was the divides between graduates and school leavers, between white voters and ethnic minorities and between young and old on national identity, equal opportunities and, particularly, immigration which drove voters' Brexit choices. Once the referendum provided the moment of awakening for these conflicts, voters became acutely aware of these new divisions. They now know what kind of people fall into each Brexit tribe and display all the classic symptoms of partisan bias when asked to judge their tribe and its opponents, seeing their own side through rose-tinted spectacles and their rivals as fools and knaves. These attachments have been consequential not only for political views, but also for social life since the referendum. Brexit partisans view political and economic information through tribal lenses and are also less willing to engage in everyday social contact with their opponents. It is the emergence of these conscious partisan identities that explains why the politics identity conflict of Brexitland really came into its own after the 2016 referendum. However, the central role of a referendum campaign in driving the emergence of this new politics raises questions about how inevitable this political awakening was, and how stable the new political alignments will prove to be.

We have no crystal ball to answer these questions, but we can draw lessons from the remarkable parallel story playing out in one constituent part of Brexitland. In Chapter 9, we look at the story of the Scottish Independence Referendum, showing how nationalism and constitutional change became focal points for identity conflicts in Scotland in 2014, as they did across Britain in 2016, but with the different Scottish context, campaign and referendum outcome critically shaping the form of the identity conflicts which emerged. In both cases, similar demographic and identity divisions presented, and in both cases a nationalist party surged to prominence in part by mobilising these divisions and promoting constitutional change. Both Scottish independence and Brexit won their strongest early support from identity conservative voters wishing to 'take back control', and in both cases the electoral success of nationalist parties advocating withdrawal from a larger union was a key factor leading to the holding of an exit referendum. Yet despite these many parallels, the politics of the Independence Referendum in Scotland has been very different to that of the Brexit conflict in England. In Scotland, a broad and inclusive nationalist political movement (the Scottish Nationalist Party (SNP)) had already risen to a position of domestic political hegemony before the referendum campaign, yet failed to persuade the Scottish to take Scotland out of the United Kingdom. In England, a narrow and exclusionary nationalist movement (UKIP) failed to break through in domestic politics, yet succeeded in persuading the English (and the British more generally) to take themselves out of the EU. Different patterns of identity attachment explain the divergent outcomes – Scottish attachments to an overarching British identity are much stronger than English or British attachments to a European identity, while negative views of England and Westminster as out-groups are much weaker in Scotland than negative views of the EU and Brussels as out-groups in England.

Scotland also offers lessons on the political aftermath of divisive referendum campaigns. New political tribes were also forged in the Scottish independence campaign, and these new tribes proved extremely potent in the 2015 general election, which re-aligned Scottish politics around the independence question. Yet this re-alignment proved fleeting, as within two years Scottish politics was shaken up once again, this time by Brexit. Voters' shifting allegiances were now driven by the combination of views they expressed on two divisive constitutional questions. The SNP's decision to campaign for a second independence referendum to keep Scotland in the EU cost it its support among the most ethnocentric Scots, who disliked rule from Brussels just as much as rule from Westminster. Meanwhile, the Scottish Conservatives staged an unexpected recovery in part by opposing the ruling SNP on both referendum issues – where the SNP was the party of an independent Scotland inside the EU, the Conservatives became the party taking a united Britain out of the EU. The further big shifts seen in 2019 underlined how volatile the Scottish context remains, as voters wrestle with two cross-cutting identity conflicts.

Chapter 10 concludes our story by looking at the electoral aftermath of Brexit in England and Wales, as seen in the

2017 and 2019 elections, and the possible paths forward after Britain's departure from the EU. The steady growth of the identity liberal electorate of graduates and ethnic minorities has provided Labour with a major source of new votes. But this influx of new identity liberal supporters came with risks for Labour, risks underlined by the party's weak performance in the 2019 elections. The growing electoral heft of identity liberals within the Labour coalition has increased the political power of identity politics to unsettle the attachments of economically left wing but socially conservative 'old left' voters, who are at odds with Labour's new educated and ethnic minority voters on identity issues. When conflicts such as immigration dominated the top of the political agenda, as they have since the New Labour years, the result has been a vicious circle for Labour, with white school leavers drifting away from a party which they saw as out of step with their values, which in turn increases the dominance of identity liberal groups in the Labour coalition, which then further alienates white school leavers. The catastrophic 2019 election result in the 'red wall' seats where traditionally Labour identifying identity conservative voters are concentrated represents the final stage in this long process, completing the departure of these voters from the Labour Party.

The re-alignment of these voters fuelled the Conservatives' 2019 election triumph, but that success brings with it a distinct but related set of challenges for the party going forward. The Conservatives have once again demonstrated their superior ability to respond to the ethnocentric anxieties of identity conservatives, benefitting once again from the political mobilisation of such anxieties by immigration and Brexit. As a result, however, demographic and cultural change is working against them, steadily eroding the identity conservative electorate at the heart of their new election-winning coalition, as catering to the anxieties of such voters puts further distance between the Conservatives and the growing identity liberal electorate. The defensive mobilisation of ethnic nationalism among identity conservative white voters in response to this decline has helped the Conservatives in the short run, but will sharpen their electoral dilemma in the long run. The Conservatives have made major short-term gains with white school leavers by embracing defensive nationalism and opposition to immigration, but as the majority governing party reshaping Britain after Brexit, they are now exposed to growing risks of counter-mobilisation from graduates and ethnic minorities opposed to the changes they are implementing.

Inevitable limitations and omissions

Electoral politics is a complex process involving the shifting preferences of great masses of citizens moved by myriad different influences. No analysis of elections and political change, no matter how detailed and rigorous, can fully do justice to this process, so there are inevitably elements of the story which have to be left out. Our account focuses on the story of demographic change, group identities and national-level shifts in political allegiances. We touch only lightly on the roles of geography and economics, which are of course important complementary influences on vote choice, though we do show at various points how these factors interact with the elements at the heart of our story. As we wish to analyse demographic and political change over the long term, we also face considerable limits on the data and measures we can use, as many of the factors we want to examine have been asked about only in a narrow or partial way over the long run. The indicators we analyse are not the whole story, they are just the part of it that is available to us to tell.[6]

---

[6] One issue is that the availability of survey data on identity conflicts depends on their salience. During periods when (for example) immigration is not on the political agenda, academics and pollsters ask fewer questions about it; some of the identity conflicts we write about – such as immigration – became organised out of politics so successfully for decades that pollsters and academics stopped asking about them, deeming them issues of little importance. This makes it hard to track the long-run evolution of attitudes on issues which rise and fall on the political agenda. Another issue is that the newer survey measures and survey experiments we and other researchers have developed and deployed in recent years often represent the first attempts to measure aspects of identity conflicts – as such they are likely to be limited and imperfect relative to more

We think of this book as an attempt to start new conversations, not to offer the final word, and therefore we hope many of the issues we raise will be explored more fully in the future by other researchers. In particular, we hope that this book will encourage British and European scholars to give more attention to ethnocentrism and its political effects; and develop better measures to separate this from the related but more widely discussed concept of authoritarianism. While authoritarianism was originally developed as a theory and set of measures used to help to explain out-group prejudice, and has continued to be closely linked to the study of groups and group conflict in American scholarship, in British and European research this link is all too often forgotten, and authoritarianism is seen instead as a form of political ideology. While there are well-validated measures of this form of political authoritarianism on most academic surveys, the measurement of ethnocentrism is much more sporadic and less consistent, forcing analysts to rely on ad hoc measures which often change from one survey to the next. As we shall show over the coming chapters, ethnocentric worldviews have a powerful impact on politics, and provide a powerful and intuitive theoretical explanation for potent political conflicts which are, at root, about group identities and group boundaries. To properly understand the group attachments and group conflicts that are driving the new identity politics of Brexitland, we need more consistent and more frequently asked measures of the ethnocentric attitudes which lie at their core.

Conclusion

Readers may expect that a book titled Brexitland, and focused on the polarised identity conflicts now dividing British society, will be a pessimistic piece. But we are not pessimists. We do not think that these new divisions will inevitably toxify politics or

established and well-tested measures, and cannot be projected backwards in time.

undermine democratic norms. We do think, though, that the conflicts laid bare on 24 June 2016 are poorly understood. Brexit does not represent the collapse of an old order or the end of British democracy, as some more alarmist commentators sometimes suggest. Instead, it represents the rise of new concerns which demand urgent attention from our political leaders. Britain might have become Brexitland, a country divided in new ways over identity and diversity, anti-racism and its limits, immigration and Brexit itself, but this is not a country that can be neatly divided between rooted and authentic 'somewhere' communities and a rootless, self-centred 'nowhere' ruling class who run things in their own interests.[7] It is not a country where disquiet about the 'destruction' of national ways of life makes the rise of reactionary national populists 'inevitable'.[8] It is not a country where anxieties about ethnic change run so deep that addressing them will obligate our politicians to enact race-conscious immigration policies, preferring 'more assimilable' white migrants.[9]

The truth is messier, but more hopeful. Although concerns about identity and social change run deep, and conflicts over these issues are here to stay, as the murdered MP Jo Cox[10] famously said there is more that unites us than divides us. Most voters share a common vision for Britain as a responsive democracy that values the rights of its citizens and responds to their needs. While many find the vast demographic and social changes of recent decades disorientating and seek reassurance from their politicians in response, they also show a tremendous capacity to adapt. Today's electorate does not think about things as did yesterday's. Tomorrow's voters will be more different still. But anyone who thinks that this capacity for change shows that

---

[7] Goodhart (2017).   [8] Eatwell and Goodwin (2018).   [9] Kaufmann (2018).
[10] Cox was murdered in the final days of the EU Referendum campaign by Thomas Mair, a man with links to various far right organisations, who at his trial explained his actions by claiming Cox's campaigns in defence of immigration and the EU showed she was a 'collaborator' and a 'traitor to white people'. Cox's murder was the first killing of a sitting MP since the murder of Conservative MP Ian Gow by the Provisional IRA in 1990.

identity politics itself is a chimera, manufactured by politicians and the media for their own ends, is also wrong. The anxieties and divisions over identity, diversity and immigration that form the basis for identity conflicts are real and rooted in fundamental differences in voters' values and outlooks. The potential to polarise and play on these divisions will always be with us. While we do not yet have the extreme 'culture war' conflicts which have blighted modern American politics, one day we might. The capacity for mutual hostility and polarised conflict is already there, latent in the electorate. The risk of this is only increased by putting our heads in the sand and pretending these destabilising divisions are the inventions of unscrupulous politicians and editors, rather than facing up to them as real tensions in the electorate which must be addressed. Identity conflicts can de-escalate if the feelings of threat which drive them up the agenda are effectively addressed, opening up space for identities to evolve and new social and political norms to develop. This has happened before – the inflammatory racism of politicians such as Enoch Powell in the 1970s is unimaginable in mainstream politics today. The volatile, polarised conflicts unleashed by the 2016 referendum may be the first necessary step down the road to more effective and responsive party politics. Brexitland is both an end and a beginning. What we make of it is up to us.

PART I

Demographic change and the emergence of new political divides over identity

2 SOCIAL CHANGE, ETHNOCENTRISM AND THE EMERGENCE OF NEW IDENTITY DIVIDES

Introduction

In 1995 Sir David Attenborough released a series, 'The Private Life of Plants', which used new filming techniques to dramatically speed up the passage of time. The results were sensational. Peaceful forest glades were revealed as whirling, chaotic worlds of dynamic change and perpetual competition. Plants formed friendships, went to war over territory and ran desperate races for access to precious light. The plant world is ever-changing, but because the change is slow, it usually escapes our notice. Social change is often like this too. Societies are in constant flux. The jobs people do, the education they have, where they come from, where they go to, how they think of themselves and what they value – none of these things are constant. Yet because such change is often slow, it goes unnoticed until a watershed moment draws attention to it. The EU Referendum was such a moment, when a shock result forced people to pay closer attention to changes long underway all around them. What people saw in the wake of the 'Leave' victory was a land suddenly divided, at odds with itself and locked into intractable conflicts: Brexitland. But the divides Brexit exposed were not new. They had been building in the electorate for years.

Two demographic shifts have been gradually reshaping British society for many decades – educational expansion and ethnic diversification. Just one generation ago a majority of the British electorate were white voters with few or no educational qualifications. University was the preserve of a privileged minority,[1] and ethnic minority communities were still small and concentrated in the largest cities.[2] Educational expansion and mass migration have since driven a slow but relentless transformation of the electorate, with the youngest generations dramatically more highly qualified and ethnically diverse than the oldest.[3] In this chapter, we examine these demographic shifts and explain how their relationship to an influential worldview – ethnocentrism – gives them disruptive political power.

Ethnocentrism is the 'view of things in which one's own group is the centre of everything'.[4] The presence or absence of ethnocentric views plays a major role in determining on which side of the Brexitland divide people fall. On one side of this divide are the voters we call 'identity conservatives' – white voters with lower levels of formal education who most frequently hold ethnocentric worldviews, making them more strongly attached to in-group identities like national identity and more threatened by out-groups such as migrants and minorities. On the other side are two 'identity liberal' groups – university graduates and ethnic minorities – who for different reasons reject ethnocentrism. The conflict between these groups runs right through the heart of the electorate, and the activation of this conflict is a major source of the political upheavals and volatility of the past decade. The new political context we call 'Brexitland' is one in which identity conflicts between the formerly dominant but now declining identity conservative group and the growing but not yet dominant identity liberal groups have become a central structuring feature of British politics. The vision of Britain each side embraces is one its opponents reject. This conflict in worldviews, once mobilised, produces polarised politics – it is hard to compromise with those whose values you abhor. But it also produces highly dynamic and competitive politics, because at the present time neither identity conservatives nor identity

---

[1] Willetts (2018).   [2] Layton-Henry (1992); Finney and Simpson (2009a).
[3] Martin (2019).   [4] Sumner (1906).

liberals are large enough groups to prevail consistently and set the terms of debate.

The polarisation of identity politics is also exacerbated by the way white school leavers, graduates and ethnic minorities are clustered in certain age groups and areas. Both ethnic and educational change are generationally structured. The British electorate today contains older cohorts dominated by ethnocentric white voters, and younger cohorts where university graduates and ethnic minorities predominate. Social norms and social experience are generationally structured,[5] with views about what is 'normal' strongly influenced by experiences in early adulthood, leaving the generations deeply divided in their experiences and their values. Many of those who grew up in a more ethnically homogeneous, socially conservative Britain have a profoundly different view of what Britain is and ought to be than members of the youngest generations, who have grown up in a much more ethnically diverse and socially liberal country.

Geography has a similar polarising effect.[6] People on both sides of the identity politics divide live in distinct locations through choice and circumstance. The migration of university graduates for study and work concentrates them in the prosperous towns and big cities where university campuses and job opportunities are found. Ethnic minorities are also concentrated in larger cities, a result of past and present migration patterns.[7] By contrast, white voters with low education levels move less often, and are becoming concentrated in more ethnically homogeneous and less economically successful rural and small-town areas.[8] These growing ethnic and educational differences between big cities and small towns are further exacerbated by a growing age gap. While the recruitment of students and young graduates is making large towns and cities younger, smaller

---

[5] Alwin and Krosnick (1991); Inglehart (1971; 1990); Inglehart and Abramson (1994); Sears and Valentino (1997); Tilley (2005); Grasso et al. (2017).

[6] Jennings and Stoker (2016; 2017).

[7] Finney and Simpson (2009b); Jivraj (2012).   [8] Jennings and Stoker (2016).

towns are rapidly ageing as these groups move away while older residents remain.[9] These trends magnify identity conflicts by increasing social segregation and reducing the level of contact and common experience between people on either side of the identity politics divide. Graduates mainly live among other graduates, in ethnically diverse places that accord with, and reinforce, their belief in a dynamic and diverse Britain. White voters with low education levels also live around similar people, in ageing and declining places which accord with, and reinforce, their sense of marginalisation and stagnation.

In this chapter we set out the demographic changes which are driving the emergence of identity politics: educational expansion and rising ethnic diversity. We then introduce the concept of ethnocentrism, the tendency to see the social world in terms of groups and group conflict; and illustrate how both educational levels and ethnicity are closely linked to this worldview. We then show how the generational and geographical polarisation in education levels and ethnic diversity serve to deepen the divides between people and places, and to magnify the political impact of the new identity politics conflicts. But while demographic change is inevitable, demography is not political destiny, as political parties have a vital role to play in determining how these new divides are mobilised into political competition.

Education: university expansion and the rise of the graduate class

Britain is in the middle of a historic transformation from a society of school leavers to a society of university graduates. This is part of an international trend evident in most developed democracies since the Second World War,[10] and which is fast spreading to other countries as they become more prosperous.[11] Higher education is widely seen as economically and socially beneficial, and there has been a near-universal tendency for

---

[9] Jennings (2017); Warren (2018).   [10] Breen et al. (2009).
[11] Altbach, Reisberg and Rumbley (2009); Schofer and Meyer (2005).

wealthier nations to invest in expanding access to it. This process was initially slow in Britain, as governments held on to an elitist model where only a small minority attended university, but then made a late and dramatic switch to mass higher education, sending university attendance rates sharply upwards. The legacy of this tortoise to hare transformation is a particularly stark generational divide in education levels.[12] The first wave of British university expansion occurred in the 1960s, but this was modest and left university attendance at around 10 per cent of each cohort. Universities then grew slowly for the next two decades, with attendance rates in the 1970s and 1980s still in the 13–15 per cent range.[13]

The second wave of university expansion was the product of reforms by the early 1990s Conservative government, in particular the 1992 Education Act, which upgraded a large set of educational institutions to degree-awarding university status. The effects were substantial: university attendance rates more than doubled from 15 per cent in 1988 to 33 per cent in 1994, and have continued to rise since. The domestic undergraduate population in 2000 was six times larger than in 1960, and by the mid-2010s university attendance rates at eighteen were approaching 40 per cent. The expansion of higher education since the early 1990s means that the British electorate is currently divided between generations born before the 1970s, who grew up with an elitist higher education system, and those born since, who have grown up with ever-expanding mass higher education provision and consumption – though access remains skewed towards the wealthy and the middle class.[14]

University expansion is one part of a broader trend of increasing access to education. The proportion of students staying on beyond the compulsory school leaving age (fifteen until 1973, sixteen since) rose from 20 per cent in the early 1960s cohorts to

---

[12] Ermisch and Richards (2016).   [13] Devereux and Fan (2011).
[14] Boliver (2011); Blanden and Manchin (2004). There is evidence, though, that the expansion since the 1990s is beginning to reduce economic divides in HE access, see Blanden and Macmillan (2016).

Figure 2.1 Share of respondents who report having no formal qualifications and who report having an undergraduate degree or more

Source: British Social Attitudes surveys 1985–2016.

40 per cent in the early 1980s and over 70 per cent among the 2000s cohort. The cumulative effect of these repeated waves of educational expansion is a slow but steady rise in the overall formal education levels of the electorate, as younger cohorts brought through a dramatically expanded education system gradually replace older cohorts where most students left school at the earliest opportunity (see Figure 2.1). The changes year-on-year are small, but their cumulative effect is striking. When Margaret Thatcher won her third election victory in 1987, seven voters in ten had left formal education at sixteen or earlier, and university graduates (8 per cent) were outnumbered five to one by voters with no formal qualifications at all (42 per cent). By the time Tony Blair won his third election victory in 2005, the

graduate share had more than doubled, but graduates were still heavily outnumbered by unqualified voters. When Theresa May faced the electorate in 2017, nearly a quarter of voters had a university degree, triple the share of Thatcher's time, and graduates substantially outnumbered the unqualified. The year 2010 was an important turning point in this process: graduates were heavily outnumbered by the unqualified in every general election held before this point, but outnumber the unqualified in every election held after it.

Racial diversity and immigration: the rise of multiracial Britain

The second great demographic change of the post-war era is Britain's transformation into a racially diverse society. While Britain has long incorporated multiple distinct national cultures within a single state,[15] and has longstanding and politically distinctive religious minorities,[16] the rise in ethnic, racial and religious diversity[17] seen since the onset of mass migration from the Commonwealth in the 1950s has been different in scale and scope to what came before.[18] Britain's shift from a nearly all-white society to a racially diverse one has occurred, like the transformation of education levels, within a single lifetime, as Figure 2.2 illustrates. A pensioner turning seventy-five in 2019 spent their childhood in a society where less than one in a hundred people was born outside Europe or belonged to an ethnic minority, while a youngster turning eighteen in the same year has only ever known an ethnically diverse Britain with large well-established ethnic and religious minority communities, a country where around one person in five belongs to an ethnic

---

[15] Colley (1992).   [16] Clements (2015); Tilley (2015).
[17] Platt and Nandi (2018); Heath et al. (2013).
[18] While ethnically and religiously distinct communities from outside Europe have existed in Britain for centuries, reflecting Britain's colonial and Imperial history (see, e.g., Olusoga, 2017), these communities were relatively small prior to the Second World War.

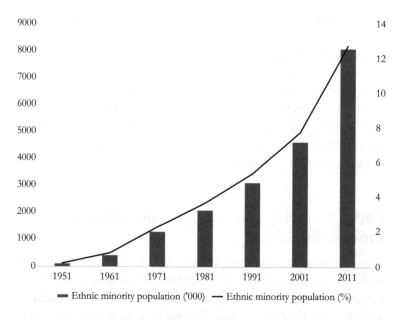

Figure 2.2 Ethnic minority population of the UK, 1951–2011

Sources: Census (1991–2011 ethnic minority population figures and 1951–2011 total population figures); Owen (1995) (1951–1981 ethnic minority population estimates).

group other than 'white British' and one in seven residents was born in another country.

This transformation is more than a matter of raw numbers. The nature of diversity has changed as minority communities have grown and become more established. In the 1950s Britain of current pensioners' youth, residents from ethnic minority groups were almost all first-generation migrants who had usually come to Britain as adults. Race and migration were conflated, racial diversity was an imported phenomenon not, outside a few districts in Britain's largest cities,[19] a home-grown aspect of mass British culture. As time passed, a 'second-generation' ethnic minority population emerged, born and raised in Britain, and with no memory of their parents' countries of birth.

[19] Olusoga (2017).

As these British-born minority communities grew and settled across a wider range of neighbourhoods, racial diversity became more embedded in everyday British social life. Black and Asian people born in Britain were less willing to accept discrimination and disadvantage;[20] and the experience of being treated differently to other native-born fellow citizens shaped, and continues to shape, their social identities and political priorities.[21] Rising diversity has thus led to new debates about the meaning of British identity, with British-born ethnic minorities favouring multicultural understandings of Britishness which recognise and include them, while older white voters still hold to an understanding of Britishness framed by the homogeneous pre-migration society in which they grew up. The idea of reversing the process of ethnic change through state-sponsored repatriation schemes remained popular with many white voters for several decades after mass migration began. Yet the absurdity of mass repatriation in a country with a large, rapidly growing British-born ethnic minority population was already obvious in the 1970s. As the West Midlands-born black British comedian Lenny Henry told television audiences at the time: 'Enoch Powell wants to give us £1,000 to go home. Suits me. It only costs me 50p to get to Dudley.'[22]

Debates over identity and diversity are now about much more than immigration and will continue to evolve as the British population changes. The 2011 Census revealed that the ethnic minority population in England and Wales was evenly split, with 48 per cent born in Britain and 52 per cent born abroad. Many of the British-born 48 per cent will be third- or even fourth-

---

[20] Heath and Cheung (2007).

[21] Nandi and Platt (2015); Heath et al. (2013); Maxwell (2012).

[22] Story cited at: www.theguardian.com/politics/2002/may/01/studentpolitics .education, last accessed 25 April 2019. The same very obvious flaw in the far right BNP's 2009 proposals for ethnic minority repatriation was pointed out live on a television panel show by a British-born ethnic minority member who asked party leader Nick Griffin: 'Where do you want me to go? This is my country, I love this country, I am part of this country, I was born here.' Despite these very obvious problems, over 40 per cent of voters as late as 1993 still supported the idea of government-sponsored repatriation schemes in polling.

generation British-born. And the boundaries between ethnic minorities and the white majority are being further blurred as majority and minority communities intermarry. The fastest growing ethnic group in Britain is those reporting a mixed racial heritage, a group for whom a bright line separation between majority white British and ethnic minority identities makes little sense.[23] The 2011 Census found that six per cent of children under ten had mixed heritage, seven times the share among fifty-somethings. This made the mixed heritage group larger than any other single minority ethnic group among Britain's youngest residents – and continued rises in mixed marriages will ensure further growth in the years to come.[24] Among the youngest cohorts, ethnic identities have become knitted together at the most intimate level, as their family heritage binds them to multiple communities.[25]

At the same time as established British-born minority communities have come of age and found their voice in society, new waves of migration have continued to bring new settlers to Britain, both from the original migrant countries and increasingly from elsewhere. Migration rates rose sharply from the late 1990s onwards, a shift big enough to constitute a 'second wave' of post-war migration. The scale and diversity of this new wave of migration is illustrated in Figure 2.3, which shows estimates of the total foreign-born population by broad region of origin. The overall migrant population nearly doubled between 2005 and 2017, rising from 5.3 million to 9.4 million. While there was substantial growth in all migrant populations, this varied a lot between regions of origin. Growth was slowest in the

---

[23] Ford et al. (2012).   [24] Muttarak and Heath (2010).

[25] In most cases, mixed/multiple ethnicities involve a combination of white British and ethnic minority heritage: 78 per cent of the 1.2 million people reporting mixed ethnic identity give such a combination, with the largest groups being white and black Caribbean (427,000), white and Asian (342,000) and white and black African (166,000). The mixed white and black Caribbean group is larger than the black Caribbean group among all the cohorts under the age of thirty, highlighting how the boundaries between the majority and the most established ethnic minority group have become very blurred among younger generations.

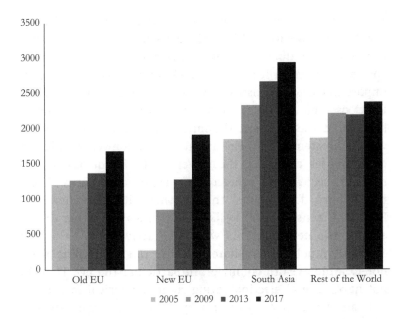

3500
3000
2500
2000
1500
1000
500
0

Old EU   New EU   South Asia   Rest of the World

■ 2005 ■ 2009 ■ 2013 ■ 2017

Figure 2.3 Migrant populations resident in Britain by broad region of origin, 2005–17

Source: Office for National Statistics.

'Old' EU migrant population (rising from 1.2 million to 1.7 million) and the diverse population from the rest of the world (up from 1.8 million to 2.4 million). The population of migrant residents born in the Asian subcontinent grew faster, nearly doubling from 1.7 million to 2.9 million. And the fastest growth of all came in the population of migrants from the new EU member states such as Poland, Romania and Lithuania – this population exploded from less than 200,000 in 2005 to nearly 2 million by 2017, a dramatic development with major political consequences, as we shall see in later chapters.

The second wave of migration to Britain has been more regionally and ethnically diverse, but it is also distinct in another politically consequential way – the new migrants are much less likely to have voting rights than those who arrived earlier.

The first wave of post-war migrants to Britain were for the most part Commonwealth and Irish citizens who possessed full political rights, including voting rights in general elections, from the day they arrived in Britain. These migrants rapidly became an important electoral constituency for politicians to court in many locations, and migrants' electoral power helped to counterbalance, at least in part, the influence of ethnocentric white voters threatened by their arrival.[26] Commonwealth migrant communities could use the power of the ballot box as one route to secure and protect their rights and status. Their British-born descendants, the vast majority of whom hold British citizenship, can do likewise. Things are rather different for the new migrants who have arrived since the late 1990s. A much larger share of these migrants come from non-Commonwealth countries, in particular the EU. They do not have general election voting rights on arrival in Britain, but can secure such rights only by becoming British citizens, which they are less prone to do than earlier waves of immigrants.[27] This marginalises the new migrants in electoral politics and skews the political debate towards those threatened by their arrival.

While the profile of British society has changed dramatically over the past few decades, these changes would not matter politically unless education or ethnic identity had an important effect on voters' values and political choices. Education levels and ethnic identity are associated with a number of differences in outlook and values, the most important of which concern ethnocentrism – the tendency to see the world in terms of groups and group conflict. It is the presence or absence of this perspective as a prevailing influence on how voters understand the world that is central to understanding how conflicts over identity arise from demographic shifts in education levels and ethnic diversity. Understanding what ethnocentrism is, why it matters to people and how to measure it, is therefore the task we turn to next.

---

[26] Saggar (1992; 2000).   [27] Murray (2016); Ford (2018).

Ethnocentrism: how educational and ethnic divides translate into political conflicts

The idea that structural changes can lead to the emergence of new conflicts between groups with different values and priorities is not a new one. There is a large academic literature mapping out how social change can drive political change in this way, the most prominent example being the work of Ronald Inglehart.[28] In a series of ambitious comparative studies, Inglehart developed a model of mass social change, with rising prosperity driving a gradual shift away from 'materialist' values focused on securing the basic essentials in life and towards a set of 'post-materialist' values focused on individual rights, self-actualisation and liberty. Inglehart argued that this is a generational process: the values individuals hold are formed in the 'socialisation' period of young adulthood and shape their political priorities for the rest of their lives. As a result, the political shift away from economic priorities towards social and humanitarian priorities lags several decades behind the economic shift from poverty to prosperity – generational change is slow, and older generations who grew up before prosperity arrived stick around in the electorate for a long time. Related arguments have built upon this influential account, proposing a similar generationally structured transformation in religious attitudes and behaviours,[29] in gender norms and gender roles,[30] and in the emergence of democratic values and institutions.[31] Similar generational value-change arguments have also been used more narrowly, to explain differences in political values and identities,[32] and shifts in these over time, with different generations retaining a lasting concern with the political problems prevalent in their youth,[33] and lasting attachments to the values[34] and political parties[35] which were dominant when they came of age.

---

[28] Inglehart (1977; 1990; 1997).   [29] Inglehart and Norris (2004).
[30] Inglehart and Norris (2003).   [31] Inglehart and Welzel (2005).
[32] Mannheim (1928); Bartels and Jackman (2014).
[33] Duffy (2013); Duffy et al. (2013).   [34] Tilley (2005); Grasso et al. (2017).
[35] Tilley (2002); Shorrocks (2016).

These accounts all share a core argument. The social, economic and political conditions people experience during their youth have a lasting impact on their politics, so changes in those conditions are followed by a much slower, generationally structured change in political allegiances and priorities. Social and economic change may be rapid, but the political change it produces comes later, and more slowly. Our account shares many elements of this story. We also focus on generationally structured social transformations – educational expansion and rising ethnic diversity – and, as in these earlier accounts, the political changes we examine are in part the product of the mobilisation of lasting differences between the worldviews of different generations, worldviews shaped by their experiences in youth. We concentrate on one aspect of this broader story – the division between those who embrace an ethnocentric worldview, with groups and group conflict at its heart, and those who reject and oppose such a view of the world. This division forms the focus of our story for two reasons.

First, ethnocentrism and identity conflicts have proven explanatory power in a range of contexts and are becoming more important as developed societies grow more diverse. The political power of group conflicts has long been evident to researchers working on American politics, where 'the color line' has been one of the most powerful of political and social divides,[36] and where race and racial attitudes are still among the strongest predictors of political choice many decades after the Civil Rights movements ended the formal segregation and disenfranchisement of African Americans.[37] More recently, conflicts over immigration and its impact on American identity have come to the fore, adding another layer of identity conflict to the long-standing 'scar of race'.[38] In Europe, a second large body of research has shown how mass immigration and the growth of

---

[36] Du Bois (1903); Myrdal (1944).

[37] Sniderman and Piazza (1993); Kinder and Sanders (1996); Tesler and Sears (2010); Tesler (2016).

[38] Sides, Tesler and Vavreck (2018); Helbling (2013).

Muslim minorities have sparked the emergence of new radical right parties which mobilise support from ethnocentric voters threatened by these developments, while views about immigration and diversity also exercise a growing influence on voters' choices between mainstream parties.[39]

There is a broad consensus in these two large research communities on a number of key points. There are deep and growing divides in white majority populations centred on identity attachments and views of out-groups. These divides have proved uniquely capable of shifting white vote choices and disrupting political alignments,[40] especially when voters perceive particular migrant or minority groups as threatening.[41] Conversely, ethnic minorities' political choices are strongly influenced by their experience of white hostility and discrimination, giving them a lasting attachment to the (usually left or liberal) parties which have fought for their political and social rights, and a lasting hostility to centre-right and radical right parties which have mobilised ethnocentric sentiments in the majority electorate.[42]

The second reason we focus on ethnocentrism is that it provides an intuitive framework for understanding many of Britain's recent political upheavals. As we show in Chapter 5, it was the activation of ethnocentric sentiments among identity conservatives that pushed immigration to the top of the political agenda in the 2000s, and it was ethnocentric voters threatened by immigration who turned against the New Labour government and then later the Conservative-led Coalition government, opening the door for UKIP in the 2010s. Meanwhile, as we discuss in Chapter 7, identity liberals – graduates and ethnic minorities – were becoming an ever more central part of the Labour Party electoral coalition, shifting the centre-left electoral coalition away from poorer, economically left wing but

---

[39] For overviews of this active research area, see Mudde (2007); Akkerman, de Lange and Rooduijn (2016); Golder (2016); Rydgren (2018).

[40] Ivarsflaten (2008); Mudde (2007).   [41] Helbling (2013); Kallis (2018).

[42] Dancygier and Saunders (2006); Bergh and Bjorklund (2011); Heath et al. (2013); Sanders et al. (2014); Sobolewska (2017).

ethnocentric white school leavers and towards better off, economically moderate but identity liberal university graduates and ethnic minorities. These emerging identity conflicts then moved to centre stage in the defining political drama of the past decade – the EU Referendum – with ethnocentric narratives of an in-group 'taking back control' from hostile and threatening out-groups defining the campaign to leave the EU (see Chapter 8). Identity conflicts also played a major role in the re-alignment of Scottish politics – with arguments about 'us versus them' used to drive the rise of the SNP, which then channelled such sentiments in a very different direction in their bid to secure Scottish independence (see Chapter 9).

The first person to name the tendency to see the world through the lens of groups 'ethnocentrism' was the sociologist William Graham Sumner in the early twentieth century. Sumner argued this tendency to attach to social groups and to denigrate rival groups was universal in human social life and explained a diverse range of otherwise puzzling behaviour.[43] A large body of research across several disciplines has confirmed this core intuition – people everywhere are indeed remarkably prone to identifying with social groups and turning even arbitrary and explicitly meaningless group contests into emotive battles of 'us versus them'.[44] But this tendency, like many aspects of personality and worldview, varies across populations in systematic and predictable ways. Political scientists and social psychologists have revealed ethnocentrism to be a stable personality orientation leading some people to be chronically prone to seeing social life in terms of attachments to in-groups and hostility to out-groups,[45] while others seldom think about social problems in terms of group conflicts. As Donald Kinder and Cindy Kam, who have studied the phenomenon and its political effects in the United States, put it, ethnocentrism is 'a readiness

---

[43] Sumner (1906).   [44] Tajfel (1970; 1981).

[45] These two sides of ethnocentrism, though they frequently overlap, are distinctive. People can and do express strong attachments to in-groups which do not generate hostility to out-groups. See Brewer (1999); Jardina (2019).

to reduce society to us and them ... a readiness to reduce society to us *versus* them'.[46]

The origins of ethnocentrism, and why it varies between people, have been much debated, with different researchers emphasising different aspects of the complex mix of psychological and sociological forces which encourage or discourage the group conflict habit. Ethnocentrism may be an aspect of the 'authoritarian personality' – a tendency to value and insist upon conformity, order and authority, and to find diversity, ambiguity and uncertainty threatening.[47] Or it may be one of a basket of tools employed by people with a 'closed' personality disposition,[48] who find a complex and unstable social world more threatening and harder to deal with than those with a more 'open' disposition.[49] Group competition can also stimulate ethnocentric thinking. People may attach to a group who share a set of goals and compete for economic resources or political influence to secure these goals. Doing so will often put them into competition with other groups seeking the same scarce resources for different goals, and the resulting conflict over resources and influence encourages ethnocentric thinking – sometimes people see an issue as a matter of 'us versus them' because it

---

[46] Kinder and Kam (2009: 8).   [47] Adorno et al. (1950); Altemeyer (1981; 2007).
[48] Johnston, Lavine and Federico (2017).
[49] This difference between 'open' and 'closed' personalities has many sources – political and moral values, perceptions of uncertainty, and the influence of basic brain structure on reactions to threat and novel situations – but all converge on a similar and stable set of different responses: a preference for the known over the unknown, for stability over change, for certainty over uncertainty, and for simplicity over complexity. Ethnocentrism may be one expression of the more general 'closed disposition' – 'closed' personality types are attracted to clearly defined, homogeneous predictable groups, who provide a source of stability and security. They are also more prone to finding new groups with different beliefs threatening, and to dislike change in the mix of groups in society, not due to any features inherent in these groups, but due to their general sensitivity to threats and aversion to novelty. Conversely, those with more 'open' personalities may tend to embrace diversity and change, in keeping with their general personality orientations, and oppose ethnocentrism because it is harmful to the kind of diverse and dynamic society that they favour.

is, indeed, a competition between groups.[50] Inequalities and hierarchies between groups can have a similar effect. When a group feels its privileges or resources are under threat from a competing group, or when a group feels its members do not get fair treatment or a fair share, then all group members will be more prone to see the world in terms of 'us versus them'.[51]

There are a number of key features to ethnocentrism which make it a valuable tool for understanding Britain's recent political disruptions. Ethnocentrism is a *stable* personality orientation, one that *varies* between individuals, and can be *activated* among those who hold it when they perceive *threats* to the in-groups they care about, particularly threats from opposed and disliked out-groups. Ethnocentric voters are sensitive to threats and will mobilise politically against them, leading ethnocentrism to become a stronger predictor of political preferences and choices when such threats are present. It is the stable links between ethnocentrism and demographic features of the electorate which enable it to translate demographic divides into political conflicts; and it is the capacity of ethnocentric 'us versus them' thinking to be activated by threats that gives ethnocentrism its disruptive 'flash' potential, with large and rapid shifts in voters' priorities and behaviour occurring when a perceived threat emerges. Both aspects are crucial to understanding the current political context, which features both long-term structural change and rapid, volatile changes in voter behaviour.

The ethnocentric worldview is stable over time. Those who express a stronger 'us against them' worldview at one point in

---

[50] Some famous and startling experiments in social psychology have shown how powerful inter-group hostilities can be stimulated by relatively modest contests: when psychologist Muzafar Sherif and colleagues (Sherif et al. 1961) set up competitions between two teams of eleven-year-old boys, they rapidly turned nasty, with insults and even blows traded as the 'Rattlers' and 'Eagles' competed for prizes. At larger scales, competition between ethnic or racial groups for resources and privilege is a powerful and well-documented factor in political conflict in many societies, conflict which has often escalated into open warfare (Horowitz 2000).

[51] Pratto and Sidanius (2001); Hagendoorn (1995).

time reliably express similar views if you ask them again years or even decades later. Political scientists Donald Kinder and Cindy Kam reviewed a range of different studies which went back to the same people repeatedly over many years and found that in all these studies ethnocentric attitudes were stable over time. Ethnocentrism behaved in this respect like many other political values, being shaped most in the impressionable years of youth, and becoming harder to shift thereafter.[52] Studies of both in-group attachments such as national identity,[53] and out-group hostilities such as racial prejudice,[54] have arrived at similar conclusions.[55]

This brings us to the second critical feature of ethnocentrism: it *varies* by education level and ethnic identity. Educational expansion and rising ethnic diversity have therefore opened up new divides between ethnocentric voters and those who reject their group-centred worldview. Education strongly predicts levels of both in-group attachment and out-group hostility in the white majority, as we shall see in the next chapter. The relationship between ethnocentrism and ethnic identity is a little more complex. Ethnic minorities are also prone to express hostility to out-groups – for example, large numbers express

[52] Kinder and Kam (2009: ch. 3).
[53] Barrett (2000); Citrin, Reingold and Green (1990); Citrin and Sears (2014).
[54] Ford (2008); Storm, Sobolewska and Ford (2017).
[55] The stability of the ethnocentric habit of mind and the variation in ethnocentrism across populations also raises the possibility that it could, perhaps, be a pre-programmed tendency, written into our genetic code by natural selection. It is a plausible speculation that early humans who formed stronger group attachments and identified and eliminated threats from competing groups more quickly could prevail over those with weaker group attachments, and hence that such a trait could spread in a population. It is, however, fiendishly difficult to figure out the genetic aspect in complex human characteristics such as political orientations and group attachments, which are likely to involve the complex interactions of many different genetic traits and environmental influences. While some researchers have attempted to estimate the genetic element in political orientations (e.g., Martin et al. 1986; Alford, Funk and Hibbing 2005; Funk et al. 2013), the meaning and credibility of such estimates remains intensely debated (see, e.g., Charney and English 2012), suggesting this is not a question that researchers can as yet answer with much confidence.

hostility to a close relative marrying someone from a different ethnic or religious group[56] – but they also tend to reject the group identities favoured by ethnocentric white voters, such as attachment to an ethnically defined nation. This is a consequence of the structural position of ethnic minorities, who are frequently the targets of ethnocentric hostility from the white majority. Ethnic minorities therefore understandably tend to reject the forms of identity and group attachment most attractive to ethnocentric white voters, as they are usually excluded from these and often face hostility from those who most strongly express them. While ethnic minorities are just as prone to ethnocentric thinking as the white majority, this tendency is less likely to find political expression among minority groups, who instead tend to align with white graduate 'conviction liberals' in an 'identity liberal' alliance of groups opposed to ethnocentric white 'identity conservatives', as we show in more detail in the next part of this chapter and in Chapter 3.

The stability of ethnocentric worldviews, and their lasting association with educational and ethnic differences, raises a paradox we need to resolve. How can stable attitudes, and very slow demographic change, account for rapid and dramatic political shifts such as those seen in Britain over the past decade? The third key feature of ethnocentrism resolves this paradox: the political influence of ethnocentric attitudes depends on the political context. Ethnocentrism becomes *activated* when ethnocentric voters perceive a *threat*, leading ethnocentric voters to rally around their threatened in-groups and mobilise hostility to the out-groups seen as posing the threat. Growing identity divides can remain latent in the electorate until ethnocentric voters perceive a threat, at which point change can happen very rapidly.[57] The most influential examination of this threat–activation dynamic comes from Karen Stenner, who works in a tradition with long historical roots, which proposes that the

---

[56] Storm, Sobolewska and Ford (2017).
[57] Sniderman, Hagendoorn and Prior (2004); Sniderman and Hagendoorn (2007); Sniderman et al. (2014).

tendency of hostility towards out-groups is a result of an authoritarian personality.[58] In a series of studies Stenner demonstrates how authoritarian voters who value social order and conformity behave no differently to others when they feel secure, but their attitudes and behaviour are transformed once they perceive a threat to the things they value.[59] Authoritarians become dramatically more intolerant towards out-groups, and they mobilise to eliminate the threat and restore the security and conformity they crave. A seemingly stable political situation can be rapidly transformed by surges in intolerance, demands for strong leadership and action against threatening out-groups.[60]

Immigration, for example, is an issue with a strong tendency to trigger such dynamic threat responses – immigrants are by definition people seeking to cross a group boundary and join a new group. Ethnocentric voters are prone to perceive immigrants as a threat to the national in-group and will mobilise to defend their national in-group when migration is a salient issue. Other issues such as national security, terrorism and war inherently involve group conflict and threats from out-groups, and all such issues tend to activate authoritarian personalities.[61] Stenner has argued that such disruptive surges in authoritarian sentiment are a structural feature of politics, and liberal democracies need to develop better mechanisms to channel and respond to them.[62]

Such threat-mobilisation dynamics have been observed for a long time. A striking early example comes from the research of British sociologist Margaret Stacey, who examined the social and political upheaval caused by an influx of immigrants into the

---

[58] See Kinder and Kam (2009) for other interpretations of the sources of ethnocentrism. See also the Introduction and Chapter 3 for our take on the relationship between authoritarianism and ethnocentrism.

[59] Feldman and Stenner (1997); Stenner (2005).

[60] A good example of this is reaction to terrorist threat embedded in survey experiments: there is a lot of literature showing this, but good places to start are Merolla and Zechmeister (2009) and Sniderman et al. (2014).

[61] Kinder and Kam (2009).   [62] Stenner and Haidt (2018).

small Oxfordshire market town of Banbury in the 1930s.[63] Stacey found ethnocentric activation in response to threat, with Banburian locals showing the same pattern of hostile mobilisation against threatening newcomers that we see in the political conflicts over immigration now playing out on a national stage. The arrival of new people who spoke differently and looked different, the subsequent pressures on existing provision and, even more tellingly, the appearance of new and alien shops on Banbury High Street triggered ethnocentric hostilities among native Banburians, who told Stacey they felt like strangers in their own town. Yet the twist in this tale is that the immigrants who settled in Banbury in the 1930s were all fellow Englishmen and women coming to work in a newly opened factory.[64] Yet because Banburians saw the issue in terms of a locally defined 'us' facing a threat from alien outsiders, their latent ethnocentric tendencies were activated, and they mobilised to defend themselves from this threat to local identity and traditions.

For insular 1930s Banburians, migrant workers coming from a few counties away were already alien enough to be seen as a threatening 'them'. In the more mobile and globalised societies of today, in-groups and out-groups tend to be more broadly defined, but the pattern of dynamic ethnocentric response to threat remains the same. As British society has undergone two massive demographic changes, three new groups of voters have emerged: one associated with higher levels of formal education and the distinct values associated with it; the second a product of growing racial and ethnic diversification; and the third arising from a formerly dominant segment of the white majority reacting defensively to decline. We now present a thumbnail sketch of these groups, and the tensions between them, to provide a summary illustration of how tensions between these

---

[63] Stacey (1960). We are grateful to Malcolm Parkes for making us aware of this remarkable work.

[64] The category of immigrants from overseas is so negligible in the Banbury study that it does not even earn its own entry in the table on origins of immigrants to the town (Stacey 1960: 13).

groups shape identity conflicts in current British politics. In the next chapter we will provide a more extensive account of these groups' identities and values, and of the political arguments which mobilise them against each other.

From demographic change to political conflict: conviction liberals, necessity liberals and identity conservatives

Educational expansion and the rise of conviction liberals

The first of the three new groups is the product of educational expansion. Education is strongly and negatively associated with ethnocentrism: the more exposure to formal education voters have, the more they reject ethnocentric notions of groups and group conflict. In particular, university graduates' attachments to social group identities are weaker and more flexible, and the groups they do attach themselves to are typically broader and more inclusive.[65] Graduates express consistently higher support for individual rights and freedoms, and consistently lower support for the conformity and authority prized by ethnocentric voters. We call this worldview 'conviction identity liberalism': a general tendency to prize individual and minority group rights, and to see diversity as a social good to be promoted. Such an outlook reveals itself in many contemporary social conflicts – it is, for example, university graduates and social liberals who are most likely to question traditional gender roles and family structures, and express the strongest support for feminism and gender equality initiatives,[66] and it is university graduates who most eagerly champion the rights of LGBT+ people to live their lives as they see fit.[67] Conviction liberals are more comfortable with complexity and ambiguity – seeing multiple shades of grey in the issues ethnocentric conservatives prefer to see in

---

[65] Surridge (2016); Lancee and Sarrasin (2015); Meesen, Vroome and Hooghe (2013); Weakliem (2002).

[66] Bozendahl and Myers (2004); Davis and Greenstein (2009).

[67] Ohlander, Batalova and Treas (2005); Schwartz (2010).

black-and-white terms.[68] The trends towards diversity, cosmopolitanism and individualism which identity conservatives find most threatening are the very social changes conviction liberals embrace and seek to advance.

Conviction identity liberals may be less attached to groups than ethnocentric people, but they also hold a distinctive stance on groups and group conflicts beyond this more individualistic worldview. Conviction liberals regard group equality and the fight against prejudice and discrimination as a key political and social value. They therefore seek to stigmatise and sanction those who discriminate against others based on group membership and oppose policies and political parties which they associate with mobilising ethnocentric motives (see Chapter 3). They also seek to internalise anti-prejudice norms, sanctioning themselves for giving in to ethnocentric impulses or prejudiced thoughts,[69] and to entrench and expand anti-racism norms in society, seeking to make discriminatory attitudes and behaviours socially unacceptable.[70]

Ethnic diversity and necessity liberal ethnic minorities

While 'conviction liberal' white university graduates oppose ethnocentrism and embrace diversity as a matter of principle, reflecting the central role of individualism and anti-racism in their personal values, the situation is more complicated for ethnic minorities. Ethnocentric suspicions of out-groups are as widespread in ethnic minority communities as they are in the white majority. Ethnic minorities,[71] in particular those of

---

[68] Johnston, Lavine and Federico (2017).

[69] Blinder, Ford and Ivarsflaten (2013); Ivarsflaten, Blinder and Ford (2010).

[70] Mark Hetherington and Jonathan Weiler, looking at a similar group (who they call 'non-authoritarians') argue that they have a distinctive conception of social justice – 'fairness as out-group preference'. That is, identity liberals tend to find attractive the idea that showing an explicit preference for currently and previously stigmatised minority groups is an important aspect of fairness (Weiler and Hetherington 2009).

[71] In the UK, the term ethnic minorities is applied to those minorities who the Census describes as 'non-white', therefore effectively making the terms ethnic minorities and racial minorities interchangeable. Although there is a lot of

Muslim origin, also tend towards the socially conservative values shared by ethnocentric voters in other areas, including religiosity, women's rights and gay rights (see Chapter 3). This social conservatism makes some ethnic minorities unlikely allies for identity liberals, who strongly support liberal stances on such issues. Ethnic minorities, however, have a distinct and powerful motive for aligning with identity liberals in conflicts over identity and diversity – they are typically the most prominent *targets* of the ethnocentric hostility expressed by white identity conservatives, and the experience of such hostility shapes their political priorities. The perception that ethnic and racial discrimination is a pervasive source of injustice is widely shared among ethnic minority voters,[72] and leads them to see their individual fates as linked to the broader status of their ethnic group. This perception of 'linked fate' is a powerful predictor of ethnic minorities' political attitudes and behaviour, leading them to align with conviction liberals who seek to politically and socially stigmatise prejudice, and to oppose ethnocentric whites who are seen as a threat.[73]

As a result of this, the place of ethnic minorities in any electoral coalition is driven strongly by the identities and value conflicts that are salient to the majority white electorate. As long as the focus of conviction liberals' attention is on racial justice and extending anti-racist social norms, and ethnocentric conservatives are politically mobilised against migrants and minority groups, ethnic minorities have a strong incentive to align with conviction liberals, even though their views on many other social issues fundamentally differ. However, this makes for a

---

debate about what makes an ethnic minority and to what extent non-whiteness or whiteness are objective – or relevant – categories, we follow the Census classification in this book (for an extended discussion see Sobolewska 2017).

[72] Heath et al. (2013).

[73] The idea of members of racial minorities thinking that what happens to other members of their racial group affects what happens to them individually has been developed in the US to describe a unique set of political attitudes of African Americans (Dawson 1996), but has since been shown to influence the political behaviour of ethnic minorities in the UK also (Sanders et al. 2014).

volatile and potentially thin coalition which could dissolve when arguments, for example, over gender equality or gay rights, take centre stage, or when the threat posed by white identity conservatives recedes due to demographic decline, a greater acceptance of minorities or the focus of ethnocentric hostility moving to other out-groups.

Decline and backlash: identity conservatives

It is crucial in understanding the politics of identity conservative voters to remember that until recently they constituted an overwhelming majority of the electorate. Before mass migration and educational expansion, ethnocentric white school leavers' views defined the mainstream. From their point of view, it is society that changed and left them behind, their only apparent fault being that they did not change sufficiently with it.[74] It is therefore no surprise that such voters tend to adopt a conservative stance, seeking to slow down or reverse social changes which they find threatening to their group and which erode its formerly dominant status.[75] Change is perceived as a loss for ethnocentric white voters: a loss of their dominant position, and a loss of the cultural conformity and continuity which they value. Many members of this group associate educational expansion and rising ethnic diversity with a loss of political status – and not without reason, as the electoral and demographic dominance of identity conservatives is indeed steadily being eroded. Such a tendency is also in keeping with these voters' ethnocentric worldview – when people are chronically prone to see politics as a conflict between 'us' and 'them', they will naturally tend to believe that the rise of new groups can be accommodated in politics only by marginalising formerly dominant groups. It is thus no wonder that slogans of restoration such as 'Make America Great Again' or 'Take Back Control' have proved resonant with identity conservative voters.

---

[74] Gest (2016); Cramer (2016).
[75] Kaufmann (2018); Eatwell and Goodwin (2018); Jardina (2019).

Ethnocentric identity conservatives are threatened by both of the rising identity liberal groups. They are threatened by the graduate class, because graduates are conviction liberals who reject their values, such as ethnically defined national belonging, and embrace social changes they oppose, such as immigration and multiculturalism. Identity conservatives are also threatened by migrants and minorities because they are attached to ethnically and culturally defined majority group identities which are eroded by mass migration and the rise of minority communities. Identity conservatives are also threatened by the general shift in social norms and values associated with the rise of both groups, resulting in a steady rise in social liberalism, and the growing stigmatisation of some of their traditional views and attachments. Although, as we show in the next two chapters, identity conservatives have also become more liberal over the long run, they lag behind other groups, and therefore find today that many views they see as unproblematic expressions of their identity attachments or concerns with change are deemed to be unacceptably intolerant by many younger identity liberals with stronger anti-racism norms. Identity conservatives are well aware of this, particularly because of the dominance of identity liberals in the media and within political elites, and often express resentment that they cannot speak their minds and express their opinions freely on issues they care about.[76] As we will describe in Chapter 3, this leads to a 'politics of racism', with conflicts between identity liberals and identity conservatives over the scope of anti-racism norms and the acceptable range of opinions on identity issues.

While these thumbnail sketches are simplified caricatures of large and heterogeneous groups, they give a sense of the tensions at the heart of the identity politics conflicts now emerging – on one side of this are rising identity liberal groups committed to diversity and anti-racism, and on the other side a declining, formerly dominant group attached to narrower

---

[76] Gest (2016).

in-group identities and threatened by rising diversity and social liberalism. We will discuss the attitudes of these three groups in greater length in the next chapter, but now we turn to look at how generational and geographical polarisation can intensify the conflicts between these groups by reducing the level of contact between group members which might promote compromise and understanding.

Identity polarisation: generations and geography

Both educational expansion and ethnic transformation are structured by generation, and the oldest British cohorts have dramatically different educational and ethnic profiles to the youngest. Both identity liberal and identity conservative voters also cluster together and live apart from the other group. Graduates and ethnic minorities congregate in big cities, while white school leavers concentrate in smaller towns and rural areas. These are polarising tendencies – identity liberals and identity conservatives increasingly live and socialise among people from their side of the identity politics divide, and apart from those on the other side. Such geographical segregation also has the potential to increase the electoral impact of identity conflicts, as the British electoral system is built around competition for control of small, geographically defined constituencies. Growing numbers of these seats are dominated either by identity liberal or identity conservative voters, giving the MPs representing them a strong electoral incentive to represent the locally dominant viewpoint, and thus helping to mobilise identity conflicts into Parliamentary politics when they arise (see Chapter 5).

The generational polarisation of identity politics is illustrated in Figure 2.4, which shows the changing proportions of under forties and over seventies who belong to the core identity conservative and identity liberal demographics. In 1986, the core identity conservative group of white school leavers was a dominant majority among all age groups, though it was smaller among the youngest cohorts. The group has steadily declined since, but the retreat has been much more rapid in the youngest age

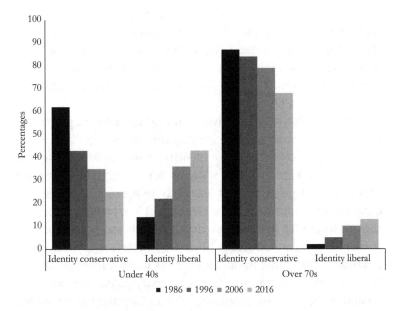

Figure 2.4 Share of under forties and over seventies belonging to the core identity conservative and identity liberal demographic groups, 1986–2016

Source: British Social Attitudes surveys, 1986–2016.

groups, who have grown up since the rise of mass higher education. The share of British residents under forty who are white school leavers fell from nearly two-thirds in 1986 to less than a third in 2016. Among those over seventy – a large and high-turnout group in Britain's ageing society – this decline was much slower. Nearly two-thirds of the oldest generations were still white school leavers in 2016. Identity conservatives are a shrinking minority in the youngest cohorts but continue to define majority opinion in the oldest cohorts. The generational rise of identity liberals mirrors the generational decline in identity conservatives. Graduates and ethnic minorities were a small minority of all cohorts in 1986, but have grown rapidly since, with the growth strongly concentrated in the youngest generations. By 1996, identity liberals made up a fifth of those under forty, by 2006 they were up to over a third, and by 2016 they had risen to nearly 40 per cent of the youngest generations, substantially outnumbering identity conservatives. As we moved into the 2010s, identity liberals were the dominant group defining mainstream opinion in the youngest generations, while remaining a minority group outnumbered by identity conservatives in all the older cohorts.

Very large generational divides have thus opened up between the youngest cohorts, where identity liberals are now dominant, and the oldest cohorts, where identity conservatives still set the tone. Such divides will be with us for a long time, because generational replacement is a very slow process. Ethnocentric older cohorts dominated by white school leavers will remain in the electorate for decades, providing a large and persistent constituency for ethnocentric politics. Conversely, while university graduates and ethnic minorities are far more numerous among the cohorts growing up since university expansion and the second wave of mass migration, it will be many years before generational replacement enables them to achieve the kind of overall electoral dominance that white identity conservatives enjoyed just a few decades ago. Both the educational and ethnic trends driving this generational replacement process are accelerating – the children attending school in Britain today are the most ethnically diverse in history, and university attendance rates continue to break records each year. As a result, the differences in the demographic composition of young and old cohorts will continue to rise in coming years, increasing the potential for generational conflict.

These differences in composition are consequential because our social lives are structured by generation – we go to school and university with people the same age, then join workplaces organised into age-structured hierarchies, with those from the same generation starting at roughly the same time and moving up the workplace hierarchies together.[77] Peers born within a few years of each other are therefore heavily over-represented within

---

[77] Alwyn and McCammon (2003).

friendship groups and social networks, and the mix of people in a generation has a big influence on our everyday social experiences. When a cohort is more ethnically diverse, diversity will seem more 'normal' to its white members. When a cohort has a higher share of graduates, university education will be seen as a more 'normal' aspiration, and the political values found among graduates will be seen as more 'normal' too. Generations dominated by identity liberals show, for example, much more liberal attitudes towards intermarriage between different ethnic groups, and have a strong social norm stigmatising expressions of opposition to such marriages.[78]

A similar polarising trend is evident when we look at where identity liberals and identity conservatives live. Britain's ethnic minorities have always been unevenly geographically distributed, reflecting the legacies of early urban settlement and chain migration. Ethnic minority communities are concentrated in larger urban areas – in particular, the largest English cities such as London, Birmingham and Manchester.[79] While levels of ethnic diversity are rising all over the country, driven by immigration, ethnic minority population growth and the internal migration of ethnic minorities,[80] the pattern of growth in minority communities has been highly uneven. Figure 2.5 illustrates this, plotting the change in local ethnic diversity between 2001 and 2011 against the starting level of local ethnic diversity.[81] The pattern is clear: the more diverse a place was in 2001, the larger the increase in ethnic diversity it has experienced since. The ethnic minority share in the least diverse places rose on average by two percentage points in the following decade,

---

[78] Storm, Sobolewska and Ford (2017); Ivarsflaten, Blinder and Ford (2010).

[79] Smaller towns and cities such as Bradford and Leicester also have very high levels of diversity due to being the focal points of particular migration flows: Bradford imported unskilled labour from Pakistan for its textile industries, while Leicester received a high share of East African Asian refugees resettling from Uganda and Kenya.

[80] Ethnic minorities, like white Britons, tend to move from inner cities to the suburbs as their ages and incomes rise (Finney and Simpson 2009b).

[81] Measured as the percentage of residents who identified their ethnic group as something other than 'White British' in the 2001 Census.

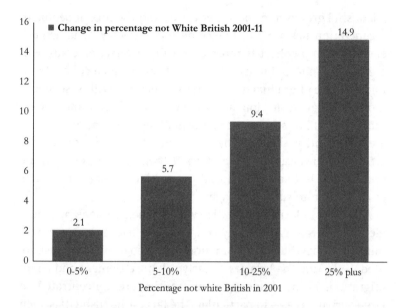

Figure 2.5 Local authority change in ethnic diversity 2001–11 by starting levels of ethnic diversity in 2001, England and Wales

Source: Census 2001 and 2011.

while in the most diverse places the increase was 15 percentage points – more than seven times as large.

With diversity rising most where it was already high, and rising least where it began low, local identities and experiences of diversity are diverging. Britain's ethnically diverse cities, led by London, are becoming 'superdiverse' places with a multitude of internally diverse migrant and ethnic minority communities,[82] where there is no locally dominant group and the white British are just one ethnic community among many. At the other end of the spectrum, a large part of the British population – and the bulk of older ethnocentric white voters – live in rural, small town and urban contexts which are still nearly mono-ethnic, with 95 per cent or more of the population identifying as white British, and with only modest growth in their small

[82] Vertovec (2007).

minority communities. The everyday experiences of diversity are diverging between communities, just as the formative experiences of diversity are diverging between generations.

Britain's towns and cities are also diverging by education levels. Mass university education now produces two major waves of internal migration in Britain every year – the first as new students move to start university, the second when new graduates move again in search of work. Both moves tend to increase the segregation of communities by education level.[83] Britain's universities are nearly all located in large towns and cities, while the students they educate come from all over the country. Each autumn, young people depart en masse from the smaller towns and rural areas where they grew up and flow into Britain's big cities and university towns to register for their degree studies. A few years later, when these same young people flow out of the university campuses, it is again the biggest cities that benefit, and the smaller communities that lose out. Most graduates either stay in the city where they have studied or move on to other large cities – particularly London – where graduate job opportunities are best.

Mass higher education is thus experienced by smaller communities as a massive loss of youth and potential – the higher a young student flies, the more likely they are to leave, and the less likely they are to return. The expansion of university education has ramped up the scale of this process, and as access rates approach 50 per cent Britain's universities now annually suck the 'best and brightest' from every community in the country into the nation's large urban areas, while those who leave school after GCSEs and A-levels typically remain where they are. Growing geographical segregation increases the disruptive political potential of identity conflicts in several ways. The first is a matter of composition.[84] As Britain's big cities and smaller communities have diverged, the common ground between different communities has shrunk and the differences between their

---

[83] Swinney and Williams (2016).   [84] Maxwell (2019).

values and priorities have grown. Where we live, like the generation we grow up in, also has a powerful and lasting influence on the social networks we form, so geographical segregation increases the contact we have with like-minded groups, while reducing everyday contact with people whose experiences and views are different. This entrenches the views that individuals encounter more frequently and marginalises opinions that, though frequently held outside the immediate peer group, or local area, are seldom encountered within it.[85]

The political impact of geographical segregation is also magnified by Britain's electoral system. Members of Parliament are elected to represent a single area and all the voters within it, so when places become more polarised by education and ethnicity, this increases the influence of distinctive local attitudes and priorities of MPs. Legislators representing ethnically diverse and graduate-heavy seats have an electoral incentive to faithfully represent the identity liberal worldview of their constituents, while MPs in seats where white voters with low education levels are locally dominant have a similar incentive to represent the ethnocentric outlook of their local voters, even if, as we show in Chapter 5, such views are often far away from such MPs' personal values.

From demographic change to political change: is demography destiny?

Is demography destiny? Can we predict the impact these dramatic ongoing demographic changes will have on our political system? Our answer is a resounding 'No', for two reasons. First, previous claims that demographic change will produce inevitable political shifts have come to grief, because they have underestimated the capacity of political actors to respond and adapt to demographic change. Four prominent examples from recent British political history illustrate this. In the wake of Labour's

---

[85] Sunstein (2002).

fourth successive election defeat in 1959, two leading researchers asked 'Must Labour lose?'[86] The authors argued the likely
answer was 'Yes', but the Labour Party begged to differ, winning
four of the next five elections. British election researchers
reflecting on Labour's repeated successes in the 1970s then
argued that demographic and generational change would further cement Labour's dominance in the contests to come.[87] Mrs
Thatcher put paid to that notion. Researchers in the 1990s,
writing in the wake of four Conservative election victories, once
again raised the existential question, asking whether 'Labour's
Last Chance' had passed, with the social changes unleashed over
many years of Conservative rule portending terminal decline for
the opposition.[88] As in 1960, this diagnosis arrived just a few
years before its refutation, in the form of a new leader, a new
strategy and renewed electoral success. Finally, researchers and
party strategists argued in the early 2010s that the Conservative
Party would struggle to secure a general election majority unless
it could improve its appeal to Britain's rapidly growing ethnic
minority communities.[89] A few years after these reports were
published, the Conservatives under David Cameron won their
first House of Commons majority in over two decades, despite
failing to improve their appeal to ethnic minority voters.[90] In all
of these cases, the parties confounded predictions of doom by
finding ways to adapt their appeal and shift their electoral
coalitions to address the effects of demographic change. There
is no inevitable read across from demographic change to
political change because parties are not passive observers, but
active agents who react to change and shape its political
meaning.

This argument applies with particular strength to identity
politics, because of the dynamic nature of identity conflicts, with
voters' preferences shifting rapidly in response to the rise and

---

[86] Abrams and Rose (1960).
[87] Butler and Stokes (1974: chs 9–11); Thorburn (1977).   [88] Heath et al. (1994).
[89] Ashcroft (2012a); Cooper (2018); see also Wheatcroft (2005).
[90] Martin (2019).

fall of perceived threats. This process provides many openings for elite actors looking to influence the political impact of identity conflicts. Parties and leaders can seek to activate or de-activate identity attachments by framing political narratives in ways that emphasise divisions between groups or focus on the values and identities that unify otherwise diverse people. As we shall see, such choices have played a large role in how parties have approached identity issues to date, and the choices they make have lasting consequences on the political form identity conflicts take. Different choices may open up new paths to resolving such conflicts in future.

For both of these reasons, we argue not that demography is destiny, but rather that demographic shifts change the *electoral resources* available to parties and open up the *potential* for new political conflicts to emerge. Demographic change creates new opportunities and new risks for parties, but does not determine the choices they make in the face of new challenges, or the consequences of these choices. Different reactions to the same trends can channel demographic change towards divergent political outcomes, as we illustrate in our analysis of the very different ways demographic divides and identity conflicts have been mobilised in Scotland (see Chapter 9). It is the choices parties have made in response to new risks and opportunities, and the mobilisation of voters in response to these choices, which have charted the road to Brexit, and beyond into the Brexitland politics of today, with the country divided as never before by identity conflicts. The story we aim to tell in the coming chapters encompasses both the changing opportunities for identity politics which have arisen from demographic change, and how the choices made by different governments have shaped the form of identity politics that has emerged. In this first section, we now move to a more in-depth review of the identity attachments and identity conflicts that define Brexit-land (Chapter 3), before examining how these divides were first mobilised a generation ago during the first wave of post-war immigration (Chapter 4).

3 DIVIDED OVER DIVERSITY: IDENTITY CONSERVATIVES AND IDENTITY LIBERALS

Introduction

Long-term demographic changes have driven the emergence of an identity politics divide, with two growing groups of identity liberals on one side and a declining, formerly dominant, group of identity conservatives on the other side. In this chapter we lay out in more detail the values and attitudes underpinning this divide and explain why identity conflicts between these groups are often intense and difficult to resolve. Two reactions to rising ethnic diversity have pulled the white majority in different directions: a process of gradual overall accommodation to change has offset by rising polarisation within the white population. As we showed in Chapter 2, successive cohorts of British voters are growing up in steadily more diverse social contexts. Each generation of white voters expresses higher levels of comfort with diversity and ethnic minorities than its predecessor. A multicultural Britain is becoming a part of 'normal' social life, but this happens slowly because each generation's sense of 'normal' is informed by the conditions when they grew up, and older generations whose norms were informed by earlier social contexts stick around in the electorate for a long time.

Both ethnic diversification and rising social acceptance of it are set to continue. As we noted in the preceding chapter, the fastest growing ethnic minority group in Britain today is the mixed ethnicity group: children with parents from different ethnic groups. Not only does this point to rising acceptance of diversity in the most intimate of social spheres, it also means the youngest cohort just arriving in the electorate features a growing group for whom ethnic diversity is a daily experience around the childhood dinner table as well as in the playground, on campus or in the office. At the time of writing (2020), the segment of the white British population who grew up before mass migration began in the 1950s, and who therefore express the strongest opposition to diversity, is elderly and declining. Conversely, the youngest voters currently joining the electorate express greater acceptance of diversity in all walks of social life than every older cohort. Within two decades, there will be virtually no voters left with any direct memory of Britain before the onset of mass migration.

While diversity is becoming more accepted overall, there are new arguments arising around the terms of this accommodation, over how and where to draw the lines between in-groups and out-groups, and what forms of group-based judgements are socially acceptable. The overall drift towards more inclusive attitudes has been accompanied by rising polarisation within the electorate. Older generations in general, and in particular white school leavers, are less exposed to diversity in their everyday lives, and often see ethnic change as threating to their understandings of British identity and culture. They favour government action to slow down or reverse this process of change. Younger generations and liberal graduates see diversity and ethnic change as both inevitable and laudable, and want to see the government focus instead on stronger action to combat the discrimination and disadvantage faced by ethnic minority groups. There are fundamental disagreements not only about the substance of policymaking in response to rising diversity, but also about how to talk about diversity. What one side sees as legitimate expressions of anxiety about the speed of change and attachment to traditional identities is criticised by the other as illegitimate expressions of prejudice. This race card politics – with fundamental disagreements over where the line is drawn in discussions of groups and group attachments – is a growing obstacle to compromise and dialogue to resolve the new political conflicts of Brexitland.

This chapter will first expand on how we measure the differences between the three identity camps, focusing on their relative tendency towards ethnocentric 'us' and 'them' thinking. Then we will tackle the question of why these differences are so hard to bridge and introduce the social norms employed by each distinct identity camp to defend their position and attack the legitimacy of their opponents. Such norms polarise discussions by denying the legitimacy of the opponent's concerns, making compromise and even basic engagement in a meaningful debate more difficult. Ultimately, it is this lack of mutual recognition and dialogue that generates the intense and polarised disputes which characterise Brexitland identity conflicts.

Identity conservatives: ethnocentrism as a political agenda

Ethnocentrism has two central aspects: attachment to in-groups and negative attitudes towards out-groups. To track the evolution of ethnocentric attitudes and identity politics over the long run, we have sought out measures which have been asked reasonably often on long-running political and social surveys. For in-group attachments, we draw particularly on measures of national identity. The nation is one of the most salient in-group identities for voters. Who does, and does not, belong to the nation is a central question in debates over diversity and immigration in Britain, as it has been in other countries experiencing mass immigration and ethnic change. National identity is also regularly asked about in surveys, so we have relatively rich data to draw upon in examining its effects. However, the nation is unlikely to be the only identity important to ethnocentric voters, and readers should bear in mind that other forms of group attachments which are not captured in the data sources available to us are also likely to matter to ethnocentric voters. The measures we use include belief in British superiority to other nations, the protection of Britain's culture and economy from foreign influence, and the notion that Britain should put its national interests before international cooperation. Later, we also make use of preferences for English or Scottish over British national identity, because both these forms of nationalism have strong and politically consequential ethnocentric elements.[1]

Out-group hostility comes in many forms, including negative stereotypes, feelings of threat, negative emotions and discriminatory behaviour amongst others, but as we wish to track the evolution of British politics over a long period, we are once again forced to focus our analysis on what is regularly available in existing data sources. The most frequently available measures of out-group hostility, and thus the ones we focus on, are 'social distance' measures capturing opposition to social contact with minority groups, self-rated racial prejudice and various measures of hostility to immigrants as an out-group.

Both in-group attachments and out-group hostility show a strong generational pattern,[2] as illustrated in Figure 3.1. Older generations consistently express stronger support for an ethnically exclusive national identity, and more opposition to ethnic minority in-laws. When we have measures asked repeatedly over many years, we find these attitudes are generally stable over time within generations, while showing large and persistent differences between generations.[3] There are also deep and enduring divides by education level and ethnicity in ethnocentrism, as Figure 3.2 illustrates. White school leavers are much more likely, for example, to agree that birth and ancestry are very important markers of 'being British' and to agree that those who do not share British culture and traditions can never be 'truly British'. By contrast, large majorities of white graduates

---

[1] See Sobolewska and Ford (2018). For a more comprehensive account of English nationalism and its political effects, see Henderson and Wyn-Jones (2020).

[2] We assume, in line with previous research, that these ethnocentric worldviews are stable over time for individual people. See, for example, Kinder and Kam (2009: 66–9). More recent work has also found evidence of high stability in hostility to immigrants as an out-group, across multiple panel studies in multiple countries, which is what we would expect if ethnocentrism is a stable aspect of voters' worldviews. See Kutsov, Laaker and Reller (2019).

[3] See the Online Appendix (www.cambridge.org/Brexitland) for details. See also Ford (2008); Storm, Sobolewska and Ford (2017).

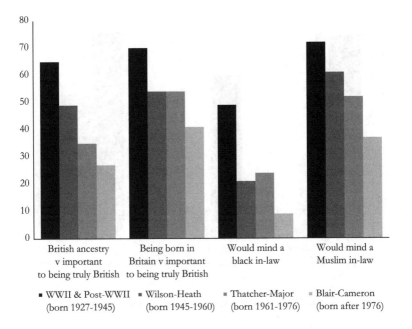

Figure 3.1 Share of people in different generations expressing ethnocentric views (percentages)

Source: British Social Attitudes, 2013.

and ethnic minorities reject birth and ancestry as markers of Britishness, and both groups are also more likely to reject the argument that the national in-group should exclude those who do not share British culture and traditions. However, while the link between demographics and identity attachments is strong, it is not perfect: there is a substantial minority of low-qualification whites who reject ethnocentric conceptions of the nation, and a substantial minority of graduates and ethnic minorities who express at least some support for them. The same patterns obtain for hostility to minority and migrant out-groups.[4]

Ethnocentric voters also have a distinctive political agenda encompassing a range of issues where groups and group conflict

---

[4] See the Online Appendix for further details: www.cambridge.org/Brexitland

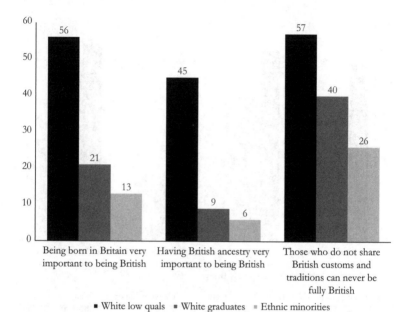

Figure 3.2 Ethnocentric national identity among white school leavers, white graduates and ethnic minorities (percentages)

Source: British Social Attitudes, 2013.

are salient. We illustrate this in Table 3.1, where we show the differences in the views of those who score highest and lowest on measures of ethnocentrism. Across a range of issues, including immigration, equal opportunities, views of the EU and views of devolution and constitutional reform, ethnocentric voters consistently favour stances which protect or enhance the position of their in-group, while opposing policies which protect or enhance the position of out-groups. Ethnocentric voters hold negative views of the EU, seeing it as a threatening out-group which constrains the sovereignty of their national in-groups. Ethnocentric voters are also strongly prone to negative views of immigrants and tend to oppose policies which support and protect ethnic minorities. On any issue framed as a conflict between in-groups and out-groups, ethnocentric voters will reliably line

Table 3.1 Ethnocentrism and views on political issues involving group conflict

Issue	Agreement with statement, high ethnocentrism	Agreement with statement, low ethnocentrism	Difference
Immigration attitudes			
Immigration should be reduced 'a lot'	83	27	56
Migration is bad for the economy	73	17	56
Migration undermines British culture	69	16	53
Asylum seekers should not be allowed to stay	46	10	36
Britain would lose its identity if more Muslims came*	88	50	38
Britain would lose its identity if more Eastern Europeans came	82	48	34
Equal opportunities/multiculturalism			
Oppose government assistance to support ethnic minority customs and traditions	72	43	29
Ethnic minorities should blend into society, not maintain customs and traditions	70	50	20
Government takes better care of ethnic minorities than the white majority*	65	30	35

Table 3.1 (cont.)

Issue	Agreement with statement, high ethnocentrism	Agreement with statement, low ethnocentrism	Difference
Euroscepticism			
Would vote to leave the EU in a referendum	62	22	40
Little or no benefit to UK from EU membership	54	23	31
UK should not follow EU decisions it disagrees with	76	40	36
Devolution/constitutional arrangements			
Support for English Parliament (England)	22	19	3
Support for English independence (England)	20	13	7
England benefits more than Scotland from UK (Scotland)	37	22	15
Support for Scottish independence (Scotland)	30	20	10

Sources: British Social Attitudes, 2013; Scottish Social Attitudes, 2013 (Scottish devolution items), items marked * from British Election Study, 2010. Ethnocentrism measured using ethnic nationalism, except on questions marked with * where self-rated prejudice is used due to data constraints.

up behind the policies seen as best defending 'us' against 'them'. The main exception is constitutional preferences – while ethnocentric Scottish voters show a stronger tendency to see the UK system as biased against them, and to favour reforming it or leaving it altogether, ethnocentric English voters do not (yet) express similar resentments about United Kingdom political institutions.[5] This could change in the future, if ethnocentric English voters come to see the other nations of the UK, or the UK's overarching political institutions, as opponents frustrating the preferences of their in-group.

While ethnocentric attitudes inform a coherent worldview and political agenda focused on conflict between in-groups and out-groups, the lines of this conflict are not drawn in the same way by all ethnocentric voters. Ethnocentrism is a tendency to divide the world into 'us' and 'them', but the nature of the boundaries used to separate 'us' from 'them' and the political and social issues seen as 'us versus them' conflicts vary between individuals and evolve over time. The political context people grow up with informs where these lines are drawn. Over time, new minority groups who are initially seen as alien and threatening come to be accepted as part of a broader 'us', with their cultural and racial differences recognised but no longer seen as a threat.[6] Even within the most ethnocentric demographic groups, there is substantial potential for tension between older and younger generations who draw the lines between 'us' and 'them' differently, with older cohorts rejecting groups that younger cohorts accept. Figure 3.3 illustrates this, showing how the share of both white university graduates and white school leavers who accept the idea of an ethnic minority in-law rises steadily among younger generations who have grown up in a more diverse Britain.

---

[5] See Henderson and Wyn-Jones (2020) for interesting discussions of why this is, and whether this situation may change in the future.

[6] Alba and Nee (2003); Alba and Foner (2015).

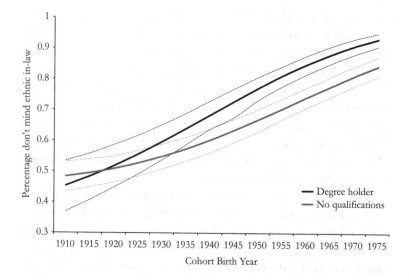

Figure 3.3 Share of white graduates and school leavers accepting the idea of an ethnic minority in-law

Source: Ford (2008).

Graduate conviction liberals: social norms and the politics of anti-racism

While views about who belongs to 'us' and 'them' shift over time and between generations, identity conservatives all share a tendency to see politics in terms of groups and group conflict. Conviction identity liberals, the first of the two identity liberal groups, are very different. This group's identity liberalism involves both the rejection of this ethnocentric worldview and the embrace of anti-prejudice social norms which stigmatise those who hold such views. Conviction identity liberals see the ethnocentric worldview, and the political stances which flow from it, as morally wrong and regard combatting the in-group bias and out-group hostility of identity conservatives as a core political value. This conviction is reflected in a commitment to strengthening and entrenching *anti-prejudice social norms* which stigmatise majority ethnocentric attitudes and behaviour as socially and morally unacceptable.[7] Identity liberals seek to protect vulnerable minorities from the ethnocentric hostility and discrimination they deplore, embracing both equal opportunities policies which aim to protect minorities from discrimination[8] and improve their representation in powerful institutions.

We use different measures to capture the normative and practical elements to conviction liberal politics. The first is a set of attitudes called 'motivation to control prejudice' which capture the degree to which people have internalised anti-racism social norms and seek to police their own behaviour in accordance with these norms. These motivations, like ethnocentrism, vary strongly with education level and generation, with younger university graduates showing the strongest commitment to anti-prejudice norms, and older white school leavers the weakest. Unfortunately, direct measures of this concept have only recently been developed so we only have them available in a handful of recent surveys. For earlier periods, we have to make use of indirect measures which can serve as a proxy for a commitment to anti-racism social norms such as positive views of migrant and ethnic minority groups, and friendship with members of these groups.

As Table 3.2 illustrates, positive views of out-groups, opposition to ethnocentrism and motivation to control prejudice are all more widespread among white university graduates than among white school leavers. Majorities of white graduates think British culture is enriched by migration, see ethnic minority migration positively, and hold positive views of ethnic minorities, all stances which most white school leavers reject. Nearly three-quarters of white graduates report having multiple migrant-origin friends compared with just a third of white school leavers (and a fifth of older white school leavers). Half of white graduates think strong patriotic feelings lead to

---

[7] Ivarsflaten, Blinder and Ford (2010); Blinder, Ford and Ivarsflaten (2013).
[8] Blinder, Ford and Ivarsflaten (2019).

Table 3.2 Positive views of out-groups and attachment to anti-prejudice social norms among white graduates and white school leavers

Issue	Agreement, white graduates	Agreement, white school leavers	Difference
Contact/positive views of out-groups			
Positive view of asylum seekers	40	12	28
Think of self as European	29	7	22
Multiple friends born outside Britain	72	35	37
Benefits of migrants from EU outweigh costs	41	13	28
British culture enriched by migration	64	16	48
Positive feelings about Muslims*	60	34	26
Ethnic minority immigration good for Britain	52	24	28
Opposition to ethnocentrism			
Strong patriotic feelings lead to intolerance in Britain	48	30	18
Strong patriotic feelings lead to negative attitudes to immigrants	53	31	22
Anti-prejudice social norms			
Acting in non-prejudiced ways towards Muslims is personally important to me	59	39	20
Using stereotypes about Muslims is not OK according to my personal values	68	44	24
I get angry with myself when I have a prejudiced thought	40	26	14
I do not want to appear racist, even to myself	68	56	12

Sources: British Social Attitudes, 2013, items marked * from British Election Study, 2010. Anti-prejudice norms measures from 'Welfare State Under Strain' survey fielded by YouGov in 2013.

intolerance or generate hostility to immigrants, while only 30 per cent of white school leavers endorse such views. Majorities of white graduates report feelings of guilt at prejudiced thoughts and strong motivations to treat minority groups equally. What characterises the conviction liberal worldview most prevalent among white university graduates is thus not just the absence of prejudice, but a positive commitment to oppose and fight discrimination.

These views in turn inform a distinctive equal opportunities and anti-discrimination policy agenda.[9] Nearly half of white graduates believe ethnic minorities should be able to keep their customs and traditions, and large majorities support greater efforts by government to ensure equal opportunities for ethnic minorities and access to public education by legal migrants. However, support for stronger multicultural or affirmative action policies is markedly lower. While a majority of white graduates believe ethnic minorities should keep their cultural traditions rather than assimilate, only a minority back government-funded efforts to support minority cultures. Similarly, while a substantial majority of white graduates support greater government effort to improve equal opportunities for ethnic minorities, only a small minority would back 'affirmative action'-style policies which explicitly target resources, university places or jobs at ethnic minorities. Britain's conviction liberals favour a kind of passive multiculturalism – they want ethnic diversity celebrated and ethnic minorities protected from discrimination, but they do not generally support interventionist policies which give minority groups preferential treatment in decisions about jobs, university places or other resources.

[9] Further details on this are provided in the Online Appendix: www.cambridge .org/Brexitland

Ethnic minority necessity liberals: discrimination, linked fate and strategic alliances

We might expect British ethnic minorities to be obvious allies of the 'conviction liberal' white graduates who embrace anti-racism norms and advocate for equal opportunities policies. The truth is more complex. While ethnic minorities share white graduates' support for anti-racism and equal opportunities, they also express some ethnocentric attitudes at similar rates to the white majority,[10] they are far more religious on average than the white population,[11] and often hold socially conservative views on family, sexual orientations and gender roles.[12] These are all factors which could potentially align them with identity conservative white voters. On the other hand, ethnic minorities strongly support policies accommodating religious and ethnic diversity and equal opportunities, and these issues are much more important for minority voters as a factor determining their political choices.[13] Even though there is great diversity within and between the different ethnic minority communities, and little evidence that their political attitudes on bread-and-butter issues differ from those of the general population,[14] ethnic minorities' intense and shared focus on prejudice and discrimination tends to align them politically with white graduates, for whom anti-racism is also a core political value. Yet this alignment is predicated almost entirely on white graduates' commitment to protect minorities and their rights, as on many other issues socially conservative ethnic minority voters and liberal individualist white graduates are poles apart. If other social issues were to rise to the top of the political agenda, such as gay rights, gender equality or teaching liberal social values to children, the coalition of ethnic minorities and white graduates would come under strain. Many European anti-immigrant

[10] Storm, Sobolewska and Ford (2017).
[11] Voas and Ling (2010); Voas and Fleischmann (2012); Lewis and Kayshap (2013).
[12] Saggar (2004); Heath et al. (2013); MORI (2018).
[13] Heath et al. (2013: chs 5 and 6).
[14] Studlar (1986); Sobolewska (2005); Health et al. (2013)

parties already seek to mobilise such tensions by campaigning heavily on secular liberals' anxieties about Muslim minorities' religiosity and socially conservative values.[15]

The importance of anti-racism and equal opportunities to the political alignment of ethnic minorities reflects a real and continuing experience of disadvantage and hostility in many areas of social life. Black and Asian minorities generally, and Muslim minorities in particular, are more likely to be targeted by police,[16] suffer at the hands of immigration officials,[17] and face discrimination when competing for university places,[18] seeking employment,[19] and trying to rent or buy a home.[20] The widespread experience of discrimination and disadvantage in many walks of life shapes ethnic minority voters' political priorities. Nearly half of respondents to the 2010 Ethnic Minority British Election Study, the most comprehensive recent survey of ethnic minority political attitudes, believed that ethnic minorities did not receive the same opportunities as white people in Britain, nearly six in ten thought black and Asian people were stopped by the police for no reason, and over 90 per cent reported that there was racial prejudice in Britain. For white identity liberals, action on discrimination is an expression of abstract values, but for ethnic minorities it is a matter of concrete personal and group self-interest. Even though ethnic minority voters are often socially conservative, they align with white liberals on issues such as those civil liberties, immigration and equal

---

[15] Betz (2016); Kallis (2018).

[16] Bowling and Philips (2007); Philips and Bowling (2017).

[17] A problem greatly exacerbated by the 'hostile environment' policies introduced by the Conservatives in 2014, which made the nation's landlords and public service providers into informal and unregulated immigration officials, by making migration status checks mandatory on all those seeking to rent property or access public services, and resulted in high-profile cases of discriminatory treatment causing major harm to the lives of elderly British ethnic minority citizens (Gentleman 2019). The application of this policy to the rental sector was judged discriminatory and in breach of human rights law by the High Court of England and Wales in 2019 (Spencer 2019).

[18] Boliver (2013; 2016).   [19] Heath and DiStasio (2019).

[20] Carlson and Eriksson (2015); Ausburg, Schneck and Hinz (2019).

opportunities where discrimination, and potential state responses to it, are salient to them.

Research into the political attitudes of minorities generally finds that even ethnic minority voters who have not personally experienced discrimination are nevertheless aware it is prevalent in British society and believe that it impacts on their lives. They are therefore strongly supportive of anti-discrimination and equal opportunity policies.[21] This perception of prejudice as a force shaping the lives of all minority group members is closely connected to 'linked fate', a belief that the fate of the individual is inextricably linked and influenced by what is happening to the wider group and how the group is treated.[22] Therefore, it is the general perception that prejudice is a social problem rather than individual experiences of discrimination that most influence ethnic minority voters' political attitudes and behaviour.[23]

Why identity conflicts are polarising: a clash of social norms

The conflicts between identity conservatives and identity liberals flow from their very different ethnocentric tendencies, the status of the majority in-group and the problems faced by minority out-groups. Yet the mere existence of such differences does not explain the polarised nature of political arguments over race, immigration and other identity issues. Such debates often evoke very strong emotions because they involve strong normative claims. In fact, paradoxically one of the most polarising aspects of identity politics conflicts stems from a point of very broad agreement. There is a general social consensus that racism is a personal failing and a social evil, so those judged racist, or

---

[21] Around 40 per cent of respondents who said they had not experienced discrimination personally in the last five years still agreed that it holds back non-white people (Ethnic Minority British Election Study, 2010).

[22] Dawson (1996); though see Laniyonu (2019) about how in Britain linked fate is less influential than in the United States.

[23] Sanders et al. (2014)

even accused of racism, face a substantial social stigma. Disagreement as to what constitutes racist, and thus unacceptable, behaviour therefore becomes very heated because all involved recognise that the stakes are high. The result is an emotive tug of war between identity liberals seeking to apply more expansive definitions of racism in order to expunge prejudice from society, and identity conservatives pushing back against such definitions, which they feel inhibit free expression of legitimate views and group attachments, and stigmatise them unfairly.

To illustrate how widespread social norms sanctioning racism are, we designed an experiment to compare the punishments people suggested for racist behaviour in an everyday social situation with those they would impose for other forms of social transgression. We asked respondents in a nationally representative survey to imagine that they were a shop manager, and that they need to decide what sort of disciplinary action, if any, to take against an employee who was rude to customers in various ways. We randomly varied the kind of rude behaviour they had to judge, with a total of four options tested: criticising mothers for not controlling their children; suggesting customers were too poor to buy the shop's goods; criticising customers for using poor English; and making racist comments towards a customer. Our design was therefore testing whether there was a distinctive stigma attached to racism, in comparison with other sources of rudeness, resulting in a stronger punitive response. We offered our respondents a range of reactions of differing severity, including dismissing the employee immediately, giving them a warning, and doing nothing.

The results, presented in Figure 3.4, confirm that racist behaviour is indeed taken more seriously than other forms of social transgression. While the majority of our hypothetical managers were not keen to tolerate rudeness on any grounds, they were more likely to dish out warnings rather than dismiss employees in most of our scenarios. Only 2 per cent would dismiss an employee for being rude about a customer's parenting. Surprisingly, given Britain's class divisions and the salience of debates over food banks and poverty in recent years, only 4 per cent

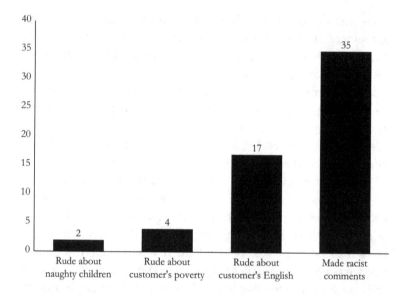

Figure 3.4 Share of respondents who would dismiss an employee for different forms of rudeness to a customer (percentages)

Source: YouGov survey commissioned by the authors, March 2018.

would dismiss an employee for ridiculing a customer's poverty. As we expected, the sanctioning of rudeness based on race is much more severe, reflecting the strength of anti-racism norms. Thirty-five per cent of respondents recommended firing the employee for making racist comments, twice as many as would react to rudeness based on language skills. This sharp rise in support for the most punitive action was mirrored by a sharp decline in those saying they would take no disciplinary action at all – while many people were happy to let rudeness about naughty children slide, virtually no one was willing to let racist comments or rudeness about language skills pass without taking action.[24]

---

[24] Given that our experiment was designed in such a way that any given respondent saw only one of these options, rather than all of them to choose

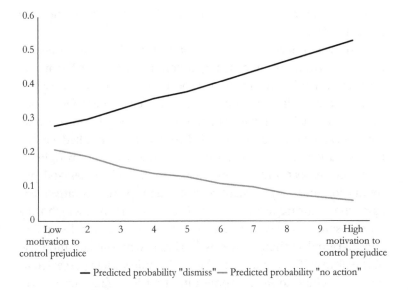

— Predicted probability "dismiss"— Predicted probability "no action"

Figure 3.5 Predicted probability of dismissing the employee and of taking no action by levels of motivation to control prejudice

Source: YouGov survey commissioned by the authors, March 2018.

The vast majority of imaginary shopkeepers, fully 97 per cent, saw racism as a transgression they should punish, an impressively broad social consensus, though people varied in how severe they thought the punishment should be. As Figure 3.5 illustrates, the strength of the sanction people apply is closely related to their own anti-prejudice norms. Those who expressed the strongest motivation to police their own prejudices also applied the toughest sanctions to others: nearly half of those at the top of the anti-prejudice scale would dismiss the racially prejudiced employee. Meanwhile, those who did not express a strong need to control their own prejudices were also more forgiving of others' transgressions – less than a third of those at the bottom of the anti-prejudice scale would dismiss the

from and compare, we can be sure that this is not an artefact of social desirability bias sometimes seen in surveys and public opinion polls.

racially offensive employee, while roughly a quarter would take no action at all.

Anti-racism norms are thus a potent force in society – people are more willing to take strong action against racist behaviour than against other forms of anti-social behaviour, and very few people were willing to ignore racism entirely. A perceived violation of anti-racism norms can therefore do real harm to someone's social position or even their livelihood. To be called a racist in today's Britain is a powerful stigma that can shut people off from the respect and support of peers and colleagues and put reputation and employment at risk. Identity conservatives are particularly aware of the power of the label 'racist', which they often resent as a means used by liberals to shut down discussion and marginalise their concerns.[25] This is why the common use of the phrase 'I'm not a racist, but ...', while widely perceived as being a prelude to saying something that is in fact racist, actually reflects invocation of a shared recognition that racism is unacceptable. It is an attempt to reach out to those on the other side of the conversation, seeking common ground and trying to neutralise an anticipated hostile response to views the speaker worries may be seen as contentious. Yet it usually has the opposite effect, alerting the other side to the fact that views they reject will be expressed. The roots of this social tension lie in an ongoing struggle to settle the boundaries separating beliefs and behaviour that should be stigmatised as racist from more benign expressions of group attachment and judgements about others. The result is a tug of war between identity liberals, who seek to broaden definitions of prejudice and strengthen the social norms stigmatising its expression, and identity conservatives seeking to defend what they see as legitimate expressions of group preferences and group attachment.

Many examples of this tug of war can be found in the political debate over immigration. Identity liberals frequently frame anxieties over migration inflows or calls for greater control as either

---

[25] Gest (2016).

direct expressions of prejudice, or efforts to legitimate racist or xenophobic motivations. A former Labour immigration minister attacked UKIP campaign posters in 2014 criticising the economic effects of immigration, featuring white workers in hard hats, as 'racist',[26] while in 2010 Labour Prime Minister Gordon Brown dismissed a voter who expressed similar anxieties about migrants from the EU as a 'bigoted woman'.[27] When Labour opposition leader Ed Miliband made a pledge to introduce immigration controls, complete with branded merchandise, this was met with a torrent of negative commentary from identity liberals, who attacked the pledge as 'pandering to racism',[28] and years later continued to reference 'Ed's racist mug' as an example of Labour appeasing prejudice.[29] Actions labelled as racist by identity liberal commentators and political activists have included: expressing anxiety about or opposition to immigration[30]; displaying symbols of English national identity such as the George Cross flag[31]; voting for UKIP in 2014 and 2015[32]; and campaigning or voting for Brexit in 2016.[33] In all of these cases, and more, the strategy employed by identity liberal campaigners has been to expand the definition of racism to include these actions directly or to achieve the same goal indirectly by ascribing racist motives to ambiguous behaviours.

Identity conservatives show the opposite tendency – looking to defend expressions of in-group attachment or hostility towards certain out-groups as expressions of 'legitimate concerns'[34] and to exclude them from the unacceptable label of

---

[26] Wintour, Watt and Carrell (2014).

[27] Carter and Wainwright (2010). Brown's successor Ed Miliband was personally congratulated by Duffy after his first conference speech, in an effort by the new Labour leader to demonstrate reconciliation.

[28] *The Guardian* (2015); Wight (2015).   [29] Goodfellow (2019).

[30] Hasan (2014).   [31] Barnett (2018).   [32] Kimber (2014).

[33] Shaw (2019); Choonara (2016).

[34] The frequent use of the phrase 'legitimate concerns' has led to this phrase itself being satirised by identity liberal political activists on social media, where it is treated as the contemporary version of 'I'm not racist but ...' A search of the phrase 'legitimate concerns immigration' by the authors in August 2019 on Twitter reveals that the most popular tweets and widely

racism. A few examples from across the political spectrum illustrate this approach. Nigel Farage, leader of UKIP and a prominent figure in the Leave.EU campaign, defended claiming that many families would not want Romanian neighbours by asserting this highlighted 'real concerns' driven by Romanian migrants' involvement in organised crime.[35] He similarly defended the deployment in the EU Referendum campaign of a poster depicting thousands of Middle Eastern refugees on the Croatia–Slovenia border in 2015, under the slogan 'Breaking Point', by claiming the poster was 'the truth' and 'an example of what is wrong inside the European Union'.[36] Boris Johnson, Prime Minister at the time of writing, defended an August 2018 article calling it 'weird and bullying' for Muslim women to wear face-covering veils, then went on to compare women who did so with 'letterboxes' or 'bank robbers', as an example of politicians 'speaking directly' about voters' concerns, something he said the public wanted to see.[37]

The defence of identity conservative stances as 'legitimate' is often combined with criticism of overly expansive identity liberal definitions of racism, a pattern of argument found frequently among Labour politicians seeking to defend efforts to reconnect with identity conservative voters against accusations of pandering to racism from their own identity liberal activists. In 2016, Labour candidate for Mayor of Greater Manchester Andy Burnham accused his party's campaigners of 'avoiding people's eyes and shuffling away' when voters raised concerns about immigration and attacked the tendency to label and stigmatise those who raised such concerns:

[The left] have a tendency to label people who speak up. Accusations of 'pandering to UKIP', xenophobia or even racism are thrown around

---

shared tweets using this phrase typically came from identity liberals criticising it, and those who use it, as seeking to advance racist arguments.

[35] BBC (2014).   [36] *The Scotsman* (2016).   [37] *The Scotsman* (2019).

quite freely. This has the chilling effect of making people who speak out fearful of doing so.[38]

The emotionally heated character of such political arguments once again reflects the high stakes in this debate. There are political risks to drawing the line too narrowly or too broadly. An overly restrictive definition of racism will underestimate its prevalence and seriousness as a social problem, weaken the case for political and social action to tackle it, and could legitimate behaviour which harms the lives and interests of minority groups. Yet there are also risks to an overly expansive definition of prejudice. If the term 'racist' is applied too broadly by one side in political debates, it may lose its sting – being seen less as a fundamental and universal taboo and more as a tool of political rhetoric. As the definition of racism and racist behaviour is broadened, it can become diluted, weakening the social consensus for action against prejudice. At the extreme of this would be a situation where radical identity liberals posit that all white people are racist, perhaps irredeemably so, with more identity conservative white voters responding by treating prejudice as a personality quirk to be tolerated, rather than a social injustice in need of urgent correction.[39] Identity conservatives have also liberalised over time, with younger generations expressing much more comfort with racial diversity than their parents, and it can therefore be alienating for them to be criticised as bigots by their identity liberal peers. They may feel, with some justification, that the goalposts are being moved, as despite adopting more tolerant views, they are still criticised as narrow-minded by identity liberals.

Identity conservative voters stung by such criticism often look to contest the expanding application of anti-racism norms by laying the counter-charge of 'political correctness' – arguing that some complaints of racism reflect overly draconian and

---

[38] Burnham (2016).

[39] This possibility is satirised in the song 'Everyone's a Little Bit Racist' in the musical *Avenue Q*.

inflexible social rules on speech and behaviour. Many people on this side of the Brexitland divide often think enough has now been said and done on the issue of racial inequalities (despite empirical evidence that these persist[40]) and see the zeal of anti-racist campaigners as excessive and oppressive, a view expressed through phrases such as 'political correctness gone mad'. Identity liberals see this invocation of 'political correctness' as a defensive deflection, used to belittle or dismiss claims about prejudice, and undermine support for policies aiming to combat it. Both sides of the identity politics divide have developed rhetorical tools to undermine their opponents' arguments, while seeking to impose their own framing on identity conflicts. Identity liberal activists attempt to police the terms of identity conflicts by deploying a more expansive definition of prejudice and stigmatising their opponents' objections as intolerance. Identity conservatives counteract this by deploying a narrower definition of prejudice and saying it is instead 'politically correct' identity liberals who are being intolerant, by seeking to marginalise those with different views.

The charge of political correctness does not carry the same sting as an accusation of racism, but it may nonetheless be influential. We tested this possibility in a second survey experiment fielded to a representative sample of voters. We presented respondents with a question about the value of diversity in London, but half were also given a statement dismissing positive views of diversity as 'the politically correct thing to say nowadays'. By comparing those randomly assigned to see the 'political correctness' treatment with those who did not, we could test whether flagging up 'political correctness' as a counter-argument would persuade people to be more openly critical of London's diversity. As Figure 3.6 illustrates, this was indeed what happened. The share saying London benefitted from diversity drops 9 per cent, while the share saying diversity either

---

[40] For recent evidence see at: http://csi.nuff.ox.ac.uk/wp-content/uploads/2019/01/Are-employers-in-Britain-discriminating-against-ethnic-minorities_final.pdf, last accessed 14 October 2019.

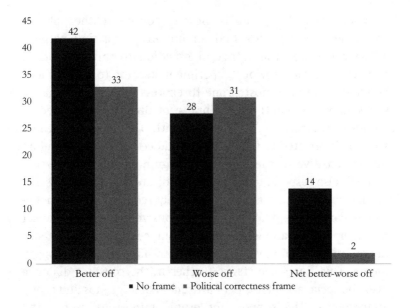

Figure 3.6 Views about the benefits of diversity, with and without 'political correctness' counter-argument (percentages): Is London better off, or worse off because of ethnic diversity?

Source: YouGov, 2015.

made no difference or made London worse off rose. The balance of support in the population shifts from overall rating diversity as beneficial to London to being evenly split between supporters and critics. Making 'political correctness' salient thus seems to achieve for identity conservatives some of what making anti-racism norms salient achieves for identity liberals – shifting opinion about which views are legitimate to express. The positions people are willing to adopt in identity conflicts depend on how the conflicts are framed. Each side has cards to play in this – voters adopt more liberal positions if they think anti-racism norms are truly at stake, but some will also adopt more conservative positions if the invocation of 'political correctness' calls the relevance of these anti-racism norms into question.

When we look at who is most responsive to the political correctness prompt, we find an initially surprising pattern. Those who express the strongest motivation to control prejudice, and were in the previous experiment keenest to fire a racist employee, are also most prone to express neutral or negative views more frequently when praise of diversity is framed as 'political correctness'.[41] This fits with the idea that those strongly motivated to follow anti-prejudice norms are therefore highly sensitive to the framing of arguments about diversity, and will also respond to cues which indicate that the expression of inclusive attitudes is not normatively required. Those motivated to control prejudice are thus responsive to the standards set by wider society, and will shift their stance in response to both liberal and conservative shifts in the framing of identity arguments. This raises the stakes further in the constant dialogue over the social acceptability of attitudes about groups and group attachments. The support for ethnic minorities' rights and policy responses to ethnic inequality will often depend on which of the two social norms prevails: anti-racism or anti-political correctness.

Conclusion

This chapter has unpacked the vexing question of how group attachments and views of racial and ethnic diversity define and divide identity conservatives and identity liberals. We have outlined the ethnocentric attitudes that form the basis of the identity conservative worldview: attachment to narrowly drawn in-groups and strong suspicions of outsiders. We have also shown how the worldview of identity liberals goes beyond simply lacking such ethnocentric predispositions, and involves embracing diversity and a focus on protecting the rights of racial and religious minorities. We have examined why it is so hard for these two groups to settle their differences, or even to engage in

---

[41] Details of this analysis are provided in the Online Appendix: www.cambridge .org/Brexitland

a constructive dialogue over identity issues. The high normative stakes of identity politics arguments make them inherently polarising. As a result, differences in worldviews can quickly become questions of legitimacy and moral worth, with both sides incentivised to police and penalise perceived infractions of social norms, and to contest the definitions and rhetoric employed by their opponents.

There is a very broad political and social consensus that racial prejudice is wrong, and that those who hold racially prejudiced views should be stigmatised. As such, the stigma attached to bigotry is powerful: accusations of racism can and do end political careers, and the perception that a party or policy is racist can erode support for it.[42] Yet while there is broad agreement that racism is a social evil and racists should be punished, there is no such consensus over how to define prejudice or how to sanction those who express it. The result is a tug of war between identity liberals, who seek to broaden definitions of prejudice and strengthen the social stigma attached to it, and identity conservatives, who seek to defend what they see as legitimate group preferences and criticise the excessive extension of anti-prejudice norms as itself an instance of intolerance. Any expression of group attachment or group judgement can become part of this 'race card politics' – with identity liberals seeking to stigmatise such expressions as unacceptable prejudices, while identity conservatives defend them as a legitimate expression of group identities and anxieties. Identity conservatives also frame these debates in emotive and polarising terms, attacking identity liberals as intolerant 'politically correct' zealots who use politicised accusations of racism to stifle the expression of legitimate viewpoints and stigmatise those who hold them.

This polarisation of debates over identity matters. When both sides are interested in policing the behaviour of their own social group, and seeking to apply their own normative framings to identity debates, people become more focused on the symbols

[42] Blinder, Ford and Ivarsflaten (2013).

and rhetoric used in the debate and cease to consider the substance of the issues they are debating. The emotional heat that identity conflicts generate makes coalition-building across identity divides is more difficult. Having laid out the general dividing lines between identity conservatives and identity liberals, we now turn to consider how the conflict between them first became activated by the issue of immigration. The origins of more recent identity conflicts over immigration and other identity politics issues, and of the political parties' reputations on these issues, lie in the heated political arguments which took place in the 1960s and 1970s, during the first wave of post-war migration. This is the story we tell in the next chapter.

4 LEGACIES OF EMPIRE: COMMONWEALTH IMMIGRATION AND THE HISTORICAL ROOTS OF IDENTITY POLITICS DIVIDES

Introduction

Political conflicts triggered by native hostility to newcomers are nothing new in British politics. As we saw in Chapter 2 with the defensive reactions of 1930s Banburians to migrants moving from elsewhere in Britain to work in their town, the activation of ethnocentrism does not even require immigrants to cross national borders. But while any influx of outsiders can trigger ethnocentric reactions, the deepest divides and most lasting conflicts have come over international immigration and the rising ethnic and racial diversity that successive waves of it have generated. This chapter tells the story of why this is so and how it came to be. We examine the first wave of sustained non-white migration to Britain from the 1950s to the 1970s, showing how conflicts over this migration became mobilised into politics. The choices taken during this wave of migration set up an identity politics alignment in the electorate, and this alignment in turn has shaped more recent identity politics conflicts over immigration. The dilemma facing this earlier generation of politicians will be familiar to those following the contemporary migration debate – policymakers agreed a liberal policy regime and unwittingly triggered an influx of migrants, then faced pressure to restrict this inflow when it activated ethnocentric hostility among the white majority, while at the same time a pressing need emerged to protect the new migrant communities from this ethnocentric hostility. The choices politicians made in response to these conflicting demands had a lasting impact, aligning identity conservative voters with the Conservative Party, which came to be seen as more willing to control the 'threat' from immigration, and aligning identity liberal voters with the Labour Party, which came to be seen as more willing to protect the rights of migrants and minorities.

There are three parts to the story, which parallel and foreshadow events in the decade leading up to the EU Referendum of 2016. The first is a large and persistent elite–mass gap on immigration, which led more liberal and cosmopolitan political elites to introduce reforms granting extensive migration rights to a large population in order to improve Britain's international position, while underestimating the scale and intensity of public hostility this would trigger. In the first wave of immigration, the goal was to secure Britain's place at the heart of a post-Imperial community of nations – the Commonwealth – and open borders between Commonwealth members was seen either as a valuable goal in itself,[1] or as an acceptable price to pay to secure lasting political influence within this community. More than fifty years later, another identity liberal-dominated political elite came to very similar conclusions when considering whether to fully open Britain's borders to migrants from the post-Communist countries acceding to the EU. In both cases, the unintended consequence of these decisions was a surge in migration as far more people opted to exercise newly granted free movement rights than political elites had anticipated, activating ethnocentric hostilities in the native electorate who perceived the new migrants as a threatening out-group.

---

[1] Emigration from Britain to Commonwealth members such as Australia, New Zealand and Canada was substantial in the early post-war years, and governments saw British emigrants as another mechanism for maintaining close and strong UK–Commonwealth links. The Commonwealth was also much more important for the British economy and British trade – and Europe much less so – in the early post-war years (see Edgerton 2018).

The second parallel between the two waves is that the ethno-centric sentiments activated by migration were successfully mobilised by political actors arguing for more radical migration restriction policies. As public opposition to immigration grew, the policy response from elites constrained by a commitment to an open borders principle and unwilling to alienate migrant-sending countries was piecemeal and slow in coming. Substantial migration continued for a number of years, and public concern remained high, but without an effective mainstream political outlet, until a new political actor mobilised ethnocentric voters behind more radical proposals and transformed the political situation. The appearance of a credible electoral threat broke the logjam, pushing one of the main political parties to embrace more radical migration restrictions, breaking with their earlier commitment to uphold open borders principles. In the 2010s, this was the story of UKIP's rise, as identity conservatives frustrated with successive governments' inability to control migration turned to the radical right and eventually forced the Conservatives to offer an option to exit Britain's open border arrangements with the EU via a referendum on Brexit. The story played out in a similar way in the 1960s as identity conservative voters, frustrated with repeated governments' unwillingness to control Commonwealth migration, turned to Enoch Powell's radical right insurgency, which eventually forced the Conservatives to concede radical reforms which effectively ended the migration rights of most Commonwealth citizens.

The final similarity between the two periods is that both also involved a substantial counter-mobilisation by identity liberals opposed to the rise of radical right actors and seeking to protect migrant minorities from ethnocentric intolerance. In the first wave, committed identity liberals within the Labour Party were pivotal in pushing through the first race relations legislation – writing anti-racism norms into British law, and laying the groundwork for a longer-run project of re-imagining Britain as a multicultural society where minority cultures are celebrated and minority rights protected. This, too, is already finding its echo in the Brexitland political cycle, with a shift towards pro-migration attitudes since 2016,[2] and the emergence of activist groups devoted to protecting the rights of EU migrants and fighting the oppressive 'hostile environment' rules applied to migrants by the Home Office since the mid-2010s. While these movements have not, as yet, had the kind of lasting legislative impact that the proponents of race relations legislation had in the 1960s, they have already shifted the balance of power on migration by activating and politically mobilising pro-migration sentiments among the much larger contemporary identity liberal electorate.

The origins of the first wave: the entanglement of citizenship and Empire

The story of the first wave begins with the British Nationality Act (BNA 1948) of 1948, one of the most liberal pieces of citizenship and migration legislation passed by a Western democracy. The BNA 1948 defined British citizenship for the first time[3] and did so in very expansive terms. A common citizenship with identical rights was conferred on all residents of Britain and of the current and former territories of the British Empire, including the vast and populous Indian subcontinent.[4] Eight hundred million people across the globe acquired full British citizenship rights, including the right to settle and work in Britain, and to

---

[2] Sobolewska and Ford (2019); Schwartz et al. (2020); Ford (2018b; 2019a).

[3] Before the Act, residents of the UK, the Commonwealth Dominions and the British colonies shared a common status of 'British subject'. However, in 1947, Canada passed legislation creating a separate Canadian citizenship, forcing the British government and the governments of other independent Commonwealth members such as Australia and New Zealand to define their citizenship and its relationship to the broader Commonwealth. For a detailed account of the legislative process and the debates which preceded it see chapter 2 in Hansen (2000).

[4] The bill defined two categories of citizenship: 'Citizenship of the UK and Colonies' and 'Citizenship of Independent Commonwealth Countries', but the rights conferred by these categories were identical (Hansen 2000: 46). There was also a separate category, also with full migration and political rights, for residents of the Irish Republic.

participate in British mainland politics from the moment they arrived.[5]

Given this remarkable openness, it is rather surprising that facilitating mass migration was not a goal, or even an expected effect, of the BNA 1948 legislation. Instead, its Parliamentary authors aimed to cement Britain's political status at the heart of an open and integrated Commonwealth of former imperial states. While close links with the former Empire were seen as essential to Britain's future prosperity and influence, mass immigration was not expected to be part of that equation, nor were all parts of the former Empire seen as equally important. The emphasis of the political elite was on maintaining close relations with the white colonial settler societies of the 'Old Commonwealth' – Canada, Australia and New Zealand.[6] In the decades prior to the BNA, the primary circulation of people within the Empire had been between Britain and these countries, and the BNA 1948 aimed to protect this system by confirming unrestricted rights to migrate to and from Britain and the Commonwealth. It was 'a fundamentally backward-looking document reaffirming the status quo as it had existed for decades'.[7] The desire was to preserve economic and political connections between Britain and the diverse global network of territories it had developed over centuries under the aegis of Empire in a new post-Imperial era of independent Commonwealth states.

It was not possible to preserve this right for the white settler states of the 'Old Commonwealth' while excluding the black and Asian majority Commonwealth states without writing an explicit 'colour bar' into the legislation, something identity liberal politicians, crafting legislation just years after a world war against a racist dictatorship, were unwilling to consider. British legislators therefore conferred a single, undifferentiated set of citizenship rights on all residents of Imperial

---

[5] This right, unlike the others, was never restricted in subsequent legislation, with important implications for electoral politics.

[6] Cannadine (2017: ch. 10).   [7] Hansen (2000: 35).

and Commonwealth territories. The policymakers who thus opened up the opportunity to migrate to Britain to hundreds of millions of people in Caribbean, Asian and African territories did not, however, give much consideration to what might happen if large numbers chose to exercise this right. The issue of migration to Britain from the current and former Imperial colonies was not mentioned once in the extensive committee and Parliamentary debates on the BNA.[8] Yet, as labour shortages developed in Britain's post-war economy, rapidly expanding numbers of black and Asian Commonwealth citizens began to exercise their rights, moving to Britain in search of better work and higher incomes. The first inflows came from the West Indies, beginning with the arrival of the famous *Empire Windrush* with hundreds of Jamaican migrants seeking work, just months after the passage of the 1948 Act.[9] As the 1950s progressed, the numbers grew and migration diversified, with flows from the West Indies augmented by arrivals from India and Pakistan.[10]

Public opposition to migration in the first wave

As Commonwealth migration flows increased, ethnocentric sentiments in the electorate were activated and strong public opposition began to manifest itself. Polling is sparse in this period, but the evidence available underscores that public opposition to 'coloured' migration, as it was then called, was intense and widespread from the outset (see Figure 4.1). Close to 90 per cent of poll respondents supported strong restrictions on

[8] Hansen (2000: 49).

[9] There are a number of popular, personal and oral history accounts of this early migration, and the reactions faced by the first Commonwealth migrants, for example, Phillips and Phillips (2009); Hall (2018); Matthews (2018); Wills (2018).

[10] In the early years after India and Pakistan became independent, their governments (under pressure from the British government) restricted their citizens' access to British passports, reducing migration flows by preventing their own citizens from exercising their Commonwealth citizenship rights. This practice ceased after an Indian Supreme Court ruling against it in 1960 (Hansen 2000: ch. 4 and p. 97).

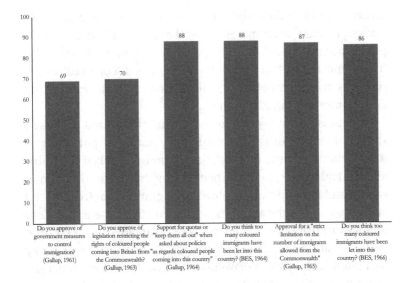

Figure 4.1 Opposition to immigration and support for migration restrictions, 1961–6 (percentages)

Source: Archive of historical immigration polling compiled by Professor Will Jennings.

Commonwealth or 'coloured' migration, and around 70 per cent expressed approval of the first restrictive legislation passed by the Conservatives in 1962. The share of the public who supported the BNA 1948 policy of full Commonwealth migration rights typically sat at around 10 per cent, while substantial parts of the public were supportive of very restrictive measures such as banning family reunion migration[11] or state-sponsored

---

[11] Pollsters only began to ask about restrictions on family reunion migration after Enoch Powell began campaigning for such restrictions, so public support for the policy may be entangled with views of Powell. Forty-three per cent of voters supported restrictions on family migration in 1968 polling, with 50 per cent opposed. When NOP ran more detailed polling on specific kinds of family members, they found large majorities supported allowing unrestricted migration of wives and dependent children, while equally large majorities opposed unrestricted migration of all other relatives (including adult children). Later polling on family migration by the British Social Attitudes survey between 1984 and 1996 found that majorities favoured 'stricter control' on the settlement of 'close relatives' in each year the question was asked.

repatriation of settled migrants.[12] This opposition was, from the outset, racially discriminatory – the overwhelming focus of public attention and hostility was migration from the West Indies and the Indian subcontinent – indeed 'coloured' migration was the issue pollsters typically asked about, rather than Commonwealth migration in general.[13]

One unusual survey conducted during this period provides a stark illustration of the discriminatory nature of public opposition to immigration. In 1967, Gallup pollsters asked the public identical questions about the benefits and harms from Commonwealth and Irish migration. Flows of migrants from Ireland were at this point as substantial as settlement from the entire Commonwealth combined,[14] and, unlike Commonwealth migration, Irish migration remained unrestricted at the time of the survey, so if public concern was driven by the actual pressures generated by migration then opposition to Irish migrants should be as high as, if not higher than, opposition to Commonwealth migrants. Yet, as Figure 4.2 reveals, Commonwealth migrants attracted much stronger public opposition than Irish migrants. Three in five voters felt Britain had been harmed by the settlement of

[12] Repatriation is another policy pollsters only began to ask about after Enoch Powell began promoting it, so public support for the policy may, like views of family reunion migration, be entangled with views of Powell. Between 42 and 64 per cent of respondents supported repatriation proposals in polls carried out between 1968 and 1978, and when Gallup asked about the idea again in 1993, it still received support from 43 per cent of respondents (though this later question referred to 'help[ing] migrants who will return to their country of origin', framing the issue as providing support to migrants who have already decided to leave Britain.

[13] It is revealing that the opinion polling companies throughout the period habitually asked questions about 'coloured' migration specifically, seeing no issue with referring to migration in racialised terms like this, and no reason to ask about any other specific categories of migrant. The pollsters were in no doubt where the locus of public concern and political debate lay.

[14] For example, Ireland was the single largest country of birth for foreign-born residents in the 1971 Census, with 709,000 Irish-born residents of Great Britain, compared with 322,000 Indian-born residents, 237,000 born in the Caribbean, 210,000 born in Africa and 140,000 born in Pakistan. There were also 632,000 residents born in Western Europe and 175,000 born in Eastern Europe, two large groups of migrants who were virtually invisible in the migration debates of this period. See Rendell and Salt (2005).

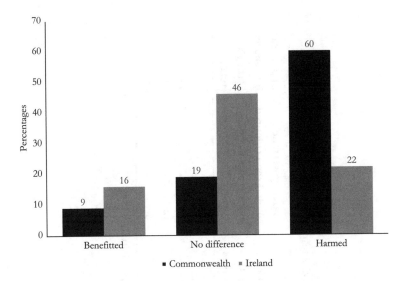

Figure 4.2 'Do you think on the whole this country has benefitted or been harmed through immigrants coming to settle here from the Commonwealth/Ireland?'

Sources: Gallup (1967); Professor Jennings historical polling archive.

Commonwealth migrants, while only a fifth felt that way about the Irish migrant population. Racially different Commonwealth migrants activated ethnocentric hostility in a way that white Irish migrants did not.

This strength of the hostile reaction to Commonwealth migration reflects the demographics of the 1960s British electorate, which was dominated in this period by identity conservatives. White school leavers – the core identity conservative demographic group – formed a large majority of the population. These voters were consistently much more likely to express ethnocentric hostility to 'coloured' migrants, and to support policies which would halt migration to Britain or repatriate already settled migrants, as Table 4.1 below illustrates by showing education divides in various immigration questions. University graduates, who were at a time a tiny minority, were much less

Table 4.1 Education gradients in attitudes to immigration and race among white respondents 1964–84

Educational qualifications	Very or fairly strong opposition to coloured immigration (1964)	Support halt to all immigration or repatriation (1970)	Support repatriation of immigrants (October 1974)	Agree 'government should send coloured immigrants back' (1979)	Oppose racial intermarriage (strongly) (1986)
No qualification	75	70	42	35	57
GCSE/O-level	63	60	36	23	45
A-level	56	47	28	14	40
University degree	33	37	17	9	37

Sources: British Election Studies (1964, 1970, October 1974, 1979); British Social Attitudes (1986).

likely to express hostility to Commonwealth migrants, and large majorities of graduates opposed all the draconian migration restriction policies proposed during this period. The migrants of the first wave faced more intense and widespread racially motivated hostility because Britain in the 1960s and 1970s was a society more dominated by the ethnocentric demographic groups most prone to such hostility.

The elite–mass divide on immigration in the first wave

Political arguments about migration in the first wave, like those today, were seldom a matter of narrow economic costs and benefits, but were a clash of outlooks between more cosmopolitan political elites concerned to maintain Britain's status in the international community and a more ethnocentric electorate opposed to the settlement of outsiders they found threatening. For Britain's post-Imperial elite, the people living in Britain's Commonwealth were part of an ideologically constructed 'us' stretching across the former Imperial territories, a community of interest defined by a common history. Britain was at the centre of a global network, so Britain should have a globalised form of citizenship which crossed continents, knitting together all those with a political and historical bond to the country.

The British public did not share this view – their sense of 'us' was much more narrowly defined, racially and territorially. 'Us' for the British public of the 1950s and 1960s was white British people born and resident in Britain. Migrants from the Caribbean and south Asia were not part of any in-group they recognised, and they saw no reason why people from thousands of miles away should have an unrestricted right to join their national and local communities. This ethnocentric opposition to Commonwealth migrants was for the most part not softened by the economic reality of post-war labour shortages,[15] or the

---

[15] Among those who saw Commonwealth migration as a valuable policy response to labour shortages was Enoch Powell, who as Conservative Health

major contribution Commonwealth citizens made to the war effort. This illustrates how immigration debates are chronically prone to activate ethnocentric concerns about groups and group conflict, which cannot be resolved with technocratic claims about economic or foreign policy benefits. In this way, too, arguments during the first wave of migration resembled, and influenced, those during the second wave.

Debates over Commonwealth migration exposed deep divides between the identity liberal minority and the majority not only over the issue of who to let in and on what terms, but also over whether migration was a political priority at all. While liberal university graduates, and much of the policymaking elite, saw the arrival of relatively modest numbers of black and Asian migrants as a trivial matter, large parts of the electorate – in particular identity conservatives – reacted with intense hostility to Commonwealth immigration from the moment it began. While most identity liberal politicians, many of whom had fought Nazi racism in the Second World War, abhorred the use of race or ethnicity to judge migrants, many of their ethnocentric constituents felt just as strongly that racial and ethnic differences were a legitimate basis for restricting migration.

These tensions between identity liberals and conservatives over immigration in the first-wave period divided the parties internally, driving a wedge between the political elites and

Minister in 1963 launched a campaign to recruit trained doctors from overseas to fill the manpower shortages caused by NHS expansion. Some 18,000 of them were recruited from India and Pakistan. Powell praised these doctors, who, he said, 'provide a useful and substantial reinforcement of the staffing of our hospitals and who are an advertisement to the world of British medicine and British hospitals' (Snow and Jones 2011). Powell continued to defend this policy even in his infamous 'Rivers of Blood' anti-immigration speech, separating temporary labour migration from permanent settlement, and denying that the former should be considered immigration at all: 'I stress the words "for settlement". This has nothing to do with the entry of Commonwealth citizens, any more than of aliens, into this country, for the purposes of study or of improving their qualifications, like (for instance) the Commonwealth doctors who, to the advantage of their own countries, have enabled our hospital service to be expanded faster than would otherwise have been possible. They are not, and never have been, immigrants' (Powell 1968).

electorates of both Labour and the Conservatives. Both parties' ruling elites tended to have stronger attachments to the Commonwealth, an intense and widely shared social norm sanctioning racial prejudice and discrimination, and a tendency to see migration and open borders pragmatically in terms of political and economic benefits. The support bases of both parties differed in all these regards – there was little attachment to Empire or Commonwealth amongst the mass electorate, whose primary loyalty was to a narrowly drawn sense of national identity defined by ancestry and birth. Social norms sanctioning expressions of racism were weak or absent in this period – as seen, for example, in the widespread and explicit use of discrimination in rental housing ('no dogs, no blacks, no Irish'), and in popular culture – 1970s television sitcoms regularly featured racial stereotypes and insults, which viewers would see as outrageous and unacceptable just a decade or two later.[16] The mass electorate, and the mass membership of both parties,[17] expressed a strong preference for white over non-white migration, with many wanting the latter completely stopped or reversed.

The first evidence of the political power of such ethnocentric sentiments came in the 1964 general election campaign in Smethwick, where the Labour Shadow Foreign Secretary Patrick Gordon Walker – a prominent campaigner against migration restrictions – lost his seat to an obscure Conservative candidate following a racially charged campaign, featuring leaflets using the slogan 'If you want a nigger for a neighbour, vote Labour'. As the defeated Labour MP left Smethwick town hall after the count, Tory supporters yelled after him: 'Where are your niggers now, Walker?' and 'Take your niggers away!'[18] While there was

---

[16] Popular family sitcoms of the late 1960s and 1970s included 'Love Thy Neighbour', where the central premise was the supposedly comic reactions of a racist white man to a black family moving in next door, and 'Curry and Chips', which featured the hugely popular white comedian Spike Milligan performing in blackface and with a heavy accent as a Pakistani migrant (Harrison 2017).

[17] Seyd, Whitely and Parry (1996).   [18] Jeffries (2014).

growing evidence of the disruptive power of this activated ethnocentric hostility, the leadership of both parties remained reluctant to respond to it. Early politicians who explicitly mobilised such concerns, such as Smethwick winner Peter Griffith, were ostracised by their fellow MPs and shunned by the parties' leadership figures.[19] While many MPs in both parties were privately worried about rising public hostility to black and Asian migrants, openly articulating or sympathising with such ethnocentric sentiments was taboo.

The political activation of ethnocentrism: Enoch Powell and 'Rivers of Blood'

The dam finally broke when, for the first time, a prominent member of the Conservative Party elite – Shadow Cabinet member Enoch Powell – broke the taboo and articulated in full the identity-based hostility to migration widely shared in the electorate in the infamous 'Rivers of Blood' speech in April 1968, which used emotive rhetoric and lurid imagery to attack liberal Commonwealth immigration policies:

> *Those whom the gods wish to destroy, they first make mad. We must be mad, literally mad, as a nation to be permitting the annual inflow of some 50,000 dependants, who are for the most part the material of the future growth of the immigrant-descended population. It is like watching a nation busily engaged in heaping up its own funeral pyre.*[20]

[19] The response to Griffiths' victory again highlights the very different priorities and values of Britain's identity liberal political elite – he was welcomed to the Commons with a searing indictment by the incoming Labour Prime Minister Harold Wilson, usually a measured and temperate speaker, who angrily denounced Griffiths' views and averred that Griffiths would 'serve his time as a Parliamentary leper'. Wilson's mark of Cain stuck. Griffiths' persistent refusal to disown an explicitly racist campaign did indeed make him into a Parliamentary leper, as Wilson predicted. He lost his bid for re-election in 1966 and, though he eventually returned to Parliament in 1979, and served another eighteen years as an MP, he was never promoted to a ministerial post.

[20] Powell (1968).

Powell was fully aware that such an open and visceral violation of anti-racism social norms would provoke a strong reaction from his colleagues: 'I can already hear the chorus of execration ... how dare he say such a thing? How dare I stir up trouble and inflame feelings ...?' However, he defended his stance by arguing that the growing opposition of white ethnocentric voters to migration was both legitimate and too important to ignore: 'The answer is that I do not have the right not to do so ... I simply do not have the right to shrug my shoulders and think about something else. What [my constituent] is saying, thousands and hundreds of thousands are saying and thinking ...'[21]

The chorus of execration Powell anticipated was indeed swift to arrive. Conservative leader Edward Heath repudiated Powell's position, sacked him from the Shadow Cabinet, and never spoke to him again.[22] This move was overwhelmingly supported by his senior Shadow Cabinet colleagues – four of whom threatened to resign themselves unless Powell was dismissed. Heath cited the 'racialist tone' of Powell's speech as the reason for his sacking, which he called 'unacceptable from one of the leaders of the Conservative Party' and 'liable to exacerbate racial tensions'. *The Times*, newspaper of record for the British ruling class, denounced Powell's speech as 'evil', calling it 'the first time that a serious British politician has appealed to racial hatred in this direct way in our post-war history'.[23]

The public response was quite different – two-thirds of voters said Heath was wrong to sack Powell, and over 75 per cent said they agreed with his views on immigration.[24] Powell received thousands of letters in support,[25] and overnight became the most widely known Conservative politician after Prime Minister

---

[21] Powell (1968).
[22] Hansen (2000: 186). Powell, however, retained the Conservative whip and was therefore able to campaign from the backbenches as a Conservative MP.
[23] *The Times*, Editorial, 22 April 1968.
[24] Schoen (1977: 37). Figures are averages across three and four polls, respectively, conducted in the weeks following the speech,
[25] Esteves (2019).

Heath himself.[26] Polling in the months before the speech already showed a large majority believed controls on immigration were not strict enough, while a substantial minority backed a 'total ban on coloured immigration'. Support for both policies rose in the wake of Powell's intervention (see Figure 4.3). There was also lower, but still widespread, public support for Powell's more controversial and draconian proposals – including banning family reunion and the repatriation of settled migrants.

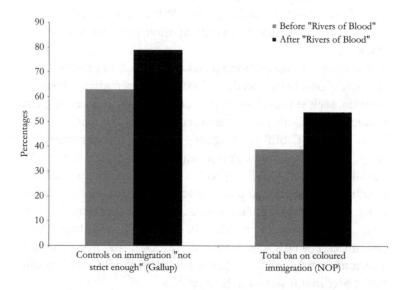

Figure 4.3 Support for Powellite positions on immigration before and after 'Rivers of Blood' speech in April 1968

Source: Jennings, Opinion polls database, 2018.

[26] Schoen (1977: 38). Just 1 per cent of voters named Powell as their preferred choice for next Conservative leader in March 1968, the month before his speech. Immediately after the speech, the figure leapt to 24 per cent, making him the leading choice. Powell remained a front runner in the eyes of the public for many months thereafter, and voters divided evenly between him and Heath when asked which of the two they would prefer as Conservative leader or PM.

Enoch Powell transformed the debate over immigration, mobilising ethnocentric identity conservatives and driving a wedge between liberal anti-racist political elites and the mass electorate. Powell's interventions were also the point at which a lasting divide emerged in the parties' reputations on immigration. Before Powell, the two main parties were seen by voters as rather similar on the issue. New migration restrictions in 1968 had been introduced by the Labour government, and the Conservative leadership – which had distanced themselves from Powell's stances – showed little initial interest in further action. But after 'Rivers of Blood', it was Powell who made the running in the migration debate. Powell continued to sit as a Conservative MP, and his association with the Conservatives led voters to see them as a party favouring strict and racialised immigration control. Powell's strident and hostile language also forced a stronger response from Labour's leadership, pushing the party into stronger defences of ethnic minorities' rights. After Powell's interventions, voters saw a clear divide between the Conservatives as the party of migration restriction and opposition to diversity, and Labour as the party of liberal migration policy and multiculturalism.[27]

We can trace the emergence of this divide in the British Election Study (BES) surveys. In 1964 and 1966, a majority of respondents, when asked which party was more likely to stop immigration, said 'neither', suggesting most voters had noticed the cross-party identity liberal consensus against strict immigration control. This changed in the wake of 'Rivers of Blood'. Nearly six out of ten respondents to the 1970 British Election Study saw the Conservatives as more likely to halt immigration, compared with just 4 per cent who named Labour.[28] Indeed,

---

[27] One of the most widely used definitions of multiculturalism was set out by a senior Labour politician, Roy Jenkins, in a speech to the National Committee for Commonwealth Immigrants in 1966, two years before Powell's campaigning on immigration began: 'not ... a flattening process of assimilation but ... equal opportunity, accompanied by cultural diversity, in an atmosphere of mutual tolerance'.

[28] This came despite Labour having passed just two years earlier one of the most controversial restrictive immigration reforms of the entire first wave, when the Labour government unilaterally revoked the migration rights of hundreds

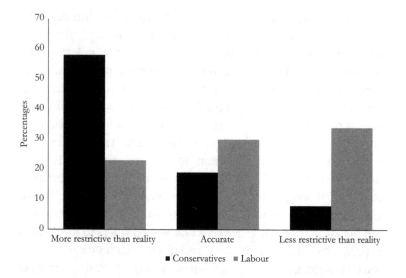

Figure 4.4 Voters' perceptions of Conservative and Labour immigration policies, 1970

Source: British Election Study 1970. The study offered respondents four options on migration policy: repatriation of settled migrants and stopping all existing migration were coded 'more restrictive than reality' for both parties; allow immediate family and a few skilled workers was coded as 'accurate' for both parties as it is the closest analogue to the proposals both made; while allowing new workers and families free entry were coded as 'less restrictive than reality' for both parties as both intended to keep in place the strict quotas on labour migration imposed since the mid-1960s, while the Conservatives proposed further restrictions on top of this.

thanks to Powell, voters in 1970 saw the Conservatives' immigration policy as a great deal more restrictive than it actually was. This is illustrated in Figure 4.4, which shows the share of voters whose perceptions about the parties' immigration policies were more restrictive than reality, accurate or less restrictive than reality. Some 58 per cent of voters in 1970 inaccurately

of thousands of ethnic south Asians living in Kenya, who only had Commonwealth citizenship, and were hence rendered stateless for forty years, until their rights were restored by the Labour government of Gordon Brown (see Hansen 2000: ch. 7).

claimed the Conservatives' policy was either to totally halt further immigration (36 per cent) or to repatriate settled migrants (22 per cent), whereas only a fifth correctly identified that Conservative policy was to 'allow immediate families and a few skilled workers'. As the share of voters who personally supported such restrictive policies was higher still (50 per cent backed a total halt, 20 per cent backed repatriation), these misperceptions, driven by Powell's rhetoric, were electorally valuable, enabling the Conservatives to attract support from ethnocentric identity conservatives. Indeed, the party was able to have its cake and eat it on immigration: Powell's widely reported polemics on the issue signalled a restrictive stance on migration, but by holding him at arm's length the party leadership could avoid fully committing itself to a strongly anti-immigration stance that would violate elite anti-racism norms and jeopardise relations with the Commonwealth. The balancing act worked,[29] bringing big gains for the Conservatives among the most ethnocentric and pro-Powell voters,[30] despite the party leadership's official disapproval of Powell and continued opposition to his most draconian proposals.

While the Conservative leadership was initially uncomfortable with Powell's high profile and fiery rhetoric, they were unable to resist the pressure for migration restriction produced by his campaigns. The party pledged to introduce new immigration restrictions during the 1970 election campaign, and Heath fulfilled this pledge within a year of taking office with the passage of the 1971 Immigration Act (IA 1971). This maintained the concept of Commonwealth citizenship, but stripped it of practical meaning by creating two classes of Commonwealth

[29] The most comprehensive analysis, by Donley Studlar, concluded that 'the Conservatives gained a net of 6.7% of the vote on the basis of the immigration issue alone' in 1970 (Studlar 1978). One of the authors re-analysed the British Election Study data from this period and came to similar conclusions (Ford 2019a).

[30] Support for Powell was heavily concentrated among voters with the lowest levels of formal education and among those expressing the strongest ethnocentric hostility to 'coloured immigrants' (Studlar 1978: 223–30).

citizens: 'patrial' citizens, with an unrestricted right to abode in Britain; and 'non-patrial' citizens, who had no such automatic right. Patriality was awarded to all those with a British-born parent or grandparent, a provision that, in effect, introduced a 'colour bar' while avoiding explicit recognition of race in immigration policy. Patriality ensured continued access to Britain for most white Commonwealth citizens (who typically had at least one British-born grandparent), while excluding most non-white Commonwealth citizens. However, to head off identity liberal criticism of racial discrimination, the Act also awarded 'patrial' status automatically to all Commonwealth citizens who had lived in Britain for more than five years, along with their families. Most already settled Commonwealth migrants of all ethnic origins therefore retained full residence rights, though in practice no effort was made to formally document such rights and thus secure them against future challenge, storing up problems which would emerge decades later in the form of the 'Windrush' scandal.[31]

Heath's 1971 legislation attempted to address the anxieties of identity conservative voters, and ensure their continuing support for the Conservatives, by stripping most black and Asian Commonwealth citizens of their migration rights. However, the legislation failed in its political goal before it was even implemented. On 7 August 1972, Idi Amin's regime in Uganda issued a decree giving tens of thousands of south Asian residents with British Commonwealth citizenship just ninety days to leave the

---

[31] The consequences of this legislative and administrative failure only became clear in the late 2010s, long after most of those who passed the 1971 Act had left politics. The failure of policymakers to anticipate that long-term resident migrants with full residence rights might at some future point need documentary evidence of their status was an oversight that proved to be disastrous decades later. Many such Commonwealth citizens, with decades of residence in Britain, found themselves unable to satisfy the Home Office of their legal status in the late 2010s, when new status check processes were introduced by the 'Hostile Environment' policies introduced by the Conservative government in 2012 and 2014. The result was often traumatic experiences at the hands of immigration officials, who treated these elderly Commonwealth citizens as illegal migrants subject to full enforcement and deportation procedures (see Gentleman 2019).

country.[32] While the previous Labour government had abandoned Kenyan Asian Commonwealth citizens when they found
themselves in a similar position four years earlier, leaving them
stateless, Edward Heath opted to uphold the anti-racist and pro-
Commonwealth principles espoused by the pre-Powell political
elite, in defiance of public opinion and despite vehement opposition from Powell himself. Heath pledged to fully honour the
passport rights of Ugandan Asians to settle in Britain. He
defended the choice as a matter of principle: '[We have] no
choice but to stand by Britain's obligation ...'[33] A massive airlift
was organised to safely remove Ugandan Asian citizens with
British passports, and the Heath government pursued an intensive diplomatic effort to ensure those without such passports
would find a safe haven in other countries ahead of Amin's
deadline.[34]

Nearly 30,000 Ugandan Asian refugees were admitted to Britain in a matter of weeks. The unexpected and rapid arrival of
large numbers of ethnic Indian refugee migrants was a scenario
likely to provoke an intensely hostile reaction from ethnocentric
white voters, and Enoch Powell wasted no time in looking to
once again mobilise such sentiments, this time against his own
party. Powell led the political campaign against the Ugandan
Asians, repeatedly attacking his own government's policy – for
example, accusing the Attorney General of 'prostituting his
office', for supporting their claims.[35] Heath, like his Labour
predecessors, discovered that Powell's speeches were more
important than Westminster legislation in driving media headlines and public perceptions on immigration. Although Heath
had passed the restrictive IA 1971 just a year earlier, the

---

[32] Amin's actions were also a reflection of ethnocentric identity politics in
action – the black majority in Uganda regarded the south Asian population,
which had settled in the country during its time as a British Imperial colony,
as an alien and threatening out-group. Much like many of Enoch Powell's
white supporters in Britain, many African Ugandans supported removing the
'threat' posed by a racially and culturally distinct migrant minority by
expelling the minority group from the country.

[33] *The Times*, 'Mr Heath Takes up Powell's Challenge', 11 October 1972.

[34] Hansen (2000: 197–200).   [35] Schoen (1977).

Ugandan Asians crisis and Powell's renewed anti-immigration campaign turned ethnocentric voters against the Conservatives, who were now seen as being 'soft' on immigration. Heath gained no credit for his restrictive reforms from ethnocentric voters, who instead were now being mobilised against him by one of his own backbenchers.

The consequences of this backlash are clear in the 1974 British Election Study. As we have seen, most voters in 1970 thought Conservative immigration policy was more restrictive than it actually was, thanks to Powell's anti-immigration polemics. Now, with Powell campaigning against his own party for being too soft on immigration, public sentiment swung the other way, as Figure 4.5 illustrates. The share of voters who thought the Conservatives favoured the strictest migration control policies – repatriation or a total halt to immigration – fell from 58 per cent in 1970 to 36 per cent in 1974. Conversely, the share who

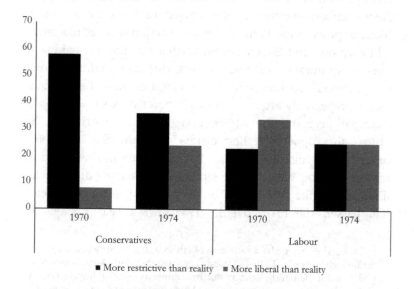

Figure 4.5 Prevalence of misperceptions about Conservative and Labour migration policies in 1970 and 1974 (percentages)

Source: British Election Studies, 1970 and 1974. See note to Figure 4.4 for details of coding.

thought Heath's Tories favoured large-scale new migration or uncontrolled entry of migrants – options never entertained by the Heath government – tripled from 8 per cent to 24 per cent. Meanwhile, the share of the electorate believing Labour favoured liberal migration policies fell, despite the party's strong support for Heath's stance on the Ugandan Asians and its opposition to the IA 1971, particularly the discriminatory ancestry rules.[36] The Conservatives' electoral advantage on immigration restriction largely disappeared, even as the Conservatives' immigration policy shifted in a restrictive direction. What Powell gave, Powell could take away. With the electorate again overwhelmingly in favour of strong restrictions on migration (73 per cent favoured repatriation or a total halt to migration in 1974), the loss of this restrictive reputation was costly. The Conservatives' 1970 lead among the most ethnocentric voters disappeared in 1974. While immigration was far from the only issue on the agenda in the turbulent mid-1970s, it is quite possible that Edward Heath's principled act of generosity to the Ugandan Asians, and Enoch Powell's fiery criticism of this generosity, contributed to the Conservatives' narrow defeat in the two elections of 1974.

After Powell: the consolidation of an identity politics divide

With the Conservatives no longer perceived as committed to immigration control after the Ugandan Asian crisis, space opened up for new parties to exploit ethnocentric sentiments. In another parallel with the politics of the second wave of immigration, the radical right surged in the late 1970s by attracting identity conservative voters who had lost faith in the

---

[36] Hansen (2000: 195–7). A number of liberal Conservative MPs also opposed Heath's migration legislation for failing to resolve the problem of stateless Kenyan Asians created by the previous Labour government, led by Bow Group chief Michael Howard, who decades later as Home Secretary would find himself on the receiving end of liberal criticism for his restrictive approach to refugee migration.

government's ability to control immigration. The extreme right and openly racist National Front, emerging as Britain's fourth largest party in the mid-1970s,[37] foreshadowed the later turn to the BNP[38] and UKIP following a similar loss of public faith in the government of the late 2000s.[39] In both cases, Conservative leaders sought to win back migration sceptics with new and stronger promises of control – David Cameron's 'tens of thousands' pledge and Theresa May's 'red line' on EU free movement echoing the earlier bid by new Conservative opposition leader Margaret Thatcher to win back ethnocentric voters in the late 1970s.

Thatcher, elected as leader in 1975, was influenced both by Enoch Powell's[40] views and by the public reaction to them. She recognised from the outset the disruptive political power of immigration, and the rewards the issue could provide to politicians able to articulate and mobilise ethnocentric anxieties. Her reflections on the issue in her memoirs are worth quoting at length:

> I felt no sympathy for rabble rousers, like the National Front, who sought to exploit race ... At the same time, large-scale New Commonwealth immigration over the years had transformed large areas of Britain in a way which the indigenous population found hard to accept. It is one thing for a well-heeled politician to preach the merits of tolerance on a public platform before returning to a comfortable home in a tranquil road in one of the more respectable suburbs, where

---

[37] Husbands (1983).   [38] Ford and Goodwin (2010); Wilks-Heeg (2009).

[39] Apart from the difference in the extremism of the anti-immigration option, with the National Front being more openly racist and violent than the later radical right parties, another interesting contrast is that while the National Front did best in London, which was the centre of migration settlement but also still had numerically dominant ethnocentric white populations in the 1970s, by the time UKIP and the BNP arrived on the political scene in the 2000s and 2010s London was far more ethnically diverse and identity liberal, and the ethnocentric appeals of the radical right only gained traction in a few districts on the fringes of the city such as Barking and Dagenham, where white school leavers were still a locally dominant group (Harris 2012; Kaufmann 2017).

[40] See, for example, Schofield (2013).

house prices ensure him the exclusiveness of apartheid without the stigma. It is quite another for poorer people, who cannot afford to move, to watch their neighbourhoods changing and the value of their house falling. Those in such a situation need to be reassured rather than patronised ... The failure to articulate the sentiments of ordinary people ... had left the way open to the extremists.[41]

Thatcher's thoughts bring together several aspects of the identity politics conflict over immigration. She, like Powell before her, was aware of the strong anti-racism norm among the political elite but, again like Powell, she did not believe such norms were shared by most voters. She attacked those propagating such norms as hypocritical – demanding acceptance of migrants while living in areas unaffected by their arrival – and defended the hostile sentiments expressed by those who she argued had to live with the disruptive consequences of migration. This account, written in 1995 and reflecting on political disputes from decades earlier, seeks both to legitimate the political mobilisation of ethnocentric sentiments and to undermine those who sought to stigmatise such mobilisation as a violation of anti-racism norms. It could easily have been delivered by a UKIP politician or Brexit campaigner defending ethnocentric opposition to mass migration twenty years later.

Mrs Thatcher's sympathy with the ethnocentric sentiments of identity conservative voters was also evident when she was leader of the opposition. In a widely reported interview with Granada's 'World in Action' programme in January 1978, Thatcher expressed sympathy with British voters who were 'rather afraid that this country might be rather swamped by people with a different culture'.[42] This had an immediate impact on public perceptions, just as Powell's interventions had ten years earlier. The share of voters who regarded the Conservatives as most likely to stop immigration, which had languished at around 30–35 per cent since the Ugandan Asians crisis,

---

[41] Thatcher (1995).   [42] Thatcher (1978).

jumped to over 50 per cent after the 'World in Action' interview, and remained at this level through to the 1979 election.[43] In the British Election Study conducted after the 1979 election this figure rose to over 60 per cent, including two-thirds of Conservative identifiers and more than half of Labour identifiers – the highest figures recorded since the studies commenced in 1964. Thatcher, like Powell, thus proved able to shift public views of the Conservatives' immigration stance by employing strong restrictionist rhetoric, aligning herself with the concerns of electorally dominant identity conservatives. Unlike Powell, however, either due to her more careful tone or her more elevated position as Conservative leader, she was able to activate such ethnocentric sentiments without suffering a significant political cost from violating elite anti-racism norms.[44]

While Thatcher made no specific policy commitments in her 1978 intervention, once elected she moved quickly to enact fundamental reform of British citizenship and immigration policy, abandoning the framework established in the 1948 BNA and replacing it with a new conception of citizenship and national identity based on heritage. The 1981 British Nationality Act (BNA 1981) not only severed Britain's citizenship links with its former colonies, it also ended an even longer-standing citizenship principle – the *ius soli* principle under which, since

[43] Figures from the historical polling database compiled by Will Jennings. An average of 34 per cent of voters rated the Conservatives as 'the party who can best handle the problem of immigration' in eight polls conducted between July 1974 and the 'World in Action' interview in January 1978. This figure rose to an average of 52 per cent in the ten polls conducted between the interview's transmission and the May 1979 election.

[44] Such norms, however, exerted an important influence on Thatcher's subsequent approach to the issue. Pressured, in particular by William Whitelaw, an important and powerful ally, she was successfully persuaded not to make similarly provocative statements on migration and race in subsequent election campaigns. Immigration did not feature at all in the 1983 and 1987 Conservative election campaigns and received only brief attention in the 1992 campaign led by Thatcher's successor John Major (Hansen 2000: 211). Strong support from identity liberal cabinet colleagues was also an important factor in the retention of largely unrestricted family migration rights for settled migrants throughout the Thatcher–Major governments.

1914, children born on British territory had an automatic right to British citizenship. Following the BNA 1981, children born in Britain to non-citizen residents have to register to obtain British citizenship, and can acquire citizenship only if they can meet residence or parental citizenship conditions.[45] The provision, like the IA 1971, stored up problems for later, as there remained a widespread assumption that people born in Britain automatically acquired British citizenship,[46] and many migrant families therefore made no effort to compile the documentation needed to secure their children's citizenship rights later on. Children born to non-citizen parents after BNA 1981 came into force, who have lived in Britain their whole lives, have often been shocked to discover once they turned eighteen that the British state regarded them as migrants who could be subject to Home Office control and exclusion from some public services.[47]

The radical reforms of the BNA 1981, and the subsequent sustained drop in migration to Britain,[48] cemented the links between ethnocentric attitudes and Conservative support which Mrs Thatcher had re-forged.[49] As Figure 4.6 illustrates, those expressing ethnocentric attitudes were consistently more likely to also express a Conservative partisan identity throughout the

---

[45] All those with right of abode in Britain under the terms of the IA 1971 were also granted British citizenship in the BNA 1981 – though, as in 1971, no effort was made to document and officially confirm these newly granted rights, so another critical opportunity to provide early Commonwealth migrants with the paperwork they needed to guarantee their citizenship rights was missed.

[46] For example, Professor J. Merion Thomas, a consultant NHS surgeon, claimed in the *Spectator* in 2013 that 'there are stories of heavily pregnant women arriving in the UK because childbirth qualifies for emergency care and the child would be British, thereby providing the mother with residency rights' (Thomas 2013). Professor Thomas called such stories 'anecdotal but almost certainly true', even though this scenario had been legally impossible for over thirty years at the time he was writing.

[47] See, for example, Bawdon (2014); Bulman (2018).

[48] This drop was not solely due to the BNA 1981 reforms, though they likely played a role. Britain suffered a severe recession in the early 1980s and experienced mass unemployment for most of the decade, making it a less attractive destination for migrants looking for work.

[49] Ford (2019b).

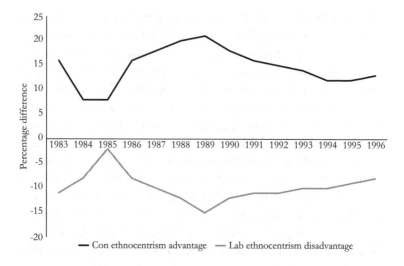

Figure 4.6 Conservative advantage and Labour disadvantage in party identification among ethnocentric voters

Source: British Social Attitudes, 1983–1996. Measure of ethnocentrism is 'Do you think of yourself as prejudiced against people of other races?' The same pattern is found with other measures of ethnocentrism (see the Online Appendix: www.cambridge.org/Brexitland).

Thatcher–Major governments of the 1980s and 1990s, a link which holds even after adjusting for the other demographic and attitudinal differences between ethnocentric voters and others.[50] Conversely, those expressing racial prejudice or other ethnocentric attitudes, such as opposition to immigration, were consistently less likely to hold Labour partisanship throughout this period. Meanwhile, the rapidly growing ethnic minority electorate showed a strong and persistent alignment to Labour, reflecting the campaigns against them and their parents by Powell and Thatcher, along with Labour's passage of race relations legislation. This powerful and lasting alignment began to tilt previously competitive or Conservative-leaning seats in

---

[50] See the Online Appendix for details: www.cambridge.org/Brexitland

England's largest cities decisively towards Labour as ethnic minority populations grew.[51]

Mobilisation on the left: entrenching anti-racism norms

Both Conservative and Labour governments passed restrictive immigration reforms during the first wave, some with black and Asian migration as the clear focus of policymakers' attention. Unhappiness with this approach was widespread among identity liberal elites and resulted in a counter-mobilisation of those most strongly committed to anti-racist norms. Identity liberals successfully pressed Labour into passing a series of Acts writing anti-racist norms into law, through pioneering race relations legislation. This legislation steadily expanded to cover more areas of life, including housing, employment and public services, and the anti-racism political debate moved from simply outlawing racially motivated discrimination to enabling fast-growing ethnic minority groups to retain many of their customs and accommodating their religious requirements. As the political and policy debate moved towards cultural recognition and providing ethnic groups with special exemptions from usual legislation (such as wearing motorcycle helmets by Sikhs[52]), Britain became one of the European leaders in implementing multiculturalism policies.[53] Unlike many continental

---

[51] For example, when Bernie Grant was elected by Tottenham as one of the first four self-identifying Black and Minority Ethnic MPs in 1987, he won 43 per cent of the vote, giving him an eight-point majority over the Conservatives on 35 per cent. The Conservative vote went into a steep and continuous decline thereafter. Thirty years later, his successor David Lammy won 82 per cent of the Tottenham vote, giving him a seventy-point majority over the Conservatives, who won just 11 per cent.

[52] The Motor Cycles (Protective Helmets) Regulations 1998; for discussion of the political and philosophical implications see Barry (2000).

[53] One of the first of these multicultural policy indices, MCP, is available at: www .queensu.ca/mcp/home. The only European country classified as more multicultural in the 1980s and 1990s was Sweden (and the Netherlands has the same score as the UK).

counterparts, but similar to the United States, British law was early to recognise indirect, as well as direct, discrimination (1976 Race Relations Act). Crucially, the choice of dealing with discrimination through the civil, and not the criminal, justice processes has meant that the burden of proof in discrimination cases has been lighter, and made it easier to raise a complaint. This choice was directly modelled on the US system of legislation,[54] and the early entrenchment of anti-racism norms in law has played an important role shaping the subsequent path of policy- and law-making in the area of race in Britain.[55]

The emergence of a distinct identity liberal political coalition was also catalysed by events in the decades between the two waves of immigration. One flashpoint was the racially motivated murder of teenager Stephen Lawrence in 1993. This case was subject to a formal inquiry headed by Sir William Macpherson, instigated in 1997 by the Labour government following a sustained and broad-based public and media campaign mobilising anti-racism norms.[56] The Macpherson report received wide press and public attention and a generally sympathetic response. It was influential in prompting further legal protections[57] against what Macpherson called 'institutional racism',[58] and a sustained campaign, unusually led by the socially conservative tabloid

---

[54] The process of how this legislation came to be inspired by the US is described in great detail in Bleich (2003).

[55] Bleich (2003).

[56] One prominent and unusual supporter of the campaign was the *Daily Mail*, a newspaper that has typically shown strong sympathies to ethnocentric anxieties about threatening migrants and minorities. The involvement of the *Daily Mail* both illustrated and helped to accelerate the growing reach of anti-racism norms.

[57] The 2000 Race Relations (Amendment) Act obliged public bodies, including the police, to promote good race relations; other changes included a new definition of a racist act, which increased the police's responsibility to investigate crimes as racist, the creation of an Independent Police Complaints Commission, and introducing diversity targets in police recruitment; in addition, criminal law's existing rules on double jeopardy were relaxed in murder cases in which new evidence came to light, in the 2003 Criminal Justice Act.

[58] Macpherson described this as 'collective failure of an organisation to provide a professional service ... through unwitting prejudice, ignorance,

press, to prosecute and jail Lawrence's suspected murderers.[59] Often dubbed the 'murder that changed Britain', the tragic death of Stephen Lawrence not only further entrenched legal protections against discrimination, but also catalysed the spread of anti-racism norms through society and politics. From mainstream news media revealing and scrutinising institutional racism in the police, Home Office and political parties, to parties across the political spectrum naming tackling racism as a key policy priority,[60] the case highlighted the potential for countermobilisation of anti-racism norms in response to extreme expressions of ethnocentric hostility. Although, as we showed in the previous chapter, the public do not always rally behind these anti-racism norms, by the 1990s they were no longer a preserve of the political elites, as they had been during the first wave of migration.

Conclusion: why did liberal immigration policies persist for so long?

Given the large majorities opposed to black and Asian migration throughout the first wave, the puzzle posed by this period is not that conflicts over immigration arose, but that relatively liberal rules governing Commonwealth migration were maintained for so long. British policymakers in 1948 granted a huge portion of the world's population rights to reside and work in Britain. It took them fourteen years to begin restricting these rights, and thirty-five years to completely curtail them. Vestiges of this liberal citizenship regime remain even today – citizens of Commonwealth countries (and Ireland) retain the right to vote and stand in British general elections from the day they arrive in Britain. This is a right very few new migrants enjoy in other

---

thoughtlessness and racist stereotyping which disadvantage minority ethnic people' (Macpherson 1999).

[59] Nineteen years after the murder, two of the perpetrators were finally found guilty of the crime and are at the time of writing serving their sentences.

[60] Uberoi and Modood (2013).

developed democracies, and a right not shared by other migrants to Britain, who cannot vote in general elections without first obtaining British citizenship.

Three overlapping factors explain this persistence. The first is legal and institutional path dependence. The 1948 choice to grant Commonwealth residents citizenship rights acted as a constraint on political elites who were reluctant to ignore or unilaterally abandon the obligations the citizenship regime created. Policymakers' refusal to write discrimination into law by creating different and unequal classes of citizens was a key factor delaying the introduction of Commonwealth migration restrictions in the 1950s, and the obligations of the state to all citizens were invoked by Edward Heath to justify his decision to assist the Ugandan Asians in 1973. We see similar path dependence emerging again some fifty years later following the EU A8 enlargement of 2004. The decision to align Britain with a large international structure – this time the EU – once again led the government of the day to forgo immigration restrictions and triggered an unforeseen influx of migrants that was opposed by ethnocentric voters. Once the decision was made, political elites again felt themselves bound by legal and normative obligations to respect citizenship rights, this time the free movement rights of EU citizens, limiting their ability to respond to rising public concern (see Chapters 6 and 7).

The second factor was foreign policy. Britain's political elites regarded close political, economic and diplomatic links with the Commonwealth as a key policy goal. With the sun finally setting on the British Empire, policymakers saw integration and cooperation across a post-Imperial 'Anglosphere' as the best way to renew Britain's place in the world. Immigration control was therefore resisted by political elites as likely to cause frictions with Britain's Commonwealth partners in the short run and weaken the bonds between Britain and its former colonies in the long run. Their successors forty years later were similarly reluctant to make a major push for reform to migration in the EU because, once again, this conflicted with central foreign policy goals. In both periods, political elites saw domestic disquiet over immigration as an acceptable price to pay for maintaining close connections with key international partners.

Finally, elite opposition to immigration control was not just a matter of policy constraint or expediency. It also reflected deeply held and widely shared elite social norms sanctioning racial prejudice and discrimination. The political classes of the 1950s– 1970s included many men who had personally fought in a global war against a racist, genocidal dictatorship. Veterans of that war abhorred the racism they associated with their Nazi adversaries, and those perceived to be mobilising similar dark forces in domestic politics were ostracised. Thus, Peter Griffiths, who ran an openly racist constituency campaign in 1964, was dubbed a 'Parliamentary leper' by the prime minister following his election, and never served in ministerial office. Enoch Powell, the first senior politician to mobilise ethnocentric opposition to migration, correctly anticipated that it would end his career in the Conservative leadership, but perhaps did not anticipate that it would also end several long-standing friendships with Conservative colleagues. Even Margaret Thatcher, the archetypal dominant and domineering prime minister, was successfully discouraged from public interventions on migration by the normative objections of Cabinet allies.

While such social norms did not, in the end, prevent politicians in either party from introducing and then extending racially discriminatory migration controls, they were still consequential. Anti-racism norms acted as a brake on the political mobilisation of hostile public sentiment by the mainstream parties, and slowed and diluted the policy responses to this ethnocentric sentiment. Normative concerns also motivated Labour politicians to balance anti-immigration legislation with equalities legislation, entrenching anti-racism norms in law. And such norms acted as a sign of things to come. Racial equality was already a core personal value for university graduates in this period and anti-racism norms would therefore only grow in political significance as university expansion dramatically increased the share of graduates in the electorate.

The BNA 1981, which came into force in 1983, brought the political story of the first wave of immigration to a close. This was a complex story of grand imperial ideals and unintended consequences, of noble stands and messy compromises, as governments of both parties wrestled with an issue that divided them internally, and where their political and ethical instincts often strongly diverged from the strongly anti-migration stance of the electorate. Yet the political legacy of these conflicts was simpler: a clear and lasting divide in the parties' reputations on immigration and diversity. The Conservatives, thanks to the strident and long-remembered stances of Powell and Thatcher in particular, became seen as the opponents of ethnic diversity and supporters of tight immigration control. The Labour Party, despite inconsistent and sometimes unprincipled positions on immigration, emerged as the party of identity liberals, migrants and minorities – in part, thanks to their passage of race relations legislation, but also simply by being the main opposition to the party of Powell and Thatcher, and thus the only viable alternative for those threatened by Conservative mobilisation of white ethnocentric hostility. This partisan alignment over race and ethnocentrism was still in place when immigration once again began to disrupt politics in the 2010s and, as we shall see, it played an important role in shaping the political impact of these new disruptions.

PART II

Identity conflicts from New Labour to the Coalition

5 THE LONG DIVORCE: PARTIES AND VOTERS PARTING WAYS

Introduction

The identity divides which took centre stage in the 2016 Brexit Referendum had been building for many years, both in terms of the changing composition of the electorate, which we described in Chapter 2, and the evolution of the links between parties and voters, which we consider here. It is not a simple or inevitable process for any latent social conflict to become mobilised into the heart of politics. As the American political scientist E. E. Schattschneider observed many years ago, politics involves the 'mobilization of bias' and at any point in time 'some issues are organized in to politics while others are organized out'.[1] When Tony Blair's New Labour came to power in 1997, conflicts over immigration, identity and the EU were marginal issues, organised out of a political debate that focused on arguments over the economy and the management of public services.[2] Twenty years later, this pattern was turned on its head. The reshaping of political competition around identity conflicts began in the New Labour era, when several long-term political trends came together to open up space for the disruptive mobilisation of identity conflicts. These trends form the focus of this chapter.

The first trend was the ideological convergence of the main political parties. The 'catch-all' New Labour created by Tony Blair and his reformist allies marked a major departure from

---

[1] Schattschneider (1961).
[2] Van der Eijk and Franklin (2004); Green (2007); De Vries (2007); Adams, Green and Milazzo (2012).

earlier patterns of party competition, which was more focused on class conflict, with Labour as the vehicle for the mobilisation and representation of working-class interests.[3] Blair's Labour adopted a more market-friendly, fiscally conservative and middle-class focused approach, reducing the ideological distance between Labour and their Conservative opponents.[4] The second, coinciding, trend was the emergence of a professionalised 'political class'[5] dominated by identity liberal graduates, while MPs with working-class and identity conservative backgrounds became much rarer, and thus the parties' elites became more remote from the everyday lives of those they governed. The third trend, which predated the first two, was the professionalisation of campaigning. A long-running shift towards centralisation and professionalisation was embraced by New Labour, with further increases in central coordination, targeting of campaigns and focus on swing votes and seats.

The ideologically moderate, performance-focused approach to politics that took hold in the New Labour years also accelerated a fourth trend: the weakening of the tribal attachments that bound voters to the traditional parties. This erosion of partisan bonds had long-term consequences, as partisanship plays a crucial role in stabilising the British political system, ensuring a core of loyal support for each party and limiting the electorate available to new competitors. Voters ceased to identify with parties they increasingly saw as ideologically indistinguishable vehicles[6] for ambitious members of an out of touch 'political class'. By the end of the Blair–Brown years, partisan attachments

---

[3] The processes of evolution of political parties from mass parties such as Labour to catch-all have long been critiqued for the resultant weakening of ties between voters and parties (Katz and Mair 1995), and New Labour seems a case in point (Evans and Tilley 2017).

[4] The problems posed by such ideologically moderate, 'catch-all' parties are not new. The famous German-American political scientist Otto Kirchheimer was already worrying about the reduction of real electoral choice and tangible opposition brought by the emergence of catch-all parties in the 1950s (Kirchheimer 1957; 1958).

[5] Cairney (2007); Allen (2013; 2018); Cowley (2012).

[6] Adams, Green and Milazzo (2012).

were at an all-time low, meaning a growing pool of disaffected voters willing to back whichever party, old or new, made them the most appealing offer at each election. This process of disaffection and disengagement proceeded further and faster with identity conservatives, and thus this was the group who subsequently provided the largest pool of volatile voters open to new options.

While political changes culminating during the New Labour years generated growing disaffection, these feelings would remain latent in the electorate until an issue emerged with the power to mobilise resentful voters and prompt a major shift in their political behaviour. Immigration provided the spark. A second wave of post-war mass migration got underway during the New Labour years and activated the ethnocentric sentiments of disaffected identity conservatives. Just as in the first wave, the political controversy over migration was an unexpected side-effect of choices made by policymakers who focused on other goals (see Chapter 4). The New Labour government saw its decision not to apply transitional immigration controls on citizens from the new Central and Eastern European EU member states in 2004 as good foreign policy, underlining Britain's commitment to the European project,[7] and good economic policy, helping to meet the needs of a growing high-employment economy. Yet New Labour's identity liberal elites, like their old Labour predecessors in the 1940s, underestimated the scale of the migration their policy shift would produce and the intensity of the public reaction it would stimulate.[8] Far from cementing Britain's place in the heart of Europe, the decision laid the ground for Britain's departure from the EU, forging a link in the minds of threatened ethnocentric voters between EU membership and uncontrolled immigration.[9] We follow the logic of these unfolding events in this chapter, first describing how gaps grew between voters and the traditional governing parties in the

---

[7] Consterdine (2017: 124–7).   [8] Consterdine (2017: ch. 3).
[9] Evans and Mellon (2019).

early New Labour years, before turning to how immigration became the issue which mobilised these gaps into new forms of political change and disruption.

Parties leaving voters: centralisation and professionalisation

The idealised model of British democracy since the Second World War was two parties with roots in different parts of society offering voters ideologically distinct solutions to the problems facing the nation.[10] While the reality was always messier, voters did usually feel that Labour and the Conservatives offered them a meaningful and consequential political choice. Three major shifts in the 1990s and 2000s[11] changed this: the ideological platforms of the parties became more similar; the competition between them became more focused on a narrow range of 'swing' seats and voters; and the politicians standing for office became more similar in background and outlook. The transition from ideological, class-based political competition to managerial, performance-based competition[12] was a major structural change to politics enacted during the New Labour governments. Tony Blair made ideological moderation a central part of his party reform agenda, weakening Labour's longstanding links to the working class and left-wing ideology in order to boost Labour's appeal to middle-class swing voters.

---

[10] Butler and Stokes (1974); Pulzer (1972); McKenzie (1956); Rose and McAllister (1983).

[11] The most comprehensive account of how New Labour's reforms shifted the structural basis of political competition in Britain is Evans and Tilley (2017). However, the phenomenon of a deepening dilemma for centre-left parties forced to choose between representing a declining working-class core electorate or marginalising such voters in order to broaden and renew their appeal was first formulated in Przeworski (1985), and has been considered in many studies of centre-left parties since (Przeworski and Sprague 1986; Kitschelt 1990; Sassoon 1996; Abou-Chadi and Wagner 2019).

[12] Clarke et al. (2003; 2009); Adams, Green and Milazzo (2012).

In order to make Labour appealing to the growing middle-class electorate, Blair abandoned his party's longstanding commitment to the nationalisation of key industries and weakened its links with trade unions, while emphasising Labour support for free-market economic policies and downplaying concerns about the inequalities in income and wealth these produced.[13] The Conservatives initial response to the shock of their crushing defeat in 1997 was renewed commitment to the image and ideology which had worked for so long. The party elected two leaders in a row – William Hague and Iain Duncan-Smith – who appealed to committed activists while alienating more moderate voters. By the middle of the second New Labour term, the persistent failure of this approach became clear to the party's leadership. The mid-term removal of 'IDS', beloved by Conservative activists but persistently unpopular with the voters, marked the beginning of a change of course, which was accelerated by the election of David Cameron as party leader in 2005.[14] New Labour's acceptance of centre-right economic ideas meant that the ideological distance between the parties on economic issues from the mid-1990s until the 2008 financial crisis was the lowest seen in forty years (see Figure 5.1). Both parties now offered a common economic agenda, focused on delivering low-inflation growth through fiscal rectitude and free markets, and using the proceeds to deliver investment in public services and moderate redistribution.[15] Voters noticed this convergence, and many began to feel that they were no longer being offered a meaningful choice.

[13] The new approach was pithily summarised by New Labour's lead strategist Peter Mandelson (a former Communist and grandson of Herbert Morrison, a senior minister in the radical 1945 Labour government), who told a US audience in 1998 that New Labour 'are intensely relaxed about people getting filthy rich, as long as they pay their taxes'. Mandelson's closing caveat was usually forgotten by New Labour's subsequent critics on the left.

[14] Bale (2010); Hayton (2012); McAnulla (2010); O'Hara (2007).

[15] The two periods of ideological consensus were quite different as the parties converged on very different terrain. The 1950s political consensus involved Conservative acceptance of the Labour agenda of redistribution, the welfare state and state involvement in the economy. The 1990s–2000s convergence was, by contrast, the result of Labour accepting the economically right-wing free market agenda and higher inequality of the Thatcher–Major era.

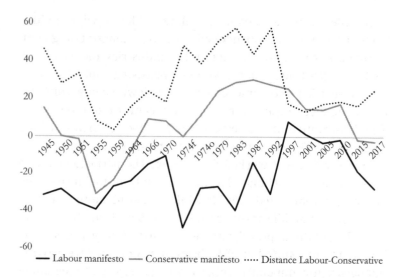

Figure 5.1 Economic ideology in the Labour and Conservative manifestos, 1945–2017

There were two elections in 1974 – 1974f refers to the February election and 1974o to the October election

Key: positive figures = more right wing; negative figures = more left wing. *Source:* Comparative Manifestos Project.

The average difference voters perceived between the parties on all ideological divides declined sharply between the late 1980s and the early 2000s, and the share of voters saying there was 'no difference' between Labour and the Conservatives rose sharply.[16]

Ideological convergence was accompanied by further professionalisation of political campaigning, accelerating shifts in parties' approaches to elections which had been evident for some time. Local political parties had traditionally deployed members and activists to knock on doors and rally support in seats all across the country in the run-up to election day. In the 1987 British Election Study, 47 per cent of respondents said that they received a house visit from a party canvasser in the run-up to the election. This practice faded in the New Labour years.

[16] See Adams, Green and Milazzo (2012); Evans and Tilley (2012a; 2012b).

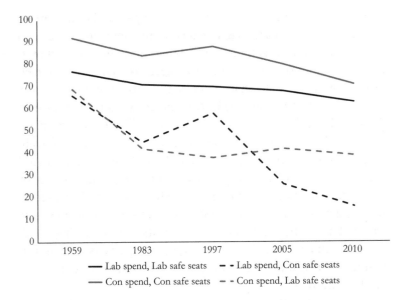

Figure 5.2 Spending by Conservatives and Labour in safe seats as a share of maximum legal limit, 1959–2010 (percentages)

Source: Johnston (2014).

By 2001, the share of voters reporting a house visit had fallen to 23 per cent, and by 2010 it was just 11 per cent.[17] Mass canvassing fell away with mass membership. A shortage of willing volunteers forced parties to prioritise, and canvassing became focused on the 'swing' votes and seats seen as pivotal to winning elections, abandoning 'safe' seats and voter groups. While many in both parties worried about the long-term consequences of this shift, chronic shortages of activists and resources left them with little choice. Both Labour and the Conservatives also sought to make greater use of data and intelligence to improve their

---

[17] The 2010 figure is even more shocking when we remember this was an election with an uncertain outcome and an unusually large number of vacant seats, meaning the parties should have seen more seats as competitive, and there were fewer incumbents who might rely on an established local reputation. Canvassing activity recovered somewhat in the 2010s, with 25 per cent of respondents reporting a house visit in 2017.

allocation of dwindling resources.[18] Campaigns became more centralised, with party HQs determining how and where to deploy money and activists, and what messages they should use. Parties were understandably eager to make use of new technologies and data that facilitated micro-targeting of voters and areas, but they also had little choice. Sustained long-term declines in resources and active members[19] forced reform on both parties. In the early post-war decades, large and well-resourced party organisations ensured voters in safe seats could expect leaflets and door knocks from both the locally dominant party and the main opposition, even when the latter's prospects were hopeless. By the mid-2000s, as Figure 5.2 illustrates, this was no longer the case: voters in safe seats were receiving steadily less contact from the locally dominant party (solid lines in graph) and heard next to nothing from their national opponents (dashed lines).

The impact of these changes fell most heavily on safe Labour seats. Safe Conservative seats tended to be relatively prosperous places, whose more politically engaged middle-class electorates could be relied upon to turn out in elections even if the parties paid them little personal attention. Safe Labour seats, however, included many of the most deprived places in Britain, where impoverished voters had little time or resources for politics. The disappearance of local Labour campaigns removed one of the main means to keep such voters informed and engaged. The consequence of the parties' retreat from such seats was soon evident, with large turnout slumps in safe Labour seats after 1997.[20] The erosion of parties' contact with voters stretched beyond the safe seats. According to surveys of election agents,

---

[18] Denver et al. (2003); Fisher and Denver (2008; 2009); Fisher, Cutts and Fieldhouse (2011).

[19] Bale, Webb and Pelotti (2019); Seyd and Whiteley (2004); Scarrow (1996). Note that following the start of Jeremy Corbyn's leadership, Labour experienced a membership increase (Bale, Webb and Pelotti 2019; Audickas, Depsey and Loft 2019).

[20] Pattie and Johnston (1998); Heath and Taylor (1999); Curtice and Steed (2001); Curtice (2005).

even in those seats that were campaign targets, and therefore received the vast majority of electoral funds and activities, the percentage of the electorate receiving face-to-face contact at the doorstep from the two main parties declined steeply between 1992 and 2010, as the parties tightened the focus of their activity even in seats where they were campaigning most. In 1992, the Conservatives canvassed 42 per cent of the electorate in their target seats, by 2010 this had declined to 35 per cent. The decline for Labour was even larger, from 53 per cent of target seat voters in 1992 to just 29 per cent in 2010.[21]

The third trend evident during the New Labour governments was the professionalisation and convergence of the social backgrounds of party elites. The parties had traditionally recruited their politicians from distinct sections of society: the Conservatives from landowners and later business and other parts of the upper middle class; Labour from the trade unions and public sector professions. Securing working-class representation was one of the purposes the Labour Party was founded to achieve.[22] However, partly as a reflection of the more managerial culture in New Labour, which ceased to prioritise working-class representation as an end in itself, and partly as a result of a broader, international trend towards greater professionalisation in party elites, both parties came to recruit more candidates from public-facing communication professions such as the media, public

---

[21] We thank Justin Fisher for making the 2010 results available to us. The 1992–2005 results are from Fisher and Denver (2008: 813).

[22] The enduring presence of a large cohort of MPs drawn from the working class on the Labour benches was a product of two influences: the existence of large and powerful blue-collar trade unions; and the central role such unions played within internal Labour Party politics. Both influences were greatly weakened in the 1980s and 1990s – the heavily unionised traditional manufacturing industries went into steep decline, while professional public sector unions – with more highly educated, middle-class members – grew in size and influence. Tony Blair's reforms to Labour's internal structures further weakened the political role of traditional blue-collar unions, marginalising their influence on internal Labour Party decisions, including candidate selection. Partly as a result of these changes, the share of MPs whose job prior to their election was in a manual labouring occupation fell from 16 per cent in 1979 to just 3 per cent in 2015 (Allen 2018: 25).

relations and the law, as well as growing numbers of career politicians who switched from supporting roles as campaign managers or policy advisers to running as candidates them-selves.[23] Labour MPs from traditional blue-collar trade union backgrounds became a rare sight in the Palace of Westminster, and even more so in the corridors of ministerial power.[24] While graduates and middle-class professionals have become a major-ity of party elites of all parties, in the 2000s there was a qualita-tive shift as a distinctive professional 'political class' emerged whose views came to define the mainstream political conversation.[25]

The growing dominance of graduates in this professional political class is illustrated in Figure 5.3, which shows the share of party candidates in each election who were university gradu-ates and school leavers. Graduates already dominated all three parties' candidate pools in 1992 – nearly two-thirds of all

---

[23] For example, see Criddle (2010; 2015). Similar trends of growing professionalisation and graduate domination of the political class have also been seen in other countries, for example, see Hakhverdian (2015); Best and Cotta (2000) and Norris (1997). However, it is also worth noting that the parliamentary party elites became more diverse in other ways – particularly in terms of gender and ethnicity – at the same time. This both reflects the greater focus among identity liberals in the political elite on securing better representation of women and ethnic minorities, and illustrates the complexity of the representation story – even as MPs were becoming less representative on some dimensions (education, previous jobs, social values) they were becoming more like the electorate on others (gender, ethnicity).

[24] The twenty-three core members of the final Cabinet of Gordon Brown included ten members who came into politics very early as special advisers or via student politics, and had very little other work experience: David Miliband, Hilary Benn, Ed Balls, Ed Miliband, Andy Burnham, Douglas Alexander, Janet Royall, Jim Murphy, Yvette Cooper and Peter Hain. Another nine members' pre-political careers were entirely in communications professions: the media (Peter Mandelson, Shaun Woodward, Ben Bradshaw); the law (Alastair Darling, Jack Straw, Harriet Harman); consulting (Liam Byrne) and higher education (Gordon Brown, Andrew Adonis). Only four had substantial experience in workplaces away from politics and communications – two (Tessa Jowell (social work, charities sector) and John Denham (charities sector)) had a background in third sector/public services work. Just two, Alan Johnson (postman) and Bob Ainsworth (car manufacturing), had any substantial experience in a traditional working-class profession.

[25] Allen (2018).

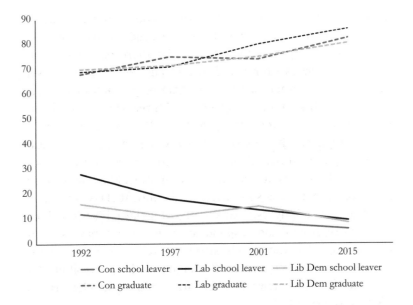

Figure 5.3 Educational background of Conservative, Labour and Liberal Democrat candidates, 1992–2015 (percentages)

Key: solid lines = school leavers; dashed lines = university graduates.
Source: Candidate surveys, 1992–2015.

candidates had degrees at a time when fewer than one voter in ten[26] had attended university. Conversely, school leavers were already very under-represented: while nearly two-thirds of voters in 1992 reported leaving school at sixteen or earlier with GCSE qualifications or less,[27] only a small minority of their Parliamentary candidates could report a similar educational experience (albeit one of those candidates was the incumbent prime minister[28]). Yet those with lower levels of education could

---

[26] The British Social Attitudes survey of 1993 found just 8 per cent of respondents had a university degree, while another 11 per cent reported some other form of post-eighteen higher education.

[27] In the 1993 British Social Attitudes survey, 35 per cent of respondents reported having no qualifications at all, and another 32 per cent reported that GCSEs or O-levels were the highest educational qualifications they had received.

[28] John Major left school at fifteen with three O-levels.

at least count on substantial representation from the Labour Party, where a third of candidates were school leavers in 1992. This was no longer so by 2001, as the share of school-leaver Labour candidates slumped to just 14 per cent, with no offsetting rise in the other parties. The share of graduates continued to rise after this, to three-quarters of all three parties' candidates in 2001, and over four-fifths in 2015. The inspiring story of Angela Rayner, who left school at sixteen as a teenage mum with no qualifications, then rose first to Shadow education secretary, and then Labour deputy leader in April 2020, was widely reported because it is so unusual in a political class dominated by academic high flyers.[29] This matters for the ability of political elites to represent and respond to voters: as we have seen in Chapter 3, education levels strongly predict identity politics stances, so when identity conflicts emerge the political elite as a whole will have views at odds with much of the electorate it seeks to represent.[30]

Figure 5.4 illustrates this point by comparing the share of each party's voters and candidates who believed equal opportunities for ethnic minorities had gone 'too far' in 1992 and in 2005. The candidates for all three main Westminster political parties were significantly more liberal than their own voters, a gap that grew between 1992 and 2005 as voters became somewhat more conservative while political candidates remained strongly liberal. The Conservative Party's candidates and voters started off relatively similar in 1992, but a gap had opened up by 2005 as Conservative voters became more sceptical of equal opportunities while the party's candidates remained more supportive. Both Labour and the Liberal Democrats show an even larger gap between universally pro-equal opportunities political candidates and voters who express more scepticism. A similar pattern emerges on the only other issue where we have sufficient data to

---

[29] For example, Newman (2016); Moss (2017); Nelson (2018; the URL to this reference is revealing).

[30] For evidence that such disconnects can generate significant citizen dissatisfaction, see Mayne and Hakhverdian (2017); Hakhverdian (2015).

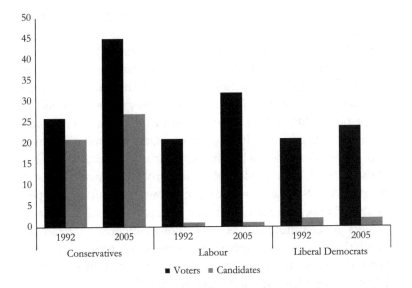

Figure 5.4 Percentage of voters and candidates who feel equal opportunities for ethnic minorities have 'gone too far', 1992 and 2005

Sources: British Election Study, 1992 and 2005; Candidate surveys 1992 and 2005. The question we use is 'Do you think equal opportunities for ethnic minority Britons have gone too far or not far enough?' The racially conservative position has been determined as people agreeing that equal opportunities have gone too far or much too far.

compare candidates and voters consistently – views of the EU. Once again, candidates from all three parties were consistently more pro-EU than their voters, meaning Euroscepticism in the electorate was persistently under-represented in the political class as a whole. The gap between voters and representatives was largest for the Labour Party.

It is thus no wonder that new political movements found themselves able to win voters away from the traditional parties once identity politics issues such as Europe and immigration rose up the agenda in the 2010s – these were issues where the views of the political class as a whole were not reflective of the spectrum of opinion in the electorate. Indeed, as we saw in Chapter 3, a similar disconnect between an identity liberal-dominated political elite and a more ethnocentric electorate also played a big role in the earlier 1960s and 1970s political disruptions over immigration.

Ideological moderation, targeted campaigning and elite professionalisation have all eroded the links between voters and parties,[31] and have particularly weakened the parties' connections to those whose backgrounds and views were not reflected in the new political class. New Labour could afford to marginalise traditional partisans in its early years, as the governing party with a popular leader delivering popular policies, but the alienation of traditional supporters posed problems once times got tougher. The New Labour political class, with an outlook shaped by shared experience of elite higher educational institutions and careers in communications professions, underestimated how much their focus on competence and moderation would weaken Labour's appeal to voters whose loyalties were rooted in traditional social identities and class politics. Such voters noticed, and disliked, the disappearance of working-class MPs and the emergence of a privileged, graduate-dominated political class.[32] The percentage of voters who agreed that the Labour Party looked after the interests of the working class fell from 89 per cent to 64 per cent between 1987 and 2010, in the wake of a sustained fall in the number of working-class Labour MPs.[33] The share saying Labour looked after big business grew from 38 per cent to 54 per cent over the same period, suggesting voters also had a pretty clear notion whose interests were being best served by Labour's shift to professionalised MPs and managerial politics.

While the rise of a professional political class eroded voters' faith in the parties' ability to represent less privileged voters, the electorate was not, on the whole, willing to reward the considerable efforts by both parties to improve the representation of women and ethnic minorities. Substantial improvements in ethnic minority representation, first on the Labour and then

---

[31] Kirchheimer (1957; 1958); Katz and Mair (1995).
[32] O'Grady (2019); Heath (2018). [33] Evans and Tilley (2017: 133–5).

on the Conservative benches,[34] had little impact on voters' perceptions of either party. A large majority of the electorate already thought that Labour represented ethnic minorities effectively in 1987, and therefore saw no pressing need for further increases in ethnic minority representation. For the Conservatives, the problem was that the 2010 change in approach by David Cameron was too transitory to produce a lasting shift in perceptions that the Conservatives were unresponsive to ethnic minority interests. The limited impact of greater representation for women and ethnic minorities[35] is itself another illustration of the growing divide between the priorities of the political elite and those of the broader electorate.[36] While ethnic and gender diversity at Westminster matter a lot to many in the political class, these forms of representation are not a high priority for most voters. Conversely, the graduate-dominated political class are more sanguine about the growing dominance of political and communications professionals at Westminster, even though many voters do see this as a problem that matters, and there is growing evidence that the disappearance of working-class MPs has had a detrimental impact on the quality of representation.[37]

Voters leaving parties: de-alignment and disengagement

New Labour's electoral approach was based from the beginning on a gamble. The architects of New Labour wagered that they could broaden their party's appeal with the middle classes while retaining the loyalties of traditional supporters with nowhere else to go. The gamble paid off handsomely in the short run,

---

[34] The Labour Party has traditionally been the leader on representation of ethnic minorities, and although it remains so narrowly today, the Conservative Party has made huge gains since 2010, see Sobolewska (2013).

[35] For new research on how younger women are much less likely to vote for the Conservative Party, see Sanders and Shorrocks (2019), and for ethnic minorities, see Martin (2019).

[36] Campbell and Heath (n.d.).   [37] O'Grady (2019); Heath (2018).

delivering the reformed party an unprecedented three House of Commons majorities, but success came at a price. As Labour and the Conservatives converged ideologically,[38] there was an unprecedented erosion of traditional political loyalties in the electorate – partisan attachments, engagement with politics and trust in politicians decayed, turnout declined and voter dissatisfaction rose. While these trends were evident across the social spectrum, they were most marked among identity conservative voters, who would later turn against traditional party politics altogether.

Strong bonds of tribal allegiance have long been the glue holding together the traditional two-class, two-party British political system. As recently as the 1980s, nearly half of the electorate reported a strong feeling of attachment to a political party, with the vast majority attached to Labour or the Conservatives (see Figure 5.5). Such bonds declined steadily in the New Labour era. Between 1989 and 2009, the share of the electorate reporting a strong party attachment fell from 51 per cent to 29 per cent, while the share reporting no partisan allegiance at all nearly doubled from 25 per cent to 47 per cent. In twenty years the British electorate went from one where a majority expressed strong party attachments to one where no attachment to any political party was the norm.

The generational decline of partisanship is even more dramatic.[39] Partisanship, like other lasting identity and value orientations, tends to be an enduring attachment formed in youth. Older generations who came of age in the era of strong

---

[38] In the New Labour period, this ideological convergence was packaged as a new 'Third Way' formula for centre-left renewal (Giddens 1998), part of an international trend followed by other centre-left parties elsewhere, for example, in the US by Bill Clinton's New Democrats and in Germany by Gerhard Schröder's SPD (Benedetto, Hix and Mastrorocco 2019).

[39] The erosion of partisanship is not simply a response to the British New Labour context. It also reflects a general decline of traditional party alignments found across Europe, with generational shifts away from traditional parties in particular found in many European countries (Dalton and Wattenberg 2002; Ford and Jennings 2020).

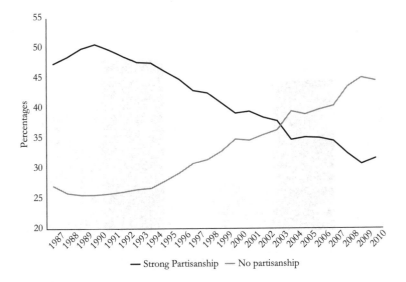

Figure 5.5 Partisan attachments in the British electorate, 1987–2010

Source: British Social Attitudes surveys, 1985–2010. Chart shows a three-year moving average.

class–party alignments[40] have tended to retain the partisan loyalties forged in that context, but partisanship has collapsed among the generations who have come of age in more recent decades.[41] This trend has been particularly pronounced among identity conservatives, as Figure 5.6 illustrates. Here we compare levels of partisan attachment during the later New Labour years among identity conservatives and identity liberals from an older cohort – the post-Second World War generation (who turned eighteen between 1945 and 1964) and the youngest cohort – the New Labour generation who turned eighteen after Tony Blair became Labour leader in 1994. While the younger cohort consistently shows lower levels of partisan attachment, the generation gap in partisanship is twice as large among identity

---

[40] Butler and Stokes (1974).   [41] Mellon (2017); Fieldhouse et al. (2019).

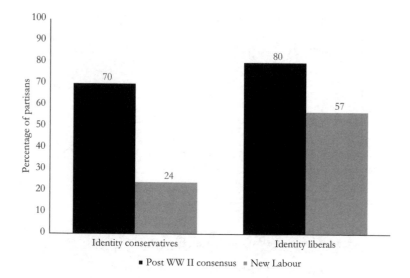

Figure 5.6 Generational differences in partisanship among identity conservatives and identity liberals, 2006–10

Figures show levels of expressed partisanship among voters who came of age in the early post-Second World War period (1945–64) with levels expressed by voters who came of age in the New Labour years (1994–2009).

Source: British Social Attitudes surveys, 2006–10.

conservatives. Seven in ten identity conservative voters from the post-Second World War cohort express a partisan attachment, a figure that collapses to barely one in four among identity conservatives from the younger New Labour cohort. By contrast, eight in ten identity liberal voters from the older cohort express a partisan affiliation, and this figure is still nearly six in ten among the younger cohort. Partisan attachments have proved even more enduring in the rapidly growing ethnic minority electorate.[42]

Generational change is a slow process, though, and as a result its power as a long-term driver of political change is often

[42] Martin and Mellon (2020).

underestimated. Even as the mighty New Labour electoral machine was delivering successive majorities, a new swing electorate was emerging, comprised of younger identity conservative voters who saw elections not as the affirmation of lifelong loyalties, but as a short-term judgement based on the choices available at each election. Many of these new swing voters were becoming convinced that neither traditional party offered them very much.

The generational decline of partisanship had important implications for the identity politics conflicts to come, as it opened up a growing gap between identity liberals, where most young voters remained bound to the traditional two-party system, and younger identity conservatives, who were growing detached from the traditional party system. These younger identity conservatives were not only floating free of traditional party bonds – they were becoming hostile to the traditional political system as a whole. Younger identity conservatives interviewed in the New Labour years expressed lower trust in government and MPs than other voters; were less happy with how British democracy operates; and were more sceptical about democracy in general.[43] Partisanship traditionally provided some buffer against such views, giving voters an emotional bond to one actor in the political system. As these bonds faded away, there was little left to stop unhappy voters turning against traditional politics altogether. The disruptive potential of alienated identity conservatives was not initially apparent because, while the discontent was plainly growing in the electorate, it had no viable political outlet. With no positive means to express their unhappiness at election time, unhappy voters found a negative alternative – abstention.

Nearly 5 million voters, or one-fifth of the entire voting electorate, dropped out of the political process between John Major's

---

[43] See the Online Appendix (www.cambridge.org/Brexitland) for more detailed analysis highlighting the concentration of these attitudes among the core identity conservative demographic of white school leavers, and the connection between identity conservative values and political disaffection.

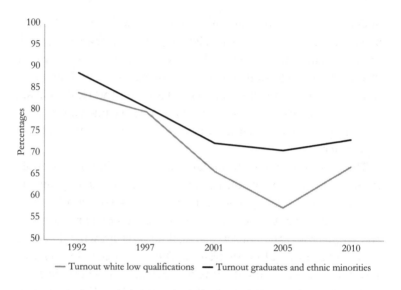

Figure 5.7 Turnout among white school leavers and among graduates and ethnic minorities, 1992–2010

Source: British Election Studies, 1992–2010.

victory in 1992 (when turnout was 78 per cent) and Tony Blair's second landslide in 2001 (59 per cent turnout). This swing from 'vote' to 'abstain' was larger than the swing from Conservatives to Labour which delivered Blair's first landslide in 1997. Many of those who gave up on the ballot box never returned: though turnout rose modestly in each election from 2005 to 2017, it was still under 70 per cent in 2017 and fell again in 2019. Every election since 1992 has seen lower turnout than all the elections from 1945 to 1992. As Figure 5.7 illustrates, this prolonged turnout slump was concentrated among white school leavers, opening up a large and lasting turnout gap between identity conservatives and identity liberals. And, as with partisanship, the shifts are even more dramatic when we break the electorate down by generation. Older generations are both more partisan and more committed to voting as a civic duty, blunting the impact of rising disaffection on their behaviour. Though many older voters were also unhappy with politics in the 2000s, a sense of social and partisan obligation kept them coming to the polls. Both partisan bonds and civic norms are weaker among younger generations, and so they expressed their political disaffection by turning their backs on elections, with the largest turnout declines of all found among younger identity conservatives.[44]

The generational differences in political disengagement help to explain why its political impact was initially so muted. We can crudely divide the British electorate into three segments: older voters, younger identity liberals and younger identity conservatives. While many older voters, particularly identity conservatives, grew unhappy with politics during the New Labour years, these voters remained bound to the mainstream political systems by the partisan attachments and citizenship norms they were socialised into when young. Younger cohorts of identity liberals were less partisan but were also more satisfied with what the mainstream parties were offering. Hence, it was among younger identity conservatives, who were both unhappy with traditional politics and less bound to it, that we find the biggest declines in turnout. Abstention, however, does not have the same kind of political impact as vote-switching, particularly when those dropping out of the electoral process are concentrated in safe seats. Politicians in the New Labour period therefore did not see a political threat from the sharp drop in turnout in this period, though the safe Labour seats where turnout slumped after 1997 included many which elected Conservative MPs for the first time in generations in 2019. A mass of unhappy voters was a necessary condition for political disruption, but it was not a sufficient one. Generating the kind of political change that would grab established political elites' attention required a political issue that could galvanise disaffected voters and mobilise them to vote for new parties. Such an issue was not long in coming.

---

[44] Details of these turnout trends are provided in the Online Appendix: www .cambridge.org/Brexitland

A flag to rally around: the second wave of immigration and the activation of identity politics

As we saw in Chapter 4, political conflicts over immigration are not new in Britain. However, the political conflicts triggered by the second wave of migration which began under New Labour have proved to be even more lasting and disruptive than those in the earlier wave of Commonwealth migration. Before we show how immigration mobilised the latent conflicts opened by demographic change and shifted the basis of party competition, we need to explain why the Labour governments of the 2000s ended up taking many of the same political risks, and making many of the same policy mistakes, as their predecessors in the first wave of migration.

Both waves of migration were the by-products of foreign policy goals – the first was a product of efforts to maintain close relations with former colonies, the second arose from efforts to build a leading position within the EU. The second wave was also the product of New Labour's unusual ideological stance with regard to immigration itself. Previous governments saw immigration in negative terms, as a source of social problems and political disruption. The Blair governments took a very different view, seeing immigration positively as a resource they could use to drive economic growth. Although they never had a fully coherent migration strategy, the broad operating principle of the first two New Labour governments was to seek a more open migration policy to attract newcomers to Britain and boost growth.[45]

---

[45] New Labour's focus on migration as an economic resource was also evident in the party's very different approach to asylum seekers. Refugees brought few immediate economic benefits, and allegedly fraudulent asylum seekers were the targets of hostile media campaigns in socially conservative newspapers such as the *Daily Mail* and the *Sun*. Labour responded to these campaigns with draconian reforms to the asylum system, which they claimed would weed out fraudulent claimants while protecting genuine applicants. Tougher criteria were applied in the asylum application process; economic support for asylum seekers was cut back; and the Home Office was granted new powers to assess claims quickly and swiftly remove rejected claimants. Researchers reviewing

The Treasury under Gordon Brown encouraged labour migration to boost economic activity and tax receipts, and faced little resistance elsewhere in government, while other reforms to family migration and student migration also made Britain more open to potential migrants through these channels.[46] Britain was already an attractive destination for migrants in this period for many reasons,[47] so these reforms had an immediate and substantial impact on migration flows. Migrant arrivals, which had averaged 300,000 per annum in the mid-1990s, rose above 500,000 per annum by 2002 and have remained above this level ever since.[48] Public concerns about immigration, which had been very low for around two decades, began to rise in tandem with this acceleration in arrivals (see Figure 5.8).[49]

Liberalised migration policies and resultant high migration levels were already generating considerable discontent in the early New Labour years. However, a key turning point came in 2004, when the Blair government opted not to impose temporary controls on migration from the new EU member states in Central and Eastern Europe, a decision that triggered a further major wave of migration to Britain from poorer EU states, intensified public anxiety about the issue, and constrained the government's ability to reverse course in response to rising public concern. This decision was heavily criticised later but was entirely in keeping with the party's approach to immigration at the time. Opening Britain's labour markets to EU migrants was seen as an uncontentious way to recruit migrant labour and generate further economic growth at a time of low

asylum decisions in this period found that bureaucratic behaviour tracked public opinion, with asylum claims rejected more frequently when public concerns were running high (Jennings 2009).

[46] Consterdine (2017); Somerville (2007).

[47] For example, rapid economic growth; tight labour markets; a high international profile in sectors such as finance and higher education; the presence of large migrant communities with links across borders from the 'first wave' of migration; and the popularity of English as an international business language.

[48] Vargas-Silva and Sumption (2018).

[49] Ford, Jennings and Somerville (2015).

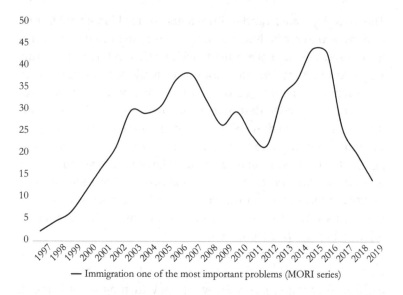

— Immigration one of the most important problems (MORI series)

Figure 5.8 Share of respondents naming migration as one of the most important problems, 1997–2018 (percentages)

Source: IPSOS-MORI political monitor polls.

unemployment. Remarkably, given its prominence in subsequent political debate, the decision was arrived at with very little ministerial or cabinet discussion, and no public consultation.[50] Prime Minister Blair and Foreign Secretary Jack Straw proposed the initiative as a way to strengthen relations with the new EU member states, which were seen as important potential allies in intra-EU debates.[51] There was little discussion of the likely migration inflows from the new member states or their possible social and political impacts.[52] Labour policymakers simply assumed that, with many EU member states opening their

---

[50] Consterdine (2017: 138–40, 177–80).   [51] Consterdine (2017: ch. 6).

[52] Erica Consterdine, who interviewed many of those involved in the decision to open to the A8, observes 'all interviewees commented that the decision would not have been made if they knew the numbers involved. In other words, the great migration from the CEE was certainly not anticipated' (Consterdine 2017: 180).

labour markets alongside Britain, migrants would come from Central Europe in modest numbers, generate some modest economic gains and have little broader impact.[53]

These assumptions swiftly proved to be wide of the mark. Almost all the established EU members imposed transitional controls on migration from the new members – only Ireland and Sweden joined Britain in fully opening up. Britain proved to be far more attractive to central European migrants than anticipated – more migrants arrived in the first two weeks than policymakers had expected in the first year. Tens of thousands of Poles, Lithuanians, Hungarians and others flowed into British airports and coach stations, attracted by plentiful jobs at wages well above those available back home. Within a decade, the Polish had overtaken more established first-wave communities from south Asia and the Caribbean to become the largest migrant origin group in Britain.[54] The wave of migration from Central Europe was unusual not just in its speed and scale, but also in its geographical scope – earlier migrants had settled mainly in urban areas where they could most easily find employment and draw on support from established co-ethnic communities. Central European migrants were different – spreading out across the whole of Britain.[55] Young Central and Eastern European workers flowed into places hitherto untouched by migration, where locals were unaccustomed to the changes it brought. The experiences of 1930s Banbury, described in Chapter 2, were repeated across the small towns of England, as the unexpected

---

[53] The Home Office commissioned research from a team of researchers on the possible impacts of A8 migration (Dustmann et al. 2003). The team concluded that inflows to the UK would be around 5,000–12,000 per annum as Britain had 'few historical links to the A8 region' (a questionable assessment given Britain's longstanding links with Poland – the country had hosted the Polish government in exile throughout the Second World War and the Communist era, and had taken in thousands of resettled Polish refugees in the 1940s, many of whom fought with the British in the Second World War), and was therefore 'not a very popular migration destination' (Dustmann et al. 2003: 58) in surveys of potential A8 migrants. However, the research was based on the expectation that Germany and most other large EU members would not impose significant restriction on A8 migration.

[54] BBC (2016).   [55] Lymperopoulou (2015); Sabater (2015).

arrival of outsiders activated ethnocentric sentiments in the local population.

Public concern about immigration intensified in the wake of this new influx, and reached an all-time high in 2007, when nearly four out of ten voters named immigration as one of the most important issues facing the nation.[56] Although public attention fell back a little as the global financial crisis unfolded, immigration remained one of the top three issues on the agenda throughout the severe recession of 2008–9. Labour's response reflected an effort to balance the need to address mounting public concerns with a continued desire to maximise the economic gains from migration. A 'points-based' system for labour migration was introduced, which awarded migrants a series of credits based mainly on skills and qualifications. This made it harder for unskilled migrants, who generated the most public opposition, to acquire visas, while keeping Britain open to skilled migrants in sectors with labour shortages.[57] This approach was, however, doomed to failure from the start because it could be applied only to migrants from outside the EU, while the inflow of unskilled migrants from poorer EU member states continued unrestricted. Central and Eastern Europe was now the main source of unskilled migrant labour arriving in Britain and the main focus of critical media and public attention, so Labour's new restrictions had little impact on public opinion, and immigration remained a highly salient issue right through to the end of the New Labour governments in 2010.

Ethnocentric activation: how immigration mobilised identity divides into politics

The growing critical attention paid to migration in the 2000s was frequently, but mistakenly, interpreted as reflecting a surge in xenophobic sentiments. Politicians addressing migration

---

[56] Blinder and Richards (2018).   [57] Gower (2018).

during the New Labour governments argued that pressures from migration on jobs, public services, rents and so on were stoking public hostility to migrants. Such arguments echoed the political rhetoric of the first wave of migration, which frequently paired 'good race relations' with 'controlled migration', implying that British natives would turn against migrants if inflows were not kept strictly controlled. Such arguments turned on the assumption that public hostility to migrants directly relates to the numbers arriving: when migration is high, intensified competition for jobs and resources, the perception that migrants enjoy an unfair advantage over natives, and ethnocentric anxiety at rapid and visible change in local and national identity and culture will all rise.[58] The truth is more complicated. Although high migration makes ethnocentric voters feel threatened and leads them to prioritise migration control, it is not accompanied by any substantial increase in hostile sentiments among those not already prone to see migrants in a negative light.

Tracking long-term shifts in views of migrants themselves, as opposed to attention to migration as a political problem, is surprisingly difficult. Although academics and pollsters have asked many questions on immigration, relatively few have been asked on a consistent basis over many years, making it difficult to track long-run trends.[59] We use four measures on the social and economic impacts of immigration asked regularly between 1995 and 2013 to build two indices capturing views of the social

---

[58] Goodhart (2017); Kaufmann (2018).

[59] While questions about immigration and immigrants are often asked in opinion polls, pollsters are not very consistent in the questions that they ask, or the way they field their polls. Comparing differently asked questions or polls with different fieldwork methods is unwise, as we cannot separate real change in attitudes from change that is an artefact of polling differences. Hence, we limit ourselves to areas where we have long-running questions and consistent fieldwork methods. Alternative analysis seeking to use more sophisticated statistical methods to combine disparate indicators suggests there was a modest but consistent negative shift in overall public sentiment about migration during the New Labour era (Ford, Jennings and Somerville 2015).

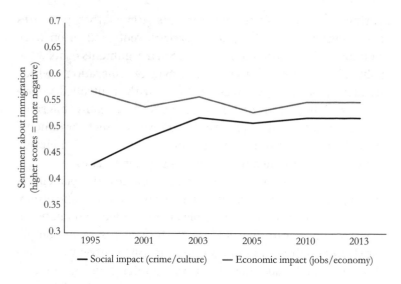

Figure 5.9 Public sentiment about immigration, 1995–2013

Sources: British Social Attitudes; British Election Studies.

and economic impacts of migration. Views of the social impacts of migration provide the closest proxy for the ethnocentric sentiment that migrants are an alien and threatening out-group.[60] Views about the economic impacts test the widely invoked assumption that voters turn against migrants because of economic pressures such as competition for jobs or economic resources.[61] Figure 5.9 shows how the two indices evolved from the mid-1990s to the early 2010s, with higher scores indicating more negative sentiment. There is evidence of a negative shift in attitudes about the social impacts of immigration between 1995 and 2003, but no change in views about economic impacts. This could reflect the initial rise in migration activating ethnocentric anxieties in the electorate, focused on migrants as a

---

[60] The measures are support for the idea that migrants increase crime, and rejection of the idea that migrants open Britain to new ideas and cultures.

[61] The two measures are support for the idea that migrants take jobs from British workers and rejection of the idea that migration is economically beneficial for Britain.

social threat. There is, however, no further negative shift in either measure after 2003, and attitudes remain stable throughout the decade thereafter despite record migration levels. While British voters have been quite sceptical about migration throughout the second wave, neither two decades of record migration inflows nor the global financial crisis is associated with any increase in negative sentiment about the economic or social impact of immigration.[62]

While overall attitudes were stable in the second wave, these averages mask deep and persistent divides within the electorate. Concern about immigration in the New Labour years was heavily concentrated among ethnocentric identity conservative voters, and opposition to immigration was already closely associated with other aspects of identity politics which would become mobilised in the next decade: assertive English national identity and Euroscepticism.[63] However, the patterns of association between identity conservatism and opposition to immigration did not change much over the course of the New Labour period, suggesting that high migration levels mobilised already existing differences in outlook between identity conservatives and identity liberals, but did not polarise these groups further.[64]

The political disruption from migration was thus not the product of a surge in xenophobic hostility to migrants, or due to growing polarisation in public views of migrants, but occurred because rising migration levels *activated* already existing anti-immigrant sentiments concentrated among identity conservative voters. These voters already had negative views of migrants well before the second wave, and the surge in migration levels led them to focus on migration as a threat and

---

[62] Voters do express more concern that migrants are taking jobs from natives in the surveys conducted after the financial crisis, but this is balanced out by greater positivity about the overall economic impact of migration.

[63] Details of this analysis can be found in the Online Appendix: www.cambridge.org/Brexitland

[64] Some researchers have found evidence of a modest increase in polarisation by education and ethnicity during this period, particularly on attitudes to the social impacts of migration. See Ford, Morrell and Heath (2012); Ford and Lymperopoulou (2017).

demand action from politicians. Identity liberals, by contrast, already had positive or neutral views of migrants before the second wave began and did not change their views in response to the sharp increase in migration levels. However, while identity liberals were happy with open migration policies in general, and with EU free movement policies in particular, they did not see maintaining Britain's open approach to migration as a political priority, and therefore did not mobilise in defence of it.[65]

Figure 5.10 illustrates this process in action, showing how attention to immigration varied with views about immigrants in the 2001, 2005 and 2010 elections. In 2001, virtually no one was focused on immigration, regardless of how they viewed immigrants. This changed dramatically in the next two elections, but the new public focus on immigration was concentrated almost entirely amongst those with negative views of immigrants. More than half of the voters with the most negative views of immigrants named the issue as the most important facing the country in 2005, and attention to immigration among this group remained very high in 2010 despite the global financial crisis. By contrast, very few voters with more moderate or positive views prioritised immigration in any of these elections, even as the issue became an all-consuming one for the most anti-migrant voters. Migration thus produced *asymmetric activation* in the 2000s – hostility to immigrants did not become more widespread, but it did become more politically influential because anti-immigrant voters became intensely focused on immigration, and very vocal in their demands for control. It was this activation of longstanding but previously latent ethnocentric sentiment which many mistook for a surge in xenophobia. In fact, what was happening, just as had occurred in the first wave of immigration, and indeed in 1930s Banbury, was the

---

[65] In part this may be because they did not see any credible threat to the open immigration status quo at this time. When such a credible threat emerged in the wake of Brexit, identity liberals did begin to mobilise in defence of open migration policies.

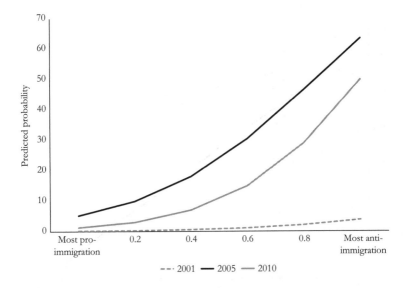

Figure 5.10 Predicted probability of naming immigration as the most important problem facing the country, by immigration attitudes by election year, 2001, 2005, 2010

Source: British Election Studies, 2001, 2005, 2010.

activation of ethnocentric hostilities to out-groups which had been there all along.

The New Labour governments were very focused on managerial performance – delivering the outcomes the public wanted to see – and immigration was their weakest link in this regard. The public rated the Labour government's performance on immigration more negatively than any other issue throughout the 2000s. Once again, the activation of ethnocentric voters was a key reason for this underperformance. The government's negative ratings with the public overall were driven by extremely negative judgements from identity conservative voters with the most anti-immigrant views, while more moderate or identity liberal voters were fairly happy with the government's record on immigration throughout the 2000s. This is illustrated in Figure 5.11, which shows ratings of Labour government performance in

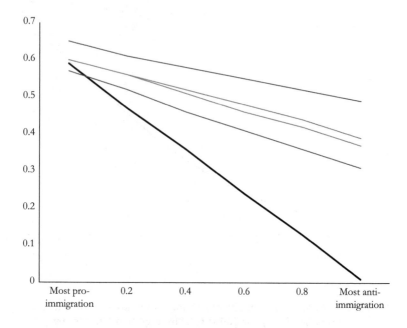

Figure 5.11 Voter ratings of Labour's performance in 2005 on asylum and other issues by sentiment towards immigrants

Key: asylum = black line; other issues = grey lines.
Source: British Election Study 2005. Lines are predicted ratings from an OLS regression model. Further details of the models are provided in the Online Appendix: www.cambridge.org/Brexitland

2005 against sentiment towards immigrants. Voters with positive sentiments towards immigrants, on the left of the graph, are as satisfied with Labour's record on immigration (black line) as they are with its records on other issues (grey lines). A very different pattern obtains among voters with the most negative views of immigrants, on the right-hand side of the graph – while they show a tendency to have more negative views of Labour across the board, their ratings of immigration performance stand out as far more negative than judgements on any other issue.[66]

---

[66] The same pattern recurs in 2001 and 2010; see the Online Appendix (www .cambridge.org/Brexitland) for details.

Identity conservatives' intense unhappiness with Labour's immigration performance also spilled over into more negative assessments of the party and its leaders. Negative sentiment towards immigrants was associated with more negative views of the Labour Party and of Labour's prime ministers throughout the 2000s, reactivating and reinforcing the longstanding identity politics party alignment over race and immigration forged in the first wave of immigration (see Chapter 4).[67] The New Labour era thus saw intensifying identity conservative dissatisfaction with government performance and leadership, driven by a belief that policymakers had persistently failed to address their concerns about high migration levels. Yet these concerns were not shared by the majority of voters, and as we showed earlier in this chapter, those most unhappy about immigration were also among the least likely to take an interest in politics or cast a ballot. The rising political disengagement of the New Labour era thus blunted the disruptive impact of immigration, as unhappy identity conservatives sat out elections, while pro-migration identity liberal voters continued to participate at very high rates.

Conclusion

In this chapter we have focused on party politics and highlighted a series of trends which came together in the New Labour era to generate space for the identity divides emerging from demographic change to be mobilised into politics. Traditional class and ideological conflicts were organised out of politics by New Labour's move to the centre ground, while the modernisation of electoral campaigning reduced the contact many ordinary voters had with political parties, and the professionalisation of political elites increased the distance between these elites and the voters they sought to represent. These changes in the party system accelerated another set of changes in the electorate, including a long-term decline in partisanship and a steady rise in political

---

[67] Details of this analysis can be found in the Online Appendix: www.cambridge .org/Brexitland

disaffection, with voters turning against a political mainstream that no longer represented their views or gave them a meaningful choice. Such discontent might have remained latent but for the final development in this period: the re-emergence of immigration as a political issue. Immigration activated ethnocentric sentiments in the identity conservative electorate, whose anxieties about the arrival of a large new out-group were stoked and reinforced by persistent negative media attention. Such voters became sufficiently unhappy about high migration levels that, as we show in the next chapter, by the end of the New Labour governments they were open to backing new parties promising radical action to restrict migration.

Policymakers were aware of rising public anxieties on migration, but they faced greater challenges in responding than their predecessors. In the first wave, the external constraints governments faced – the citizenship and migration rights of Commonwealth residents – were within their power to amend or to remove. Which is what, by stages, they did. A series of restrictive reforms phased out Commonwealth migration rights between 1962 and 1981. In the second wave, it was not within domestic policymakers' power to alter the policy most responsible for generating public discontent from 2004 onwards: free movement rights within the EU. As a result, there was no mechanism to relieve the electoral pressure, and instead discussion of immigration was forced into an 'all or nothing' framework – voters either had to accept uncontrolled immigration as the price of EU membership, or seek to fundamentally redraw Britain's relationship with Europe in order to achieve immigration control.

Another crucial difference between the two waves of immigration is that during the first wave, the core identity conservative demographic of white school leavers was the largest group in the electorate for both main parties, who therefore had a strong electoral incentive to respond once migration activated ethnocentric sentiments in this group. In the second wave, identity liberal graduates and ethnic minorities were a much larger and rapidly growing part of the electorate, particularly in the Labour electoral coalition (see Chapter 7), while a graduate-

heavy political class dominated by communications professionals and career politicians gave identity liberals an outsized voice
in the political elite. Resistance from identity liberal elites made
immigration control a more difficult issue to pursue, and few
university-educated politicians regarded doing so as a priority.
This resulted in a very different political dynamic: ethnocentric
concerns steadily rose, but the governing Labour Party was
internally divided over how to respond, so such concerns were
not effectively addressed. This lack of response further intensified identity conservative voters' anxiety and helped to turn
them against mainstream politics.[68]

Yet, despite growing polarisation over immigration, no great
political earthquake occurred in the New Labour years. There
were tremors, certainly, but the traditional British party system
remained more or less intact. A critical stabilising factor was the
Conservatives' reputation for immigration control, which gave
the main opposition the capacity to channel much of the rising
discontent into mainstream politics. Voters angry about immigration in the 2000s still had an obvious place to go – they could
back the Conservative Party, who had a long-established reputation for strict migration control dating back to the first wave of
immigration, and the strong anti-immigration stances of Enoch
Powell and Margaret Thatcher. The Conservative opposition
gained politically from their traditional association with migration control, though their choice to appeal to ethnocentric anxieties with undeliverable promises of draconian restrictions
would set the stage for the next, more dramatic phase of political disruption.

[68] McLaren (2013).

6 THE IDENTITY CONSERVATIVE INSURGENCY AND THE RISE OF UKIP

Introduction

The conditions for a major rupture to traditional party politics were all in place before 2010. The bonds between voters and parties were fading; a large segment of the electorate was losing faith in traditional British politics; and immigration had again emerged as a powerful disruptive issue. There were plenty of warning signs. Both the BNP and UKIP had grown rapidly through the 2000s and secured nearly 1.5 million votes between them in 2010, a record level of support for the radical right.[1] The 2010 election campaign was volatile, with a massive surge in support for the Liberal Democrats after the first televised leaders' debates when leader Nick Clegg attacked the 'two old parties ... making the same promises, breaking the same promises'. Polls immediately afterwards gave Clegg an approval rating of over 80 per cent, making him briefly the most popular party leader since Winston Churchill,[2] and highlighting the hunger for new political options among a public tired of the two traditional governing parties.[3]

---

[1] However, neither party came close to winning a Westminster seat. The electoral system may thus have blunted the early influence of the radical right on mainstream politicians.

[2] Oliver and Smith (2010).

[3] The Liberal Democrats were once again punished by the first-past-the-post electoral system, ending up with a net loss of two seats despite increasing their

Yet, in the end, the election of 2010 did not end up being a watershed where voters turned against the traditional parties. David Cameron's Conservatives secured a large increase in vote, and a large lead in seats, though they fell short of a Commons majority. The resurgent Conservatives then formed a coalition government with the Liberal Democrats, whose campaign polling surge had melted away on election day. Widespread discontent did not deliver a political earthquake, and instead one of the traditional parties of government took over from the other, albeit in an unusual coalition arrangement. In part, this reflected the context of the 2010 election, fought in the wake of the worst economic crisis for generations. Voters and politicians alike were focused on the traditional arguments over economics, public spending and redistribution which had traditionally framed competition between Labour and the Conservatives. Tellingly, after peaking in 2007, by 2010 immigration was no longer top of the most important issue list in the British Election Study, displaced by economic concerns.[4] But the Conservatives also derived a critical benefit in 2010 from their long-standing reputation for migration control, reinforced by new campaign pledges for major cuts to migration, which enabled them to mobilise discontented identity conservatives.

The 2010 election delayed the mobilisation of identity conflicts, but not for long. The 2010–15 Coalition government proved to be a tipping point, with identity conservatives and identity liberals switching in large numbers to parties better aligned with their preferences. There are two parts to this story, which we tell in the next two chapters. The first, told in this chapter, is the emergence of a distinctive new party that mobilised identity conservatives: UKIP.[5] The second, which we focus on in the next chapter, is the reshaping of the Labour party electoral coalition by the simultaneous arrival of identity liberal

vote share to 23 per cent, the best result by a third party since the SDP/Liberal Alliance's first election in 1983.

[4] Whiteley et al. (2013).

[5] Ford and Goodwin (2014b); Goodwin and Milazzo (2015).

voters and departure of identity conservative voters. Labour lost a large cohort of white school leavers to UKIP in this period, but this loss was offset by a major influx of white graduates alienated by the Liberal Democrats' decision to join the Conservative-led Coalition government. In addition, the fading of discontent about New Labour's foreign policy brought Muslim voters back into the Labour fold. The demographic basis of Labour support therefore changed dramatically between 2010 and 2015, even as the party's overall popularity remained broadly stable. Meanwhile, the Coalition stripped the Liberal Democrats of two traditional sources of appeal – anti-government populism and anti-Conservative tactical voting – and thus the majority of their support. What remained after the party's 2015 collapse was a much smaller but more socially and ideologically distinctive Liberal Democrat electorate.

The 2010–15 Coalition government is thus the period when the mobilisation of identity politics divides begins to restructure British party competition. By the end of this period, England and Wales had one party dominated by identity conservative voters, issues and ideology – UKIP – and two parties where identity liberals were dominant (the Liberal Democrats) or becoming so (Labour). The Coalition government was also the period when Scottish politics re-aligned around identity conflicts, though this was a very different journey, one we take up in Chapter 9. Only the governing Conservatives proved able to weather the mobilisation of identity conflicts effectively. Though they lost substantial identity conservative support to UKIP, the quirks of the first-past-the-post electoral system, and the gains they made at the expense of their junior coalition partners blunted the electoral effects of this in 2015. David Cameron was able to deliver one more unexpected Commons majority in 2015 using the competent leadership and economic performance approach pioneered by his New Labour predecessors.[6]

---

[6] Though their reputation with identity conservatives was damaged by their failure on immigration, the Conservatives also continued to make appeals to this group in both policy and messaging during the 2015 campaign in an effort

UKIP's breakthrough during the Coalition was not a coincidence. It followed directly from the Conservatives' failure to deliver on their promise to deliver swingeing cuts to immigration. This pledge, always undeliverable because of the institutional constraint of EU membership, shredded a decades-old reputation for migration control in less than two years, and broke the longstanding link between ethnocentric sentiments and Conservative support. Nor was it an accident that UKIP was the vehicle identity conservatives chose to express their discontent. UKIP was an established hard-Eurosceptic party with a track record of success in European Parliament elections and longstanding links to Eurosceptic Conservatives. UKIP was therefore seen by large parts of the electorate as a legitimate political actor with a coherent political agenda. This made them a more effective outlet for discontent because (unlike the BNP) they were not seen as an organisation that existed solely to stoke and mobilise hostility to migrants and ethnic minorities, and hence could not be easily stigmatised as a racist party. UKIP also profited from the link between the Conservatives' failure on immigration and the constraints imposed on Britain by EU membership – precisely the kind of constraints UKIP had long argued were intolerable. The link between immigration and EU membership proved to be the party's golden ticket.

Riding on reputation: the Conservatives and immigration under New Labour

Immigration was a recruitment opportunity for the Conservative opposition throughout the New Labour governments. As Figure 6.1 illustrates, the party enjoyed strong ratings on the issue, particularly amongst identity conservative voters and the

to head off the challenge from UKIP. Tough crime and immigration policies were again emphasised, along with the high-profile pledge of a referendum on EU membership (Cowley and Kavanagh 2015).

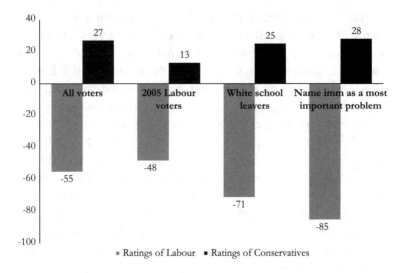

Figure 6.1 Ratings of the Labour government and Conservative opposition on immigration, 2010 (difference in percentages)

Source: British Election Study, 2010.

voters most concerned about immigration.[7] Immigration was consistently the issue where the Conservatives enjoyed their largest (or only) advantage among voters who had backed Labour in the previous election. Large parts of the electorate, including many Labour voters, considered immigration to be an important political priority, were unhappy with the incumbent government's performance, and thought the Conservatives would do a better job. There was no other issue on the agenda in the 2000s where the Conservatives had this triple advantage.

The Conservatives were aware of their leverage on immigration from early on in their long spell of opposition, and repeatedly sought to capitalise on the issue. In 2001, William Hague warned of Britain being 'swamped' by a 'flood' of 'bogus' asylum seekers, echoing the rhetoric employed by Margaret Thatcher in

---

[7] The same pattern holds in the 2005 British Election Study. In 2001, the same pattern obtains with regard to ratings of the Labour government, but the BES did not ask voters to rate the Conservatives' issue performance.

1978.[8] Immigration was even more prominent in the 2005 Conservative campaign,[9] when Michael Howard made immigration control a central policy focus, and the party ran hundreds of billboards with the tagline 'It's not racist to impose limits on immigration'.[10] This slogan highlighted how the politics of immigration was not just an issue of numbers and control, but was already also about broader conflicts over identity attachments and anti-racism norms, with identity liberal activists and voters framing opposition to immigration as an expression of prejudice, while identity conservative voters and politicians sought to push back against this framing and defend the legitimacy of immigration control (see Chapter 3).

The response from Labour Prime Minister Tony Blair to the Conservatives' 2005 campaign illustrates that Labour's leadership, too, recognised the disruptive potential both of immigration anxieties in general, and of the Conservatives' argument that demands for immigration control were being unfairly stigmatised. Blair's campaign speech on the issue embraced the theme of immigration control, underlining that he regarded it as a legitimate public preference, and that Labour would prioritise extending the use of controls '[so] that those who stay illegally are removed'. But Blair also attacked the Conservative charge that immigration concerns were being marginalised:

> *Their campaign is based on the statement that it isn't racist to talk about immigration. I know of no senior politician who has ever said it was. So why do they put it like that?... It is an attempt deliberately to exploit people's fears, to suggest that, for reasons of political correctness, those in power don't dare deal with the issue, so the public are left with the impression that they are being silenced in their concerns, that we are blindly ignoring them or telling them that to raise the issue is racist, when actually the opposite is true.[11]*

---

[8] Saggar (2001).   [9] Green and Hobolt (2008); Butler and Kavanagh (2005).
[10] There is some evidence that the Conservatives' strong focus on this issue increased voters' attention to it during the campaign (Norris 2006).
[11] Blair (2005).

While Blair's diagnosis of the problem was accurate, his government did not (and, after 2004, could not) offer the kind of draconian controls identity conservative voters concerned about immigration wanted to see. Nor, strangely, did New Labour pursue changes which might have helped offset the losses of anti-migration voters – in particular, providing an easier route to citizenship for non-Commonwealth migrants, so that, as in the first wave, the rapidly growing EU migrant community could in time join the electorate as a substantial new constituency with a strong interest in supporting EU free movement policies.[12]

With mass migration continuing during Labour's third term, the salience of immigration hit new highs in 2006–7, and though attention faded somewhat in the wake of the financial crisis, immigration remained a pressing concern for many as the 2010 election approached. The Conservatives once again sought to press home their advantage on the issue with Howard's successor David Cameron, though by instinct and background a social liberal,[13] promising to reduce migration. Cameron's pledges implied more radical restrictions than previous Conservative leaders had proposed. Cameron announced in January 2010 that his party 'would like to see net immigration in the tens of thousands rather than the hundreds of thousands. I don't think that's unrealistic.'[14] However, as Cameron and his Home Secretary Theresa May would soon discover, such radical cuts to migration were hopelessly unrealistic while Britain remained an EU member, given its attractiveness to migrants from poorer EU member states. However, this constraint was not initially recognised by identity conservative voters, amongst whom Cameron's pledge proved very popular.

The electoral value of the Conservatives' advantage on immigration during the New Labour governments is illustrated in Figure 6.2, which shows how views of immigration were associated with the chances of switching from Labour to the

---

[12] Ford (2018).   [13] Bale (2010).   [14] Cameron (2010).

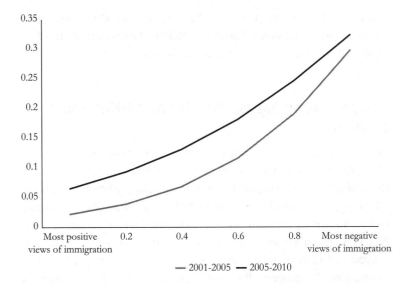

Figure 6.2 Predicted likelihood of switching from Labour to the Conservatives by attitudes to immigration, 2001–5 (grey) and 2005–10 (black)

Source: British Election Study face-to-face surveys, 2005, 2010. Figures show predicted probability of a voter who reported backing Labour in the previous election switching to the Conservatives.

Conservatives in 2001–5 and in 2005–10. In both elections, voters with the most anti-immigration views were much more likely to defect to the Conservatives – between a quarter and a third of the most anti-immigrant Labour voters switched in both elections, while fewer than one in ten of those with pro-migration views made such a switch. In 2005–10, immigration was a stronger predictor of switching away from Labour than economic issues despite the financial crisis,[15] as voters blamed Labour for high immigration while seeing the financial crisis as a global issue. Opposition to immigration won the Conservatives a steady stream of identity conservative recruits from Labour throughout the 2000s. But these new recruits' demands for total

[15] Evans and Chzhen (2013).

control of migration could not be met, and as these were distrustful and politically disaffected voters, they would be hard to hold on to if their hopes were disappointed.[16]

Early warning signs: the BNP and UKIP under New Labour

The Conservatives were not the only party profiting from identity conservative discontent over immigration in the 2000s. Both the BNP and UKIP also grew substantially during the New Labour governments, mobilising ethnocentric sentiments to secure record shares of the vote in the 2005 and 2010 elections.[17] The BNP was the successor to the 1970s far right National Front, and shared the openly racist and violent reputation of this earlier movement.[18] However, following the election of Nick Griffin as leader in 1999, the BNP sought to play down its most extreme past beliefs in an effort to build a broader base of support.[19] This strategic refocus coincided with the first surge in public concern about immigration, and with a rise in anxiety about terrorism and Islamic extremism, giving the BNP two potent campaign issues.

The BNP's new approach paid some dividends – by recruiting support from intensely ethnocentric and politically disaffected parts of the electorate, it grew into the most successful far right party in British history thus far,[20] with general election support rising tenfold over the decade from 47,000 votes in 2001 to 564,000 in 2010. The BNP had even greater success in local and European Parliament elections, where lower turnouts and lower stakes provided greater opportunities for newcomers and

---

[16] The problem of radical right competition for voters on the immigration issue is one centre-right parties in many of the more open, proportional political systems of Western Europe had already been grappling with for some time, see Bale (2003).

[17] Ford and Goodwin (2010); Ford, Goodwin and Cutts (2012).

[18] Copsey and Macklin (2011); Goodwin (2011).   [19] Goodwin (2011).

[20] Ford and Goodwin (2010).

protest parties.[21] However, after failing to win any seats in the 2010 general election, the BNP rapidly disintegrated as Griffin lost his ability to control more extreme elements who wanted to return to violent, street protest politics. Within a few years, nearly all BNP elected representatives in local government and the European Parliament were gone.

The rise of the BNP from a tiny fringe outfit to a mass political party in the 2000s, and its swift collapse thereafter, highlights the power both of ethnocentrism and of anti-racism social norms. The BNP's growth was driven by recruitment of the most ethnocentric voters, who held strongly hostile and often openly racist views about immigrants and ethnic minorities, in particular British Muslims.[22] The BNP's emergence was thus an early sign of the disruptive potential of activated ethnocentric sentiments.[23] Yet the party's racist and fascist history also put a low ceiling on its appeal, reflecting the power of the other side of identity politics: anti-racism social norms. BNP politicians were pariahs, shunned by all the other parties, including the radical right UKIP, whose leadership repeatedly rebuffed approaches by BNP figures and banned former BNP members from UKIP membership.[24] Party leader Nick Griffin's sole appearance on the flagship BBC programme 'Question Time' attracted protests outside the TV studio, and Griffin faced a universally and intensely hostile reception from the other panellists on the show and from questioners in the studio audience. Such stigmatisation was

---

[21] BNP support in local elections rose from 3,000 votes for seventeen candidates in 2000 to 350,000 voters for over 750 candidates in 2007, the year when the salience of immigration hit an all-time high. At its peak, the BNP had over fifty councillors spread over more than twenty local authorities, and a seat on the London Assembly. The European Parliament, with its proportional electoral system, proved to be an even greater opportunity. BNP support rose nearly sixfold from 103,000 votes (1.1 per cent of the total) in 2001 to 940,000 votes (6.3 per cent of the total) in 2009, when the party returned two MEPs (Cutts, Ford and Goodwin 2011).

[22] Ford and Goodwin (2010).

[23] Wilks-Heeg (2009); John et al. (2006); John and Margetts (2009).

[24] Ford and Goodwin (2014b: ch. 3).

effective: voters who had internalised anti-racism norms rejected the BNP, even when they shared its core concerns about immigration and identity.[25] Despite Griffin's efforts, the BNP could not escape its long history of racism and violent extremism. Many of the activists knocking doors for the BNP were the same people who had been throwing punches for the party in earlier decades,[26] and a stream of stories about candidates' violent and extremist past deeds cast doubt on the party's claim to have moderated. The BNP's toxic reputation ultimately doomed its electoral strategy to failure in Britain's mainly first-past-the-post political system, where victory requires broader electoral coalitions than it was capable of building.

UKIP also experienced rapid increases in support during the 2000s. The party was founded in 1993 and secured over 100,000 votes in the European Parliament elections of 1994, the last contested under the first-past-the-post electoral system. It managed a similar showing in the general election of 1997, when it was overshadowed by the similarly hard Eurosceptic but better funded 'Referendum Party' founded by billionaire Sir James Goldsmith.[27] UKIP were among the first to profit from the 1999 switch to using proportional representation in British European Parliament elections, more than quadrupling their support to nearly 700,000 votes, enough to return their first three MEPs (including a young Nigel Farage). The European

---

[25] Anti-racism norms were associated with rejection of the BNP, even among voters with ethnocentric concerns about immigration, and the activation of anti-racism norms leads voters who would otherwise support discriminatory policies to reject these policies if these were associated with the BNP (Blinder, Ford and Ivarsflaten 2013).

[26] Goodwin, Cutts and Ford (2012).

[27] The Goldsmith family have a century-long history of involvement in British politics. Sir James' father Frank Goldsmith was a Conservative MP, representing Stowmarket from 1910 to 1918. Sir James himself sat as an MEP for a French Eurosceptic party from 1994 until his death in 1997. His son Zac went on to be a Conservative MP for Richmond Park from 2010 to 2016, when he was deposed in a by-election by the Liberal Democrats running a strongly anti-Brexit campaign. He narrowly regained the seat in the 2017 election, then lost it again in 2019. Sir James' brother Teddy Goldsmith was a co-founder of the British Green Party.

Parliament thereafter became strategically important to UKIP, enabling it to mobilise Euroscepticism to return large cohorts of MEPs every five years, and thereby secure considerable EU resources and media attention in between European Parliament campaigns.

UKIP support in general elections also grew through the 2000s, more than doubling from 391,000 in 2001 to 920,000 in 2010. The party secured more votes in each of these elections than the BNP, although this vote was spread thinly across more seats. The lack of local strongholds reduced the party's domestic influence as, while the BNP represented a credible local threat in some pockets of the country,[28] UKIP were not a viable challenger anywhere despite a larger national vote. The party fielded many council candidates, but these were spread haphazardly across the country, with no effective local organisations to back them.[29] UKIP secured many votes but very few councillors and no influence. Of the two fringe right parties in the 2000s, the BNP looked in many respects the more effective domestic electoral force, despite lower overall support.

UKIP's subsequent eclipse of the BNP and consolidation of the identity conservative vote underscores the critical importance of anti-racism norms and party reputations. In domestic elections UKIP was mobilising the same kind of voters, with the same kind of concerns, as the BNP.[30] Yet UKIP, though less well organised in domestic elections, was able to secure a larger overall vote because it was more widely seen as a legitimate political choice. UKIP's primary focus was not immigration, but Europe: the party was founded to secure Britain's exit from the EU, and its

---

[28] The BNP's strongest general election results came in Oldham and Burnley in 2001, two economically depressed Northern mill towns with deep and longstanding local tensions between the white majority and a large Muslim minority; and in Barking and Dagenham and Rainham in 2005 and 2010, in an area with a very strong local white working-class identity built around the Ford car works and large council estates, which was undergoing very rapid ethnic change due to the inward migration of large immigrant populations and ethnic minority populations moving eastwards from inner London (Gest 2016).

[29] Ford and Goodwin (2010: chs 2 and 3).

[30] Ford and Goodwin (2014b); Ford, Goodwin and Cutts (2012).

success in European Parliament elections reinforced its image as a credible outlet for Euroscepticism.

UKIP's history and reputation thus made it harder for mainstream party elites to stigmatise it as racist and extreme. Many Eurosceptic politicians regarded UKIP as a legitimate political outfit, most of the national media treated the party as such, and the electorate picked up on such cues and followed suit. UKIP thus exemplify a paradoxical finding regarding radical right parties mobilising ethnocentric sentiments across Europe: nearly every successful radical right party has started as something else, before shifting on to immigration and other identity politics conflicts. A history of campaigning on other issues provides such parties with a 'reputational shield' against the charge of intolerance – they cannot easily be stigmatised as agents of hatred.[31] This matters because many identity conservative voters are internally conflicted – though they have ethnocentric anxieties, they also do not want to think of themselves, or be thought of by others, as enablers of bigotry. A veneer of legitimacy is therefore a vital resource for radical right parties, as by escaping the stigma of racism they can appeal to a much broader electorate. UKIP's well-entrenched reputation as a Eurosceptic party provided it with a veneer of legitimacy and made it better placed to profit from the activation of ethnocentric sentiments than the toxic BNP.

The early warning signs of a potential identity conservative revolt against the mainstream parties were thus very clear. However, both parties' prospects were limited as long as the Conservatives' longstanding reputation for migration control enabled them to lock down most identity conservative votes. This last aspect of the political environment was about to change, opening up a powerful new opportunity to radical right insurgents just at the moment when the organisational collapse of the BNP enabled UKIP to consolidate its position as the main competitor on the radical right.

---

[31] Ivarsflaten (2006).

Betrayal: the failure of the immigration pledge and the opening of the electoral market

While Labour remained in office, the Conservatives could have their cake and eat it on immigration: pledging radical cuts without having to confront the costs and constraints involved in delivering them. This changed when the 2010 Coalition government returned the Conservatives to office, and the party's political advantage on migration began to unravel almost immediately. This was not for want of effort. The Coalition government passed a range of migration control policies and rule changes, including ending visas for skilled migrants without a job offer; an annual cap on skilled migrants *with* a job offer; substantial increases in the financial requirements for those wanting to bring a foreign spouse to Britain; tougher financial and language requirements on foreign students and restrictions on their ability to work in Britain after their studies or bring relatives to the country; restrictions on new migrants' access to welfare benefits; and restrictions on migrants' ability to appeal decisions refusing their right to stay in the UK.[32] The Conservatives strengthened enforcement procedures and broadened their scope, imposing much tougher reporting and inspection regimes on employers and educational institutions looking to recruit migrants, and drastically expanding migration enforcement to encompass landlords, health care providers and other providers of public services via what became known as the 'hostile environment' regime.[33]

---

[32] For further details on the range of migration policy changes introduced during the Coalition, see Hampshire and Bale (2016) and Gower (2015).

[33] The phrase, which has since become politically notorious, was initially coined to refer to how expanded checks were supposed to make Britain a 'hostile environment' for *illegal* immigrants, but the instruments created to achieve this goal were very blunt. A wide range of employers and service providers with no knowledge of migration policy and rules found themselves legally obliged to undertake migration status checks on all those seeking to use their services or work with them. When combined with Britain's unusually complex past citizenship and migration regimes (see Chapter 4), and the lack of any universally held or accepted forms of identification documents in

There was a lot of policy and enforcement activity focused on restricting migration, but this persistently failed to produce the drastic numerical reductions the Conservatives had promised. After falling modestly in the first two years of the Coalition, net migration began to rise again.[34] In particular, substantial EU migration continued. The government's new controls could not be applied to EU migrants, and the now established inflows from Central and Eastern Europe to Britain were boosted by increased migration from older EU member states, where unemployment had surged in the wake of the Eurozone debt crisis.[35] The government was also unwilling to impose stricter controls on foreign students coming to British universities from outside the EU, due to the risk of damaging the finances and international competitiveness of a key strategic sector.[36] Yet, perversely, Home Secretary Theresa May also resisted calls to exclude

Britain, this was a recipe for disaster. Many lifelong legal British residents (in particular, Commonwealth citizens who had exercised Commonwealth citizenship rights to migrate to Britain without any documentation many decades earlier) were suddenly confronted by demands for proof of status they could not meet. They were thrown out of jobs and houses, or denied urgent health care, and when they appealed their situation to the Home Office they found themselves facing the threat of deportation from the country they had lived in legally as citizens for decades. This situation, known as the 'Windrush crisis' was an entirely predictable consequence of the rule changes introduced by the 2010–15 government, but only came to light several years later, when Theresa May, who had developed these rules and overseen their implementation as home secretary, was Prime Minister.

[34] Far from reducing net migration below 100,000 a year by the end of its term of office, the Coalition failed even to reduce migration below the average of 250,000 per year during the final term of the Labour government. By 2014, net migration was running at over 300,000 per year.

[35] Migration Observatory (2016).

[36] The government was, however, willing to impose draconian new rules on non-university educational institutions. The Home Office revoked licences for over 800 educational institutions sponsoring migrants coming to study from outside the EU between 2010 and 2014. The vast majority of these were further education colleges and English-language schools. Migrant numbers in these sectors fell by over 80 per cent between 2010 and 2014 (Blinder and Fernandez-Reino 2018; Home Office 2019).

student migrants from official migration targets,[37] despite widespread evidence that voters either saw foreign students as beneficial or did not see them as migrants at all.[38] May defended this decision by claiming that many student migrants overstayed their visas – claims later shown to be false.[39] Restrictions on the migration of skilled workers from outside the EU were also watered down in the face of intense lobbying from employer groups.[40] When push came to shove, ministers were unwilling to inflict substantial economic harm or create recruitment problems for businesses, universities or public services such as the NHS. Yet without policies that imposed such disruption, hitting the net migration target was impossible. The government was neither willing to introduce the harsh restrictions necessary to hit the net migration target, nor to admit to the public that the target could not be hit. The Conservatives thus bound themselves to a policy pledge that was doomed to fail. And fail it did, on a regular schedule. By making an official statistical measure (the net migration rate) the goal of policy, the Conservatives encouraged the entire political and media class to focus on this measure and highlight the government's failure when new data arrived.

A strange new political ritual therefore developed. Every three months, the Office for National Statistics would publish a new quarterly migration report, which would show net migration continuing to run well above the government's target. A torrent of negative media coverage would follow, highlighting the massive difference between current migration levels and the government's pledge, and framing this as a major policy failure. Government ministers dutifully reiterated their commitment to

---

[37] This change was recommended by five different Parliamentary committees during the Coalition, as it has been criticised as damaging to one of Britain's largest exports industries (Hampshire and Bale 2016: 157).

[38] Ford and Heath (2014); Blinder (2015).

[39] Stewart, Mason and Grierson (2017).

[40] Hampshire and Bale (2016: 155–7). In particular, highly paid workers and intra-company transfers were excluded from the new restrictions, meaning that large globalised firms could continue to recruit globally.

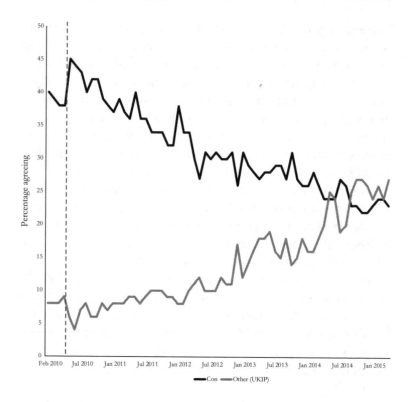

Figure 6.3 'Which party is best able to handle immigration?' 2005–14

Key: dashed vertical line marks beginning of Coalition government.
Source: YouGov.

the target, and pledge to do better in future, while making none of the radical changes required to achieve their stated goal. The government thus set themselves up to be pilloried again three months later, when new migration statistics would once again confirm their failure to hit the target, and the cycle would start over. This rinse-and-repeat ritual of failure destroyed the Conservatives' reputation for migration control very rapidly. The party began their term in office with a huge advantage on the issue: nearly 50 per cent of voters rated them as the best party to address immigration, while only around 10–15 per cent preferred Labour (see Figure 6.3). By the midpoint of the Coalition the share of the electorate who saw the Conservatives as the

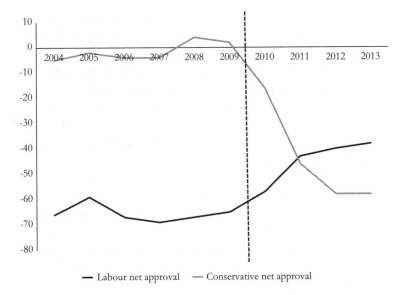

— Labour net approval   — Conservative net approval

Figure 6.4 Net approve–disapprove ratings for handling of migration, Conservatives and Labour, 2004–13

Source: British Election Study Continuous Monitoring Survey, 2004–13. The questions asked approval of 'asylum' but other data sources confirm that views of this match up very closely with views of migration policy more broadly.

best party on migration had nearly halved. Labour registered no gains, and instead growing numbers of anti-immigration voters turned to the radical alternative approach offered by UKIP.

The same dramatic collapse in voter faith is evident in the monthly surveys conducted by the British Election Study in this period, as shown in Figure 6.4. The Conservatives' net approval ratings on migration was around zero in the years prior to the Coalition, meaning equal numbers of voters approved and disapproved of their approach. The balance of opinion shifted very rapidly after the Coalition government began, falling from +2 in 2009 to −58 in 2012. The swing against the Conservatives was even larger among the core identity conservative electorate of white school leavers. Net approval ratings of the party among this group dropped a whopping 73 points from −2 in 2009 to

−75 in 2012, and by the midpoint of the coalition more than half of white school leavers felt the Conservatives were performing 'very badly' on immigration.

The evaporation of voters' longstanding faith in the Conservatives on immigration was not, however, accompanied by much rekindling of enthusiasm for Labour on the issue. Instead, for the first time since the 1960s, a large part of the electorate felt neither traditional party could effectively handle immigration. Around a third of respondents in regular YouGov polling said no party could be trusted to deal with it, while a growing minority began to name UKIP as the only party able to address it.[41] The share of voters who disapproved of both parties' immigration policies nearly doubled from around 20 per cent in 2009 to almost 40 per cent in 2013, and once again such a 'plague on both your houses' sentiment was most widespread among identity conservatives.[42]

There was also broader political fallout, with the government's persistent failure on immigration further eroding the public's trust in politicians generally and strengthening the links between political distrust and hostility to mainstream parties.[43] The salience of immigration, which had dropped during the financial crisis and recession, began to rise again after 2011 as public faith in the government's pledge to control it collapsed. Immigration would remain at the top of the public's political agenda thereafter all the way through to the EU Referendum vote in 2016. This resurgence in concern about immigration was, however, different in a crucial way from earlier periods of public concern: voters now linked the Conservatives' inability to control immigration with Britain's membership of the EU, recognising that EU free movement rights were a key reason the government could not deliver effective control.[44]

---

[41] Dennison and Goodwin (2015).
[42] This figure comes from the British Election Study monthly Continuous Monitoring Study surveys.
[43] McLaren (2013).   [44] Evans and Mellon (2019).

Mobilising the backlash: UKIP during the Coalition

This was an unusually propitious moment for a challenger able to combine a strong anti-migration stance with trenchant hostility to the EU. While UKIP had already grown into Britain's most successful fringe right-wing party by 2010, the collapse of identity conservatives' trust in the Conservatives on immigration expanded the party's appeal. UKIP support in polls more than doubled in the first half of the Coalition, from an average of less than 5 per cent in 2010 to well over 10 per cent in early 2013. The party was virtually absent from Scotland, and very weak in London, while in the English regions where most Conservative and Labour marginal seats were found, UKIP was polling in the mid- to high teens.

UKIP achieved its first domestic political breakthrough a few months after Cameron's pledge to hold a referendum on EU membership, winning over a hundred local council seats in the May 2013 elections, beginning a virtuous circle where electoral and polling success drove increases in media attention, which in turn helped the party further increase its support.[45] This was repeated in 2014, when Britain went to the polls in European Parliament elections. The BNP's collapse meant UKIP had the radical right Eurosceptic field all to itself, and the party duly capitalised, coming in first place with nearly 27 per cent of the vote.[46] The defection of two Conservative MPs a few months later kept up the virtuous circle, delivering UKIP its first Westminster by-election wins. UKIP's seemingly relentless rise in the polls and in local, European and Westminster elections was one of the main stories on the political agenda throughout the second half of the Coalition.

While the largest group of recruits to UKIP throughout this period were 2010 Conservative voters, the party's growth was

---

[45] Murphy and Devine (2018).   [46] Geddes (2014); Vasilopoulou (2016).

also fuelled by the defection of voters from all the mainstream parties, particularly if we look back further than one election cycle. A substantial chunk of UKIP support came from voters who had backed Labour in 2005, then the Conservatives in 2010; another chunk came from voters who had backed the Liberal Democrats in 2010.[47] UKIP voters' past politics were diverse, but their demographic background, attitudes and priorities were not. UKIP's support came overwhelmingly from ethnocentric white school leavers with very negative views about immigration and the EU.[48] UKIP consolidation of votes from this electorate was a matter of both luck and leadership. While UKIP's core issue was opposition to the EU, the party had also been a long-standing critic of open migration policies and the failures of the political class, positions which endeared it to disaffected identity conservatives. The party was also fortunate to have a leader in this period, Nigel Farage, who proved adept at packaging these three issues together into a resonant populist narrative and communicating this message on national media. Farage's argument that both immigration control and political renewal in Britain were impossible without leaving the EU was plausible and appealing to identity conservatives, and Farage missed no opportunity to hammer this message home in regular media appearances.

UKIP's mobilisation of identity conservative voters in England and Wales is illustrated in Figure 6.5. The party quintupled its support among white school leavers between the 2010 general election, when it won 5 per cent of this group, and the European Parliament elections in 2014, when it was backed by around 25 per cent of such voters. UKIP was much weaker among the core identity liberal demographics – graduates and ethnic minorities. Education and ethnicity were the strongest demographic predictors of UKIP support throughout the Coalition government,[49] underscoring how the party mobilised one side of the identity politics divide. It is a similar story when we look

[47] Evans and Mellon(2014; 2019).   [48] Ford and Goodwin (2014b: chs 5 and 6).
[49] Ford and Goodwin (2014b: ch. 4).

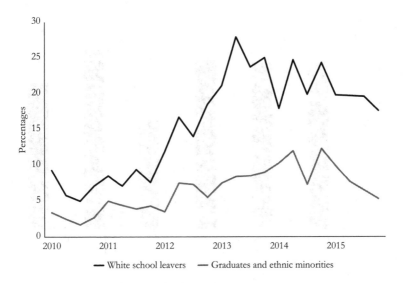

Figure 6.5 UKIP support among white school leavers, and among graduates and ethnic minorities in England and Wales, 2010–15

Source: BES/NSF Continuous Monitoring Study. Note that data availability issues mean that in 2014–15 only education divides are captured.

at the attitudes which predicted UKIP support, as illustrated in Figure 6.6: negative views of immigration, salience of immigration, English identity, views of equal opportunities for ethnic minorities and authoritarianism are all very strong predictors of UKIP support. These demographic and attitudinal measures of identity conservatism do a much better job of explaining UKIP support than any other economic or social factors,[50] particularly in domestic elections.[51] UKIP during the Coalition were, first and

---

[50] Full details of these regression models are provided in the Online Appendix: www.cambridge.org/Brexitland. See also, for example, Ford and Goodwin (2014b); Ford, Goodwin and Cutts (2012); Goodwin and Milazzo (2015); Fieldhouse et al. (2019: ch. 5).

[51] UKIP's support in European Parliament elections was slightly different, due to its success in recruiting 'strategic Eurosceptics', highly Eurosceptic but otherwise fairly typical Conservative voters who backed UKIP as a protest vote against the EU (Ford, Goodwin and Cutts 2012).

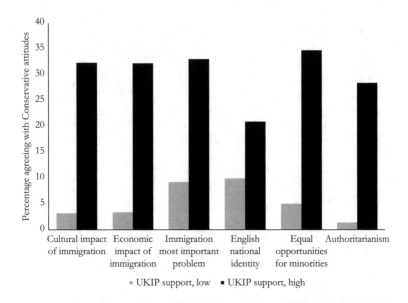

Figure 6.6 Identity conservative attitudes and UKIP support, 2014

Source: British Election Study internet panel, 2014–18, waves 1 and 2: UKIP vote intention is measured at wave 2 and all identity conservatism measures at wave 1.

foremost, a vehicle for identity conservative voters to revolt against mainstream politics.

UKIP's success at recruiting identity conservative voters from across the political spectrum is illustrated in Figure 6.7, which shows how the chances of switching to UKIP from each of the three traditional parties change as we move from the most identity liberal attitudes on the left of the chart to the most identity conservative attitudes on the right-hand side.[52]

---

[52] The figures are predicted probabilities from logistic regression models of switching to UKIP in 2014 general election voting intentions questions for each party's 2010 supporters. The measure of identity politics attitudes includes attitudes to the economic and cultural impact of immigration, English national identity, views of equal opportunities for ethnic minorities and authoritarianism. Full details of the models are provided in the Online Appendix: www.cambridge.org/Brexitland

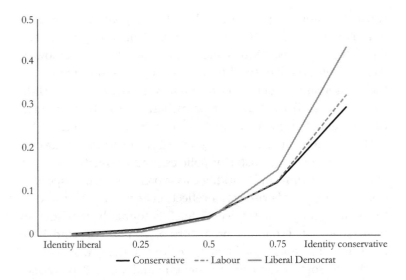

Figure 6.7 Identity conservatism and predicted probability of switching to UKIP in 2014 among 2010 Conservative, Labour and Liberal Democrat voters

Source: British Election Study internet panel, 2014–18.

The rates of switching from every party to UKIP rise sharply as we move towards the identity conservative end of the spectrum. The predicted chances of a 2010 Conservative voter with the most identity conservative attitudes switching to UKIP in 2014 were nearly three in ten. The predicted rates of switching to UKIP among 2010 Labour and Liberal Democrat voters with the most identity conservative attitudes were even higher.[53] The Conservatives lost more support to UKIP because, having recruited unhappy identity conservatives in large numbers in 2010, they were much more exposed to competition on this flank. However, identity conservatives also provided a substantial part of the 2010 support base for both Labour and the Liberal Democrats too. For example, 38 per cent of 2010 Labour

---

[53] However, fewer Labour or Liberal Democrat voters hold strongly identity conservative attitudes.

supporters and 35 per cent of Lib Dem supporters expressed negative views about the cultural impact of immigration (the figure for the Conservatives was 66 per cent). While the flow of identity conservatives to UKIP had the largest overall impact on the Conservatives, defection of identity conservatives to UKIP also helped shift the Labour support base decisively in an identity liberal direction, as we shall see in the next chapter.

UKIP's surge in the middle years of a Conservative government implementing austerity policies, and its relative success with lower-income and working-class voters, has led to speculation that the party's rise was a reflection of public anger at cuts to welfare and public services.[54] Such accounts have tended to focus solely on economic predictors of UKIP's rise, and have neglected the impact of identity politics divides, which often overlap to some extent with economic and social deprivation, but are much more powerful predictors of UKIP support. For example, UKIP's tendency to do better among older voters, working-class voters and lower-income voters is almost entirely accounted for by the differences in education levels and ethnocentric attitudes between these groups. Once differences in education are statistically controlled for, there are no remaining class or income differences in UKIP support. A white working-class school leaver is no more likely to support UKIP than a white middle-class school leaver. A poor ethnocentric nationalist is no more likely to back UKIP than a rich ethnocentric nationalist. And so on.

Similarly, while there is some evidence that UKIP performed better among economically pessimistic voters, and in particular competed effectively with Labour for the support of voters most opposed to austerity cuts (as we shall see in the next chapter), economic perceptions are also weak predictors of UKIP support compared with identity politics demographics and attitudes. It is certainly possible that anger at austerity cuts may have increased UKIP support among the minority of voters directly

---

[54] See, for example, Fetzer (2019).

exposed to them, and thus boosted support for the party at the margins.[55] But among the large majority of voters who were not exposed directly to the effects of welfare cuts, identity conservative attitudes, including ethnocentric hostility to immigrants, national identity attachments, views of equal opportunities, Euroscepticism and so forth, were much better predictors of UKIP support than any measure of economic circumstances or attitudes.[56]

The nature of UKIP's dramatic rise, and the context in which it occurred, closely fit the 'authoritarian dynamic' argument laid out by Karen Stenner to explain how seemingly stable political systems can be upended when latent sentiments in the electorate become activated. Stenner argues that rapid and disruptive mobilisation of authoritarian voters is most likely when such voters perceive an urgent threat to their identity or values, and believe that political elites have failed or are incapable of resolving that threat. A dynamic like this played out with identity conservative voters during the Coalition. These voters perceived an urgent threat from immigration, and lost faith in the ability of the Conservative-led government to address their concerns. Threatened identity conservative voters reacted by mobilising behind a new party that promised radical action to resolve the threat. There was little the Conservatives, or anyone else, could do to fight this dynamic, because no one could offer the kind of draconian controls necessary to dramatically cut immigration while Britain remained an EU member.

Hijacking the agenda: UKIP's impact on the Conservatives

The EU had long been a toxic issue for the Conservatives. The party that had once branded themselves the 'party of Europe' and, under Prime Minister Edward Heath, had taken Britain into

---

[55] Fetzer (2019). For some criticisms of the article's framing and the issue of marginal impacts, see McKay and Bailey (2019).

[56] See the Online Appendix (www.cambridge.org/Brexitland) for details.

the European Economic Community (as it was then called), had since travelled in one direction only, with 'Eurosceptics' opposed to some or all of the European political project exercising a steadily growing influence within the party. Arguments over Europe roiled the party under every leader from Margaret Thatcher onwards.[57] It is thus no surprise that David Cameron, elected in 2005 with a mandate to renew the Conservatives' electoral appeal, told his party it needed to stop 'banging on' about Europe if it wanted to reconnect with voters.[58] However, Cameron also recognised the power of arch-Eurosceptics within the party, and made a major concession to their views by agreeing to withdraw the Conservatives from the European People's Party, the main centre-right party grouping in the European Parliament, aligning them instead with a smaller grouping of Eurosceptic nationalist parties.[59]

Cameron's bargain proved to be a poor one – the Eurosceptics, in a pattern familiar to Cameron's predecessors, banked the leader's concession but offered little in return. They were soon 'banging on' about Europe again, encouraged to do so by UKIP's rise in the polls. Meanwhile, Cameron's departure from the European People's Party left him and his party marginalised in EU political institutions, which would prove costly when Cameron later sought to renegotiate the terms of Britain's EU membership. Although Cameron and many of his closest allies were Eurosceptic themselves, their flexible and pragmatic form of Euroscepticism was distrusted by the more extreme parts of his party. The emergence of UKIP, an insurgent party with consistently socially conservative, Eurosceptic and nationalist views, strengthened the hand of these hard Eurosceptics by enabling them to argue that a more radical stance was needed to hold the Conservative electorate together. Although, as we

---

[57] Indeed, it was an argument over Europe that triggered Mrs Thatcher's downfall in 1990.

[58] On how Europe became a toxic issue for the Conservatives in the 1990s, see Evans (1998).

[59] The largest other member of this grouping was 'Law and Justice' (PiS), the controversial populist radical right ruling party of Poland.

have seen, UKIP's success was more to do with immigration and ethnocentrism than with the EU, its reputation as a strongly Eurosceptic party encouraged Conservatives to see their new competitor through the lens of Europe. At the same time, the collapse of the Liberal Democrats blunted the original electoral incentive driving Cameron's 'modernisation' strategy. The need to attract and retain socially liberal, pro-EU voters looked less pressing with the Liberal Democrats, the main local competitor for many Conservative MPs, electorally moribund. While it was the failure of the Conservatives on immigration which sparked UKIP's surge, once UKIP grew, its rise was framed by Conservative Eurosceptics as reflecting British voters' demands for reform of Britain's relationship with the EU.

UKIP's rapid rise put mounting pressure on Cameron to adopt a harder line on Europe. Eurosceptic backbenchers were an effective pressure group within the Conservative Party due to their longstanding willingness to rebel against the party leadership on Europe, disrupting the government's broader political agenda and making the party look divided in the eyes of the electorate. Such rebellions had caused trouble for every party leader since John Major, who faced a series of historic backbench revolts over the Maastricht Treaty that created the 'European Union' with substantially expanded powers in 1992.[60] The Coalition parliament saw no fewer than forty-nine rebellions over the EU with more than a hundred different MPs rebelling over European issues at some point.[61] Cameron was losing ground fast, having been heavily criticised for an ineffectual attempt to block an EU-wide treaty agreement to shore up the Euro in late 2011, which left Britain looking isolated and weak. The perceived failure of Cameron's moderate Eurosceptic position shifted the dividing line within the Conservatives. The party had previously been split between Eurosceptics, who wanted a more distant relationship within the EU, and Europhiles, who wanted a closer engagement. Now the main dividing

---

[60] Cowley and Norton (1999).   [61] See, for example, Cowley and Stuart (2013).

line was between soft Eurosceptics, who wanted a looser relationship within the EU, and hard Eurosceptic 'Better Off Outers', who wanted to take Britain out of the EU altogether.[62]

For the 'Better Off Outers', UKIP was less an electoral threat and more a potential ally or even an alternative political home. UKIP had longstanding links with the Eurosceptic wing of the Conservative Party, from whom it recruited many activists and funders.[63] High-profile donors, activists and politicians defected to UKIP in substantial numbers. Three of UKIP's early leaders were former Conservative politicians, while Nigel Farage himself was a Conservative member until 1992.[64] Three former Conservative peers were taking the UKIP whip by the midpoint of the Coalition,[65] and a Conservative MEP defected in 2012. UKIP therefore represented a growing threat to the Conservatives not only as a competitor for votes, but as an attractive alternative home for funders, activists and legislators. The difference was that while voters saw UKIP primarily in terms of immigration control, Conservative elites saw the party mainly through the prism of their own Euroscepticism. Under mounting internal pressure to address the UKIP threat, Cameron made a major shift in stance, offering the 'in or out' referendum on EU membership that hard Eurosceptic backbenchers had long demanded.[66] Cameron made this pledge in January 2013, promising to renegotiate Britain's EU membership if the Conservatives won a Parliamentary majority in the next general election, and then offering the British people 'a very simple in or out choice to stay in the EU on these new terms, or come out

---

[62] Lynch (2015).

[63] Three of UKIP's leaders in the 2000s – Jeremy Titford, Roger Knapman and Malcolm Pearson – were former Conservative politicians and activists, as were many of the party's biggest funders in this period (Ford and Goodwin 2014b: ch. 1). Another former UKIP leader – Craig Mackinley – defected to the Conservatives in 2005, and defeated UKIP leader Nigel Farage in the South Thanet constituency in the 2015 general election.

[64] Farage has confirmed he was a Conservative member until the signing of the 1992 Maastricht treaty (BBC 2006).

[65] Lynch and Whittaker (2013).   [66] Lynch (2015).

altogether'.[67] Cameron's concession reflected a recognition that the pressure from UKIP without and hard Eurosceptics within could not be relieved by anything less. Cameron also believed the referendum promise needed to be made early, because defeat to UKIP in the European Parliament elections already looked likely to Conservative pollsters, and a change of policy after that could end up boosting UKIP, who would argue they had forced the PM's hand.[68]

Cameron's hope was that a referendum pledge delivered on his own terms would relieve internal and external pressures. By giving Eurosceptic MPs the exit referendum they had long craved, he could bring them back into line. And by making a Conservative vote the only viable route to an EU referendum, Cameron could return UKIP voters to the Tory fold. Both hopes swiftly proved forlorn. Eurosceptic backbenchers continued to distrust Cameron, and as before banked his concession before making new demands, trying to force the prime minister to legislate for an EU referendum even before the next election, legislation which (as they well knew) was impossible to pass while the party governed in coalition with the strongly pro-EU Liberal Democrats.[69] The EU referendum pledge also did not satisfy UKIP voters, whose primary demand was immigration control, and who had lost trust in a prime minister who had already failed to deliver this. Far from reducing the appeal of UKIP, Cameron's shift in stance may have increased it, as his concession in the face of rising UKIP support may have led identity conservative voters to see UKIP as an effective vehicle to pressure Conservative leaders into more radical positions. Cameron's referendum pledge also increased UKIP's credibility and its political profile, and shifted the political agenda to the party's core issue of EU membership.

UKIP received a further boost in 2014 with the arrival of another immigration-related policy shift beyond the government's control – the ending of temporary controls on migration

[67] BBC (2013).   [68] Bale (2018).   [69] Bale (2018).

from the two newest and poorest EU members, Romania and Bulgaria. This became a major focus of UKIP campaigning, with Nigel Farage framing migrants from these countries as impoverished and criminal, and reminding voters of the government's inability to prevent their arrival. UKIP support rose sharply again and, as we have seen, the party secured record results in local and European Parliament elections in 2013 and 2014, despite Cameron's referendum promise. In September 2014, two Conservative MPs – Douglas Carswell and Mark Reckless – defected to UKIP, successfully calling and winning by-elections fought under their new party's banner. The Conservatives had hoped to 'shoot the UKIP fox'; instead, the fox was in the henhouse, wreaking havoc.

Conclusion: how UKIP changed politics without winning at Westminster

UKIP's performance in the 2015 general election was both dramatic and disappointing. The party's national vote gains were extraordinary. UKIP support rose nearly ten percentage points to 12.6 per cent in the 2015 election, the strongest general election performance by a party other than the Conservatives, Labour or Liberal Democrats since the Labour–SDP split in 1983 (and the second strongest ever recorded since the introduction of the universal franchise). Yet despite all these votes – nearly 4 million in total – UKIP returned only a single MP to Westminster, Douglas Carswell, and even he was a recent and semi-detached Conservative defector[70]. This extraordinary disparity between votes and seats underscores the power of the British first-past-the-post electoral system to shape the meaning of election results and, in particular, the powerful influence of geography under this system. If Britain had conducted its general election using the

---

[70] Carswell defected again in March 2017, leaving UKIP to sit as an independent. He stood down at the subsequent 2017 general election, and his seat of Clacton reverted to the Conservatives. UKIP collapsed to third place, well behind Labour on just 7.6 per cent of the vote.

regional list proportional representation system that it employs for European Parliament elections, UKIP would have been by some margin the third largest party in the House of Commons after 2015, and would have held the balance of power in the legislature. Yet because the revolt of identity conservatives was evenly spread across England and Wales, UKIP remained at the margins of elite politics, represented by a single MP and unable to exert any direct influence on the legislative process.

Yet a focus solely on MPs returned to Westminster and formal influence on legislation understates UKIP's broader political significance. UKIP's most significant electoral impact was in activating identity conservatives as a coherent and distinctive political force, mobilised behind a radical right party focused on two issues: the EU and immigration. Hostility to immigrants did not increase during the Coalition, but its political impact was transformed. The substantial minority of British voters with the most negative views of migration mobilised behind a single radical right insurgent party, giving them a loud and clear new voice in politics, while the majority with more moderate or accepting views of immigration were scattered across the political spectrum. In a sense, this was the pendulum swinging in the opposite direction to the previous decade. Under New Labour, identity conservative voters were present in large numbers in each party's support base, but their views were marginalised and under-represented by a political class dominated by identity liberals. Now, mobilised behind a single party that catered exclusively to their worldview, identity conservatives were able to exert a disproportionate impact on the media and political agenda, pulling the governing Conservatives in a Eurosceptic direction and driving growing attention to ethnocentric voters' anxieties about immigration. This, in turn, created a virtuous circle for UKIP, as greater attention to its core issues of immigration and the EU increased its profile and credibility, enabling it to grow its support, which in turn drove more favourable coverage.[71]

[71] Murphy and Devine (2018).

While UKIP's impact on Westminster was limited by the first-past-the-post electoral system, which effectively repelled the insurgents, the party had a huge indirect political impact. Conservative Eurosceptics used UKIP's rise to successfully push their own agenda on a reluctant prime minister, securing a historic commitment to a referendum on Britain's EU membership. Within Labour, UKIP's rise encouraged the belief that it was only those on the conservative side of the identity politics divide who had the numbers and motivation to disrupt election outcomes. Labour therefore also sought policies designed to appease identity conservatives, though with little success as they had even less credibility on immigration than the Conservatives. But Labour failed to give serious attention to the possibility of instead mobilising voters against UKIP and the ethnocentric values it represented. Labour failed to make a strong positive case for either immigration or Europe in this period. The Liberal Democrats, shell-shocked by the collapse in their support during the Coalition, were also unable to mount an effective effort to mobilise identity liberal voters or to defend liberal, pro-European values against the UKIP challenge. This left both parties in a weak position when, just a few years later, they needed to defend EU membership and open immigration policies in a referendum campaign. This failure to build a convincing response to UKIP also reflected a failure by Labour to understand how the ground on which it stood was shifting. The 2015 election was historic for another, less noted reason: it was the first election in which graduates and ethnic minorities outnumbered white school leavers in the Labour electorate. This shift was less visible than UKIP's surge, but it was just as consequential for politics in the years to come.

7 CHANGE WITHOUT RECOVERY: HOW THE COALITION CATALYSED LABOUR'S DEMOGRAPHIC TRANSFORMATION

Introduction

The 2010–15 Parliament featured a lot of churn, as voters reshuffled their preferences. British Election Study researchers found such electoral volatility was the highest in at least fifty years.[1] More than one in ten voters switched their support to UKIP during this period, with most backing the party for the first time. This 'revolt on the right'[2] was more than matched by a reshuffle on the liberal left, as one in eight voters switched their support from the Liberal Democrats to someone else. The Greens also secured a record vote in 2015 by recruiting disaffected identity liberals.[3] And in Scotland, the party system was completely upended in the wake of the 2014 referendum, a political earthquake we will consider in Chapter 9.

All of these changes reflect, in part, the growing importance of identity politics divides as a driver of political choice. UKIP's dramatic emergence was driven, as we have seen, by the mobilisation of identity conservative voters – ethnocentric voters opposed to immigration, to the EU and to rising ethnic diversity. Meanwhile, the decision to enter the Coalition collapsed the

---

[1] Mellon (2017); Fieldhouse et al. (2019).   [2] Ford and Goodwin (2014b).
[3] Denver (2015).

heterogeneous alliance of opposition voters the Liberal Democrats had built, resulting in a flow of anti-establishment voters from them to UKIP, and a larger flow of disappointed identity liberals to the Labour and Green parties. At the same time, the traditional alliance of ethnic minority voters with Labour was restored, as Muslim voters alienated by Labour's foreign policy in the 2000s returned to the fold, and growing anxieties about the political mobilisation of white ethnocentrism by the Conservatives and UKIP further cemented other ethnic minority voters' allegiance to Labour. Labour's gains among identity liberals were offset by losses of white school leavers to UKIP, and taken together these twin trends accelerated the long-running shift in the balance of Labour support. By 2015, graduates and ethnic minorities outnumbered white school leavers in the Labour electoral coalition for the first time ever.

The identity liberal vote did not, however, fully consolidate behind the Labour Party in this period. The Liberal Democrats were greatly weakened, but still a substantial force. Their remaining support was heavily concentrated among university graduates, and identity liberal values now predicted support for the party more strongly. Meanwhile, an insurgent party on the identity liberal left – the Greens – grew their support to record levels largely by recruiting heavily among younger white graduates. Identity liberal support remained rather fragmented because there was – as yet – no issue that mobilised and unified such voters in the way immigration did for identity conservatives. Identity liberalism remained politically latent, as many voters with views diametrically opposed to identity conservatives did not have a unifying cause to mobilise them in the way that immigration mobilised identity conservatives.

The accelerating transformation of Labour's electoral coalition generated new frictions for the party. Labour was founded as the party of the working class, and many within it continued to see the representation of poorer and more economically insecure voters as their mission. The loss of white school leavers, often poorer voters hit hard by government austerity policies, to the Conservatives and UKIP was seen by many within Labour as a major political failure, prompting much soul-searching in Labour intellectual circles.[4] Electoral geography also played into this discussion. Many of the constituencies with the largest concentrations of identity conservative voters were Labour-held seats, a legacy of the party's deep roots in former industrial and mining communities. The MPs representing such seats naturally prioritised retaining the loyalties of such voters, and regularly voiced concerns about the leakage of support to the radical right. The younger graduates and ethnic minorities flocking to Labour's banner were clustered together in big city and university seats, and their geographical concentration reduced their electoral influence, as they piled up enormous majorities for Labour incumbents but were less important to Labour candidates fighting marginal or target seats. Labour's electoral geography meant that a shift from identity conservative to identity liberal support had disruptive electoral implications, even if the party's overall support levels remained the same. Long-held seats in places with a deep historical and cultural affinity to Labour were put at risk by the loss of identity conservatives, while the recruitment of identity liberals brought fewer new seats into play, often serving instead to pad out Labour majorities in already safe seats.

In this chapter we tell the story of how Labour's electoral coalition changed in the Coalition years and consider the new problems these changes brought for the party. This shift in the demographic profile of Labour support had an important impact on how the party responded to the identity conflicts which emerged subsequently in the EU Referendum and its aftermath, when the identity liberal voters Labour had attracted became

---

[4] The Blue Labour movement associated with Maurice Glasman offered early and influential analysis of this issue (Glasman et al. 2011; Davis 2011; Geary and Pabst 2015). Others subsequently pursued the question of Labour's decline among traditional working-class voters from other angles (see, for example, Pecorelli 2013; Cruddas, Pecorelli and Rutherford 2016; Hunt 2016). Many of these analyses highlighted the importance of identity attachments in political choice.

strongly mobilised behind the cause of Remain. We also look at Labour's steady loss of identity conservative voters directly to UKIP under the Coalition, which accelerated the long-running decline of this group within Labour. By 2015, Labour was for the first time a party in which identity liberal demographic groups and identity liberal value orientations were dominant. However, these new identity liberal voters were less loyal to Labour than the ageing partisans they were replacing, and Labour faced credible competition for these identity liberal recruits on more than one front.

Red to purple: UKIP's challenge to Labour during the Coalition

UKIP's rise proved more problematic for Labour than anticipated by some in the party, who initially cheered it as an opportunity to 'split the right'[5] and reopen Conservative divisions over Europe.[6] This line of thinking relied on two assumptions: that UKIP's success was primarily driven by Euroscepticism; and that UKIP's support came exclusively from voters who would otherwise be solid Conservatives.[7] Both were mistaken. UKIP, as we have seen, mobilised identity conservatives who perceived high immigration as threatening, and had long been unhappy with politics. UKIP's surge helped to keep the political conversation focused on immigration, keeping the spotlight on an issue where Labour's reputation remained weak with identity conservatives. Parties usually have an opportunity to rehabilitate their reputations in opposition, as voters' attention turns to the

---

[5] As late as 2014, senior advisers to Ed Miliband were briefing journalists that a strong UKIP performance could be the key to a Labour general election victory (Kirkup 2014).

[6] For a review of early Conservative–UKIP competition over Europe, see Lynch and Whittaker (2013).

[7] For a critical review of analyses making this case, see Roberts, Ford and Warren (2014). Conservative pollster Lord Ashcroft also recognised early that his colleagues had misunderstood UKIP's rise, which was not as much about Europe as they assumed (Ashcroft 2012b).

failings of the incumbent government and past errors fade from memory.[8] Labour, however, proved unable to repair in opposition the public distrust on immigration built up during the New Labour governments. Despite considerable and sometimes controversial efforts to address the party's weakness by new leader Ed Miliband, a majority of poll respondents continued to give Labour negative ratings on immigration in 2013, halfway through the Coalition, making it comfortably Labour's worst issue.[9] Fewer than one voter in ten rated Labour as the best party to address immigration.[10]

The rise of UKIP therefore posed real problems for Labour, complicating efforts by the new leader Ed Miliband to reconnect with disaffected identity conservative voters with a more radical left-wing policy offer on issues such as inequality, redistribution and regulation of markets.[11] These were areas where Labour's new message resonated well with identity conservatives, who were frequently older voters with relatively few skills and qualifications, who often faced chronic insecurity in the labour market and were more exposed to austerity spending cuts. But immigration drove a wedge between Labour and identity conservatives, undermining the party's efforts to rebuild bridges and capitalise on disaffection with the Coalition government.

As Figure 7.1 illustrates, although the Conservatives did lose a lot of their 2010 support among, for example, those who felt austerity cuts had gone too far,[12] it was UKIP who benefitted

---

[8] Governing parties face a consistent reputational cost – the longer they are in government, the more negative voters become about them (see, for example, Paldam 1986; Sanders 2005). However, there is no evidence that opposition parties consistently recover once out of government (Green and Jennings 2012). Labour's failure to recover on immigration is thus one example of many.

[9] This finding comes from analysis of the Continuous Monitoring Study. Details in the Online Appendix: www.cambridge.org/Brexitland

[10] See, for example, Kellner (2012) and our analysis of changing public perceptions on immigration in Chapter 6.

[11] Bale (2015).

[12] A similar pattern is found with regard to those with negative views of the economy and the state of the NHS, and with those expressing higher levels of economic insecurity. See the Online Appendix (www.cambridge.org/Brexitland) for details.

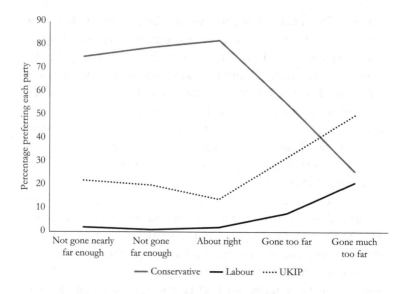

Figure 7.1 2014 vote preferences of 2010 Conservative voters, by views of national austerity cuts

Source: British Election Study internet panel, 2014–18, wave 2.

most. By 2014, Labour was winning over nearly one in five of 2010 Conservative voters who thought austerity spending cuts had gone 'much too far', but UKIP were winning nearly half. Immigration was the key reason for this. Defections among voters unhappy with the Conservatives' record on austerity and other issues skewed heavily towards UKIP if such voters also prioritised immigration as a problem, and towards Labour if they did not. The problem for Labour was that an awful lot of unhappy 2010 Conservative voters continued to see immigration as a priority, giving UKIP a major advantage in the competition for their support. UKIP, and the persistent concerns about immigration they exploited and helped to keep on the political agenda, thus stood in the way of Labour's strategy of building a broad anti-austerity coalition. Labour could not win anti-austerity identity conservatives to its banner as long as such voters were focused on immigration and therefore saw UKIP as a better option.

UKIP was a threat to Labour's existing electorate as well as a competitor for new recruits. Identity conservative voters remained an important part of Labour's electoral coalition in 2010: around four in ten Labour voters in the 2010 election were white school leavers, and ethnocentric attitudes were widespread amongst this group. These Labour identity conservatives were typically voters whose aversion to the Conservatives in 2010 outweighed their unhappiness with Labour on immigration and other issues. The toxic reputational legacy of Thatcherism[13] was likely a factor for many of these voters, particularly those living in the post-industrial towns and cities hit hardest by economic decline during the Thatcher–Major governments.[14] UKIP did not have the same reputational baggage, and therefore had the potential to reach disaffected Labour identity conservatives unwilling at this point to consider a Conservative vote.[15] As UKIP's surge gathered momentum during the Coalition, the defection of identity conservative voters became a significant problem for Labour (as Figure 7.2 illustrates by showing the 2014 vote preferences of 2010 Labour voters by levels of concern about immigration). Labour held on to nearly 90 per cent of voters who had never expressed concern about immigration as a political problem. But the party lost nearly one in three of its 2010 voters who had at some point[16] named immigration as a political priority, with the vast majority of defections going to UKIP. We find similar patterns if we look at other identity politics attitudes, such as views about the impact of

---

[13] A 2019 YouGov poll revealed that more than a third of voters named 'overseeing the decline of mining and manufacturing' as the biggest failing of the Thatcher government. Such feelings are no doubt more intense in the communities where such industries were once concentrated. See Smith (2019).

[14] See, for example, Dorling (2014); Fieldhouse (2014). Toxic reputations do not, however, last forever, as Labour painfully discovered in 2019 when the very same 'red wall' seats that had shunned the Conservatives in 2010 saw huge swings to the party among Brexit-supporting Labour voters.

[15] Ford and Goodwin (2011); Ford and Goodwin (2014a).

[16] Defined as those who had ever named immigration as the most important problem in any of the first three waves of the British Election Study panel conducted during 2014.

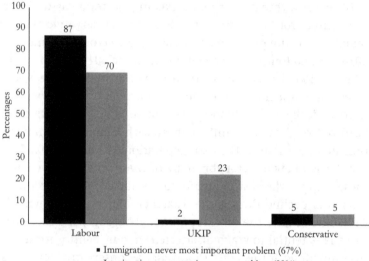

Figure 7.2 2014 vote preferences of 2010 Labour voters, by salience to immigration

Source: British Election Study internet panel, 2014–18.

immigration, attachment to English identity or opposition to equal opportunities for ethnic minorities.[17] In all cases, 2010 - Labour supporters with the most identity conservative attitudes were most likely to switch to UKIP over the course of the Coalition.

Labour leader Ed Miliband had hoped that a more radical anti-austerity 'One Nation' Labour could rebuild a broad coalition of middle-class progressives and poorer socially conservative voters, renewing Labour's appeal in opposition. This did not happen, and Nigel Farage's entrance onto the political scene is a big reason why. UKIP's emergence during the Coalition hampered Labour's ability to mend fences with these voters in several ways. The radical right insurgents competed effectively with Labour for 2010 Conservative voters who were now angry

[17] See the Online Appendix (www.cambridge.org/Brexitland) for details.

about austerity cuts, while also winning over a significant chunk of Labour's 2010 electorate. Even though UKIP did not campaign much on austerity, their populist anti-politics messages appealed to such voters' disaffection and distrust. A related problem was that ethnocentric voters often held negative stereotypes of welfare claimants, believing welfare assistance often went to undeserving out-groups such as immigrants or irresponsible 'scroungers'. As such, while they agreed with the principle of redistribution, they were also willing to support welfare cuts if they thought these took money away from people they saw as undeserving of help. Both of these problems were exacerbated among voters with strongly anti-immigration attitudes – who distrusted Labour following their failure to control migration in the 2000s, and were most attracted to UKIP's anti-immigration message. It was a different story among the middle-class identity liberals who had provided the backbone of Liberal Democrat support before the Coalition, and now provided the main source of Labour recruits in opposition.

The Liberal Democrats' collapse and Labour's consolidation of white graduates

The Liberal Democrats' decision to enter a Coalition with the Conservatives posed severe electoral risks for the party as it undercut the main arguments the party had used to grow support over the previous two decades.[18] The Liberal Democrats had three traditional sources of appeal: they were a vehicle for discontent with both of the traditional governing parties[19]; they won 'tactical votes' from Labour supporters seeking to oust Conservative MPs in areas where Labour was weak[20]; and they offered a politically distinctive package of socially liberal, reforming and decentralising policies.[21] The decision to enter Coalition robbed the party of appeal on all three fronts. The Liberal Democrats could not function as a credible outlet for

---

[18] Fieldhouse and Russell (2005).   [19] Belanger (2004).
[20] Fisher (2004); Pattie and Johnston (2011).   [21] Curtice (2007).

anti-establishment sentiment when they sat at the heart of government. The majority of Liberal Democrat MPs who represented areas where the Conservatives were the main local opposition could no longer campaign for anti-Conservative tactical votes while serving in a Conservative-led government. And it proved hard for the Liberal Democrats to convince voters that they were advancing a distinctive liberal and reforming policy agenda as junior partners in the Coalition. The Liberal Democrats' plans for electoral reform were watered down in Parliament, and then decisively defeated in a 2011 referendum.[22] Elsewhere, while the party's moderating and reforming influence on policy was noted and praised within the political class,[23] it was largely invisible to the broader electorate, who instead saw the Liberal Democrats as enablers of regressive Conservative policies such as austerity spending cuts and immigration controls, including policies such as the steep hike in tuition fees for undergraduates which the party had pledged to oppose in the 2010 election campaign.[24]

Liberal Democrat support had grown steadily during the New Labour governments, increasing from 17 per cent in 1997 to 23 per cent in 2010, with much of this growth coming from former Labour voters unhappy with the incumbent Labour government, but ideologically opposed to the Conservatives.[25] The party won a swathe of urban and university seats in 2005, often on huge swings, by mobilising students, ethnic minorities and social liberals angry at the Labour government's decisions to join the US-led invasion of Iraq and to increase university tuition fees.[26] This earlier success at recruiting disaffected but also strongly anti-Conservative former Labour voters made the Liberal Democrats very vulnerable once they joined forces with a Conservative government. Liberal Democrat support fell sharply, mirrored by

---

[22] Laycock et al. (2013).

[23] For a detailed academic assessment of the Coalition and the role of the Liberal Democrats within it, see Beech and Lee (2015). For an elite insider's reflections on the Liberal Democrats' role in the Coalition, see Clegg (2017).

[24] Butler (2019).   [25] Curtice (2007).

[26] Fieldhouse, Russell and Cutts (2006).

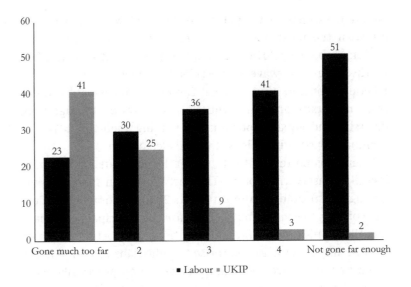

Figure 7.3 Rates of switching to Labour and UKIP in 2014 among 2010 Liberal Democrat voters, by views on equal opportunities for ethnic minorities (percentages)

Source: British Election Study internet panel, 2014–18.

a large rise in Labour support, immediately after the Coalition government began in May 2010. By early 2011, Liberal Democrat support had levelled off at around 10 per cent, less than half the level of a year earlier, while Labour support had risen from below 30 per cent to over 40 per cent.[27]

Much of this swing was the result of identity liberal voters switching in large numbers from the Liberal Democrats to Labour. Figure 7.3 illustrates this process, showing how the rates of switching to Labour and UKIP among 2010 Liberal Democrat voters varied with their views on equal opportunities for ethnic minorities. The more liberal voters' views are on this core identity politics issue, the greater their rate of defection to Labour

---

[27] Ford, Jennings and Pickup (2011); Fieldhouse et al. (2019: ch. 7).

(and to the Greens). Over half of 2010 Liberal Democrat supporters with the most liberal views on equal opportunities were
backing Labour by 2014, and another 16 per cent had switched
to the Greens. A wave of post-Coalition defections from the
Liberal Democrats thus enabled Labour to consolidate support
from university graduates with liberal views on immigration,
diversity and equal opportunities, making them by 2014 the
dominant party with this part of the electorate.

There was no respite for the Liberal Democrats among more
identity conservative voters. The party lost even more support
among the substantial minority of its 2010 electorate with identity conservative views, but in this case the principal beneficiary
was UKIP. This flow of votes directly from the Liberal Democrats
to UKIP might come as a surprise to politicians in both parties,
given how far apart their ruling elites are on practically every
political issue. However, it reflects the longstanding appeal of
the Liberal Democrats as a vehicle for protest and rejection of
the political status quo.[28] Once the Liberal Democrats became
part of the governing political establishment, they ceased to be
credible as an outlet for political protest, and the substantial
cohort of 'anti-politics' Liberal Democrat voters, typically identity conservatives, provided additional eager recruits to UKIP's
insurgency.

Another group of voters who abandoned the Liberal Democrats during the Coalition were ethnic minority voters, particularly British Muslim voters. The longstanding Labour loyalties of
ethnic minority voters came under considerable strain during
the later years of the New Labour government, with Muslim
voters in particular incensed by the Blair government's participation in the invasions of two majority Muslim countries, and its
passage of authoritarian anti-terrorism legislation whose effects
fell primarily on their community.[29] The Liberal Democrats'
opposition to the Iraq War made them an effective outlet for
Muslim anger, and the party secured some very large swings in

---

[28] Belanger (2004); Lebo and Young (2009).   [29] Martin (2017).

areas with large Muslim communities in 2005,[30] helping them to victories in constituencies such as Rochdale, Manchester Withington and Brent East. Muslim voters were also the main group powering the 2005 rise of a new radical left party, Respect, whose founder, the controversial former Labour MP George Galloway, secured a surprise victory in Bethnal Green and Bow. Four other Respect candidates scored above 15 per cent of the vote in 2005, all in seats with large Muslim populations, briefly suggesting the possibility that a new party could establish itself to represent the distinctive politics of Britain's Muslim community. The moment proved fleeting as Respect were plagued by internal conflicts, many relating to the behaviour of Galloway, and lost more than half of their votes and their only seat in 2010.[31]

In 2005–10 Labour faced a threat on one flank from parties mobilising opposition to their foreign policy among Muslims, and on the other flank from the Conservatives, who under David Cameron made a concerted effort to increase their appeal to better-off, middle-class and socially conservative ethnic minority voters, in particular by fielding far more ethnic minority candidates in winnable seats than hitherto.[32] Their efforts brought some modest gains, particularly among Indian ethnicity voters, the most economically prosperous ethnic minority group, and one that had long been somewhat more receptive to the party's appeals.[33] The Conservatives' efforts to appeal to ethnic

---

[30] Curtice, Fisher and Steed (2006); Curtice (2007).

[31] Galloway himself made a brief surprise comeback in the 2012 by-election in Bradford West – another seat with a very large Muslim population – but lost the seat again at the 2015 general election, by which point Respect were electorally moribund, fielding just four candidates. Another former leader of Respect, Salma Yaqoob, re-joined the Labour Party and staged an unsuccessful campaign to be Labour's 2020 candidate for Mayor of the West Midlands combined authority (she was defeated by Liam Byrne, a Cabinet minister in the New Labour governments that Yaqoob had campaigned against in the 2000s).

[32] Although there is little evidence that ethnic minority candidates made a direct difference (Martin 2017), they may have helped indirectly, by helping to repair the Conservatives' reputation with ethnic minorities.

[33] Martin (2019).

minorities and recruit more minority candidates may also have helped the party with some white identity liberals, by making more credible the party's claim to have become more representative of a diverse, multicultural Britain – though the Conservatives' restrictive approach and hostile rhetoric on immigration tended to undercut such claims.

It is difficult to assess Labour's performance with ethnic minorities over the 2005–15 period as representative surveys of Britain's ethnic minority electorate are relatively rare. There are only two comprehensive surveys of ethnic minority political behaviour, conducted in 1997 and 2010. For other elections we have to piece together evidence from less representative or reliable data sources and examine the pattern of election results in the seats where ethnic minority voters are concentrated. Nevertheless, the overall trend across such data sources is consistent – Labour support from ethnic minorities recovered under the Coalition, with most of the votes lost during the later New Labour years returning from the Liberal Democrats and Respect, whose support among ethnic minorities collapsed. By 2015, lopsided majorities (75 per cent plus) of all ethnic minority communities except Hindu Indians were once again solidly behind Labour, and even among Hindu Indians Labour was by a large margin the most popular party, with support levels around 50 per cent.[34]

This consolidation of ethnic minority support is also reflected in constituency voting patterns. Swings against Labour in the most ethnically diverse constituencies were typically above the national average in the 2005 election, suggesting that Labour was paying a price for its controversial foreign policy with ethnic minority voters.[35] It was a different story, however, in 2005–10, when Labour support held up better in the most diverse seats than elsewhere,[36] and again in 2010–15,[37] when Labour support in the most ethnically diverse seats rose more than nine points,

[34] Martin (2019).   [35] Curtice, Fisher and Steed (2006: 239–40).
[36] Curtice, Fisher and Ford (2016: 391–2).
[37] Curtice, Fisher and Ford (2016: 395–6).

more than three times the increase achieved in the seats with the smallest ethnic minority populations. By 2015, Labour held sixty-seven of the seventy-five seats in England and Wales where the white population share was below 75 per cent, and these sixty-seven Labour MPs had an average majority of 30 per cent.[38]

The past versus the future: the geographical conundrum created by Labour's changing electoral coalition

The flows of votes to and from Labour during the Coalition accelerated the demographic trends that had long been reshaping the party's support base. The share of identity liberal graduates and ethnic minorities within the Labour coalition rose sharply as Muslim voters and white graduates returned to the party following the collapse of the Liberal Democrats and Respect. Meanwhile, the defection of white school leavers to UKIP accelerated their long-running decline in the Labour electoral coalition. As a result, though Labour's overall support was relatively stable from 2010 to 2015, the mix of voters backing the party was rapidly changing. The situation was akin to filling a bath with cold water, then opening the plug and turning the hot tap on at the same time. The level of water remains static, but the temperature of the water changes rapidly, as cold water exits at the bottom to be replaced by hot water coming in at the top. Figure 7.4 illustrates how the composition of Labour's electorate shifted between 1997 and 2015. The share of graduates and

[38] The exceptions were Harrow East (39 per cent white in the 2011 census); Hendon (55 per cent white); Croydon Central (61 per cent white); Finchley and Golder's Green (66 per cent white); Kensington (68 per cent white); Cities of London and Westminster (69.5 per cent white); Uxbridge and South Ruislip (69.7 per cent white); and Enfield Southgate (just under 70 per cent white). Three of these seats were lost in 2017, and of the remaining five, two have large concentrations of Jewish voters who, unlike other ethnic and religious minorities, tend to align with the Conservatives (Barclay, Sobolewska and Ford 2019). The current Conservative leader and prime minister at the time of writing, Boris Johnson, represents one of the three remaining seats (Uxbridge and South Ruislip).

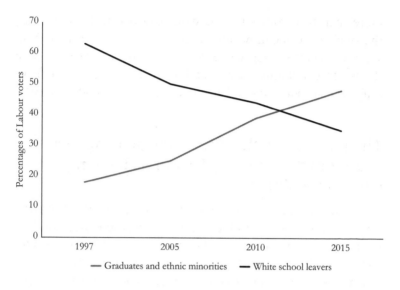

Figure 7.4 Share of Labour voters in England and Wales who are white school leavers (black) and graduates/ethnic minorities (grey)

Source: British Election Study face-to-face surveys, 1997–2015.

ethnic minorities in Labour's voter base had already more than doubled during the New Labour years, but even in 2010 these groups were outnumbered by identity conservatives. This changed decisively in 2015, which was the first election in which the two identity liberal groups outnumbered the identity conservative group among Labour voters. Graduate and ethnic minority populations are set to continue their rapid growth, while white school leavers will continue to decline. The new dominance of identity liberal demographic groups in the Labour vote coalition is likely to continue in elections to come.

The same trends are evident when we look at the attitudinal side of the identity politics divide – Labour's electorate shifted over the course of the 2001–15 period from one where identity conservative views predominated to one where identity liberal views were dominant. Figure 7.5 illustrates this using views about the cultural impact of immigration. In 2005, Labour

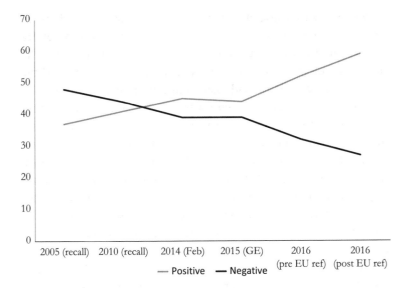

Figure 7.5 Views of the cultural impact of immigration among Labour voters, 2005–16 (percentages)

Source: British Election Study internet panel, 2014–18.

voters with negative views about immigration outnumbered immigration enthusiasts, and in 2010 the two groups were almost equal in size. A majority of Labour voters were immigration liberals by the time the EU Referendum got underway and this share rose to two-thirds of the Labour vote by the autumn after the Brexit vote. Similar trends are evident when we look at views of the EU and about equal opportunities for ethnic minorities[39] – identity liberals rose to dominance for the first time during the Coalition, and were already the largest group in the Labour electorate before the EU Referendum campaign began. Yet, although demographic and political trends were pulling Labour's electoral centre of gravity ever further towards identity liberal views and votes, the party's history and electoral geography made this transformation both complex and politically fraught.

---

[39] See the Online Appendix (www.cambridge.org/Brexitland) for details.

The problem these demographic shifts pose for Labour is simple to state but hard to resolve. Labour had risen to dominance in the urban and university seats with the largest populations of identity liberal graduates, students and ethnic minorities. But Labour had also traditionally been dominant in declining post-industrial areas with large concentrations of identity conservative white school leavers. Its support in such communities had been slowly declining but most still returned Labour MPs in 2015. When identity politics conflicts emerged, these put the large and growing cohort of Labour MPs representing the most identity liberal seats at odds with the equally large, though slowly declining, cohort of Labour MPs representing the most identity conservative seats. The local electorates for these two cohorts of MPs are drawn from opposite poles of the identity politics spectrum, making compromises acceptable to both groups very hard to find once identity politics conflicts become salient and polarised, as happened with immigration in the decade before 2015 and with the EU and Brexit from 2016 onwards.

There are 123 seats in England and Wales where the 2011 Census recorded a share of 26 per cent or more of local residents with no qualifications, less than 15 per cent of local residents were ethnic minorities and less than 10 per cent were students. These can be considered the most demographically 'identity conservative' seats. Such seats include many post-industrial towns and cities which Labour has dominated electorally and culturally for generations, including Welsh valleys seats such as the Rhondda and Cynon Valley; former mining areas such as Bolsover and Ashfield; and post-industrial towns such as Rotherham and Wigan. Labour's support in such seats declined by 10 percentage points on average in 2005–10 and recovered by an anaemic average of 1.6 points between 2010 and 2015. UKIP significantly outperformed in such areas in these seats in 2015, securing an average of nearly 20 per cent of the vote. Labour's performance was thus well below its average showing elsewhere in these seats throughout the 2005–15 period, yet political dominance entrenched for generations dies hard, and Labour continued to hold on to most of these seats throughout 2005–15, winning ninety-nine in 2005,[40] eighty-two in 2010 and eighty-one in 2015. These are also areas with outsized historical and symbolic significance, in a party where history and symbols matter deeply.[41] They are seen by many within Labour as the 'traditional working-class heartlands' the party was created to represent and serve, and so their loss weighs heavily.[42] Yet the relentless outflow of identity conservative voters has steadily eroded Labour's once mighty majorities in these constituencies,[43] and intensified the desire of the politicians representing them to halt or reverse the identity liberal positions which were antagonising their already disaffected local supporters, and putting their seats at risk.[44]

There are another 128 seats in England and Wales where students constitute more than 10 per cent of the local resident population registered by the 2011 Census. Such seats, typically in big cities and university towns, also have above average numbers of university graduates and public sector professionals. These are the most identity liberal constituencies. Labour have also dominated these seats since the mid-2000s: the party won ninety-five of them in 2005, seventy-six in 2010 and eighty-seven in 2015. And in these seats Labour's position is steadily improving. Labour's vote fell by four points in such seats between 2005 and 2010, half the average loss elsewhere, then rose by seven points between 2010 and 2015, double the average gain elsewhere. Many of the Labour Party's seat gains from both the

---

[40] These are notional figures calculated for the 2010 boundaries.

[41] Jobson (2018).

[42] Many of these seats finally fell in December 2019, in between the first draft of this book and the final draft, provoking agonised discussion within the Labour Party.

[43] For an analysis of Labour's decline in such areas between 2005 and 2017, see Jennings and Stoker (2017).

[44] Once lost, such seats have also proved hard to recover – Labour lost thirty-nine seats in England and Wales with an above average share of voters with no qualifications and a below average share of ethnic minorities in 2010. It did not win back a single one of these seats in 2015. In most cases, the Labour vote fell further in 2015. The justified fear that such seats would be very hard to get back once lost provided another reason for Labour MPs representing similar areas to resist liberal stances on identity politics conflicts.

Conservatives and Liberal Democrats in 2015 came in such areas, and most of the Conservative MPs remaining in such seats saw their majorities slashed between 2005 and 2015. Labour MPs representing these seats, and ambitious candidates and activists seeing an opportunity to gain more of them, were understandably keen to take a strong liberal stance on identity politics issues, in line with their local electorates.

When the slow but relentless aggregate shift in Labour support away from identity conservatives and towards identity liberals interacted with the distribution of Labour seats, the result was a polarised conflict between two very different sets of places, setting MPs defending declining majorities in identity conservative seats at odds against MPs and candidates seeing the tide turn Labour's way in identity liberal seats. It would not be possible for any Labour leader to fully satisfy both groups, yet nor would it be possible for any Labour leader in the political context of the 2010s to secure a Commons majority without retaining most of the Labour seats in both groups, because Labour's dominance at both poles of the identity politics spectrum was offset by weakness in the more moderate and mixed seats in the middle. Labour won eighty-seven of the 128 England and Wales seats with the largest student populations in 2015, but just seventy-eight of the 318 seats with small student populations (down from 132 in 2005). Similarly, Labour won sixty-seven of the seventy-five England and Wales seats with the largest ethnic minority communities in 2015, but just seventy-seven of the 276 seats where the population was more than 95 per cent white (down from 110 in 2005). In 2010–15, Labour was winning the liberal bastions and holding on against the demographic tide in the most identity conservative seats, but was unable to appeal to the places in between where Parliamentary majorities are won and lost.

A more demanding electorate?

Labour's consolidation of support from identity liberal voters during the Coalition caused significant frictions within the party's Commons delegation, yet put it on the right side of long-term demographic change, as the party attracted stronger support from groups whose electoral power was steadily growing. But this change was not without costs. Labour's identity liberal new recruits were less firmly attached to the party than the partisan loyalists it has been shedding since the New Labour years (see Chapter 5), and many had attractive alternative choices available, as several competitor parties operated in the same liberal left political space. Labour's new electoral coalition was therefore less reliable than its old one – the identity liberals the party had recruited were not partisan stalwarts and could easily leak away again if Labour failed to give them what they wanted.

Around a fifth of Labour's overall 2015 vote in England and Wales came from voters who had backed the Liberal Democrats in 2010, while another tenth came from voters who did not turn out in 2010. As Figure 7.6 illustrates, these new recruits – roughly a third of Labour's 2015 electorate – had much weaker levels of attachment to their new party than voters who backed Labour in both elections. Less than one in five of the voters who backed Labour in both 2010 and 2015 reported weak or no identification with Labour, and the figure among younger loyalists was only a little weaker (despite the much lower levels of partisanship among young voters overall). But nearly four in ten of those who switched to Labour in 2015 after sitting out the 2010 election reported having little or no attachment to their new party. Loyalties are even weaker among recruits from the Liberal Democrats – nearly six in ten of the voters who switched to Labour after voting Liberal Democrat in 2010 reported little or no identification with their new party. The voters Labour gained during the Coalition had no strong bonds to their new party; they would be open to new offers if the political climate changed again.

Other appealing choices were available for these voters. The Liberal Democrats' socially liberal, pro-immigration and pro-EU stances were inherently appealing to identity liberal voters, though this was offset by the negative effect of their coalition

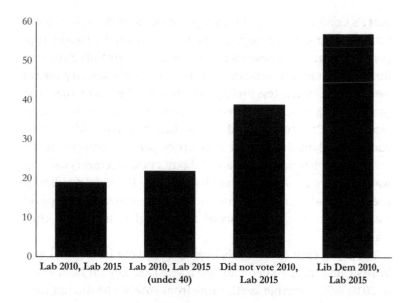

Figure 7.6 Share of different groups of 2015 Labour voters who expressed little or no Labour partisanship (percentages)

Source: British Election Study internet panel, 2014–18.

with the Conservatives. The Green Party also offered a similar mix of liberal policies on immigration, the EU and other social issues, combined with an environmentalist stance also popular with many identity liberals. And in Scotland and Wales, nationalist parties with a range of identity liberal policy stances were also available. The greater openness of Labour's new recruits to these alternatives is illustrated in Figure 7.7, which shows how likely different groups of 2015 Labour voters rated their chances of ever voting Liberal Democrat during the waves of the British Election Study panel conducted between 2014 and 2017. Voters who backed Labour in both 2010 and 2015 (solid black line) gave the Liberal Democrats consistently low ratings, though their views of the party gradually rose in later waves. Voters who had stayed home in 2010, then backed Labour in 2015 (dashed black line) were somewhat more tempted by the Liberal Democrat alternative, but the most distinctive group are those who

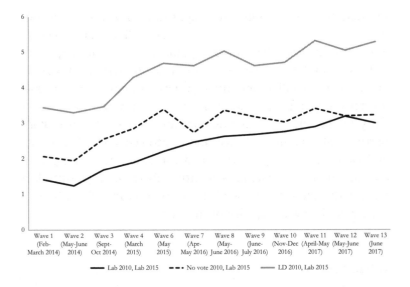

Figure 7.7 Probability of ever voting for the Liberal Democrats among different groups of Labour 2015 voters, 2014–17

Source: British Election Study internet panel, 2014–18. Voters rate their probability of ever voting for parties on a 0–10 scale.

Labour won over from the Liberal Democrats in 2015 (grey line). These voters retained a much more positive view of the Liberal Democrats throughout the BES panel period, rating themselves on average a whole point more likely than Labour loyalists to vote for the Liberal Democrats at some future election. It is a similar pattern with the Green Party,[45] and while we do not have sufficient numbers to test the pattern for Scottish and Welsh nationalists, there are good reasons to suspect that Labour's new identity liberal recruits found these parties more attractive, too, when available.

Intense competition for identity liberal voters was already evident in the 2015 election. The surge in Green support in 2015 was driven by younger university graduates with cosmopolitan identities who combined very liberal views on

[45] See the Online Appendix (www.cambridge.org/Brexitland) for details.

immigration, the EU and equal opportunities with strongly left-wing views on economic issues and (naturally) strong environmentalist stances. The remaining Liberal Democrat support in 2015 was similarly skewed towards graduates with liberal views on all the most salient identity conflicts – immigration, Europe, diversity – though Liberal Democrat voters were less consistently to the left on economic and environmental issues. Both parties' political elites shared and reinforced such identity liberal views, expressing a strong and consistent pro-immigration and pro-EU line. If Labour's identity liberal new recruits lost faith in the party, their friends in the Greens and Liberal Democrats would be waiting with open arms.

Conclusion

Ed Miliband's five-year mission as Labour leader was to transform the party's appeal in opposition and restore it to popularity and government.[46] Although he failed in the latter aim, he succeeded in the former, though not in the way he expected. Although Labour won a similar share of the vote in 2015 as it had in 2010, the voters it won at the end of the Coalition were quite different from those it was winning before. Labour collapsed in Scotland (see Chapter 9), while in England and Wales it lost white school leavers to UKIP and the Conservatives while gaining graduates and ethnic minorities from the Liberal Democrats and elsewhere, accelerating the long-run shift in the party's support and meaning identity liberal voters were, for the first time, dominant in the Labour electoral coalition. Yet this accelerating shift caused major frictions within the Labour Party, putting MPs and ambitious candidates competing in identity liberal areas where the party was rapidly advancing at odds with MPs defending traditional post-industrial seats with large concentrations of white school leavers, fighting to defend their seats against the tide. The emergence of divisive identity politics

---

[46] Bale (2015).

conflicts would inevitably pit these two groups of Labour MPs against each other, as the former sought to mobilise identity liberals while the latter struggled to hold on to identity conservatives.

This transformation brought new problems in its wake. The first was one Labour had struggled with before: geographically concentrated support. In the traditional class politics era, Labour was often at a disadvantage because its strongest demographic groups – unionised workers in traditional industries – clustered together in places where those industries were based.[47] This meant a poorer return of seats for the votes Labour won, as many were wasted racking up towering majorities in mining and mill towns. New Labour had reversed this pattern, by spreading Labour support across suburbia and the south of England.[48] Now the curse of concentration was returning in a new form – students, graduates and ethnic minorities also tend to cluster together in the same city centre constituencies. Most such seats were already represented by Labour MPs, who saw their majorities soar. But elsewhere in the country the relative paucity of graduates and minorities left the party struggling, and at a disadvantage to the Conservatives, whose vote was more effectively spread.[49] Labour's new recruits also brought with them the germ of a second new problem. As we have seen, New Labour's electoral majority winning strategy in the 2000s relied on a gamble that traditional left-wing and working-class voters would remain loyal even if the party ceased to offer them much, as they had nowhere else to go. This would be a much harder trick to pull off with its post-Coalition electoral base, as

[47] This concentration of Labour voters created a persistent electoral system bias against Labour in the 1950s and early 1960s. See Johnston and Pattie (2006: ch. 8).

[48] Blair and Brown did more than overcome the electoral system disadvantage of earlier times, instead the system swung in Labour's favour, giving the party a large and persistent advantage during the New Labour years (Johnston and Pattie 2006).

[49] The problem was compounded by Labour's collapse in Scotland, meaning large numbers of Scottish Labour votes were 'wasted' in seats where the party came second to the SNP. For further details see, for example, Curtice (2015b).

the new identity liberal voters the party attracted lacked the strong partisan bonds of traditional supporters in the New Labour era, and attractive alternatives were available to them if Labour lost its lustre.

Labour's new identity liberal coalition gave it the potential to grow in the long term, but at the cost of internal division and instability in the short term. Yet it was largely achieved by default – the defection of former Liberal Democrats alienated by the Coalition – rather than through active mobilisation on Labour's part. And Labour would face a serious dilemma if an issue emerged that mobilised identity liberals as strongly as immigration mobilised identity conservatives. On the one hand, this could open opportunities to the party in traditionally Conservative-voting prosperous middle-class areas with lots of identity liberal university graduates. On the other hand, an even stronger association of the party with identity liberal voters and causes would intensify the party's vulnerability in its impoverished post-industrial heartland seats. Nor was this dilemma a matter simply of raw seat numbers. Many Labour activists and MPs would see a shift in the party's centre of gravity towards prosperous suburbia as a threat to Labour's traditional identity and purpose, even if the party came out ahead on the deal electorally. Yet spurning the opportunity presented by an identity liberal uprising would risk sending these voters, who had no great loyalty to Labour, into the arms of a competitor party, without any guarantee of reversing the long-term decline in identity conservative seats. Shifting to a clear identity liberal stance risked an internal crisis for Labour in the short run. But failing to shift could risk an existential crisis in the long run. In 2016, the issue arrived that would force Labour to choose, as the country geared up for a vote on EU membership. That vote, and its effects, are the focus of the next chapter.

PART III
Brexitland

8 BREXITLAND AWAKENED: IDENTITY POLITICS AND THE EU REFERENDUM

Introduction

Britain did not become Brexitland on 23 June 2016. The people who ended up on opposite sides of the Brexit argument had been drifting apart for decades, with growing differences in values and priorities deepened by mutual misunderstanding and lack of dialogue, as we discussed in Chapter 3. The deep public distrust of the political class, which we highlighted in Chapter 5, and which the Leave campaign mobilised, had been building since at least the 1990s; the impression that voters were being denied meaningful choice by political parties' offering identikit MPs and policies had been widespread since the early 2000s; the disruptive electoral potential of immigration had been in evidence since at least the 1970s; and, although systematic evidence is sparser, the battle to police the political debate between those seeking to extend anti-racism social norms and those attacking them as oppressive 'political correctness' has also been going on a long time. The association between views of immigration and attitudes towards the EU was also in place well before 2016, and was instrumental in driving the rise of UKIP and bringing the referendum itself onto the political agenda.

But 23 June 2016 still mattered. The EU Referendum was a moment of awakening, when the two sides of Brexitland became fully aware of the divides that set them against each other, and these divides were crystallised into a concrete conflict with a name – 'Brexit' – and two tribes of antagonists – 'Leavers' and 'Remainers'. The growing electorate of identity liberals who until now had no common group identity or unifying political cause forged both in their lost battle against Brexit. Before 23 June these voters did not feel very strongly about the issues such as immigration, national identity and Europe which had mobilised identity conservatives over the previous decade. But defeat is a powerful motivator, and the threat of Brexit made the cause of continuing within the EU a powerful flag for these voters to rally around. A new identity was forged – 'Remainers' – a group now conscious of itself with a common agenda and a strong sense of grievance. The dynamics on the 'Leave' side were a little different – many identity conservative voters had already developed a distinct agenda and political identity before the referendum, through their focus on immigration and mobilisa-tion behind UKIP. But before the referendum they saw them-selves as protesters voicing their discontent from the margins at political developments they felt they had little power to stop.[1] Now they saw themselves, often for the first time, as holders of a powerful democratic mandate, one they could wield to dictate the political agenda.

Both referendum identities were reinforced by mutual hostil-ities and stereotyping – 'Leavers' attacked 'Remainers' as metro-politan elites stuck in a bubble of privilege, 'citizens of nowhere' out of touch with the values of their own country, and in the extreme saboteurs unwilling to accept defeat bent on undermin-ing the democratically expressed will of the majority.[2] 'Remai-ners' attacked 'Leavers' as naive fools who did not know what they were voting for, taken in by hucksters and bigots, whose referendum victory was based on lies and corruption, and in the extreme attacked them as authoritarian nationalists bent on

---

[1] McKenzie (2017).

[2] Some headlines from 'Leave'-supporting newspapers in the months after the referendum include 'Out of touch elite will do anything to keep us in the EU' (*Express*, October 2016); 'Enemies of the People' (*Daily Mail*, November 2016); and 'Unstoppable march of Theresa May could foil the bitter Remoaners ...' (*The Sun*, October 2016).

impoverishing the nation and destroying the institutions of representative democracy.[3] After 23 June, there was no going back. New tribes rallied under new flags, and Brexit identities were swiftly entrenched. As we shall see, the Brexit battle lines were drawn right along the demographic and attitudinal identity politics fault lines which had been building in the electorate for decades hitherto.

The 2016 vote for Brexit was a historic turning point, and stimulated an intense debate among academics looking to understand the drivers and meaning of the choices voters made. Researchers have examined the referendum from a wide range of angles, including the relative roles of culture and the economy[4]; why surprisingly large numbers of ethnic minorities voted Leave[5]; the role of austerity spending cuts[6]; the role of authoritarian social values[7] or of a broader social conservatism[8]; the role of economic and demographic divides[9]; the role of social and geographical inequalities[10]; and the role of campaigns and leaders.[11] There will doubtless be plenty more to say on the diverse motives of the coalitions assembled by 'Leave' and 'Remain', each of whom secured nearly half of the national voting electorate in a vote with the highest turnout since 1992. No single factor or small set of factors can provide a complete account of such a complex event, and our analysis here does not attempt to do so. Instead, we focus on the aspects of the Brexit political conflict relevant to our broader story: how the referendum campaign activated and mobilised identity conflicts; the role played by identity politics divides in motivating voters and

---

[3] Headlines from 'Remain'-supporting or leaning newspapers in late 2016 include '"A frenzy of hatred": how to understand Brexit racism' (*The Guardian*, June 2016); 'The biggest vote of a generation was based on a lie ...' (*Independent*, June 2016); 'Let's be alarmist: Brexit could take us back to the very worst of Europe's intolerant past' (*New Statesman*, July 2016).
[4] Hobolt (2016); Norris and Inglehart (2019); Jennings and Stoker (2016).
[5] Begum (2018); Martin, Sobolewska and Begum (2019). [6] Fetzer (2019).
[7] Kaufmann (2016). [8] Evans and Menon (2017).
[9] Goodwin and Heath (2016). [10] Dorling, Stuart and Stubbs (2016).
[11] Clarke, Goodwin and Whiteley (2017).

structuring the referendum outcome; and how the aftermath of the EU vote led to the awakening of Brexitland, as the new Brexit political identities cemented identity conflicts at the heart of politics and began to re-align voters' political preferences.

We tell this story in three parts. First, to underline how distinctive the 2016 voter alignments were, we travel back to the general election one year before. This was an election where all the elements of a new political cleavage between identity conservatives and identity liberals were in place except one: a consciousness among both identity conservatives and identity liberals of themselves as distinct groups with opposing interests.[12] While there were considerable shifts on identity grounds, as we have seen in previous chapters, the influence of these shifts was greatly reduced by the way they interacted with local political geography, which in turn was still structured by long-standing class and economic divides.

Secondly, we show how the EU Referendum vote was completely different. Here was a closely fought, high-stakes national poll on a question where identity conflicts were central, and where the geographical distribution of votes did not matter to the outcome.[13] The referendum stimulated a mass mobilisation of voters on identity politics grounds in both camps, producing a new alignment of political forces. The dividing lines of class, income and economic ideology which still structured choices between the Conservatives and Labour in 2015 played virtually no role in the referendum a year later. Instead, it was identity politics conflicts which divided 'Leave' from 'Remain'.

Thirdly, we consider the new 'Leave' and 'Remain' identities forged in the referendum campaign, and their political effects. We show how voters understand the social and political meaning of these new Brexit tribes, and how their attachment to these

---

[12] Bartolini and Mair (1990).
[13] The referendum result was decided by a simple total of the votes cast on each side, making the geography of the vote irrelevant to the outcome.

tribes has driven shifts in their political attitudes and behaviour from the moment the referendum result was announced. These new Brexit identities are more powerful than fading attachments to the traditional parties and may yet catalyse a complete restructuring of British party competition, a possibility we consider in greater depth in Chapter 10.

Setting up the storm: the 2015 general election

The 2015 election presents a puzzle. UKIP's mobilisation of identity conservatives angry about immigration impacted on all parties during the Coalition, but it clearly hit the Conservatives hardest. Yet despite this, it was the Conservatives who emerged victorious in May 2015, unexpectedly securing a Commons majority. How were the Conservatives able to survive, even thrive, despite the mobilisation of conflicts which split the party internally, and the mass defection of identity conservative voters to UKIP? The answer lies in how these newly mobilised identity divides interacted with the older divides which traditionally structure British party competition, and in the central importance of geography in shaping results in the British electoral system. The interaction of new divisions and established local voting patterns which caused such headaches for the Labour Party in 2015 (see Chapter 7) provided the Conservatives with several important advantages: UKIP's even spread blunted their impact on Conservative candidates' prospects, while the Liberal Democrats' concentration in Conservative-friendly areas made the Tories the biggest beneficiaries of their coalition partner's collapse, even though most former Liberal Democrat voters switched to Labour and the Greens.

Geography blunted the electoral impact of UKIP on the Conservatives in several ways. First, UKIP's support was thinly spread across the country, reflecting the even spread of the white school leavers who provided its core support. While the party did enjoy higher votes in some areas, particularly along the east coast, it was seldom able to concentrate support enough to be a viable threat to incumbents.[14] As a result, while there were large Conservative to UKIP swings in many Tory seats, Conservative MPs typically had large enough majorities to weather these swings without difficulty. UKIP's only elected MP – Douglas Carswell – was the exception who proved the rule: as a Conservative defector with an established local profile running in a seat with possibly the most UKIP friendly demographics in the whole country, he had everything running in his favour.[15] Secondly, many of the largest concentrations of identity conservative voters were in post-industrial seats where Labour had long been dominant, and the Conservatives were already weak. In such seats, the net effect of mass defections from the Conservatives to UKIP was often to replace a weak and ineffectual local Conservative opposition with a weak and ineffectual local UKIP opposition. Thirdly, the Conservatives had some success in squeezing the UKIP vote in the key marginal seats, where Conservative defections to UKIP could have shifted the local balance of power in favour of the local Labour challenger. The British Election Study found that the Conservatives secured a substantial late gain of support from UKIP in such seats during the final weeks of the election campaign.[16]

Geography cut the other way with Liberal Democrat support, helping the Conservatives to gain seats from the Liberal Democrat collapse even though few Liberal Democrat voters switched to the Conservatives. Liberal Democrat support was not evenly spread across the country – in most of the seats where they were in first or second place, they faced off against the Conservatives. Most of the Liberal Democrat MPs elected in 2010 represented seats where the Conservatives were in second place locally and

---

[14] Ford and Goodwin (2014b: ch. 6).

[15] Ford and Goodwin (2014c). Carswell's seat of Clacton is also another example of the long-term drift of identity conservative communities away from Labour. Labour secured 45 per cent of the vote in its predecessor seat of Harwich in 2001. By 2015, the local Labour vote had fallen to 14 per cent.

[16] Green and Prosser (2015) note a net 2.6 point Conservative gain from UKIP in Conservative–Labour marginal seats in the final months before the election.

Labour were out of contention.[17] The Conservatives were able to capture many of these seats in 2015 despite a flat or declining vote, as support for the incumbent Liberal Democrat MP scattered in multiple directions, enabling the second place Conservative candidate to triumph simply by holding steady.

While the mobilisation of identity politics had a major effect on vote choices in 2015, playing a central role in the rise of UKIP and the decline of the Liberal Democrats in England and Wales, and the rise of the SNP and decline of Labour in Scotland (see Chapter 9), the Conservatives were able to prosper because the traditional economic dividing lines that had long structured British choices continued to exercise a powerful influence, creating a geography that worked to the Conservatives' advantage.[18] However, this apparent return to political normality proved to be fleeting. The Conservatives' Commons majority meant they were now committed to a referendum on EU membership, and that referendum rapidly became about far more than the narrow question on the ballot paper.[19] The campaign over Britain's EU membership fully unleashed the identity

---

[17] Some of these were in rural and peripheral areas of Liberal Democrat historical strength, such as rural Wales and south west England. Others were suburban seats in the south of England where the Liberal Democrats had tactically squeezed the local Labour vote over several election cycles to make the competition a local two-party contest with the Conservatives.

[18] The Conservatives had a further unusual and widely underestimated advantage in 2015. They had gained 100 seats in the 2010 election, the most new seats the party had won in a single election since 1931. The Tories therefore had an unusually large number of new incumbent MPs running for re-election for the first time. Such new incumbents usually accrue a personal vote as they build personal links with their new seats, and attract support from grateful local constituents they have helped. This 'incumbent bonus' effect was unusually large in 2015, as much as five percentage points in the marginal seats won by the Conservatives in 2010, and was spread over a large cohort of new incumbents. Estimates suggest that stronger Conservative performance in such seats, most likely driven by the incumbent bonus, may have saved the party ten seats or more. See Curtice (2015b); Curtice, Fisher and Ford (2016); Pattie and Johnston (2017).

[19] This is a common feature of referendums. See, for example, Hobolt (2009); Renwick (2017).

politics conflicts which had been building for a generation or more, and the outcome divided the British electorate in new ways. Stances on EU membership symbolised conflicting views about the kind of nation Britain was, is and would become in future. The referendum contest over EU membership became the first national campaign in which identity politics conflicts, not conflicts about economics, or social class or public services, were the primary dividing line in the electorate. The narrow and unexpected leave victory rapidly entrenched the referendum conflict in the minds of voters, and implementing Brexit became the main issue on the political agenda, ensuring that the new conflicts the referendum unleashed would persist for years to come.

Framing the choice: the referendum campaign

Identity conservatism and Euroscepticism have been linked for as long as Britain has been part of the European project. Identity conservatives favour protecting the autonomy and boundaries of the national in-group, putting them at odds with a political project premised on the pooling of political authority and the dilution of national sovereignty. Nor is this pattern unique to Britain – education divides in attitudes to the EU have been observed all over Western Europe for many years,[20] and have become steadily larger as the EU integration project has grown in scale and scope.[21] Identity conservative attitudes such as ethnic nationalism, authoritarianism and negative views of migrants and minorities have been reliably associated with Euroscepticism for decades in Britain and elsewhere in Europe.[22] Figure 8.1 illustrates this by showing the share of voters with high and low levels of identity conservative attitudes expressing support for either leaving the EU or reducing its powers in 2003, well before the idea of a referendum on departure became a live issue. Substantial majorities of those with identity conservative views, however these were measured, were already Eurosceptic

---

[20] Hooghe and Marks (2017); Kriesi et al. (2012).   [21] Hakhverdian et al. (2013).
[22] Carey (2002); McLaren (2002); Carl, Dennison and Evans (2018).

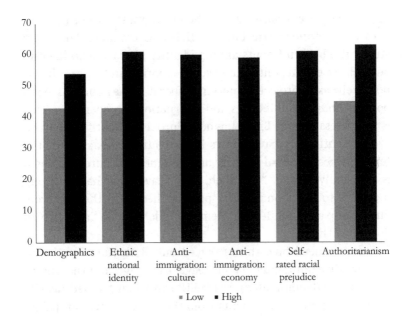

Figure 8.1 Identity conservative attitudes and Euroscepticism in 2003

Source: 2003 British Social Attitudes. We used this survey because it asked a particularly wide range of relevant measures. The same patterns shown here are also found in earlier and later data sources. Connections between Euroscepticism and identity conservatism go back further still – similar relationships can be found in surveys conducted in the 1980s. Chart shows share saying either that EU powers should be reduced or that Britain should leave the EU altogether.

at this point, while those with identity liberal views were much less likely to express negative views about the EU.

Given these strong and longstanding associations between identity divides and Euroscepticism, which were intensified by the growing linkage between EU membership and high immigration,[23] the EU Referendum campaign was always likely to polarise voters on identity grounds. Yet a campaign that mobilised identity divides handed an important advantage to the 'Leave' side owing to another longstanding feature of British attitudes to Europe. While identity conservatives across Europe

---

[23] Evans and Mellon (2019).

tend to be more negative about the EU, in most European countries such ethnocentric Euroscepticism is counterbalanced by strong pro-EU sentiments among identity liberals, who identify with 'Europe' as a political and social identity, and regard the EU positively as a project promoting liberal values such as open borders, individual liberties and international cooperation. This is much less true in Britain, where European identification and pro-EU sentiments have always been relatively weak, while the link between national identity attachments and Euroscepticism is unusually strong.[24] As such, the 'Leave' side had a strong incentive to focus on identity politics themes in their referendum campaign, while the 'Remain' side had an incentive to downplay them.

This is indeed how things played out. Both the official (and Conservative-dominated) 'Vote Leave' campaign and the unofficial (and UKIP-dominated) 'Leave.EU' campaign focused heavily on identity politics arguments from the outset. Leave campaigners employed classic ethnocentric themes – portraying the EU as a threat to the political autonomy of the national in-group, and EU immigrants as a threatening out-group. The slogan 'take back control' was perfectly pitched to ethnocentric voters' twin desires to defend the autonomy of the in-group and to police its borders. 'Leave' material referred repeatedly to the need to exert control over 'our' borders, 'our' laws and so forth – framing Brexit as the defence of the national 'us' from a threatening EU 'them'. The official Leave campaign also made a number of misleading claims about Turkey's possible accession to the EU – with prominent assertions on its website and in campaign materials that Turkey was imminently 'joining the EU' and that Britain could not stop this.[25] Though Turkey was an official applicant for EU membership, its membership bid had languished for many years and had little support from either the

---

[24] Carl, Dennison and Evans (2018); De Vries (2018).
[25] See at: www.bbc.co.uk/news/uk-politics-eu-referendum-36353013, last accessed 3 September 2019.

EU or the current Turkish leadership,[26] and the UK government had an official veto which it could have used to prevent Turkey's accession. The Vote Leave website and multiple other materials drew attention to Turkey's 76 million-strong population, and linked this to immigration by presenting maps with very large arrows drawn from Turkey to the UK.[27] The message was not subtle, not accurate and clearly aimed at stoking ethnocentric voters' anxieties by convincing them that if Britain remained in the EU millions of people from a large and relatively poor Muslim country would shortly have a right to migrate to Britain and would exercise that right in large numbers.

The Leave campaign also claimed that continued EU membership would embroil Britain in the European refugee crisis, which it claimed the EU had made worse, and that the arrival of criminal or extremist elements among the refugee population would threaten British security.[28] Although the official campaign distanced themselves from it, an infamous poster unveiled by the unofficial Leave.EU campaign headed by UKIP leader Nigel Farage depicted Syrian refugees massing on the Slovenian border with the headline 'Breaking Point: the EU has failed us all',[29] tapping into the same sentiment. The message from both the Vote Leave and Leave.EU campaigns was that continued EU membership would leave Britain open to a tidal wave of refugee migration, overwhelming public services and threatening public order. Such adverts were another transparent effort to activate

---

[26] Turkey began formal negotiations in 2005, but has completed just one of thirty-five 'chapters' in this lengthy process. Negotiations have been stalled since 2006 due to Turkey's refusal to allow free movement of goods between it and Cyprus, a longstanding EU precondition for negotiations to progress. There is little interest in pursuing EU negotiations from the current Turkish government, and Turkish public opinion is lukewarm at best. See at: https://fullfact.org/europe/turkey-likely-join-eu, last accessed 3 September 2019.

[27] See at: www.voteleavetakecontrol.org/why_vote_leave.html, last accessed 19 August 2019.

[28] See at: www.voteleavetakecontrol.org/briefing_immigration.html, last accessed 19 August 2019.

[29] See at: www.bbc.co.uk/news/uk-politics-eu-referendum-36570759, last accessed 19 August 2019.

ethnocentric sentiments in the public by associating the EU with the uncontrolled arrival of racially and religiously distinct migrants, reminiscent of the anti-immigration rhetoric of Enoch Powell and his supporters in the 1960s and 1970s described in Chapter 4. Though these were not, of course, the only messages deployed by the 'Leave' side in the campaign, such ethnocentric and anti-immigration arguments were prominent and widely reported.

While the Leave campaign mobilised ethnocentric sentiments, the official Remain campaign – 'Britain Stronger In Europe' – did not follow suit by seeking to make a positive case for European identity in order to mobilise those who strongly identified with Europe in defence of EU membership. Instead, the arguments for staying in the EU were resolutely pragmatic and transactional, building a case based on Britain's economic interests and the risks of disruption, which fell flat by comparison with the emotive and value-laden tone of the Leave campaign. The most rousing call to Remain that the official website managed to include – on the website's front page, no less – was a half-hearted quote from the financial affairs journalist and pundit Martin Lewis: 'I'm generally risk-averse, and that pushes me *just* towards an IN vote for safety.'[30] Similarly equivocal and half-hearted support for Remain was offered by the leader of the Labour Party, Jeremy Corbyn, who declared himself 'seven, or seven and a half', out of ten, for Remain in a live TV interview,[31] refused to do any joint events with David Cameron or other Conservative Remainers, and took a holiday in the middle of the referendum campaign.[32] Given that Conservative Prime Minister David Cameron was also, prior to the referendum

---

[30] See at: www.strongerin.co.uk/#mUF3h2iUx1FOJLx1.97, last accessed 19 August 2019 (emphasis added).

[31] See at: www.bbc.co.uk/news/av/uk-politics-eu-referendum-36506163/corbyn-i-m-seven-out-of-10-on-eu, last accessed 20 September 2019.

[32] For further details of Corbyn's semi-detached approach to the campaign, see Shipman (2017: ch. 19). Phil Wilson, the chair of the 'Labour In for Britain' Parliamentary group wrote a scathing critique of Corbyn's lack of engagement with the EU Referendum campaign in the wake of the Leave victory, see Wilson (2016).

campaign, a Eurosceptic who had repeatedly criticised the EU as a political project, this left identity liberals with no committed pro-Remain cues from the parties they traditionally backed, and left the Remain campaign without political leaders making a positive case for their cause. Despite a clear view on the Remain side, both from journalists and many civil society organisations, that the Leave campaign's messaging was frequently xenophobic and violated anti-prejudice social norms, the Remain campaign was not able to mobilise tolerance and inclusiveness as core values to rally its own supporters around. This activation of the EU as a symbol of identity liberal values only came later, when it was too late to change the referendum result, as we shall see in Chapter 10.

Brexitland awakens: identity divides and 2016 vote choices

When we look closely at the structure of the EU Referendum vote choice, it becomes clear that the Leave campaign's focus on identity conflicts prevailed over the Remain campaign's focus on pragmatic economics. The referendum split the country almost exactly in two – 52:48 in favour of the Leave side – and the new split was very different to the divides which had previously structured British politics in general elections. To illustrate this, we make use of the British Election Study internet panel to compare the attitudes, values and demographics associated with 'Leave' and 'Remain' voting in 2016 with those associated with the choice between Labour and the Conservatives the year before. We narrow our focus here to look at just voters who chose the Conservatives or Labour to make a more direct comparison between two binary choices: Labour and Conservative; Leave and Remain. Conservative voting is compared with Leave voting because it was the Conservatives who called for the EU Referendum, Conservative politicians who took the leading roles in the official Leave campaign, and a Conservative prime minister who embraced the cause of Brexit after the referendum result.

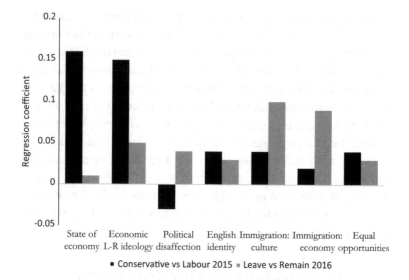

Figure 8.2 Impact of various motivations on voting for Conservatives vs Labour in 2015 and for Leave vs Remain in 2016, England and Wales only

Source: British Election Study internet panel, 2014–2020.

In Figure 8.2 we illustrate the differences between the two elections with a graph showing the impact that a diverse selection of motivations had on choices in 2015 and 2016. Economic motivations had the largest impact on choices between the Conservatives and Labour in 2015 – both economic left–right ideology and assessments of economic conditions had a very large effect on general election choices. The effects of both were much weaker in the EU referendum a year later. We find the opposite pattern for immigration attitudes – these had a modest impact on choices between the Conservatives and Labour in 2015, but a very large impact on EU Referendum choices in 2016. Other forms of identity divide such as English nationalism and views of equal opportunities had similar impacts in both votes, highlighting the growing mobilisation of identity politics discussed in the previous two chapters. However, the impact of one motivation was reversed between 2015 and 2016: voters who were dissatisfied with British democracy were more likely to back Labour over the Conservatives in 2015, but such motivations encouraged Leave support the following year. The divided loyalties of the politically disaffected would become an issue once again in 2017, as we shall see in Chapter 10.

Economic perceptions and economic ideology have long loomed large in general elections[33] (as discussed in Chapter 5), and 2015 was no exception. Perceptions about the national economy and traditional left–right economic ideology (bosses versus workers, state versus market and so on) strongly predicted voters' choices between the Conservatives and Labour. It was therefore natural for the strategists heading the Remain campaign, seasoned veterans of many general election contests, to assume that a focus on economic arguments was to their best advantage. The lesson from past general elections was that if you convinced voters that Remain was the economically beneficial choice, you were well on your way to victory. But the 2016 referendum did not play out this way. We illustrate this in more detail in Figure 8.3, which shows the relationship between economic perceptions and vote choices in the two elections in more detail. Views of the national economy had a powerful connection to vote choices in 2015, shown by the black line. Voters with negative views about the current state of the economy backed Labour over the Conservatives by large margins in 2015, while economic optimists heavily favoured the incumbent Conservatives. But such economic perceptions had no relationship to choices in the EU Referendum the following year, shown by the grey line. Those who thought Britain's economy was booming voted the same way as otherwise similar voters who saw an economy in crisis. It is a similar story with economic ideology: ideologically left-wing voters who wanted a larger, stronger state, stronger unions and a more regulated market voted just the same as otherwise similar voters in favour of a low-tax, low-regulation, free market 'Singapore-on-Thames'. The Remain campaign's quest to tie EU

---

[33] See, for example, Clarke et al. (2003; 2009).

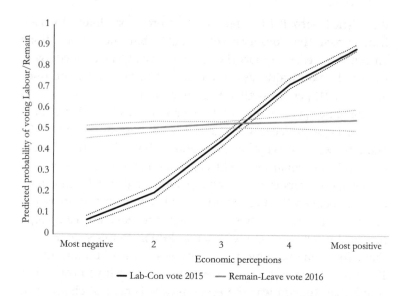

Figure 8.3 Relationship between economic perceptions and vote choices between Labour and the Conservatives in 2015 and between Leave and Remain in 2016

Source: British election study internet panel, 2014–18.

membership to traditional economic motivations was a flop. In 2016, it was not the economy, stupid.

When we look instead at the central identity politics conflict – immigration – the pattern is reversed, as Figure 8.4 reveals.[34] While the economy moved to the margins in 2016, immigration conflicts moved to centre stage. Immigration was influential in 2015 (shown by the black line), reflecting its growing political mobilisation over the previous decade. But the impact of immigration attitudes on EU Referendum vote choices, shown by the grey line, was much stronger. The most anti-migration voters

[34] For ease of presentation we combine the effects of attitudes about the economic and cultural attitudes to immigration. Both are stronger in the EU Referendum model than in the 2015 Conservatives versus Labour model. Full details are provided in the Online Appendix: www.cambridge.org/Brexitland

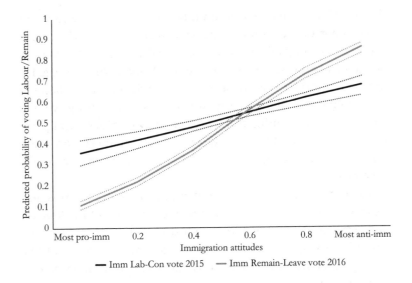

Figure 8.4 Views about immigration and vote preference between Labour and the Conservatives in 2015, and between Leave and Remain in 2016 in England and Wales

Source: British Election Study internet panel, 2014–18, England and Wales only.[35]

split 60:40 towards the Conservatives over. Labour, but split 90:10 towards Leave over Remain, while the most pro-migration voters favoured Labour over the Conservatives by a narrow margin in 2015, but broke overwhelmingly for Remain in 2016.

The structure of the EU Referendum vote was thus fundamentally different to that seen in general elections. Traditional divides on economic perceptions and ideology, which had long structured choices between Labour and Conservative, had little impact on the choice between Remain and Leave.[36] Conversely,

---

[35] For the statistical details of the models see the Online Appendix: www .cambridge.org/Brexitland

[36] This is not to say that economics played no role in the EU Referendum. The economic disadvantage of many Leave voting areas was certainly influential, although the pathways linking long-term disadvantage and referendum vote choices are complex, and overlap with the impact of identity conservatism, with identity conservative demographic groups often concentrating in these

the new identity divides over immigration, national identity and equal opportunities, which were a secondary factor in the choice between Labour and Conservative in 2015, were the strongest predictor of choices between Leave and Remain 2016. In the EU Referendum, the latent identity divides in the electorate became fully mobilised as the primary factors structuring voters' choices. The restraining influences of party loyalties, local political cultures and first-past-the-post electoral incentives were removed, and the full political potential of identity conflicts became clear.

The central role of identity divides in the referendum is also clear when we look at the demographic structure of the Remain and Leave electorates. Figure 8.5 illustrates this. We present the results of a simple statistical model[37] testing the impact of five demographic factors – social class, income, education level, ethnicity and generation – on predicted support for the Conservatives over Labour in 2015 and on Leave over Remain in 2016. The differences in the demographic patterns of Conservative versus Labour and Leave versus Remain support are stark, underscoring how the referendum choice split the electorate in new ways. As a result, the Conservatives' post-referendum embrace of Brexit had considerable disruptive potential, offering them opportunities with demographic groups who had traditionally shunned the party, while putting the Tories at odds with other groups who were traditionally strong supporters.

The marginalisation of traditional economic conflicts in the EU Referendum is evident when we look at the impact of class and income, the two leftmost pairs of bars in the chart. The middle classes and the wealthy heavily favoured the

areas (see also McKay 2019; Goodwin and Heath 2016; Jennings and Stoker 2016). Secondly, there is evidence that those personally affected by austerity due to cuts to their benefits were more likely to vote to Leave, possibly making a small, but significant, difference to the overall result (Fetzer 2019).

[37] We use the same dataset – the British Election Study Internet Panel, 2014–18 – to maximise comparability here. However, other datasets – for example, the British Election Study face-to-face survey and the British Social Attitudes face-to-face survey – confirm the pattern of differences we identify here. See the Online Appendix (www.cambridge.org/Brexitland) for further details.

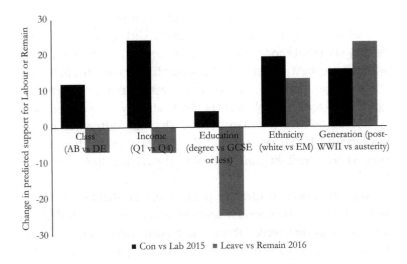

Figure 8.5 Demographic divides in support for Conservatives vs Labour in 2015 (black) and Leave vs Remain in 2016 (grey) in England and Wales

Source: British Election Study internet panel, 2014–18 (England and Wales only); bars show predicted differences in support with all other demographic factors held at their means.

Conservatives over Labour in 2015 – Conservative voting was twelve points higher among middle-class 'AB' groups than working-class 'DE' groups even after controlling for other demographic differences, and twenty-four points higher among the richest quarter of the electorate than among the poorest quarter. In the EU Referendum one year later, both relationships are much weaker and run in the opposite direction: Leave voting is around seven points lower among the wealthy than the poor, and among the middle class than the working class.

While traditional economic divides had less impact on Brexit choices, the EU Referendum opened up new divisions by education and generation. The differences in the impact of education are dramatic. In 2015, graduates leaned slightly more towards Conservative than school leavers, with a four-point gap between the groups after controlling for the other

demographic factors.[38] In the EU Referendum a year later the
two education groups were poles apart, with graduates voting
twenty-six points more Remain than school leavers. Education
was the weakest of the five demographic factors in 2015, and
the strongest in 2016. As we have seen, differences between
graduates and school leavers had already been gradually
reshaping politics for many years. The vast difference in the
two groups' Brexit choices had the potential to accelerate that
process as Brexit became the central dividing line in British
politics.

Another aspect of identity politics, ethnic divides in voting
behaviour, were by contrast somewhat smaller in 2016 than in
2015, though they were substantial in both years. The ethnic gap
in Conservative–Labour voting was twenty points, with white
voters backing the Conservatives and ethnic minority voters
breaking heavily for Labour, continuing their longstanding
alignment with the party. But the ethnic gap the following year
was somewhat narrower – white voters were thirteen points
more Leave voting than ethnic minorities. There were many
more ethnic minority Leave voters in 2016 than ethnic minority
Conservative voters in 2015. Longstanding ethnic minority suspicions of the Conservative Party seem not to have fully trans-
ferred to the Leave campaign, despite the prominence of
Conservative politicians and Leave campaigners' embrace of
ethnocentric themes and messages. It is not clear why this did
not happen.[39] One factor may be Labour's relatively low profile
in the campaign, meaning ethnic minority voters did not receive
clear political cues on the EU Referendum from the party they
trusted most. Another factor may be minority voters' more
extensive contact with the immigration system, which generated resentment towards EU citizens who were given free

---

[38] The education gap was larger in earlier elections, with graduates leaning more
strongly to the Conservatives and school leavers leaning towards Labour. The
small gap in 2015 reflects the ongoing identity politics shifts discussed in
Chapters 6 and 7, with identity liberal graduates migrating towards Labour
while school leavers defected from the party.

[39] See Martin and Khan (2019) for further discussion of this issue.

movement rights while ethnic minority employers and families had to navigate a bureaucratic and expensive migration control system.[40] The idea that leaving the EU might lead to more equal treatment of all migrants, with greater control of European migration and more liberal rules for Commonwealth migrants reflecting their home nations' historical connections to Britain, was popular among ethnic minority voters. The post-referendum embrace of Brexit may therefore have offered the Conservatives an opportunity to renew their appeal to ethnic minorities. However, incoming Prime Minister Theresa May, the architect and administrator of the draconian immigration system which produced the 'Windrush' scandal, was uniquely ill-suited to capitalise on this opportunity.

The overall generational pattern of voting is similar in both years: both the Conservatives in 2015 and 'Leave' in 2016 did better with older generations. But the generation gap grew between 2015 and 2016. This mainly reflects distinctive behaviour among the youngest 'austerity' generation – voters who had turned eighteen since the beginning of the Coalition in 2010. This youngest cohort of voters narrowly favoured Labour over the Conservatives in 2015, but backed Remain over Leave by an overwhelming margin. The narrow victory for Leave, and the government's embrace of the referendum mandate, thus put the Conservatives strongly at odds with the youngest voters, a tension which the Labour Party would successfully capitalise upon in the years after the EU Referendum, as we will see in Chapter 10.

Two tribes go to war: the emergence of Brexit political identities

The EU Referendum split the British electorate along new lines. Traditional economic conflicts moved to the margins, and identity conflicts moved to centre stage. But the referendum was also (at least in theory) a one-off event, with the nation as a whole

[40] Begum (2018; 2019).

rendering its opinion on a single constitutional question. The new divides it laid bare could have faded away again once the vote was done, with voters' minds turning back to other things. If the status quo Remain side had won, this may have been the outcome. But a narrow victory for Leave made a return to politics as usual impossible. The vote for Brexit mandated the British government to embark on the most complex international negotiation in modern British history,[41] and required a vast domestic political effort to unpick the effects of four decades of European integration in British laws, policies and institutions. The vote to leave made it certain that Brexit would dominate the political agenda for years.

The choices of June 2016 also had a lasting impact on the mass electorate. The battle over Brexit crystallised new political identities – Remain and Leave were more than expressions of how people voted, they had become a central part of how people saw themselves. Voters on both sides of the Brexit debate now had a sense of themselves as distinct social groups with their own values and priorities, and views about who their opponents were and what they stood for. These new Brexit partisan identities were more strongly held and more widely shared than fading attachments to the traditional political parties, and became a driver of larger and more lasting changes in attitudes and behaviour, as voters began to see parties and policies through the lens of their newfound Brexit tribes. There are three aspects to this new phenomenon of Brexit partisanship: voters developed a clear sense of 'Leave' and 'Remain' as social groups; they developed clear group-based judgements, seeing their own group positively, and their rivals negatively; and these group identities and group judgements began to influence their political preferences and choices. We consider each in turn.

---

[41] See O'Rourke (2018) and Shipman (2018) for detailed accounts of the first stages of this process, and Evans and Menon (2017) for an account of the early political ramifications.

We start with voters' awareness of the referendum tribes as distinct social groups. Voters need to have a clear sense of who a political grouping represents if they are to form a sense of attachment to that group, and a sense of rivalry and hostility towards its competitors. We have seen that the referendum result divided the electorate in new ways, with education and age divides moving to the fore, and economic divides fading into the background. Did voters recognise and understand these new divisions? Were they able to correctly characterise the demographics of the new 'Leave' and 'Remain' tribes? To find out we presented survey respondents with a randomly ordered list of nine attributes, some of which were demographic factors strongly associated with referendum vote choices. Figure 8.6 presents whether voters volunteered 'working class', 'old' and 'young' as descriptions of Leave and Remain voters.[42] Voters have a clear understanding of the 'Leave' electorate as older and more working class, and of the 'Remain' electorate as younger. What is more, both 'Remain' and 'Leave' voters agreed about these characterisations of the two tribes.[43] Voters had clear and accurate ideas about the social character of the two Brexit tribes.

Consensus about who is on each side of a divide is not, on its own, enough to give a divide political power. The divide also has to matter to people. And the Brexit divide does: voters do not treat Leave and Remain as records of how their fellow citizens voted one summer's day, but as much broader expressions of who people are and what they value. When voters have such

---

[42] Space constraints on the survey prevented us from testing a wider range of characteristics.

[43] The one exception to this pattern was 'well off', the last of the four demographic characterisations we asked about. This is in itself revealing. The lack of clarity about into whose camp the 'well off' fell might reflect the weaker links between economic status and vote choices in the EU Referendum than in general elections. But a different possibility emerges when we break down the responses by voters' own referendum votes. Both sides are eager to characterise their opponents as 'well off' and reluctant to describe themselves in this way. This suggests that the 'well off' are seen in negative terms, perhaps as a group who are protected from the impact of political choices they inflict on others.

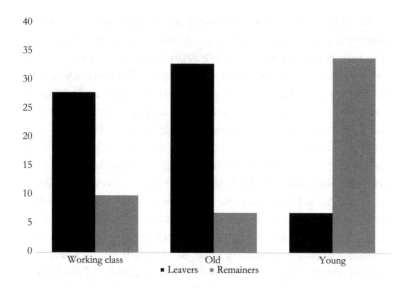

Figure 8.6 Share of voters describing 'Leavers' and 'Remainers' as working class, old or young (percentages)

Source: YouGov, 2019.

strong bonds to a political tribe, this can have a powerful influence on their behaviour, as they come to see politics in terms of a competition between their tribe and its opponents. As we discussed in Chapter 5, similar emotional attachments to parties have played an important role in structuring British politics for many decades, and the decline in British voters' partisan attachments is an important driver of the more volatile and unpredictable politics we see today.[44]

The EU Referendum conjured new political identities with similar emotional power into existence overnight. The words 'Remain' and 'Leave' had no political connotations before September 2015, when these terms were proposed by the Electoral Commission and accepted by the government as answer categories for the EU Referendum question. Yet just a year after this some 88 per cent of respondents in the British Election

[44] Green, Palmquist and Schickler (2004); Fieldhouse et al. (2019).

Study reported feeling close to either Remain (45 per cent) or Leave (43 per cent), a level of identification far above that expressed towards the traditional governing parties.[45] 'Leaver' and 'Remainer' rapidly spread as terms used by both sides to affirm their own in-group and to denigrate the other side, reflecting the two classic dynamics of social identity: emotional attachment to the in-group and hostility to out-groups.

Researchers surveying voters in 2017 found symmetrical stereotypes had already become widespread – both 'Leavers' and 'Remainers' saw their own side as intelligent, open-minded and honest, while describing their opponents as selfish, hypocritical and closed-minded.[46] Not only were these new Brexit identities more widely shared in the British public, they were also more intense. American political psychology researchers have developed measures designed to capture the emotions associated with partisans, using questions like 'when I talk about the [partisan identity] side, I usually say "we" instead of "they"', and 'when people criticize the [partisan identity] side, it feels like a personal insult'. Such measures capture the degree to which partisans have internalised political loyalties as part of how they see themselves and imagine how others see them. As Figure 8.7 reveals, such emotional attachments were much stronger in the 'Remain' and 'Leave' tribes than they were among partisan supporters of the traditional political parties.

Stronger partisan attachments are also revealed in the descriptions voters apply to 'Leavers' and 'Remainers' as groups. Members of both Brexit tribes attach positive descriptions such as 'patriotic', 'tolerant' and 'reasonable' to their own side and negative ones such as 'selfish' or 'intolerant' to their opponents. Figure 8.8 presents two of these characteristics to illustrate the general pattern: both Leavers and Remainers rated their group as 'reasonable' while considering the opposing Brexit tribe

---

[45] Fifty-four per cent of voters in the same survey spontaneously reported an identification with the Conservatives (28 per cent) or Labour (27 per cent).

[46] For further evidence on the rich content and wide-ranging influence of the new Brexit political identities, see Hobolt, Leeper and Tilley (2018).

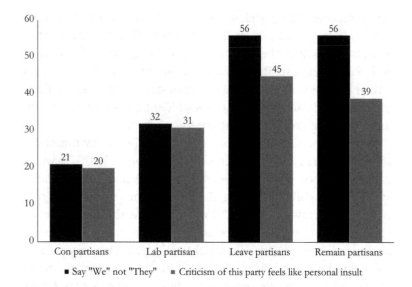

Figure 8.7 Expressions of emotional attachment to parties and referendum sides, autumn 2016 (percentages)

Source: British Election Study internet panel, 2014–18, wave 10 (autumn 2016).

'intolerant'.[47] The EU Referendum changed the way in which voters understood British political competition, creating new tribal affiliations that now play a central role in structuring how they see the ebb and flow of political debate. Both sides in the referendum have formed into tribes, developing loyalties to their own side and hostility to their opponents. A referendum that was supposed to settle the Europe question in British politics has instead restructured British politics around views of the Europe question.

What social and political impact did these new Brexit tribes have? We devised a simple experiment to test the impact of

---

[47] A similar pattern occurred on our other items with one exception: Remainers were less likely to draw a clear difference between the two groups on patriotism, perhaps because for Remain supporters this is not such a straightforwardly positive characteristic. See the Online Appendix (www.cambridge.org/Brexitland) for more details.

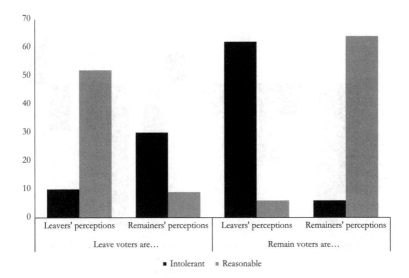

Figure 8.8 Share of Leave and Remain voters rating each Brexit tribe as 'intolerant' and 'reasonable' (percentages)

Source: YouGov, 2019.

these new attachments relative to other social identities. Groups who dislike each other usually avoid social contact, whether through living near each other, marrying or befriending each other, and even working with each other, thus creating social distance between each other.[48] Our experiment therefore set out to compare the social distance expressed by Leavers and Remainers towards the opposing tribe, and to compare it to the frictions generated by other more established social divisions such as immigration, ethnicity, social class and political partisanship. We asked our respondents to compare two hypothetical families vying to move in next door and say which one the respondent would prefer to move in. We gave the respondents ten randomly varied pieces of information about each family, and then

---

[48] Social distance measures are often used to assess prejudice and intolerance between groups (see Ford 2008 for a review).

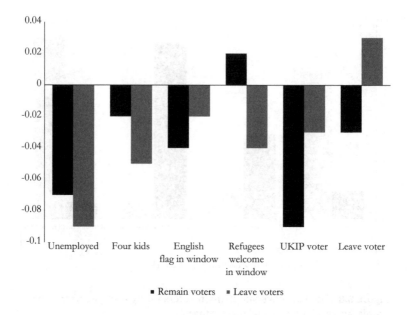

Figure 8.9 Relative impact of neighbour characteristics on probability of being welcomed (above 0) or shunned (below 0) as a new neighbour (average marginal effect)

calculated which characteristics had the biggest relative impact on which potential neighbour respondents preferred.[49]

The referendum preferences of prospective neighbours had a powerful impact on whether people wanted them moving in next door. Both Leavers and Remainers preferred fellow tribe members as neighbours and sought to avoid sharing a fence with Brexit opponents. Referendum choices had a bigger impact than cultural indicators, such as hobbies or holiday destinations, and identity indicators, such as migration status and country of birth, though less effect than disclosing that the potential neighbours were unemployed. We also included some other political characteristics, some of them related to identity politics, such as

[49] We asked each respondent to look at three pairs of families to increase statistical power, for details of how we asked this question and how we analysed it, see the Online Appendix: www.cambridge.org/Brexitland

displaying a 'refugees welcome' sign or an English flag in the window, some to traditional party politics, such as who the new neighbours voted for at the last election. A vote for either of the main parties had no consistent impact on how Remainers or Leavers viewed a new neighbour. However, a past vote for UKIP had a larger negative effect on Remainers' views than anything else. Both Remainers and Leavers also reacted to the political symbols of the 'refugees welcome' sign and the English flag: Remainers had a stronger objection to English flag wavers than Leavers, and Leavers disliked the prospect of neighbours who displayed a 'refugees welcome' sign in their window, while Remainers reacted positively to this (Figure 8.9).

The new Brexit identities were also beginning to change how voters saw politics, acting as a lens through which they perceived all aspects of the political situation. The attitudes of the two Brexit tribes diverged after the referendum result on a remarkably wide range of issues. The British Election Study, which went back to the same panel of people at regular intervals, enables us to see this process unfolding in real time. The 'Leave' tribe, buoyed by victory in the referendum, found new causes for optimism wherever they looked, developing a growing hostility to the parties they associated with 'Remain' (particularly the Liberal Democrats, but also Labour) and a growing attraction to the Conservatives after their embrace of Brexit under new leader Theresa May. The 'Remain' tribe moved in the opposite direction in all respects – becoming gloomier about the state of the economy and society, more hostile to the Brexit-embracing Conservatives, more attached to Europe and more positive about the Liberal Democrats as an openly pro-EU party.[50]

There is also a clear link between the strength of Brexit identities and the divergence in the views of the two Brexit tribes after the EU Referendum. Figure 8.10 illustrates this by using

---

[50] Further details on these analyses are provided in the Online Appendix (www .cambridge.org/Brexitland). Brexit partisanship is associated with shifts in assessments of the main parties and shifts in reported vote choice between parties.

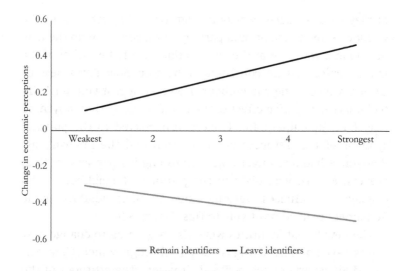

Figure 8.10 Change in views about Britain's economic performance between spring 2016 (pre-EU Referendum) and spring 2017 by strength of Leave or Remain identity, England and Wales

Source: British Election Study internet panel, 2014–20, England and Wales only.

voters' views about the economy. As we have seen, such views had in the past been closely linked to voters' choices in general elections, but were not linked to the choices voters made in the EU Referendum. However, after the referendum result was announced, a new link emerged between referendum choices and economic perceptions, not because economic perceptions influenced Brexit choices, but because Brexit choices began to influence economic perceptions. The Brexit tribes began to see the economy through partisan lenses. 'Leave' voters, who thought departure from the EU was an opportunity for renewal, became more positive about the economy after June 2016, while 'Remain' voters, who felt Brexit would cause serious economic harm, became more pessimistic. And the stronger voters' attachment to their Brexit tribes, the larger the post-referendum divergence in their economic perceptions, as shown by the black and grey lines in the graph. By spring 2017, the economic perceptions which have long been a central barometer of government performance were instead being driven in part by Brexit loyalties. Strong Remainers had become filled with economic gloom, while strong Leavers were convinced that happy days were here again.

This divergence of the Brexit tribes also impacted on their political preferences. In the immediate aftermath of the referendum, Remain-identifying voters developed more favourable views of the Liberal Democrats, and Remainers who had previously voted Conservative became more hostile to the party after it embraced the Leave cause under new leader Theresa May. Conversely, Leave identifiers became more positive about the Conservatives once Theresa May became leader, and Leave voters who had backed Labour or the Liberal Democrats in 2015 began switching to the Conservatives. Both of these shifts were more pronounced among those expressing the strongest attachments to their Brexit tribes.

The political power of Brexit flowed through two channels. Brexit mobilised longstanding identity divides, and it created new political identities with a force of their own. Voters now saw themselves as 'Leavers' and 'Remainers' and began to see politics in terms of these newly acquired tribal loyalties. Brexit partisanship informed how voters saw the political situation, and what they wanted to do. This effect stretched well beyond Brexit itself. Those who identified with 'Remain' began to see trouble everywhere – economic decline, social disorder and rising intolerance. Those who identified with 'Leave', by contrast, had a spring in their step and saw sunshine wherever they looked – a strong economy, restored sovereignty and a renewed democracy. The polarised outlooks produced by seeing the world through tribal lenses drove divergence in political preferences, over and above the effects of the identity conflicts activated in the original EU Referendum. From the moment the EU Referendum result was announced, it opened up new fractures in the electorate and created new political loyalties, putting additional strains on the traditional governing parties, as these new Brexit divides ran right through the middle of their electoral coalitions.

Conclusion

When he decided to call the EU Referendum, David Cameron worried that the campaign would 'unleash demons'.[51] Indeed it did. Although the identity conflicts of Brexitland have deep roots, Brexit marked the opening of a new phase in British politics, as these conflicts intensified and became central to British voters' political identities. Identity conflicts were nothing new in British politics, as we have seen, but before the EU Referendum they exercised only a minority of voters, making their disruptive political effects easier to contain. Ethnocentric identity conservatives mobilised in large numbers against traditional party politics in 2015, but the impact of their uprising was defused by their dispersal across the country. Identity liberals, though many shifted from the Liberal Democrats to the Labour Party in the same period, did not mobilise behind a single cause in the same way or to the same extent, and the geography of political competition meant their drift towards Labour ended up helping the Conservatives. Meanwhile, for most of the voters not focused on immigration, 2015 was still an election fought on the traditional grounds of economic ideology and economic competence. The Conservatives advantage on this terrain was enough to deliver a parliamentary majority and conveyed an impression of business as usual, despite the dramatic rise of two nationalist parties in different parts of the UK and the dramatic collapse of their coalition partners.

Brexit was different – a contest where identity conflicts were the primary dividing line. This played into the hands of a Leave campaign who embraced emotive and divisive identity themes from the outset, helping them to overcome a Remain campaign whose economics and risk-focused message fell flat. The referendum result changed the stakes yet again. It came as a shocking wake-up call to hitherto complacent identity liberal voters, giving them a cause to fight for and the flag of 'Remain' to rally

---

[51] Oliver (2016).

around. Victory also galvanised politically disaffected identity conservatives, who also rallied to defend their political cause and ensure the referendum mandate was implemented, coming to see 'Leave' as the cause that would turn the tide of social change their way.

This crystallisation of referendum choices as political identities created a new political environment, with two new tribes aware of who they were, what they stood for and what they opposed. Although we do not yet know how the new Brexit tribes will align with Britain's existing party divisions in the long run, they demonstrated a powerful disruptive capacity from the outset. Brexit identities were stronger than the traditional party attachments, provoking from the off powerful feelings of attachment and rivalry, and beginning to reshape voters' political perceptions across the board. 'Leavers' and 'Remainers' did not just see Brexit differently. They saw British society, the British economy and British politics differently. And the more strongly they identified with their cause, the more their views differed. Resolving these differences posed a new and difficult challenge for any political party with aspirations to bridge the Brexit divide.

The story of Brexit divides we have told here is the story of England and Wales. In Scotland, deep new divisions had already emerged before the Brexit debate even got underway, as a consequence of another closely fought constitutional contest: the 2014 referendum over Scottish independence. The story of the Scottish independence referendum involves all the same elements as that of the Brexit referendum – a closely fought campaign which mobilised identity politics divides, created new referendum identities and re-aligned politics around a constitutional conflict. Yet there are important differences in the Scottish story which help us to understand the role played by political choices and historical context in shaping the electoral coalitions formed by referendums, and their subsequent impact on politics. In the next chapter, we turn our attention to Scotland, and examine how distinctive choices and circumstances have shaped a very different identity politics re-alignment there since 2014.

9 DANCING TO A DIFFERENT TUNE: IDENTITY POLITICS AND POLITICAL CHANGE IN SCOTLAND, 2007–19

Introduction

The Brexitland political drama laid out in the previous chapters is very much an English and Welsh story. The underlying drivers of political disruption – demographic change, partisan de-alignment, identity politics conflicts and a polarising referendum campaign – were also all present in Scotland, but they have combined to produce a very different story in Britain's northernmost nation. In this chapter we turn to this distinctive drama, examining how and why Scotland has followed a different path, and what this can tell us about the role of historical legacies and party choices in shaping how social change is channelled into political competition. The upending of politics in England and Wales during the 2010s unfolded in three stages. First, disaffected voters mobilised behind a new entrant after losing faith in the incumbent government; then a divisive and closely fought referendum split the electorate on identity grounds; then a general election fought in the aftermath of this referendum began to re-align party choices around the new political identities forged by the referendum. Each of these stages has an analogue in Scotland over the same period, yet at each stage distinct political traditions and party choices have led to different outcomes.

The same patterns of stronger attachments to the smaller nation and suspicion of a larger political union exist among identity conservatives in Scotland with regard to Britain as exist among identity conservatives in England[1] with regard to the EU. But Scots, or at least most Scots, also feel a stronger sense of affinity and loyalty to Britain than the English feel to the EU. This loyalty to Britain provides a counterweight to Scottish separatist sentiments which has no analogue in England with regard to the EU. And such loyalties to Britain were concentrated among older Scots, while in England it is the older generations who expressed the strongest antipathy to the European Union. In the two referendums, the higher turnout rates of older voters magnified the impact of British affinities in Scotland, and of Eurosceptic antagonism in England.

The parties mobilising separatist sentiments in Scotland and England have very different histories, reputations and political strategies. The political champion of Scottish independence has for many decades been the Scottish National Party (SNP), a larger and more established party than UKIP, the chief political vehicle for Euroscepticism in England.[2] The SNP broadened its electoral support after devolution reforms brought in a separate Scottish Parliament in 1999, becoming the governing party of Scotland in 2007, and governing with a majority from 2011 to 2016. While UKIP focused on carving out a narrow, radical right electoral niche and pressuring the mainstream parties from outside the

---

[1] We focus primarily on the Scotland–England comparison. Wales cleaves closely to the English pattern in most cases, but has some distinctive features of its own which we do not have the space to cover here. Our findings are fairly similar with or without the inclusion of Wales. For discussion of distinctive Welsh trends in politics around and after the EU Referendum, see Osmond (2017); Awan-Scully (2018); McAllister and Awan-Scully (2019); Wyn-Jones (2019).

[2] The SNP was founded in the 1930s, and since 1967 it has had a continuous presence in Westminster (McLean 1970), but it is only since devolution that it has risen to become a force capable of first challenging and then supplanting the locally dominant Labour Party: the SNP were the second in Scotland from the establishment of the Scottish Parliament in 1999, and have been the first-placed party in Scottish elections, and the governing party in the Scottish Parliament, since 2007.

Westminster legislature, the SNP sought to channel Scottish nationalist sentiment into a broader majority coalition. Their electoral platform combined economically left-wing and ethnocentric themes, portraying the SNP as the true defenders of a socially and economically progressive Scotland threatened by right-wing, 'English Tory' rule.[3] This proved a remarkably effective strategy, enabling the SNP to recruit support from both sides of the identity politics divide, mobilising Scottish identity conservatives by framing the English and the Conservative Party as threatening out-groups, and attracting economic left wingers and identity liberals by promoting a left-liberal agenda of redistribution and social progressivism for Scotland.

The 'exit' campaigns in the two referendums were also very different. The 2016 'Leave' campaign focused on activating and mobilising ethnocentrism, polarising voters around identity issues and entrenching identity politics divides. The 2014 Scottish independence 'Yes' campaign, orchestrated by the governing SNP, looked to build a broader support base by crafting a message that appealed to identity liberals, economic progressives and ethnocentric Scottish nationalists alike. The campaigners, taking their cue from messages honed by the SNP for many years, framed Scottish independence as an opportunity to build a more economically left-wing and socially liberal Scotland freed from the constraints of reactionary English politics.[4] One goal of this campaign, and one where it was particularly successful, was to boost the appeal of independence to working-class, economically left-wing and traditionally Labour-supporting Scots strongly opposed to austerity policies they saw as imposed by English politicians and voters.[5]

The two exit campaigns also differed in their outcomes: the 'Yes' campaign fell short, while the 'Leave' campaign narrowly

---

[3] The SNP developed this formula relatively early, even before devolution began. See Brand, Mitchell and Surridge (1994); Levy (1995).

[4] Wiggan (2017); Béland and Lecours (2016).

[5] Mooney and Scott (2015); Pattie and Johnston (2017); Fieldhouse et al. (2019: ch. 8).

succeeded. The differing balances of attachments conflicted voters felt played a key role in this. The stronger British loyalties and high turnout of older Scots, and the unionism of migrants to Scotland from the UK and elsewhere, helped tip the 2014 referendum against Scottish independence. In the Brexit campaign the high-turnout grey vote had no attachment to Europe and broke heavily for Brexit, and most of the large and pro-EU European migrant population resident in Britain was not eligible to vote. The political aftermaths of the two campaigns were also different, as the new referendum political identities interacted with the differing party systems of England and Scotland. In England, as we shall see in greater detail in Chapter 10, Brexit identities aligned unevenly with the traditional parties of government, helping to produce, first, a dramatic resurgence of two-party politics in 2017, then the first substantial Conservative majority in a generation in 2019. In Scotland, the SNP rose to new heights of dominance on the back of defeat as 'Yes' identifiers aligned strongly with the SNP, while 'No' partisans scattered across three unionist parties. Then Brexit shook everything up again less than two years later, setting Eurosceptic identity conservatives who opposed rule from Brussels and Westminster alike against cosmopolitan nationalists seeking independence to keep Scotland in the EU.

The demographic roots of 'exit' politics: Scotland and England compared

When nations group together into a larger union, the citizens living within each participating unit have dual loyalties: to the smaller member nation, and to the broader union.[6] Campaigns to exit a larger political unit force people to choose between these allegiances. Those whose loyalty to the smaller unit is strong, or who have a strong hostility to the larger unit, will be more easily attracted to the exit option. Those who feel a strong

---

[6] See, for example, Henderson (2007).

loyalty to the larger unit, or at least see it as benevolent or beneficial, will be more inclined towards maintaining the union. The mix of loyalties in the electorate is therefore a critical factor on which the fate of exit campaigns turns. While the initial support for Scottish independence and Brexit came from similar voters with similar resentments, the two electorates were very different in terms of their loyalty to the larger unit – attachment to Britain was widespread among Scots, while attachment to the EU was much scarcer in the British referendum electorate. British attachments were a valuable resource for the 'No' campaign in 2014, while the absence of European affinities was a problem for the 'Remain' campaign two years later.

Identity conservative voters formed the demographic core of both exit movements. The Scottish electorate was not immune from the trends we described in Chapter 2, and despite lower levels of ethnic diversity, and a somewhat slower educational expansion, the two opposing identity camps have evolved in similar ways. Levels of ethnocentrism in Scottish society are comparable with those in the wider UK, as we show in Figure 9.1. Similar shares of Scots and English express ethnocentric attitudes on national identity, immigration and diversity. The Scots are a bit less likely to express hostility towards migrants and Muslims, but placed somewhat more emphasis on ancestry and birth in defining Scottishness than the English placed on these things when defining Britishness.[7] All of these attitudes show the same splits by education and ethnicity in Scotland as they do in Britain as a whole.

The proportion of ethnocentric voters is comparable in Scotland and England, and ethnocentric voters in both contexts tend to view larger political unions with more suspicion. In both

---

[7] Academic surveys have not asked identical questions about the meaning of national identity about English identity specifically, but work by the think tank 'British Future' in 2012 suggested that the English gave slightly greater weight to ancestry and birth in defining their national identity than either the Scottish or the Welsh (British Future 2012), though a later survey suggested that ethnic perceptions of English identity had fallen sharply in the 2010s (Denham 2019).

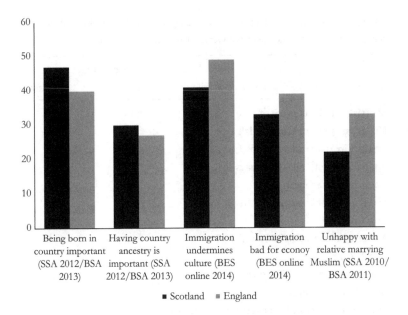

Figure 9.1 Ethnocentric attitudes in Scotland and England (percentages)

Sources: British Social Attitudes; Scottish Social Attitudes; British Election Study online panel; all residents of Scotland and England included in these surveys are included.

countries, the most ethnocentric demographic group, white school leavers, expresses stronger loyalties to the smaller national unit, and greater hostility to both the citizens and political institutions of the larger political unit. This is illustrated in Table 9.1, where we compare Scottish 'Angloscepticism' – negative views of the English and of British political institutions – with English Euroscepticism. The comparison is imperfect, as in most cases identical questions have not been asked, but the measures are close enough to highlight some broad patterns. White school leavers adopt an ethnocentric stance towards migrants from elsewhere in the larger union in both contexts. English school leavers oppose Eastern European migrants as an alien and threatening presence in their nation; many Scottish school leavers feel similarly about English migrants. White school leavers in both countries also dislike

Table 9.1 Scottish Angloscepticism and English Euroscepticism compared: out-group hostility and negative views of union institutions

	White school leavers	Others
Scottish Angloscepticism		
Negative views of the English		
English in Scotland take jobs from Scots	40	23
English in Scotland will always feel more English than Scottish	75	65
Scotland would lose its identity if more English came	36	26
Negative views of British political institutions		
'Almost never' trust UK government to work in Scotland's interests	37	27
Little or no trust in UK government to make fair decisions	47	31
Scotland gets less than its fair share of UK government spending	49	36
English Euroscepticism		
Negative views of Europeans		
Britain would lose its identity if more Eastern Europeans came	79	47
Costs of EU migration outweigh the benefits	67	47
Would mind if a close relative married an Eastern European	24	10
Negative views of EU political institutions		
Little or no benefit to UK from EU membership	59	32
UK should not follow EU decisions it disagrees with	75	55
EU should have much less power than member states	36	23

Sources: Scottish Social Attitudes, 2011; British Social Attitudes, 2013; all residents of Scotland and England in these surveys are included.

and distrust the political institutions of the larger union. Scottish identity conservatives distrust Westminster and think it short-changes them; English identity conservatives similarly distrust Brussels and see little benefit from Britain's EU membership. While distrust of political unions is a common theme, Euroscepticism in England appears to be stronger and more widespread than Angloscepticism in Scotland. Roughly a third of Scottish identity conservatives think English migrants are a threat to Scottish identity, but four in five English identity conservatives feel that way about Eastern European migrants. Nearly half of Scottish white school leavers think their country is short-changed by the UK government, but more than two-thirds of their English counterparts see little benefit from EU membership. While suspicion of outsiders frames ethnocentric views of both political unions, the EU attracts a lot more suspicion in England than the UK does in Scotland.

Political unions involve dual identities – attachments both to the member nation and the broader union. Separatist nationalism acts as a centrifugal force, pulling the constituent nation away from the union. Bonds of attachment to the larger unit act as a centripetal force which counteracts this. Here, also, Scotland's relationship to Britain differs crucially from England's (and Britain's) relationship to Europe. The English loom large in Scotland as a politically and culturally dominant rival, and efforts to distinguish Scotland from England have long played an important role in Scottish nationalism. Yet counterbalancing this is a centuries-long political union, with generations of close cultural and economic integration, and many prominent political defenders, most notably the long-dominant Scottish Labour Party. Britain's membership of the EU is much more recent: many older British voters in the 2016 EU Referendum grew up before Britain's EEC membership began in 1973. And though the British economy is now closely integrated with Europe, there has been much less integration at the cultural and political level – the EU is still widely seen as an alien institution, and its everyday politics are rarely reported, save to ridicule its processes and

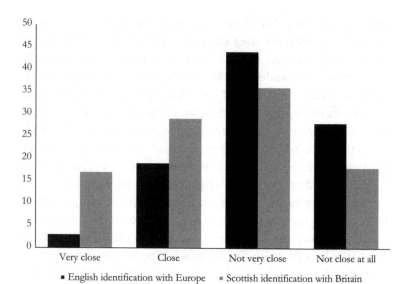

Figure 9.2 English identification with Europe and Scottish identification with Britain (percentages)

Sources: British Social Attitudes, 2013; Scottish Social Attitudes, 2011. The questions used are not identical and so were recoded to enable comparison. The English were asked to rate 'How close do you feel to Europe?' on a four-point scale. The Scots were asked 'How British do you feel' and given a seven-category scale to which to respond. We have recoded the scale to enable comparison (1–2 = 'not close at all'; 3–4 = 'not very close'; 5–6 = 'close'; 7 = 'very close').[8]

regulations.[9] There have never been many strongly Europhile voices in British politics or the media, so the case for a common European cultural or political identity is rarely heard in British public life.[10]

The different levels of positive identification with the two unions are illustrated in Figure 9.2. Nearly half of residents of Scotland felt either very close or close to Britain, but only a fifth

[8] The overall pattern identified here is robust to other coding choices, and other measures of both concepts confirm that Scottish identification with Britain is stronger and more widespread than English identification with Europe (see Carl, Dennison and Evans (2018) for more discussion of the latter).

[9] Forster (2002); Daddow (2012).   [10] Copeland and Copsey (2017).

of the English felt a similar degree of closeness to Europe. At the other end of the scale, around a quarter of the English said they were 'not close at all' to Europe, but only about a sixth of Scots felt similarly about Britain. The ties of common identity bind the Scottish to Britain much more than they bind the English to Europe. The strength of Scottish attachment to a broader British identity is also clear in 'Moreno' survey questions[11] which ask Scots to express the relative strength of their dual Scottish and British identities. Around one in three reject British identity outright, declaring themselves 'Scottish not British'. The rest split between a third who say they are 'more Scottish than British', meaning their Scottish identity is primary, but they still feel an attachment to Britain, and another third who rate British identity as equally or more important to them than Scottish identity.[12] A substantial majority of Scots thus express some attachment to Britain, bonds of common identity which posed an obstacle to the Scottish independence campaign.

The generational distribution of union attachments, illustrated in Figure 9.3, posed a further problem for Scottish independence campaigners, while offering an opportunity to Brexiteers. Strong identification with Britain is more common among older Scots, in particular identity conservative older Scots. Those growing up in the immediate post-Second World War era were socialised into a stronger and more unified overarching British identity, while younger generations growing up in the more polarised recent political context were socialised into a more oppositional Scottish identity. By contrast, strong European identity, indicated here by respondents volunteering 'European' as one of their main identities, is more common among younger English voters and is particularly weak among

---

[11] Named after a Spanish researcher who developed this question to examine the levels of identification with so-called 'stateless nations' like Scotland and Catalonia (Moreno 2006).

[12] Details of these results are provided in the Online Appendix (www.cambridge.org/Brexitland). See also Sobolewska and Ford (2018); Curtice, Devine and Ormston (2013). Unfortunately, similar 'Moreno' questions are not available for European and British identity.

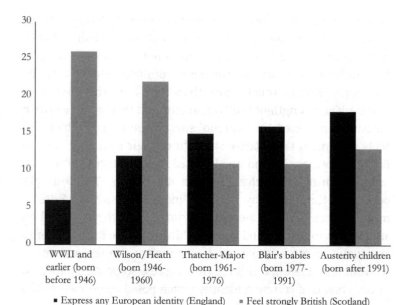

Figure 9.3 Generational distribution of volunteered European identity in England and strong British identity in Scotland (percentages)

Sources: British Social Attitudes, 2013; Scottish Social Attitudes, 2011.

the post-Second World War cohort who came of age before Britain joined the EU. These generational differences weigh heavily in referendums because of the strong generational gradient in turnout – older voters turn out more than younger ones, so the attachments of the old are magnified in the voting electorate, while the attachments of the young are diluted.

The two forms of separatism also differ in their connections to other political values. The political dominance of England in the UK system, and the absence of devolved political democratic institutions in Scotland before 1999, has reinforced the belief, already a mainstay of SNP campaigning for many years,[13] that

---

[13] The SNP had adopted left of centre economic policy positions and been seen as a left of centre party by Scottish voters, since at least the 1980s. See Lynch (2009); Paterson (2006).

English voters and politicians were imposing right-wing economic policies on Scotland against the will of Scottish voters.
The repetition of this argument by both of the dominant political parties in Scotland – Labour and the SNP – has encouraged
Scots to believe that they are more left wing than the English,
although in fact this is much exaggerated.[14] This narrative has
helped to link together left-wing economic ideology with Scottish nationalism in the minds of Scottish voters. Scots who
prioritise Scottishness over Britishness express more left-wing
views than Scots with a stronger British identity.[15] This link is
reinforced in both directions. If left-wing Scottish voters perceive
right-wing economic policy as imposed by English-dominated
governments, this encourages them to adopt a stronger, more
exclusive Scottish identity. And if Scottish nationalist politicians
argue left-wing economic values are what set Scots apart from the
English, then this encourages nationalist voters to adopt progressive economics as a badge of Scottish identity. Both routes bring
Scots to the same destination – a coalescence of nationalism and
left-wing economic values not found in England.

The links between economic ideology and Euroscepticism are
more complicated, reflecting the more confused signals sent by
the political system. Exit from the EU was initially more popular
among the most economically left-wing English voters, the
legacy of debates over Europe in the 1970s and 1980s, when
many of the most prominent Eurosceptics were radical left-wing
politicians such as Tony Benn, who attacked the EU as inherently hostile to radical left-wing economic policy, while free
market right-wing politicians defended the EU as offering opportunities for free trade and economic integration. This changed in
the 1990s and 2000s when the most prominent critics of Europe
were Conservative politicians and media figures otherwise
broadly on the free market right, while the centre-left Labour

---

[14] Henderson (2014; 2007); Curtice and Ormston (2011), though see Pattie and
Johnston (2017) for a partial defence of Scottish distinctiveness.
[15] Analysis of this link can be found in the Online Appendix: www.cambridge
.org/Brexitland

Party became more consistently, though often rather quietly, pro-EU. Yet while the Conservative right did begin to portray EU regulations and institutions as an impediment to trade and growth, this framing was neither as prominent nor as successful as the linkages made in Scotland between economic policy and English Conservative governments. As a result, the links between economic ideology and support for the exit option were much weaker in England than in Scotland.

Mobilising support for the exit option

In Scotland, as in England, the mobilisation of identity politics into the party system began with a party campaigning to defend an in-group against threatening out-groups. But while this initial dynamic was similar, there were large differences between the SNP and UKIP strategies which influenced the form of this mobilisation, and its impact on the political system. The SNP were the main opposition party in Scotland from the outset of devolved Scottish Parliament elections in 1999 and sought to broaden their appeal by mobilising a range of political and economic resentments against the Scottish Labour government. The SNP sought to define themselves as more effective defenders of Scottish interests than a Labour party they claimed focused on England. This framing proved to be very effective, enabling the SNP to mobilise anti-Westminster resentments from both ethnocentric Scottish nationalists and more radical voters unhappy with New Labour's moderation. Attachments to Scottish identity, desires for stronger Scottish political institutions, and resentments against unfair treatment by Westminster were all strong predictors of SNP support in 2007,[16] and when combined with the party's successful efforts to portray

[16] Brand, Mitchell and Surridge (1994) also show that they were in 1992, although in the 1990s these feelings were also equally strong predictors of Labour support, thus making a powerful point that the reputation gained from devolved Scottish politics has helped the party to 'own' this issue more effectively in the 2000s.

themselves as a credible alternative government were sufficient to propel the SNP to a narrow election victory.[17] This was very different to the situation in England, where similar discontents were mobilised by a radical right party which lacked credibility as a competitor for government, and had no devolved institutions where it could compete for English power. UKIP therefore focused on an outsider strategy, polarising voters and seeking to put pressure on the governing parties.

Scottish Liberal Democrat support collapsed during the Coalition government in Scotland much as it did in England (see Chapter 7), and growing disaffection with the governing Conservative Party was evident among identity conservative voters in both contexts. But the distinctive Scottish party system drove these shifts in public sentiments in a different direction after 2010. The Conservatives were already very weak in Scotland – they collapsed in 1997, losing all their Scottish Westminster seats, and flat-lined in subsequent elections. The Scottish Conservatives were similarly marginal in devolved elections, coming a distant third in the first three Scottish Parliament polls, just ahead of the Liberal Democrats. The primary political competition in Scotland was the battle between Labour and the SNP for control of the Scottish government, a competition the SNP now framed around the question of who could best defend Scottish interests from a hostile, English, Conservative-dominated Westminster government.

The SNP was well placed to win this battle, as it had already developed a potent political narrative fusing nationalist sentiment and populist distrust of the Westminster government with centre-left ideology and a reputation for strong and effective leadership. When the SNP Scottish government faced the judgement of voters in 2011,[18] it had three key advantages which

---

[17] Johns, Mitchell and Denver (2009); Hassan (2009).

[18] For an academic account of the 2011 election result, see Johns, Mitchell and Carmen (2013; 2014). For a broader account of the SNP's rise to power, see Johns and Mitchell (2016).

propelled it to a stunning majority victory.[19] First, the SNP could now appeal to a much larger pool of disaffected voters, in particular Scottish voters angry at the previous Westminster Labour government over the financial crisis, and Scottish Liberal Democrats alienated by their party's Westminster coalition with the Conservatives. Secondly, the SNP's argument that Scotland needed a strong defender of its national interest was more persuasive to Scottish voters with a Conservative-dominated, austerity-focused government in charge at Westminster. Thirdly, four successful and broadly popular years in charge of the Scottish government had made the SNP more credible generally as a party capable of delivering effective devolved rule.

The potency of 'English/Tory/Westminster' as an overlapping set of out-groups against which to mobilise, and the effectiveness of the SNP in framing themselves as the best defenders of Scottish interests, enabled the SNP to expand across the board, gathering together the disparate discontents of voters who in England scattered in several directions. The SNP won over a large chunk both of the collapsing Liberal Democrat vote and of the ethnocentric, economically left-wing and anti-Tory Scottish Labour vote.[20] Scotland's nationalist party was able to bring together a broad coalition encompassing both identity liberals and identity conservatives, all of whom found something to like in the idea of a Scottish government that stood up to English Conservatives. This electoral strategy of bridge-building and

---

[19] The victory was particularly stunning because the Scottish Parliament's mixed-member proportional system was supposed to make majority single party rule very hard to achieve given the traditional fragmentation of Scottish political preferences. This victory was also historic in the sense that it enabled the SNP to pursue a referendum on Scottish independence, something impossible before this due to a blocking majority of unionist legislators in the Scottish Parliament.

[20] Whereas, in England, economically left-wing but ethnocentric voters were typically focused on immigration and were most likely to switch from Labour to the Conservatives in 2010, and then from both traditional parties to UKIP in 2014–15 (see Chapter 6).

broad coalitions was repeated during the referendum campaign which followed.

The 2014 Independence 'Yes' campaign had some similarities with the 2016 Leave campaign – both sought exit from a larger political unit and, in both cases, the strongest initial support for exit came from ethnocentric voters.[21] But while the Leave campaign, as we saw in Chapter 8, pursued a polarising strategy that sought to maximise identity conservative mobilisation by fusing ethnocentric hostilities to the EU and to migrants and minorities, the Scottish independence 'Yes' campaign ran in the opposite direction, downplaying ethnocentric themes and seeking to attract identity liberals by portraying independence as a cause that would advance liberal and multicultural values in Scotland. The difference was reflected in the coalitions the two causes built and in the form of nationalism they mobilised. The Leave campaign polarised the electorate on identity lines, with messages which appealed strongly to identity conservative voters but alienated identity liberals. The independence referendum 'Yes' campaign mobilised support on both sides of the identity politics divide by offering something for everyone: appealing to Scottish identity conservatives by offering a means to free Scotland from English political control, and to identity liberals by pledging to use independence to build a more inclusive and multicultural Scottish society.

These different approaches were associated with different outcomes, as illustrated in Figure 9.4, which shows the levels of support for the exit option the year before and the year after the two referendums among the demographic groups on opposite sides of the identity politics divide – white school leavers and graduates plus ethnic minorities. Support for Scottish independence began higher among white school leavers (30 per cent) than among graduates and ethnic minorities (23 per cent), but

---

[21] Detailed analysis of the links between ethnocentrism and support for Scottish independence pre-2014 is provided in the Online Appendix (www.cambridge.org/Brexitland). Support for leaving the EU had long been strongest among ethnocentric identity conservative voters, as discussed in Chapter 8.

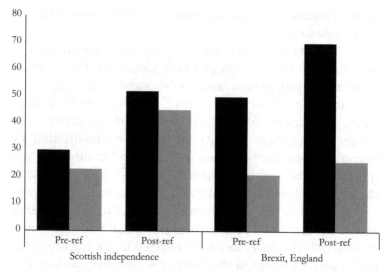

Figure 9.4 Support for exit options before and after the referendums among white school leavers and graduates/ethnic minorities (percentages)

Sources: Scottish Social Attitudes, 2013 and 2015; British Social Attitudes, 2015 and 2017.

support rose by similar amounts on both sides of the identity politics divide after the referendum campaign. Support for Brexit began much higher among English white school leavers (50 per cent) than among graduates and ethnic minorities (21 per cent), and the referendum campaign deepened this divide, winning many new recruits to the Brexit cause from the white school leaver group (support rose by twenty points) but virtually none among graduates and ethnic minorities (support rose five points). The 'Yes' campaign managed to persuade large numbers on both sides of the identity politics divide, while the 'Leave' campaign grew support by driving identity conservatives and identity liberals further apart.

It is a similar story when we look at ideological divides: the 'Yes' campaign built a broad tent, while the Leave campaign polarised. Figure 9.5 shows the increases in support for the

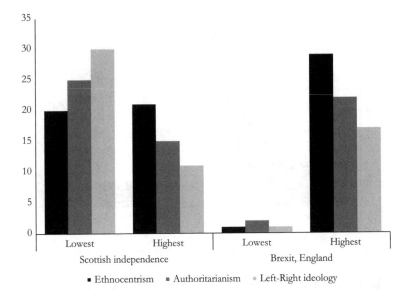

Figure 9.5 Change in support for the exit options before and after the Independence and EU referendums, by levels of ethnocentrism, authoritarianism and left–right ideology (percentages)

Sources: British Social Attitudes, 2015 and 2017; Scottish Social Attitudes, 2013 and 2015 (except authoritarianism 2011 and 2015).

exit options among those scoring in the lowest and highest quarter of the public on three ideological dimensions: ethnocentrism, authoritarianism and economic left–right ideology (where 'lowest' means most left wing and 'highest' most right wing).[22] When we look at the results for Scotland, on the left, two things are clear: support for independence grew more among those on the left-liberal side of all three ideological divides, but independence also became substantially more popular in the most ethnocentric–authoritarian–conservative parts of Scottish society. The story with Brexit in England is different in both regards: the substantial rise in support for leaving the EU comes entirely from ethnocentric–authoritarian–conservative

---

[22] Further details on the analysis summarised here are provided in the Online Appendix: www.cambridge.org/Brexitland

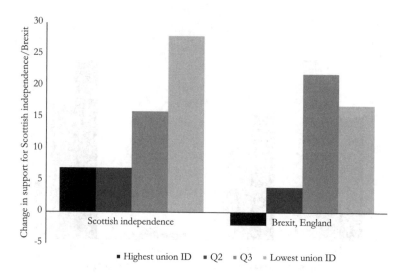

Figure 9.6 Change in support for exit option before and after referendum campaign by level of union identity

Sources: Scottish Social Attitudes, 2013 and 2015; British Social Attitudes, 2015 and 2017.

groups. Support barely rises at all among left-liberals, meaning the campaign for Brexit deepened divides in England along all three of these ideological dimensions.

While both referendums' exit campaigns succeeded in increasing support for separation, they could not alter the underlying patterns of voter attachment to the larger political unit. Expressions of British identity in Scotland, and European identity in England, were little different after the referendum than they were before.[23] And such bonds were consequential in both contexts, as we illustrate in Figure 9.6, which shows the increase in support for the exit option at different levels of identification with the larger union. Support for both exit options grew strongly among those who identified least with Britain and Europe – the light bars on the right. But both exit campaigns struggled to persuade voters who identified most

[23] Analysis on this point is presented in the Online Appendix: www.cambridge .org/Brexitland

with the larger union (dark bars on the left) – support for Scottish independence grew modestly among those who felt strongly British, while support for Brexit fell among English voters who identified most with Europe.

Why 'Yes' failed but 'Leave' succeeded

The Scottish Yes campaign sought a broad base of support for independence, bridging ideological and identity politics divides, while the campaign for Brexit polarised the electorate by seeking to maximise mobilisation of already sympathetic voters. Why did the narrow campaign succeed and the broad campaign fail? Three factors played a key role: union identities, turnout differentials and voter eligibility. Scottish voters' attachments to Britain proved too strong and widely shared for the independence campaign to overcome. Independence was overwhelmingly rejected by the many Scots who saw themselves as equally or more British than Scottish, and the 'Yes' campaign only won around half of those who said they were 'more Scottish than British'. Only the minority of Scots who rejected British identity altogether – the 'Scottish, not British' – voted decisively for independence, and they were not numerous enough to deliver a victory for the 'Yes' campaign.[24] The 'Leave' campaign, even though it was narrower and more polarising, won a similar majority among those who rejected European identity, but this was a much larger group.[25] While in Scotland, the question 'Scotland or Britain?' forced most Scots to choose between two attachments which mattered to them, such internal conflict was rarer when 'Leave' campaigners asked voters to choose between Britain and the EU. Exit referendums require decisively breaking with a larger unit, and weaker bonds are easier to break.

---

[24] Detailed analysis on this point is provided in the Online Appendix: www .cambridge.org/Brexitland

[25] Carl, Dennison and Evans (2018).

The importance of layered loyalties and dual identities is also underscored by the different roles played in the two referendums by those whose migrant or ethnic minority status gave them a unique perspective on these questions. Migrant voters, whose movement across borders generates complex, multiple identities, favoured the union side in both exit referendums. But though far more international migrants reside in England than in Scotland, the impact of migrant voters was greater in the Scottish referendum for two reasons. First, the two referendums did not apply the same voter eligibility criteria. The Scottish independence referendum gave a vote to all British, Irish, EU and Commonwealth citizens resident in Scotland, while not offering a vote to those born in Scotland but living elsewhere. This enfranchised a large migrant electorate who leant against independence while excluding the Scottish-born emigrant electorate, including Scottish-born British citizens resident elsewhere in the UK, who were potentially more pro-independence. The EU Referendum, by contrast, applied the same franchise used in UK general elections,[26] and therefore excluded several million EU citizens resident in Britain.[27] These disenfranchised British residents with the strongest bonds of identity to Europe and the strongest personal and group interest in British EU membership continuing.

Secondly, a group not normally thought of as migrants at all – those who had moved internally from one constituent nation of the UK to another – proved pivotal in the Scottish campaign. A large part of the Scottish population in 2014 – roughly one resident in ten – was born elsewhere in the UK, usually England.[28] These internal migrants had a much stronger sense of British and/or English identity, they seldom shared

[26] With some exceptions – residents of Gibraltar were able to vote, for example. Residents of Gibraltar were eligible to vote even though they do not participate in UK elections, because Gibraltar was also within the EU.

[27] British voters resident abroad but still registered or able to register in the UK were also eligible to vote, provided they had lived overseas for fewer than fifteen years.

[28] The 2011 Scottish Census recorded 514,000 Scottish residents born elsewhere in the UK, 9.7 per cent of the total population; 459,000 of these were born in England.

independence campaigners' concerns about English cultural influence or political dominance, and they were strongly opposed to independence.[29] While most sources suggest a narrow majority of Scots born in Scotland backed independence in 2014, this was offset by the large pro-union majorities among voters born elsewhere, in particular those who had come to Scotland from England.[30] The Scottish campaign to depart a political union dominated by England might have been successful if Scotland had proved less attractive to English internal migrants.

The different generational structure of British and European identity attachments also affected their influence on the outcome, magnifying the impact of British identity in the Scottish referendum, while diluting the impact of European identity in the EU Referendum. As we have seen, older generations of Scottish voters express a stronger sense of British identity, while the youngest Scots are most likely to reject British identity altogether. The pattern of European attachments runs in the opposite direction – weak or absent in the oldest generations, and strongest in the youngest. As we show in Figure 9.7, the generational breakdown of support for the exit option in Scotland was the mirror image of that in Brexit. Identity attachments were one big reason why. While it was young Scots who felt least attachment to Britain, and who were therefore most supportive of leaving it, in England it was the oldest who had the least attachment to the EU and were keenest on Brexit.

These generational differences were magnified by turnout differences, with older voters turning out at higher rates in both referendums. In Scotland, that skewed the electorate on polling day towards the status quo option, despite the exceptionally

---

[29] Support for independence before the referendum among those born in the rest of the UK in the Scottish Social Attitudes survey was, at 18 per cent, half the level expressed among those born in Scotland. Post-referendum differentials in support by UK country of birth cannot be ascertained in this survey as the question is no longer asked.

[30] The 2014 Scottish Referendum Study found 51 per cent of Scots born in Scotland voted 'Yes', but only 32 per cent of Scots born in England did so. Analysis of the aggregate results shows that the share of voters in the local authority who were born elsewhere in the UK was a strong predictor of the 'No' vote share in that authority (Ayres 2014).

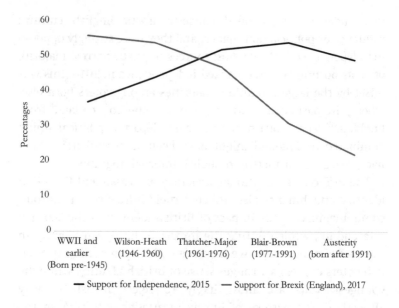

Figure 9.7 Generational distribution of support for the two exit options

Sources: Scottish Social Attitudes, 2015; British Social Attitudes, 2017.

high overall turnout. A post-referendum poll estimated turnout was 54 per cent among 18–24-year-olds, 72 per cent among 25–34-year-olds and a whopping 92 per cent among those aged over 55.[31] The traditional age gap in turnout also manifested in the Brexit Referendum, but in this case skewed the electorate towards the exit option favoured by older voters. Estimates from a large post-referendum poll by IPSOS-MORI found turnout of registered voters was around 64 per cent among 18–34-year-olds but 78 per cent for those aged over 55.[32]

---

[31] Curtice (2014).

[32] Skinner and Gottfried (2016). The differentials in turnout are even larger if we also take into account differences in voter registration – older voters are more likely to be on the register than younger ones.

Two stones thrown in the pond: the impact of two referendums in quick succession

The passionate and divisive campaigns fought in 2014 and 2016 both forged new political identities with the potential to disrupt party politics, and this disruption was also shaped by the different political contexts in which these referendum identities emerged. The 2015 general election came less than a year after the independence referendum, making 2015 a dramatically different contest in Scotland. The referendum dramatically increased the salience and popularity of Scottish independence. This was a boon to the SNP, who were closely identified with the cause. Newfound devotion to the independence campaign overrode many 'Yes' voters' traditional loyalties to the Scottish Labour Party, producing a massive wave of political change, as 'Yes' voters switched not just their votes but their partisan allegiance en masse from Labour to the SNP.[33] SNP support and partisanship rose by around twenty points among 'Yes' voters in the aftermath of the referendum, while Labour vote and identification fell by double digits.[34]

The independence campaign finally broke longstanding partisan bonds which had kept identity conservative, left-wing nationalist voters in the Scottish Labour camp.[35] Unionist voters, though a bigger group, were not affected by the referendum in the same way and continued to divide along traditional class, regional and religious lines between Labour, the Conservatives and the Liberal Democrats. This gave the SNP a major advantage under the ruthless logic of first-past-the-post, as a united independence vote triumphed over a larger but fractured pro-union vote nearly everywhere.[36] While the surge in support for independence in the 2014 referendum campaign was not enough to win a referendum with only two options on the ballot, it was

---

[33] Fieldhouse and Prosser (2018); Fieldhouse et al. (2019: ch. 8).
[34] Figures come from the British Election Study internet panel, comparing wave 1 (February 2014) with wave 6 (post-2015 election).
[35] Brand, Mitchell and Surridge (1994).   [36] Dennison (2015).

sufficient to deliver a landslide in a general election fought against divided opposition: the SNP won 95 per cent of Scotland's Westminster[37] seats with a shade under 50 per cent of Scottish votes.

However, this dominance proved to be transitory. Scottish voters did not just live in Scotland, they also lived in Brexitland. The EU Referendum following just a year after the SNP's landslide acted as a second massive stone thrown into Scottish political waters, disrupting the waves of change rippling out from the first stone. The 2017 general election brought further radical changes to Scotland, upending the political order just established in 2015, but also proceeding very differently to the EU Referendum aftermath elsewhere in the UK. In England and Wales, as we consider in more detail in Chapter 10, the ruling Conservatives adopted the polarising approach of the Leave campaign and pushed for an uncompromising 'hard Brexit'. This initially mobilised remain partisans behind the Labour opposition who, despite their own confused stance on Brexit, were seen as the only viable means of opposing a disruptive departure from the EU.[38] Then, in 2019, the Conservatives achieved at the second attempt what the SNP had managed in 2015 – winning a major election victory by unifying one side of the referendum divide more effectively than their opponents could unify the other.

In Scotland, the new divide introduced by Brexit initially drove a wedge into the broad coalition constructed by the SNP during and after the independence campaign. Many of the ethnocentric Scots who had backed independence in 2014 as a means to throw off English rule also backed Brexit in 2016 as a means to throw off European rule. The identity liberal Scots who

---

[37] The SNP's three failures were Orkney and Shetland, distant islands where a culturally very distinct electorate had longstanding Liberal Democrat loyalties; Dumfriesshire, Clydesdale and Tweedale, a large rural seat on the border with England with large concentrations of British-identifying pensioners and English-born voters, which narrowly remained Conservative; and Edinburgh South, a middle-class suburban seat where the SNP started in a distant fourth place but still ran the Labour incumbent close.

[38] Ford, Goodwin and Sobolewska (2017).

had backed independence as a route to a more tolerant and multicultural Scotland vehemently opposed Brexit as the vehicle of narrow, intolerant (and English) nationalism. The SNP was forced to choose a side in the Brexit fight, and by choosing to back a second referendum to keep Scotland in the EU,[39] they changed the meaning of the independence cause. Ethnocentric Scots opposed to rule by outsiders were now forced to choose which dragon they most wanted to slay – Westminster or Brussels. Many chose Brussels. Support for independence fell by double digits among the most ethnocentric and Eurosceptic Scottish voters in the aftermath of the EU Referendum, while holding steady among the most identity liberal and pro-EU voters.[40] After Brexit, the independence 'big tent' could no longer hold together. The SNP, whose own political elite and activist base was strongly pro-EU, may have underestimated how much support they were receiving from voters who disliked Brussels' rule as much as they resented Westminster's.

The Scottish electorate in 2017 was split by two referendums into four groups. Two of these groups had a clear party representative. The SNP's position of 'Yes and Remain' – an independent Scotland within the EU – was shared by 31 per cent of the electorate, a large group but well below the nearly 50 per cent of voters the SNP had won in 2015. In the opposite corner was 'No and Leave' – keeping Scotland in the UK as it departed the EU – a stance held by 20 per cent of Scottish voters. This was the clear position of the post-Brexit Scottish Conservative Party, who were Unionist and pro-Brexit. The other two positions did not align

[39] SNP leader Nicola Sturgeon made it clear in the days after the EU Referendum result that Scotland's vote for Remain, married with the UK vote for Leave, made a second independence referendum highly likely. She first officially called for a second referendum on Scottish independence in March 2017, initially saying this should be held between autumn 2018 and spring 2019. A second referendum has not happened at the time of writing (spring 2020), but the SNP leadership has reiterated its continued desire to hold one, with Sturgeon stating in April 2019 her desire to see one held before the end of the current Scottish Parliament term in 2021.

[40] Details of this analysis are provided in the Online Appendix: www.cambridge .org/Brexitland

clearly with existing party stances, and thus had no clear political outlet. Those holding the strongly ethnocentric 'Yes, Leave' position (15 per cent of the total), wanted Scotland free from rule by outsiders in both Westminster and Brussels. This put them at odds with the Holyrood SNP government over Brexit and with the Westminster Conservative government over Scottish independence. Such voters had to decide which of the two exit projects they saw as a priority. Meanwhile, 'No, Remain' voters – the largest group in the Scottish electorate with 34 per cent of voters, were also at odds with both governing parties, because they were committed to the status quo on both constitutional questions, while both the Scottish government and the British government were committed to change, as was the internally divided but officially Brexit-accepting Labour Party.[41]

The two main shifts in Scottish voting choices between 2015 and 2017 were a sharp decline in support for the SNP and a sharp rise in support for the Conservatives.[42] Figure 9.8 breaks down these shifts by our four Scottish voting tribes. The SNP lost ground across the board, also reflecting growing disaffection with a party that had governed Scotland for a decade. But their decline was steepest among 'Yes, Leave' voters, suggesting the SNP's pro-EU stance alienated such voters despite their support for independence. The Conservatives made some progress in all groups, but their gains were much stronger among 'Leave' voters, and they surged among the 'No, Leave' voters who shared both of the party's constitutional positions, rising nearly forty points from 30 per cent to 68 per cent.

The surge in support for the Scottish Conservatives meant two clear packages of constitutional choice were available to Scots after 2016–17: the SNP were the main party for supporters of independence, but packaged this with support for EU membership; the Conservatives were now the strongest unionist party,

---

[41] 'No and Remain' was, however, consistent with the position of the Scottish Liberal Democrats.

[42] Labour continued to flounder, recovering only a few percentage points after its historic collapse in 2015.

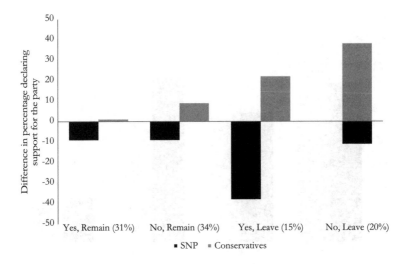

Figure 9.8 Change in support for the SNP and Conservatives 2015–17 by referendum choice combinations

Source: British Election Study internet panel, 2014–20.

but packaged this with support for Brexit. In 2017, a large part of the Scottish electorate did not support either of these packages. This began to change in 2019, as voters' views moved into alignment with the packages available. The share of voters who backed the SNP's package of 'independence and Remain' jumped between 2017 and 2019, rising from 32 per cent to 42 per cent of Scottish voters.[43] Support for the Conservatives' package of 'Union and Brexit' also rose slightly. Meanwhile, the share of Scots backing the combination of union and Remain, the most popular choice of Labour voters in 2017 and the Liberal Democrat stance in both elections, fell from 33 per cent to 24 per cent. The consistently ethnocentric minority package of 'independence and Brexit', which had no party backers, also fell slightly.

---

[43] These figures exclude 'don't knows', but the same strong rise in 'Yes, Remain' support is evident if 'don't knows' are left in.

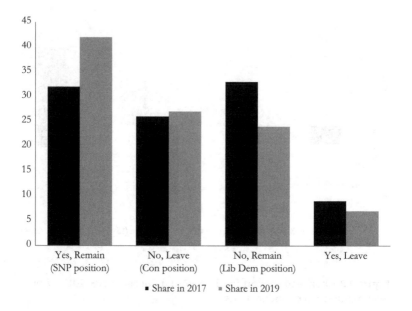

Figure 9.9 Combinations of independence and Brexit positions among voters in Scotland in 2017 and 2019 (percentages)

Source: British Election Study internet panel, 2014–19.

Initial results from the Scottish Election Study paint a similar picture: Scottish voters whose stances on independence and Brexit were at odds with their preferred party in 2017 tended to resolve this tension by bringing their Brexit stances into line with those of their preferred party (Figure 9.9).[44] They did so because, on the whole, more Scots saw the independence question as primary and the Brexit debate as secondary. As a result, the SNP went to the polls again in 2019 in a much stronger position than two years earlier – the share of the Scottish electorate who shared both of their constitutional preferences was now much larger. It was this growth in the support for the SNP's unique package of an independent Scotland within the EU which

---

[44] See Johns et al. (2020) for more analysis of this question.

accounts for the party's 2019 rebound.[45] The Conservatives were able to hold steady in 2019 even as support for both of their constitutional causes declined by strongly increasing their support among Scots who shared their package of referendum preferences. Scottish Labour faced the worst of both worlds. The best group of voters for the party in 2017 were unionist Remainers, but in 2019 this group was shrinking, and they were losing support to the more vocally pro-EU Liberal Democrats amongst those who were left. The Liberal Democrats' hope of reaping gains in the UK's most Remain-voting nation through an uncompromising pro-EU platform were also disappointed, as growing numbers of Remain-voting Scots now prioritised independence as the route back to the EU, and therefore backed the SNP instead.

The unprecedented volatility seen in Scotland over the past two elections may continue in future cycles. The meaning of Brexit partisan identities may change once Scotland departs the EU along with the rest of Britain. A costly and chaotic departure may further increase support for Remain and the alignment of pro-EU and pro-independence sentiments, as alienated Scottish voters seek a route back to the EU. Yet a relatively smooth Brexit transition could also further disrupt Scottish voters' alignments, as Brexit conflicts fade away and voters' attention returns to the unresolved independence argument. If the Conservative majority government at Westminster continues to reject demands for a second independence referendum, the SNP will seek to exploit this by reactivating their longstanding ethnocentric narrative, mobilising Scottish voters against a hostile English, Tory, Westminster government. If the Westminster Conservative government responds by mobilising English nationalist resentments against the Scots, it will place the Scottish Conservatives in an awkward position. They have

---

[45] The SNP support actually fell slightly from 87 per cent to 82 per cent amongst 'Yes, Remain' voters between 2017 and 2019, but this modest fall was more than offset by the large increase in the group's size. The SNP won a slightly smaller slice of a much larger cake.

prospered as the main voice of British unionism, but such a reputation will be hard to maintain if a more strident brand of English nationalism comes to the fore in the Westminster party. Meanwhile, Scottish Labour and Liberal Democrats will hope that growing alienation from the Conservative Westminster government, and perhaps growing disaffection with the SNP's endless campaign on independence, will enable them to recover their position as the standard-bearers of a more progressive unionism. Much will depend on how the allegiances of Scottish voters shift as the identity conflicts which now dominate their politics continue to play out.

Conclusion

At the end of our analysis of demographic trends in Chapter 2, we warned that despite its fundamental role in driving political change, demography is not destiny. Scotland provides a powerful illustration of this. Although it has been going through the same demographic changes as its southern neighbours, and although similar ethnocentric arguments have been mobilised into politics in both contexts, the resulting political outcomes have been very different. The latent potential for identity conflicts can build up in similar ways in different countries, but its political expression can and will diverge depending on their history and the choices made by their politicians. Ethnocentric sentiments in England were mobilised by a young upstart party, UKIP, using divisive arguments to grab attention and voters in a context where they had little chance of significant representation and influence. The same sentiments in Scotland were channelled into a longstanding tug of war between Scotland and England by a long-established nationalist party, the SNP, who had spent decades making and reinforcing their political arguments to build a large and loyal electoral base.

The SNP, as first the main opposition and then the main governing party of Scotland, had an incentive to build and defend broad electoral coalitions, and so sought to build a 'big tent' electoral coalition for its brand of identity politics, both in

Scottish elections and in the independence referendum. UKIP, as an attention-seeking radical outsider, had an incentive to build a narrow but intensely loyal coalition, and use this as a weapon to put pressure on the parties of government. The 'Leave' campaign followed the same blueprint. Yet, despite a much more inclusive and broader campaign, Scottish attachments to the institutions and identities they shared with the 'auld enemy' were too strong for the independence campaign to overcome. A narrower and more divisive referendum campaign succeeded where the contrasting campaign for Scottish independence had failed, in part because attachments to Europe in England were far weaker than the bonds to Britain felt by most Scots.

Comparing the Scottish and English experiences of identity politics highlights a number of key points where context, history and party strategies influenced the paths taken. In both countries there was a large identity conservative electorate whose ethnocentric sentiments were a dominant political motivation. But the party systems of the two neighbours channelled these sentiments into different causes and coalitions. In England, ethnocentric anxieties were focused on immigration and the EU, and were mobilised on the political right, first, by the Conservatives' pledge to control immigration, then by UKIP exploiting the backlash when the Conservative government failed to deliver. In Scotland, ethnocentric sentiments were mobilised by the political left, and were focused on overlapping national, institutional and political out-groups: England, Westminster and the Conservatives. The SNP, aspiring to build a broad governing coalition, sought to offer something for everyone. Their political narrative married together ethnocentric resentments of the English with centre-left economic ideology and promises of a liberal, multicultural Scotland freed from the shackles of English intolerance. Negative views of migrants and minorities were (and are) roughly as widely held in Scotland as in England and Wales, but they were ignored by the SNP, who directed ethnocentric voters' resentments towards London and the Tories. This proved to be just as effective with identity conservatives and enabled the party to mobilise them while also

keeping identity liberals on board. Nor was Euroscepticism pol-
itically mobilised in Scotland, though many ethnocentric Scots
shared their English peers' suspicion of Brussels, because the
SNP saw the EU as a counterweight to English dominance, and
Europhilia as another means to appeal to identity liberal voters.
Widespread hostility to the Conservatives and UKIP, seen by
Scottish voters as English nationalist parties, meant there was
little prospect of the SNP being outflanked by a xenophobic or
Eurosceptic insurgent, and enabled them to keep ethnocentric
voters focused on the 'standing up for Scotland against England'
narrative. The result was that the 'Yes' campaign increased
support for independence across the social and political spectrum, while the 'Leave' campaign consolidated and concentrated
support for Brexit among already sympathetic groups and
deepened the social and ideological divides between supporters
of the cause and opponents.

Yet this bridge-building strategy by the 'Yes' campaign faced
two major obstacles not encountered by Brexiteers. First, Scottish attachments to Britain were much stronger and more widespread than English attachments to Europe – a contrast that was
particularly stark among older voters. The grey vote in the
Scottish referendum broke heavily to the unionist cause; the
grey vote in England broke heavily for Brexit. In both cases,
older voters got their way, in part because they turned out in
higher numbers. Secondly, there was a large electorate in Scotland whose migration across borders – from England, Europe or
elsewhere – encouraged blurred identities and multiple loyalties. Such voters were less supportive of separatist campaigns
which force them to choose between their identities and voted
heavily against independence and Brexit. But in the Brexit campaign, the section of the population who felt such conflicting
loyalties most keenly – EU citizens resident in Britain – were
largely excluded by administrative fiat from the EU Referendum,
denied a vote regardless of the length of their residence in
Britain.

Both the independence and EU referendums forged new identities with the power to disrupt existing voting patterns. Yet

here, again, the impact of this disruptive new force was shaped by the context into which it was unleashed. In Scotland, the SNP were able to harness independence partisanship in the 2015 general election to rise to a position of unprecedented political dominance, because they monopolised one side of the binary independence debate, while the unionist side was politically fragmented. In England, as we shall see in Chapter 10, the Conservatives were similarly able to harness Brexit partisanship into a dominant political position, at the second time of asking, by unifying the 'Leave' side behind their vision of hard Brexit, while Remain voters were more fragmented. In Scotland, this initial 2015 re-alignment proved to be the first of three exceptionally volatile elections, as Scottish voters' preferences continued to shift in response to evolving dual debates over Scotland's membership of the UK and of the EU. The Scottish experience suggests that the volatility already seen in England since 2016 is unlikely to end with the 2019 Conservative general election victory. The aftershocks from constitutional earthquakes reverberate for many years.

10 BREXITLAND AFTER BREXIT: THE ELECTORAL FALLOUT FROM THE EU REFERENDUM

Introduction

Brexit dramatically intensified the mobilisation of identity conflicts. In the first two general elections held since the shock 'Leave' win, identity divides have reshaped party competition in England and Wales. As a result, these two general elections have been among the most volatile in British political history, delivering the largest campaign swings ever recorded in 2017, then in 2019 delivering the first substantial Conservative majority for over thirty years. We first examine how identity politics conflicts drove these volatile shifts. Then, we show how the intensification of these conflicts after Brexit has laid bare the long-running tensions in both governing parties over how to adapt to demographic change. Finally, we consider some possible scenarios for the future evolution of identity conflicts after Brexit, as the parties continue to wrestle with these dilemmas.

The deepening of identity politics divides since the EU referendum has posed problems for both parties. Many Conservatives now believe that Boris Johnson's 2019 triumph demonstrates that a hard-line, nationalist, anti-immigration and Eurosceptic approach is an election winner, and regard Theresa May's failure in 2017 as the one-off product of an incompetent leader bungling a sound strategy. This account risks neglecting the structural problems thrown up by the alienation of identity liberal Remain voters, who swung away from the Conservatives in 2017, costing the party its majority, and did not return in 2019. The costs of this alienation were mitigated in 2019 by widespread dislike of Jeremy Corbyn and the fragmentation of 'Remain' votes in 2019 between Labour, the Liberal Democrats and others. Such factors may not be present at future elections. The ongoing demographic transformation of the electorate will pose mounting problems for a Conservative Party now more allied than ever with a declining identity conservative electorate, and at odds with the fast growing identity liberal groups.

Labour interpreted their 2017 surge as a vindication of Jeremy Corbyn's strategy of radicalism and Brexit ambiguity. This strategy proved costly in 2019, when the cumulative decline of Labour support washed away once mighty Labour majorities in the former mining and industrial towns of England. The fall of this 'red wall' leaves Labour facing a huge electoral task if it is to return to power, yet renewing the party's appeal to the more identity conservative people and places Labour lost in 2019 will be difficult. Labour is now more closely aligned with identity liberal voters and values than ever before. The party's electoral heartland has over the 2010s shifted to the big, ethnically diverse English cities where identity liberal voters congregate, and the party membership, that has a powerful influence on policy, is overwhelmingly dominated by identity liberals.[1] Yet while the identity liberal electorate is large enough to dominate Labour's losing electoral coalition in 2019, it remains at present too small, and too geographically concentrated, to deliver election victories for the party in the near future.

Identity politics will pose problems for both parties in elections to come, as they wrestle with the demographic changes which continue to transform the electorate and with the new Brexit partisan identities which have given political force to

---

[1] For more on the views of Labour Party members, see Bale, Webb and Pelotti (2019).

these divides since 2016. Both parties have been split internally
by Brexit and identity conflicts, and both face potential competition from insurgents mobilising the poles of the identity politics
spectrum. Conservative strategists worry that the forces of
radical right nationalism unleashed by immigration and Brexit
could once again be mobilised against their party unless they are
appeased. Yet aligning with such forces carries its own long-
term risks. The identity conservatives won over by the promise
to 'get Brexit done' and impose controls on immigration are
distrustful and hard to please, and have little partisan attachment to the Conservatives. Yet focusing too heavily on this
group's priorities risks further alienating the rapidly growing
identity liberal electorate. Meanwhile, Labour face an intense
pressure to renew their appeal to 'Leave'-voting people and
places following the party's worst defeat in terms of seats won
since 1935, yet doing so risks angering the 'Remain'-voting identity liberals who now dominate the party's electorate and membership. With partisan attachments continuing their relentless
decline, and political volatility at an all-time high, the greatest
fear of all is political extinction. If either party proves unable to
accommodate new conflicts, it risks being destroyed by them,
like the Liberal Party in the 1920s or Scottish Labour in the
2010s. The identity conflicts of Brexitland, which have already
transformed both traditional parties, could yet end one or both
as parties of government.

A Brexit re-alignment? Identity conflicts in the 2017 and 2019 elections

The EU Referendum was the first time the electorate split primarily on identity politics lines, creating electoral dilemmas for
both parties. Each now had a dominant Brexit faction – 'Leave'
for the Conservatives, 'Remain' for Labour – but also a large
Brexit minority. Each had a hard choice to make: should they
embrace the cause of their majority Brexit faction, offering a
clear stance on the dominant issue of the day but at the risk of
alienating their minority faction? Or should they seek to keep

both sides on board with a compromise offer? The two parties came to opposite conclusions. The Conservatives embraced the 'Leave' cause of their majority faction, while Labour sought to bridge the Brexit divide with compromise offers. Both parties increased support in 2017, but Labour's gains were larger, suggesting the party's bridging strategy was more effective. The Leave voters attracted by the Conservatives' promise of an uncompromising hard Brexit strategy were enough to return the party to government, but the loss of alienated Remainers cost the Conservatives their Commons majority.

Yet the 2017 result flattered to deceive, with Labour's overall advance masking a hollowing out of support in formerly rock-solid Leave-voting seats with large concentrations of identity conservatives. After two years of mounting public frustration at Brexit deadlock, Labour's compromise stance could no longer hold together polarised voters. The party's support fell back on both sides of the Brexit divide in 2019, as ardent Remainers became as frustrated with the party's equivocation as ardent Leavers. Labour's seat losses in 2019 were concentrated in what became known as the 'red wall' – a swathe of former Labour heartland seats with large concentrations of identity conservative voters and very high 'Leave' votes. The Conservatives' strategy worked at the second time of asking – Boris Johnson secured a large Commons majority by rallying Leave supporters behind the promise to 'get Brexit done'. The Conservatives, like the SNP in 2015, were able to win a big first-past-the-post victory by consolidating support on one side of a referendum divide behind a clear pledge of change. Yet this victory has changed the balance of power in the Conservative electoral coalition, posing new problems for the party in elections to come.

The choices made by both parties reflected the different constraints they faced. To govern is to choose, and an ambiguous stance on Brexit was not sustainable for the governing Conservative Party, who had to negotiate a Brexit deal with the EU, and then pass legislation to implement it. Yet by the same token, the Conservatives had much greater influence over which Brexit options were on the political agenda than Labour, who had to react to the legislative and negotiating choices made by the government. The convoluted and divisive Brexit negotiations have been recounted at length elsewhere[2] and need not detain us. The key point is this: faced with a spectrum of possible Brexit outcomes, Theresa May's government focused on the 'harder' forms of Brexit which were most acceptable to identity conservatives,[3] delivering maximal national sovereignty and control of immigration.[4] May ignored 'softer' forms of Brexit outcome more acceptable to identity liberals, which would have maintained closer economic integration with Europe, shared more sovereignty and kept more open migration policies. The political logic of this was clear. The Conservatives had lost a swathe of identity conservative voters to UKIP in 2015, and those same voters had overwhelmingly backed Brexit the following year. A Brexit that delivered on these voters' priorities – sovereignty and control of immigration – could be used to win them back while also bringing over Labour 'Leave' supporters who thought along similar lines.

While the Conservative government polarised the Brexit divide, the Labour Party sought to bridge it. Labour held many of the seats with the highest 'Leave' votes in the country, in particular a swathe of former industrial and mining communities in the Midlands and north of England. Many of the MPs representing these areas regarded it as essential that Labour respect the popular mandate for Brexit. Jeremy Corbyn and his leadership team were sympathetic to this argument, as many were themselves either longstanding Eurosceptics,[5] or were

---

[2] See, for example, Shipman (2017; 2018); O'Rourke (2018); Evans and Menon (2017).

[3] Hobolt (2016); Goodwin and Milazzo (2017); Clarke, Goodwin and Whiteley (2017).

[4] In May's own words this was framed as 'taking back control of our laws, our borders and our money' (May 2018).

[5] Reflecting an older divide in the Labour Party dating back to the 1970s and 1980s, in which radical left-wingers allied with Tony Benn, such as a young Jeremy Corbyn, opposed the EEC as a capitalist club whose rules would prevent the development of radical socialism.

convinced by the argument that the 2016 result had to be respected. Yet Labour MPs also represented most of the seats with the largest 'Remain' majorities in England and Wales, and politicians from these seats were adamant that Brexit was a mistake. Many became supporters of a second referendum on EU membership in the 2017–19 Parliament, with some so committed to this approach that they also opposed efforts to develop a cross-party 'soft' Brexit compromise. Corbyn's strategy for resolving these internal tensions was to embrace the mildly pro-Brexit position of the median voter, even at the risk of antagonising strong 'Remain' supporters who by 2017 were providing a majority of Labour's votes. It was a move reminiscent of one made by an earlier Labour leader. In 1997, Tony Blair gambled that he could move his party to the right on economic issues while retaining the loyalties of working-class left wingers with nowhere else to go. After the EU Referendum, Corbyn moved his party to a Brexit-accepting position designed to retain 'Leave' voters, gambling that 'Remain' voters, alarmed by May's rhetoric and hard Brexit policy, would recognise Labour as the only viable alternative. This 'Brexit Blairism'[6] was designed to blunt the Conservatives' appeal in 'Leave' seats, while also allowing Labour to capitalise on alarm about May's hard Brexit proposals in 'Remain' areas.

The first general election verdict on the parties' Brexit strategies presented a paradox: both parties posted impressive gains in support, yet neither really won. Both therefore received a mixed signal about their strategies for dealing with the Brexit dilemma. The Conservatives achieved their biggest increase in vote share since 1983, and their biggest total vote share since 1979. Yet Theresa May failed to meet the expectations raised by her snap election decision, and instead of an enhanced Parliamentary majority, she was left with no majority at all. Labour secured their biggest increase in vote share since 1945, and their

[6] Ford, Goodwin and Sobolewska (2017).

biggest total vote share since the second Blair landslide of 2001, yet remained in opposition. Jeremy Corbyn won just four more seats in 2017 than Gordon Brown had managed seven years earlier.[7] The very different world of Scottish politics was crucial in tipping the overall balance – Labour's failure in Scotland is a key reason why its 2017 recovery in votes did not translate into greater seat numbers, while the resurgence of the Scottish Conservatives furnished the seats Theresa May needed to secure a majority for her government with outside support from the Northern Irish Democratic Unionist Party.

Figure 10.1 illustrates why the Conservatives fell short in 2017, and why Labour were able to gain from their fuzzy 'Brexit Blairism'. The Conservatives made large gains among Leave voters, increasing their share by more than fifteen percentage points, but these gains were offset by a five-point loss among Remainers. This effect was even stronger among voters with a strong Brexit partisan identity.[8] Labour, by contrast, managed to increase their support on both sides of the Brexit divide in 2017, posting a double-digit gain amongst Remainers while also making a modest advance among Brexiteers. Labour's performance among Leave voters was critical to the overall election result, enabling Labour incumbents in many Leave-voting areas to cling on even as the local Conservative vote surged. Conversely, the Conservatives' embrace of a hard Brexit came back to haunt them in strongly Remain seats, as their vote collapsed and Labour's surged, leading to shock defeats in places such as Kensington and Canterbury that were considered safe for the party.

Both main parties were able to advance simultaneously in 2017 thanks to a collapse in the vote for smaller parties. UKIP lost more than four-fifths of their support, falling from 3.9

---

[7] Labour won 262 seats in 2017 under Corbyn with 40 per cent of the vote. They had won 258 under Brown from 29 per cent of the vote.

[8] The effect on Brexit identity strength was weaker for Labour, thus confirming that Brexit was more strongly related to Conservative voting. Details in the Online Appendix: www.cambridge.org/Brexitland

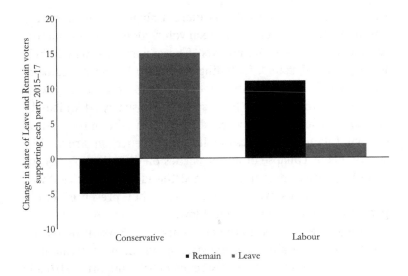

Figure 10.1 Changes in Conservative and Labour support, 2015–17 in England and Wales among 'Remain' and 'Leave' voters

Source: British Election Study internet panel, 2014–19.

million votes in 2015 to under 600,000 in 2017, while the Greens lost more than half of their support, falling from a record 1.1 million in 2015 to just over 500,000. The SNP also fell back substantially, as we saw in Chapter 9, and Liberal Democrat support also declined again in 2017. The consolidation of support from smaller parties took the combined Conservative and Labour share of the vote in 2017 to its highest level since 1970. More than half of 2015 UKIP voters, overwhelmingly Brexit-backing identity conservatives, switched directly to the Conservative Party.[9] Yet the Labour Party was also able to consolidate

---

[9] Data from the British Election Study internet panel. Theresa May's Conservatives won over half of the 2015 UKIP voters who had previously voted Labour or Liberal Democrat in 2010, and did even better with 2010 Conservatives who had switched to UKIP: over 70 per cent of the 2010 Conservative voters who had defected to UKIP in 2015 returned to their former party in 2017.

the Remain electorate with its more ambiguous Brexit stance, winning over six in ten 2015 Green voters along with substantial numbers of Liberal Democrats. These were overwhelmingly identity liberal voters, including many 2010 Liberal Democrat voters who had backed the Greens in 2015 because they were alienated by the Coalition but also unimpressed by Ed Miliband's Labour.[10] These voters were attracted by the more radical Corbyn Labour Party, despite its ambivalence on Brexit. The simultaneous collapse of minor parties on opposite poles of the identity politics spectrum deepened the identity politics divide between the Conservatives and Labour, but prevented either party from landing a knockout blow.

Both parties reacted to the ambiguous 2017 result by recommitting to essentially the same strategy in the next Parliament. Theresa May's government now relied on the support of strongly Eurosceptic backbenchers and MPs from the Democratic Unionist Party for its majority, steering May even more towards an uncompromising 'hard Brexit', or even a 'no deal Brexit', with Britain leaving the EU without an agreement in place when the legally mandated negotiating deadline arrived.[11] After May

---

[10] More than half of the voters who switched from the Liberal Democrats in 2010 to the Greens in 2015 backed Jeremy Corbyn's Labour in 2017.

[11] Article 50 of the 2009 Lisbon Treaty is the legal mechanism by which a member state can depart from the EU. Once triggered, it provides two years to negotiate the terms of exit, though this deadline can be extended by mutual consent. Hence, once Theresa May triggered Article 50 in March 2017, she set up a deadline for Brexit negotiations in March 2019. Failure to agree the terms of exit by this point, or ask for extra time, could lead to a very economically disruptive 'no deal' Brexit. May agreed terms with the EU, but failed repeatedly to have her Withdrawal Agreement ratified by the House of Commons, and so asked for the Article 50 deadline to be extended, eventually pushing it back to October 2019. Her successor, Boris Johnson, negotiated a new Withdrawal Agreement, but failed also to fully ratify this before the new deadline, and was forced by Parliament to ask for a new extension. After the extension was agreed, Johnson succeeded in calling a new general election, fought on the slogan 'get Brexit done'. When he was returned with a large Parliamentary majority, he was able to fully ratify his Withdrawal Agreement, meaning Britain formally left the EU on 31 January 2020. However, both parties agreed a 'transition period' during which new trading and regulatory arrangements would be agreed, and which can also be extended. At the time

failed three times to secure a Commons majority for her deal, Boris Johnson campaigned for and won the Conservative leadership by promising an even more combative and uncompromising approach. Both 'Remain' and 'Leave' voices in the Labour Party were emboldened by the 2017 result. The large swings to Labour among Remain voters encouraged pro-EU Labour activists and MPs to advocate a second referendum, with the aim of reversing Brexit altogether. Yet many Labour MPs from Leave-voting areas had clung on despite large local swings to the Conservatives, and they were equally adamant that Labour needed to accept the referendum result and implement some form of Brexit. Corbyn and his Shadow Cabinet team once again sought to bridge this divide, which ran through every level of Labour politics, with an ambiguous policy, favouring a vaguely defined 'Labour Brexit deal' while also seeking to leave open the option of a second referendum.

The two parties thus went into the 2019 election with broadly the same stances as in the 2017 election. The Conservatives sought a strong mandate to deliver a Brexit deal focused on the priorities of identity conservative voters: national sovereignty and immigration control. Labour sought to placate both sides: promising 'Leave' voters that they would negotiate a better Brexit deal, and 'Remain' voters that any such deal would be subject to another referendum. Yet the context of 2019 was very different to 2017. May sought a mandate to negotiate; Johnson sought one to 'get Brexit done', by implementing a deal already agreed with the EU and which a majority of MPs had already backed.[12] In 2017, the Brexit process was young enough that both sides could find something to like in Corbyn's ambiguity:

of writing (May 2020) this transition period is due to expire on 1 January 2021, at which point new rules will govern UK–EU relations.

[12] Johnson secured a Commons majority for his deal at its 'second reading', a crucial Parliamentary hurdle never cleared by Theresa May. However, MPs then rejected his accelerated schedule for debating the detail of the Bill, put to them in a 'timetabling motion'. Johnson was unwilling to accept a longer process of debate and amendment, and therefore pressed for, and eventually secured, an early election.

Leavers could see him as a vehicle for a better Brexit deal, while Remainers could argue a strong Labour vote was the only way to soften Brexit or stop the process altogether. In 2019, with a deal agreed with the EU but stalled in Parliament, such ambiguity was no longer credible. Pressure from Remain activists and MPs alarmed at an imminent Brexit forced Labour to commit to a second referendum, yet holding a second public vote on Brexit was anathema to Leave supporters, frustrated by repeated delays to the process, and convinced that a second referendum would prevent Brexit happening at all.

The cumulative effect of the two elections, as Figure 10.2 illustrates, was to dramatically increase the alignment of the Conservative and Leave causes. Theresa May's embrace of a hard Brexit in 2017 won over many Leave voters, while costing the Conservatives support among Remainers. Boris Johnson's

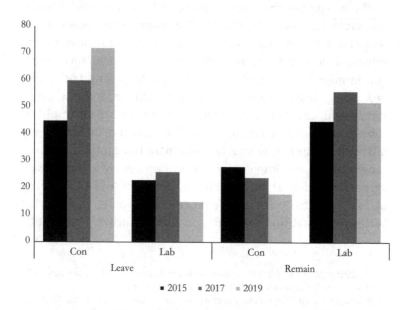

Figure 10.2 Conservative and Labour support among Leave and Remain voters, 2015–19 (percentages)

Source: British Election Study internet panel, 2014–19.

campaign to 'get Brexit done' pushed the same process further: Conservative support increased again among Leave voters, while falling again among Remain voters. Conservative support among Leave voters rose twenty-seven points from 45 per cent in 2015 to 72 per cent in 2019, while support among Remainers fell eleven points from 29 per cent to 18 per cent. In both 2017 and 2019, the gains the Conservatives made among Brexiteers more than offset Remain losses, enabling the party to keep increasing its overall support. The cumulative gains this produced tipped the balance in 2019 in many seats where the party fell short in 2017, and were thus one reason the Conservatives won a large Commons majority in 2019 with the same strategy that had fallen short just two years earlier.

Another decisive factor in 2019 was the reversal of Labour's fortunes. Corbyn's ambiguous 'Brexit Blairism', which had delivered gains on both sides of the Brexit divide in 2017, now saw the party decline amongst both Leave and Remain voters in 2019. Labour support dropped by four points from 56 per cent to 52 per cent among Remainers between 2017 and 2019, leaving the Remain vote far less consolidated behind Corbyn than the Leave vote was behind Johnson. Labour lost even more ground among Leave voters, dropping from 26 per cent to 18 per cent. Leave voters offered an immediate Brexit resolution by the Conservatives no longer saw much attraction in Labour's promise of further delay and another referendum, while Remain voters alienated by Labour's long resistance to holding a second public vote were no longer willing to back the party over more clearly pro-EU alternatives such as the Liberal Democrats or the SNP. In 2017, the Conservatives' Leave gains were blunted by an overall rise in Labour support across the board. In 2019, the opposite dynamic kicked in, with the impact of further Tory Leave consolidation magnified by an across-the-board Labour decline in support.

Both post-Brexit elections featured record levels of direct switching between Labour and the Conservatives, highlighting how Brexit has catalysed a re-alignment of politics around identity divides. This is evident in demographic predictors of

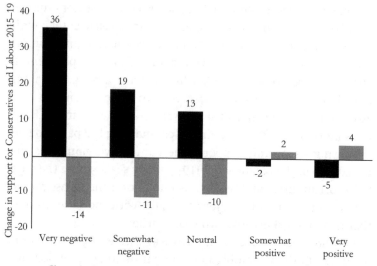

Figure 10.3 Changes in support for the Conservatives and Labour, 2015–19, by views about the cultural impact of immigration

Source: British Election Study internet panel, 2014–19.

switching, with white school leavers and older voters most likely to switch directly from the Conservatives to Labour in both elections, while university graduates and the young were more likely to switch in the opposite direction. The patterns are even clearer when we look at identity politics values and attitudes. Authoritarianism, English nationalism, views of equal opportunities and, particularly, views of immigration all strongly predict rates of switching between Labour and the Conservatives in both 2017 and 2019.[13] This is illustrated in Figure 10.3, which shows the cumulative change in support for Labour and the Conservatives between 2015 and 2019 by voters' views about the cultural impact of immigration. The overall swing to the Conservatives since 2015 is driven by huge rises in support for the party, and

[13] Further details of these various effects are provided in the Online Appendix: www.cambridge.org/Brexitland

declines in Labour, amongst those with negative views of immigration, with huge swings to the party among the most identity conservative voters. Pro-immigration voters, by contrast, show a modest swing to Labour over the same period.

The story of 2017 and 2019 underlines the difficulty of re-aligning politics around new conflicts, even when they are very salient. The Conservatives mobilised one side of the identity politics divide effectively in 2017, but could not fully neutralise the other motives and loyalties influencing voters, or overcome in a single leap decades of weakness in the Labour leave seats where identity conservative voters were concentrated. Yet, while the 2017 campaign failed on its own terms, it provided the platform for the 2019 victory, when further consolidation of Leave support finally put the party over the top in many Labour seats.

This two-cycle story of re-alignment is found repeatedly when we look at the links between identity politics and post-Brexit voting. Voting patterns in 2017 began to shift away from the pre-Brexit patterns of economic voting and towards the identity conflicts which framed the EU Referendum. This process proceeded further in 2019, but with a key difference – identity conservative voters continued to shift towards the Conservatives, but Labour could no longer offset this with gains amongst identity liberals. In Figure 10.4 we illustrate how the relationship between economic assessments and vote choices evolved from 2015.[14] In 2015, shown by the black line, there is a very strong link between economic judgements and choices between the Conservatives and Labour: those who think the economy was doing well favoured the incumbent Conservatives heavily, while economic pessimists aligned with Labour. This relationship is completely absent in the 2016 EU Referendum, represented by the light grey solid line. In the two elections since the referendum, marked by the two dashed lines, the link between

---

[14] Details of the statistical modelling in this and subsequent analysis are provided in the Online Appendix: www.cambridge.org/Brexitland

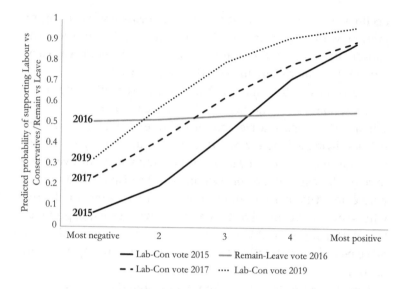

Figure 10.4 Economic perceptions and vote choices, 2015–19

Source: British Election Study internet panel, 2014–19.

economic assessments and vote choices is altered.[15] The Conservatives gain ground among economic pessimists in both elections, while remaining dominant among economic optimists.[16]

---

[15] The reduction in economic effects may also be larger than it appears because, as we saw in Chapter 8, after the EU Referendum voters started to see economic trends through the lens of the Brexit partisanship, and therefore part of the link between economic variables and vote choices may in fact reflect Brexit attachments. For example, many of those expressing positive views of the economy in 2017 (and backing the Conservatives) may in fact be 'Leave' voters who became more optimistic after 2016 due to their Leave partisan attachments rather than any other shift in economic conditions, and who were backing the Conservatives due to their Brexit stance rather than their economic record. Similarly, many 2017 Labour-backing 'Remain' voters would be people who became more negative about the economic situation after the EU Referendum, but it was their Brexit attachments driving the link between their economic views and vote choice, not the economic views themselves.

[16] The same patterns are evident in aggregate results data. Although Labour railed against austerity and welfare reform, the poorest voters and the areas hardest hit by budget cuts swung to the Conservatives (Curtice et al. 2018;

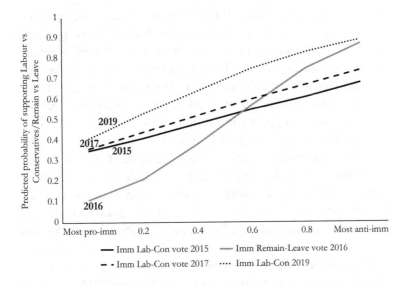

Figure 10.5 Attitudes to immigration and vote choices, 2015–19

Source: British Election Study internet panel, 2014–19.

As we shall see, it is the mobilisation of identity conservatism which enabled the party to gain ground amongst the voters who were most unhappy with their economic record.

The mobilisation of identity conservative opposition to immigration was central to the Conservatives' advances after the EU Referendum, as we have seen. This point is further illustrated in Figure 10.5, which shows the relationship between views of immigration and vote choices between 2015 and 2019 while controlling for other influences on vote choice. As we saw in Chapter 8, the link between immigration attitudes and EU

Goodwin and Heath 2016). Conversely, fear of a Corbyn government did not put off the richest people and most privileged places – the largest swings to Labour in England and Wales came among the best-off voters and the wealthiest seats (Curtice et al. 2018). Although see Jump and Michell (2019) for how this might all be mediated by educational levels, which, as we say in Chapter 2, are also unevenly distributed geographically.

Referendum vote choices was extremely strong, and symmetrical – voters hostile to immigration backed Leave by large margins, while pro-immigration voters aligned with Remain. There was already a link between immigration attitudes and general election vote choices before the EU Referendum, but it became steadily stronger after 2016. The Conservatives greatly increased their support from immigration sceptics, while holding steady among immigration liberals.

Identity politics was not the only factor in 2016. The 'Leave' campaign also proved very effective in mobilising political disaffection, with strong 'Leave' victories among voters who felt British democracy was not working, or that politicians did not care about 'people like me'. Here we find a substantial difference between 2019 and earlier elections, as illustrated in Figure 10.6. While political disaffection was associated with support for 'Leave' in 2016, such disaffection was in both 2015 and 2017 associated with a preference for Labour over the Conservatives. But in 2019, a Conservative message crafted by leading figures from the 2016 'Vote Leave' campaign shifted this. The Conservatives dramatically improved their performance among the most politically disaffected, but without losing support among the contented. The previous negative relationship between political disaffection and Conservative voting disappeared: the dotted line in Figure 10.6 which represents the 2019 election is almost completely flat. While Boris Johnson's mobilisation of identity conservatives was an extension of Theresa May's 2017 gains, his ability to rally the politically disaffected brought something new to the table.

The political impact of post-Brexit shifts in voting behaviour was critically influenced by their interaction with established local voting patterns. We do not have space for a comprehensive survey of electoral geography in 2017 and 2019,[17] but three

---

[17] Curtice et al. (2018) gives a good summary for 2017.

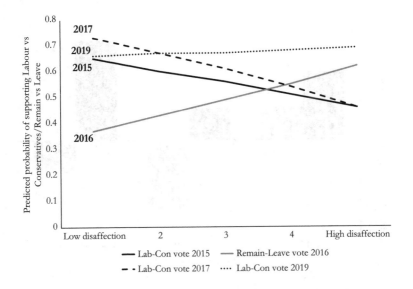

Figure 10.6 Political disaffection and vote preferences, 2015–19

Source: British Election Study internet panel, 2014–19.

short case studies help to illustrate how identity politics and electoral geography have interacted since the vote for Brexit.

The first is the fall of the 'red wall' in 2019. Many of the most identity conservative-dominated seats in England and Wales returned Labour MPs with daunting majorities in 2015, as we noted in Chapter 7, and many of these seats had returned Labour MPs for generations. These seats – Leave-voting yet with enduring and powerful attachments to Labour – were dubbed the 'red wall' in 2019. The Conservatives made serious inroads in many such seats in 2017, but in most the local Labour majorities were simply too large to overturn in one election cycle. But the foundations of the wall were eroded, and a further push in 2019 brought it down, as Figure 10.7 illustrates. Here we show the average change in the two parties' vote shares in the eighteen Labour seats which elected their first Conservative MPs since at least 1945 in 2019. The Conservatives' vote share in these

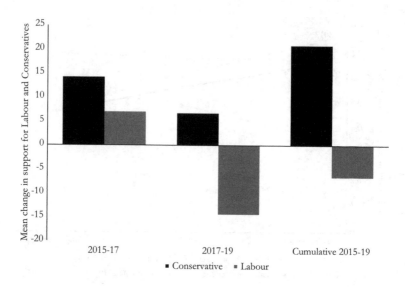

Figure 10.7 Average vote changes, 2015–19, in the eighteen 'red wall' seats which elected their first Conservative MPs since at least 1945 in the 2019 general election

Source: BBC general election database, 2019.

seats rose by fourteen percentage points on average in 2017. While Theresa May's success in rallying identity conservatives was somewhat offset by a seven-point average rise in the Labour vote, the net effect was a large swing to the Conservatives, which left these seats more marginal. Then, in 2019, a smaller seven-point average rise in Conservative support was magnified by a Labour slump, with the incumbent party falling by an average of fourteen points. Over the course of the two elections, these seats saw a whopping fourteen-point swing from Labour to the Conservatives, but it required a huge two-cycle mobilisation of pro-Brexit sentiment to overhaul large Labour majorities, and generations of local anti-Tory sentiment.

A mirror image to this cumulative erosion of Labour support in the 'red wall' can be found in the Conservatives' sustained loss of support in identity liberal, remain-leaning seats in the south east of England. There are thirty-four seats won by the Conservatives in 2015 where the party's support has cumulatively fallen by five percentage points or more over the two post-Brexit elections, even as the party has gained ground nationally. All of them voted to Remain in 2016, all but two are in London or the south of England, most have large concentrations of identity liberal demographic groups, yet the majority (twenty of thirty-four) were still Conservative-held in 2019. While the party has hung on in these seats, the cumulative effect of identity liberal defection has made once rock-solid Conservative seats such as Wimbledon, Esher and Walton, and the Cities of London and Westminster into battlegrounds where the forces of demographic change will continue to work against the incumbent Conservatives in the future. If the Conservatives remain focused on the identity conservative voters of their newly gained 'red wall' seats, Conservative MPs in this 'blue wall' risk falling victim to the same cumulative demographic and electoral trends as their Labour 'red wall' colleagues. In most of these seats the Conservatives' local opponents, however, are not Labour but the Liberal Democrats.[18] The 'blue wall' presents an opportunity for them to re-establish themselves as the voice of cosmopolitan, pro-EU identity liberals in the wealthier parts of England.

Labour's relative absence from these new Remain battlegrounds in south east England reflects a third interaction between identity conflicts and geography: the growing concentration of Labour support in ethnically diverse big cities and graduate-heavy university towns. Labour's cumulative loss of identity conservative Leave voters and seats has further tilted its electoral coalition towards graduates and ethnic minorities, and both groups are strongly clustered in the same sets of seats,

---

[18] The Liberal Democrats were in second place in seventeen of the thirty-two seats where Conservative incumbents defending majorities under 20 per cent experienced a decline in their vote share in 2019, and twelve of the fifteen seats where those declines were largest. The Liberal Democrats saw dramatic vote gains of ten or even twenty percentage points in most of these seats.

most of which already had Labour MPs by 2015. As Labour faded away after Brexit in the towns of England, it rose to a position of unprecedented dominance in the largest cities. Twenty-five MPs achieved majorities of 30,000 votes or more in 2017, all of them were Labour MPs representing big English cities, and all but one achieved majorities of 24,000 again in 2019 even as Labour's national support slumped.[19] Although the Conservatives won nearly 65 per cent of England's constituencies in 2019, most of the safest seats in England were once again Labour-held. Labour MPs have fifteen of the twenty largest majorities, and twenty-eight of the top forty. While such local popularity is doubtless gratifying for incumbents, concentrated support harms Labour's electoral prospects under first-past-the-post, as extra votes cast piling up huge majorities do nothing to win Labour new seats. The geographical concentration of Labour-supporting identity liberal groups therefore puts the party at a disadvantage.[20] In addition, the concentration of Labour voters in safe seats increases the geographical polarisation of identity conflicts – constituents' views on immigration, national identity, Brexit and other issues in Labour strongholds are increasingly at odds with the views on these issues found in the marginal seats Labour needs to target to achieve election victory.

The ghosts of elections past: reputations and temptations

In 2002, a newly appointed Conservative chairman stunned members at the party's annual conference by attacking the party's history of 'demonising' ethnic minorities, which she said had given the Conservatives a toxic reputation as 'the nasty party'. Theresa May was not alone that year in voicing concerns about a 'toxic' Conservative Party at odds with a changing

[19] All of the MPs in question represented seats in London, Manchester, Birmingham, Liverpool or Bristol.
[20] See Curtice et al. (2018: 481–8).

electorate. Shadow Chief Secretary to the Treasury Oliver Letwin condemned the unrepresentativeness of the party, while party Vice-Chairman Andrew Lansley called for an 'A list' of candidates to improve the representation of women and ethnic minorities. In 2002, the Conservatives were struggling electorally following two landslide defeats, and their negative reputation with ethnic minorities and identity liberals as a party 'out of touch' with a diverse and increasingly liberal Britain was seen as a key problem for the party. Yet this toxic reputation proved hard to shift, because Conservative politicians – including Theresa May herself – have repeatedly indulged the temptation to appeal to ethnocentric sentiments for short-term political gain.[21] While responding to identity conservative anxieties has repeatedly delivered short-term gains, it also reinforced distrust of the Conservatives among identity liberals, posing a long-term electoral risk to the party. Thus, in 2019, nearly two decades after Theresa May's ground-breaking speech, the Conservatives' first ethnic minority leadership candidate Sajid Javid was still criticising the toxicity of his party, which had 'gone backwards with ethnic minority voters', many of whom 'simply don't trust our motivations'.[22] Two generations after their departure from frontline politics, the ghosts of Enoch Powell and Margaret Thatcher still haunt the Conservatives.

The most visible policy to renew the Conservatives' appeal to identity liberal voters was David Cameron's effort to stand more women and ethnic minorities in winnable seats.[23] This required

---

[21] Ironically, May herself proved to be one of those most eager to cater to such sentiments once in high office, with her policies and political messages as both home secretary and prime minister squarely focused on appealing to ethnocentric voters threatened by immigration and social change.

[22] Quoted in the *Daily Telegraph*, 6 June 2019, available at: www.telegraph.co.uk/politics/2019/06/09/sajid-javid-tories-have-gone-backwards-ethnic-minority-voters, last accessed 27 April 2020.

[23] This was the most visible Cameron policy proposal in this area, but not the only one. Policy pledges on tackling racial discrimination in job searches and university admissions followed, see at: www.telegraph.co.uk/news/politics/11953841/Big-employers-agree-to-hide-names-on-graduate-job-applications-to-end-discrimination.html.

overcoming scepticism among constituency parties, who saw it as a threat to their autonomy, and though calls for such a policy began in the early 2000s, sustained efforts did not get underway until the 2010 election. But Cameron's focus on diversifying Conservative candidates did have a lasting impact.[24] The number of ethnic minority Conservative MPs rose from two in 2005 to eleven in 2010 and twenty-two in 2019, while female Conservative MPs went up from forty-nine to eighty-seven in the same period. Cameron hoped these changes would help the party look more 'in touch'. Recruiting a more diverse cohort of MPs is strategically valuable to the Conservatives: such policies can help their image with white identity liberals without harming them with identity conservatives. It is much easier for the party to defend themselves from allegations of racism when the policies being criticised are delivered by an ethnic minority minister and supported in Parliament by ethnic minority MPs.

Yet elite diversity has proved insufficient to repair the Conservatives' reputation with ethnic minority voters, whose distrust of the party is more deep-rooted and multifaceted. BAME voters polled by Michael Ashcroft were still mentioning contentious statements by Enoch Powell and Margaret Thatcher when explaining their suspicions of the Conservative Party in 2013, decades after both had departed from politics.[25] Addressing such distrust would require more radical efforts. Yet going further presents the Conservatives with a problem. The anti-immigrant stances of Powell and Thatcher not only entrenched a toxic reputation for hostility to migrants and ethnic minorities, they

---

[24] See Sobolewska (2013). Although this policy was not implemented as initially envisaged through a list of priority candidates, it was nonetheless successful. Britain's first ethnic minority Chancellor and Home Secretary, Sajid Javid, and the second ethnic minority Home Secretary, Priti Patel, were both selected for safe Conservative seats in 2010 after it was introduced.

[25] Ashcroft (2012a). Comments included: 'Thatcher called Mandela a terrorist. How can I vote for someone like that?', 'If you go back to the rivers of blood speech, Enoch Powell, there was no one in the Conservative party denouncing him and saying this isn't the way forward', and 'Stephen Lawrence. Who was in power with Stephen Lawrence?'

also won the party enduring support from the ethnocentric voters most threatened by immigration and cultural change.[26]

While Conservative reformers have recognised the need to appeal to a steadily liberalising and diversifying electorate, their longstanding support from identity conservatives makes such reforms risky and increases the temptation to push ethnocentric messages instead. David Cameron's modernisation efforts on gay marriage and ethnic minority representation were undercut by campaigns against immigration and speeches about the alleged 'failure' of multiculturalism.[27] Home Secretary Theresa May's harsh approach to immigration ignored the warnings of Party Chairman Theresa May's 2002 speech, and undercut the credibility of Prime Minister Theresa May's efforts to address the 'burning injustice' of ethnic minority disadvantage through a wide-ranging Racial Disparity Audit. The 'Windrush' scandal, in particular, did lasting harm to the Conservatives' efforts to renew their appeal, as elderly ethnic minority citizens who found themselves unable to prove their right to reside in Britain were subjected to all manner of indignities and mistreatment by a hostile Home Office.[28]

Both Cameron and May had sincere reforming ambitions yet ended up reinforcing the Conservatives' 'nasty party' reputation.

---

[26] The Conservatives' temptation to appeal to ethnocentric white voters was also something minority voters in Michael Ashcroft's focus groups cited as a reason to distrust the party. For example, one noted: 'There has been a move to embrace multiculturalism, but at the same time there has been a quiet majority of white people who are saying, actually we are forgetting who we are. And as a result of the backlash, that's why I think [Cameron] made this speech about multiculturalism. He's realised that by going on about it, trying to work on one group in society, he has ignored this other group.' Another put it more bluntly: 'It's how they look at us. They always have and do today. They will never change.'

[27] Cameron's 2011 Munich speech on the alleged failure of multiculturalism was another incident noticed by Michael Ashcroft's focus groups, highlighting how sceptical ethnic minority voters are highly sensitive to signals which they read as evidence of Conservative hostility. One said of the speech: 'It didn't make me feel welcome, to come out with comments like that.' Another drew a direct comparison between Cameron's speech and Enoch Powell's earlier, much more incendiary speeches.

[28] Gentleman (2019).

Enoch Powell's ghost has still not been exorcised, and with images of traumatised and helpless black pensioners treated as strangers in their own land now burned onto the public consciousness, the task will be all the harder for Boris Johnson and his successors. Yet demographic change will continue to increase the electoral cost of alienating identity liberals and ethnic minorities in years to come. Perhaps this is why, despite having a very patchy past record on race and women's rights,[29] Boris Johnson appointed the most ethnically diverse cabinet in British history at the beginning of his term in office, including giving two out of the four top jobs to ethnic minority front benchers.[30]

Labour face their own identity politics dilemmas. Since 2010 many in the party have argued that a decisive break with the legacy of the Blair–Brown governments was needed to reconnect with the socially conservative white school leavers who turned against politics in the New Labour years[31] (see Chapter 5). Labour's efforts on this front have so far proved ineffective, and a key reason is the power of anti-prejudice social norms among identity liberal voters. Whenever senior Labour politicians during Ed Miliband's period as leader sought to engage with identity conservative concerns on immigration, a loud chorus of condemnation would rain down from identity liberal activists, attacking such measures as either inherently prejudiced or designed to appease prejudice.[32] Identity conservative voters

---

[29] Boris Johnson's most famous faux pas on the issue of race and gender was comparing burka-wearing Muslim women with letterboxes, available at: www.telegraph.co.uk/news/2018/08/05/denmark-has-got-wrong-yes-burka-oppressive-ridiculous-still.

[30] Home Secretary the Rt. Hon. Priti Patel and Chancellor the Rt. Hon. Rishi Sunak are both of ethnic minority origin, as was the chancellor's predecessor Sajid Javid, also appointed by Boris Johnson.

[31] The need to reconnect such voters to the Labour Party was a major theme of the 'Blue Labour' movement during the Miliband opposition, and of two major reports on the 2015 general election defeat by John Cruddas and Margaret Beckett.

[32] See, for example, Bale (2015) on the divisions between 'beer drinkers' and 'wine drinkers' over how Labour should respond to immigration and the UKIP threat during Ed Miliband's leadership.

are also sceptical of such initiatives, seeing them as insincere gesture politics from Labour politicians who do not share their concerns, a perception that is reinforced by identity liberal critics who often make the same claim. As we explained in Chapter 5, working-class Labour MPs whose social and educational background makes them credible communicators with identity conservative voters are all but gone. Tristram Hunt, former MP for Stoke Central, provides a good example of the problems Labour face. Hunt clearly took the issue of identity politics seriously – he edited a book on how to reconnect with the working class by embracing English patriotism – yet he was a hopeless vehicle for this message. Cambridge born, privately educated in London, Hunt was a university academic and think-tank researcher with no connection to Stoke before becoming its MP. He sought to represent a seat where most voters never went to university and unemployment was twice the national average. Hunt's efforts to represent the identity conservatism of his Stoke constituents may have been sincerely motivated, but they rang hollow with voters who knew that these were not views identity liberal people like him typically held.[33] Such scepticism was reinforced by the much more negative attitudes towards identity conservative stances and symbols shown by other identity liberal Labour MPs, such as Emily Thornberry's mocking of the display of an English flag on a constituent's house.[34]

A slightly different dynamic set in under Jeremy Corbyn's leadership, particularly after the EU Referendum. Corbyn repeatedly expressed scepticism about free movement migration policies, though the roots of his opposition lie less in electoral calculation than in economic ideology. Corbyn and his allies had long seen EU free movement as a policy that strengthens the

---

[33] See at: www.politics.co.uk/blogs/2016/05/24/tristram-hunt-s-patriotism-will-not-back-the-working-class, last accessed 27 April 2020.
[34] See at: www.theguardian.com/politics/2014/nov/21/emily-thornberry-resignation-explain-outside-britain, last accessed 27 April 2020.

hands of employers at the expense of (native) workers.[35] Soon after the referendum result, Corbyn started signalling a willingness to end free movement rights, saying Labour was 'not wedded' to free movement as a 'point of principle'.[36] Within months, this firmed up into a position of ending free movement, with Brexit Secretary Keir Starmer arguing that 'reasonable management of migration and moving away from free movement has to be part of the referendum result'.[37] This stance was confirmed in Labour's 2017 election manifesto, which stated baldly that 'free movement will end when we leave the European Union'.[38]

Yet Corbyn, like Miliband, found it was hard to restore Labour's credibility to identity conservative voters despite this more restrictive stance on immigration, their most salient concern. Corbyn's migration stances, like Miliband's before him, provoked strong criticism from identity liberal Labour politicians and activists, which in turn reinforced identity conservatives' concerns that they were not sincere or sustainable. One of Corbyn's most vocal critics was his own Shadow Home Secretary Diane Abbott, creating an interesting symmetry between Labour's identity politics struggles and those of the Conservatives a few years earlier. Just as the credibility of David Cameron's liberalising efforts was undermined by the strongly anti-immigration stance of his Home Secretary Theresa May, so the credibility of Jeremy Corbyn's restrictive stances on EU migration was undermined by the strident identity liberalism of his Shadow Home Secretary Diane Abbott. Corbyn himself also muddied the waters, sometimes retreating from anti-immigration positions in the wake of criticism and offering

---

[35] This was a widespread objection to the single market of those on the 'Old Left' of the Labour Party in the 1970s and 1980s, and is also a position shared by some of the more ideologically left-wing union leaders close to Corbyn.

[36] Jeremy Corbyn interview with Laura Kuenssberg, January 2017, available at: www.bbc.co.uk/news/uk-politics-38561501, last accessed 19 September 2019.

[37] Mason and Asthana (2017).

[38] Labour Party (2017). This stance was the most restrictionist stance taken on EU immigration by any Labour leader since Britain had joined the EEC in the 1970s.

much more liberal rhetoric and positions on other aspects of migration policy such as refugees. Sceptical identity conservatives could find plenty of reasons to doubt the sincerity of Labour's responses to their concerns.

Paths through Brexitland: three scenarios for the future of British politics

The axis of political competition has shifted since 2016, as the new political identities forged in the Brexit debate have intensified the mobilisation of identity conflicts. But will these new alignments last? As we saw in Chapter 9, Scottish politics in 2015 was upended by the 2014 independence referendum, only for the sands to shift again just two years later in the wake of the Brexit vote. The changes produced by polarising shocks such as referendums may prove to be short-lived, particularly in a political environment which is itself rapidly changing. While Brexit may create a more lasting divide, with debates over Britain's relationship with the EU rolling over many years, and partisan 'Leave' and 'Remain' identities enduring in the electorate, this outcome is not certain. Nor is it certain that the identity conflicts polarised by Brexit will continue to be funnelled into traditional two-party conflict between Labour and the Conservatives. New parties could once again disrupt politics by mobilising voters on one pole of the identity politics divide.

In this final section we consider three possible scenarios for the future path of British politics as identity politics divides continue to reshape the electorate and reconfigure political competition: fragmentation, restoration and replacement. In the fragmentation scenario, identity conflicts prove impossible to contain within a two-party system still structured around economic divides, and voters become split between three, four or more substantial parties. This scenario would be chaotic given Britain's first-past-the-post electoral system, which only awards seats to the local winner. Many constituencies would become unpredictable multi-sided fights, and the relationship between parties' vote shares and seat totals could become chaotic. But because the British electoral system heavily rewards whichever side in a fragmented competition manages to consolidate most, this pattern of competition may prove unsustainable, as both voters and parties seek more united fronts in order to win. Fragmented politics might produce wild and chaotic interludes, but unless the British electoral system is changed it will also be hard to sustain.

The potential for fragmentation was underlined by developments in summer 2019, when two years of deadlocked polling was upended within months, as the broad electoral coalitions assembled by Labour and the Conservatives in 2017 and held together for eighteen months thereafter unravelled in the wake of Theresa May's failure to ratify a Brexit deal ahead of the initial March 2019 deadline.[39] The resulting extension of the Brexit negotiations obliged Britain to take part in European Parliament elections fought under a proportional system and stimulated a rapid fragmentation of British politics, as voters on both poles of the identity politics spectrum defected to challenger parties. Former UKIP leader Nigel Farage returned to front-line politics at the head of a new outfit, the Brexit Party, which mobilised identity conservatives with demands for an uncompromising and immediate 'no deal' exit from the EU. On the Europhile side, the Liberal Democrats targeted identity liberal Remain partisans with a tribal pro-EU campaign fought under the slogan 'Bollocks to Brexit'. Both parties secured huge surges in support, and in the June European Parliament poll both Labour and the Conservatives recorded their worst ever performances in a nationwide election since the introduction of the mass franchise. By mid-summer, Westminster polls conducted in the wake of the European Parliament election shock were showing the first four-way national tie in vote shares ever recorded.

---

[39] This deadline was the product of Article 50 of the Treaty on European Union, which provides member states who notify the EU of an intention to withdraw from the Union with two years to negotiate the terms of their departure. Theresa May sent Britain's Article 50 notification on 29 March 2017, automatically setting 29 March 2019 as the deadline for the two-year negotiation period.

As Figure 10.8 illustrates, this four-way split in fact reflected the growing division of the electorate into separate Remain and Leave 'blocs'– with Labour contesting the Remain vote with the Liberal Democrats, the Greens and the SNP, while the Conservatives and the Brexit party vied for Leave voters' support.[40]

A four-way contest is perfectly sustainable in European elections, fought using a proportional seat allocation system (and indeed many European countries with proportional electoral systems have very fragmented party systems), but it is hard to sustain in the Westminster first-past-the-post system, which heavily punishes fragmentation. The awarding of seats to whoever comes first locally hands disproportionate advantages to broad consolidated parties over fragmented rivals.[41] Parties and voters alike are aware of these incentives. Voters try to figure out which parties are viable in their constituency, and many whose preferred national party has no chance locally will switch their support to a more viable local option.[42] Parties with overlapping priorities and support bases have a strong incentive to cooperate or even merge in order to maximise their electoral prospects (as happened with the Liberal and Social Democratic parties in the 1980s).

As we show in Figure 10.8, the fragmentation which peaked in the middle of 2019 reversed very rapidly, as both traditional parties took steps to see off the threat from new challengers in the run up to another general election. The Conservatives, under new Prime Minister Boris Johnson, took an even more uncompromising approach to Brexit to squeeze out the Brexit Party, while Labour sought to counter the Liberal Democrat surge

---

[40] For further analysis of the implications of this 'bloc politics', see Carella (2019).

[41] The Conservatives were able to win huge Westminster majorities in 1924 and 1931 with around half of the vote, and the SNP won all but three of Scotland's seats in 2015 with just over half of the vote. Conversely, parties who achieve very substantial support, but are not big enough or geographically concentrated enough to top the poll anywhere often emerge with next to nothing, as happened to the SDP in 1983 and to UKIP in 2015.

[42] See, for example, Fisher (2004).

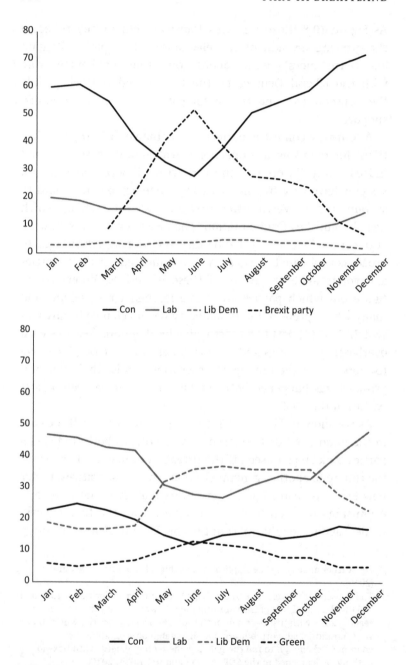

Figure 10.8 Party support in 2019 among Leave voters (top graph) and Remain voters (bottom graph) (percentages)

Source: YouGov.

among Remain supporters by firming up its support for a second referendum.[43] The four-party split of summer 2019 did not last long, but just as extreme weather events highlight the destabilising effects of global warming, so this extreme volatility highlighted the destabilising effects of long-term demographic change. The waning of voter loyalties and the emergence of new identity divides has made the large parties' broad coalitions more unstable. Triggering events such as the emergence of a new political issue, internal splits in a party or an unusual election campaign can rapidly produce new bouts of fragmentation. While such fragmentation is unstable, as all parties know that broad alliances are the route to victory, efforts to combat it when it emerges can themselves produce rapid political change. One future path for British politics could be unpredictable cycles of fragmentation and consolidation, as parties struggle to square the need for broad coalitions with the growing internal tensions building such coalitions produces.

In the restoration scenario, such instability is averted and political competition instead reverts to a more predictable iteration of the traditional fight between Labour and the Conservatives. This could occur because identity conflicts fall down the agenda, for example, if a sustainable Brexit end state arrives and conflicts over immigration fade with the implementation of a new migration system. Although identity divides will persist in the electorate, in this scenario they return to a more politically latent state, exercising weaker influence as voters' attention returns to traditional questions such as economic policy, management of public services and the competence of political leaders. There is already evidence that the most polarising identity politics conflict of the last two decades – immigration – may be fading. Immigration was the top priority for identity conservative voters for fifteen years prior to the EU Referendum, but

---

[43] See at: www.independent.co.uk/news/uk/politics/remain-alliance-labour-coalition-lib-dems-conservative-boris-johnson-election-a9076951.html, last accessed 27 October 2019.

since the Brexit vote such concerns have gone into steep and sustained decline, falling to a twenty-year low in 2019.[44] This was not just a matter of public attention shifting elsewhere. Views about immigrants and the impact of immigration became substantially more positive in the years after the referendum, among Remain and Leave voters alike.[45] The Conservative government's plan to introduce new migration rules which apply uniform selection criteria to all labour migrants could reinforce this trend, as a selective migration system focused on the potential economic contribution of migrants as the main criterion for entry is consistent with the preferences of voters on both sides of the identity politics divide.[46]

What has happened with immigration could also happen with Brexit. While at the time of writing Britain is divided as never before into mutually hostile Brexit tribes, the importance of these new political identities could be driven by perceptions on both sides that they are engaged in a high-stakes battle with an uncertain outcome. If Britain arrives at a stable Brexit end state, Brexit conflicts could rapidly dissipate as voters' minds turn elsewhere. Leavers may cease to focus on the issue once Britain is formally out of the EU if they decide the 'job is done'.[47] Remainers may find that the new status quo is not as awful as they had anticipated, and may lose interest in what would no longer be a short-term fight to prevent Britain leaving the EU, but instead a longer and harder campaign to gradually move

[44] In IPSOS-MORI polls from January–September 2019, an average of 15 per cent of voters named immigration as one of the nation's most important problems, the lowest annual average recorded since 2000 (11 per cent). See the Online Appendix (www.cambridge.org/Brexitland) for details.

[45] See Ford (2018a); Schwartz et al. (2020).

[46] For quantitative research, see Ford and Mellon (2019); Ford and Heath (2014); Ford, Morrell and Heath (2012). For large-scale qualitative research providing richer detail on the nature of contributions voters favour, see Rutter and Carter (2018).

[47] Indeed, the salience of Brexit has already fallen sharply in the months since Boris Johnson secured a new Withdrawal Agreement with the EU, declining in the MORI polling series from a peak of 65 per cent in September 2019 to 47 per cent in January 2020, the month the new Withdrawal Agreement became law. This was the lowest figure recorded for eighteen months.

Britain back into the EU orbit. Traditional economic and public services issues such as poverty, the NHS, education and housing, which have been steadily rising up the public agenda in the years since the EU Referendum, could swiftly return to the centre of attention with Leavers and Remainers alike as the long period of all-consuming focus on Brexit wrangling comes to an end.[48] This, in turn, could prompt a new bout of political disruption, as voters who aligned with parties over their immigration and Brexit stances reassess them based on new priorities.

However, the restoration scenario is also possible if the identity politics conflicts of recent years continue. Negotiations over relations with the EU might remain contentious and incomplete, immigration levels may remain high, and new identity conflicts may rise up the agenda again. If such conflicts persist, the electoral reconfiguration of the past four years may continue and become further entrenched. The resulting Brexitland Labour and Conservative parties will be very different to their pre-Brexit iterations. Labour's electoral strategy would likely become more focused on adding swathes of what we have dubbed the 'blue wall', where identity liberal and Remain-leaning graduates and professionals congregate, to the party's big city strongholds. The Conservatives would seek to complete their takeover of the 'red wall' post-industrial and coastal towns where identity conservatives congregate in the largest numbers.

Such shifts could worry activists in both parties, who may see them as being at odds with their parties' traditional identity and purpose, or as a 'hostile takeover' by factions they oppose. Conservative activists would worry that a party built around a core electorate of economically insecure, politically alienated and ethnocentric white school leavers will no longer promote free market policies, or effectively represent the aspirations of wealthier, more upwardly mobile voters. Labour activists would fear that a party dominated by middle-class professional identity liberals and focused on the prosperous suburbs where they

---

[48] The share of voters naming each of these issues rose in IPSOS-MORI polling between 2016 and 2019.

congregate will gravitate once again towards the middle-class friendly 'Blairite' economics of New Labour, while neglecting poorer voters and marginalised communities which no longer provide the backbone of Labour support. Two-party politics would survive in this scenario, but activists in both parties may wonder if the price paid for survival is too high.

The final scenario, replacement, would kick in if the traditional governing parties prove unable to accommodate or resolve identity conflicts. If they fail, one or both could die off as voters shift en masse to parties better able to reflect their concerns. While the disappearance of established governing parties is a rare event in mature democracies, it is by no means unknown, and collapse can be swift when it comes. In Canada, which operates a similar first-past-the-post electoral system to Britain, the incumbent Progressive Conservative Party lost two-thirds of its support and all but two of its seats in 1993, and never recovered, later being subsumed into the Reform Party which had overtaken it.[49] Closer to home, the Liberal Party was one of the two governing parties in Britain for many decades prior to the 1920s. The Liberals proved unable to accommodate the new class divides rising in politics, and after a turbulent decade which featured three elections in three years, Liberal–Conservative competition was replaced by Labour–Conservative competition.[50] The Scottish Labour Party, which won a plurality of Scottish Westminster seats in every election from 1959 to 2010, collapsed more recently, unable to find an effective voice in a political competition structured around the question of independence. Scottish Labour was wiped out at Westminster in 2015 and has been a marginal force in Scottish politics ever since.[51]

---

[49] Clarke and Kornberg (1996); Laycock (2002); Belanger and Godbout (2010).
[50] For two of the most influential accounts, see Adelman (1995) and Taylor (2005).
[51] Scottish Labour lost all but one of its forty-one seats in 2015, won just seven seats in 2017 as the SNP fell back, then lost six of these again in 2019 as its vote fell to a new record low. These were the worst three results for Labour in Scotland since the introduction of the mass franchise (see Chapter 9). Labour's

There are some signs that a future extinction scenario is not so far-fetched. Voters' attachments to both main parties have been declining for decades, as we saw in Chapter 5. Brexit partisanship is for now much stronger and more widespread, just as independence partisanship was in Scotland prior to the collapse of the Scottish Labour Party. Voters have been exceptionally volatile in the past decade – the last time electoral volatility was this high was around the time of the Liberals' demise in the 1920s.[52] Yet even in these turbulent times, it will most likely require a further intensification of identity conflicts to upend completely patterns of party competition which have been entrenched for generations. Party replacement is thus most likely if we see another period of sustained mobilisation around an identity conflict. A major constitutional shock such as a breakdown of negotiations with the EU or conflict between England and Scotland over Scottish independence could provide the stimulus for such mobilisation, or it could come through renewed conflicts over immigration and diversity, which have proved to be capable of prompting lasting party system change elsewhere in Europe. If the traditional parties find themselves unable to adapt, it could produce a more lasting political re-alignment, with new parties promoting uncompromising positions on opposite poles of the identity politics spectrum rising to prominence.

The sudden disappearance of a governing party could also be enabled by the peculiar incentives of the British 'winner takes all' electoral system. Voters are reluctant to back upstart parties even when they prefer them, because they fear such parties cannot win locally, so they stick to backing whichever of the traditional governing parties they find least objectionable. In normal political circumstances, this tendency promotes political stability, protecting the traditional parties and suppressing

---

vote also slumped to an all-time low in the 2016 Scottish Parliament election, and has continued to decline in polling for Scottish Parliament elections since.
[52] Fieldhouse et al. (2019).

support for newcomers. But if an upstart party manages to overtake one of the established parties in polls or election contests, this can set off a feedback loop as voters start to believe the insurgent is now a viable alternative, and they no longer have to accept second best. We can think of this as an electoral 'Tinkerbell effect'[53] – if people believe new parties can win, that belief can become self-fulfilling. If people cease to believe the old parties are unbeatable, this can make them beatable.[54] If another bout of constitutional or ethnocentric conflict tipped the polling balance in favour of identity politics insurgents, such a feedback loop could make the shock fatal for one or both traditional parties.

While this risk cannot be discounted entirely, it is also hard to quantify, and it is hard to tell which party is more exposed to it. The indicators available paint a mixed picture. One is the geographical distributions of support for new and old parties. Labour and the Liberal Democrats currently have quite distinct pools of strength – each tends to be strong where the other is weak. This pattern, if maintained, could make co-existence a more plausible outcome than replacement if Liberal Democrat support took off among identity liberal voters. By contrast, both UKIP and the Brexit Party tended to be strongest where the Conservatives were also strong, making it harder for either to break through initially, but also increasing the risk of Conservative collapse if support for a future identity conservative challenger in the UKIP or Brexit Party mould reached a 'tipping point'.[55]

Demographic change also offers mixed indications – while the growth of identity liberal groups may make a national party built around their interests more plausible in the long run, defensive mobilisation by identity conservatives threatened by such change has so far proved more potent, fuelling the rise of

---

[53] In J. M. Barrie's 'Peter Pan' play, the fairy Tinkerbell's powers depended on the audience. The more the audience believed in her, the stronger she became.

[54] Academics have observed this effect in majoritarian systems, first described by Maurice Duverger as the 'psychological effect' of the first-past-the-post system, see Blais and Carty (1991).

[55] See Carella (2019) for more analysis on this point.

two radical right insurgents in the past decade. We should also not underestimate the power of chance and political accident in a non-linear electoral system where narrow advantages feed on themselves. In 1922–3, the Liberals fell just one percentage point short of the Labour Party for two elections in a row, but this was enough to put them decisively behind Labour in seats won and set them on a downward spiral. A narrow votes or seats advantage could easily feed on itself once again, enabling an insurgent party to leverage a narrow victory into a lasting political re-alignment. Such events may look unlikely, even from the vantage point of today's unsettled politics, but they have happened before. No governing party has a right to govern, or even to exist. The voters of Brexitland may yet form themselves into new political tribes.

Conclusion: unstable coalitions, uncertain outcomes

The traditional two parties, Labour and Conservatives, have so far weathered the disruptions unleashed by the rise of identity conflicts. But more disruptions are likely to follow. The white school leavers the Conservatives have attracted in growing numbers since the mid-2000s with appeals on immigration, Europe and assertive nationalism will continue their long demographic decline. The Conservatives' need to repair their toxic reputation with ethnic minority voters will grow ever more urgent as the population continues to diversify. The electoral risks posed by a reputation for intolerance towards immigrants and minorities will also rise as the wide identity liberal population who take a dim view of such intolerance continues to grow. Both groups may be joined by another migrant-origin electorate with similar concerns if long-term EU residents seek or are granted British citizenship in large numbers after Brexit. While the growth of identity liberal groups should offer opportunities for Labour, they are still too small and too geographically concentrated to win elections for the party at present. Both parties will therefore still face pressures to reach out to a wider pool of voters and build broader, but less stable, electoral coalitions.

Political parties must always think ahead, forming strategies to win the next election, but they can never fully escape the past. The legacies of earlier campaigns, policies and reputations with different social groups all haunt parties and constrain their options. This chapter has outlined the choices and risks for the political parties as they seek to chart a way forward. Many of the issues we have identified reflect problems repeatedly thrown up by the mobilisation of identity conflicts: internal divides, unstable electoral coalitions and tensions between short-term temptations and long-term needs. Brexit has amplified these problems, with unpredictable electoral implications. The 2017 and 2019 elections are a case in point. The Conservatives succeeded in winning by gradually becoming the party of Leave while Labour failed to become the party of Remain. But the resulting voter alignments may not last even to the next election, whenever that might be. We identified three possible paths forward from this uncertain moment, including one that may look unlikely after three years of ceaseless Brexit battles: that identity conflicts may dissipate and our politics return to traditional arguments over the economy and public service delivery. As we have seen in Chapter 4, levels of ethnocentric threat can go down as well as up, and there are early signs already that concern about immigration is falling. Brexit may follow suit if a stable end state arrives.

Regardless of what happens in the longer term, in the short term electoral volatility is set to continue, and the deeper differences in values and priorities which generate identity conflicts will continue to grow. Brexit is the biggest identity politics disruption to date, but it is unlikely to be the last, even if identity conflicts become latent again for a time. Demographic change will continue, and the parties will have to keep adapting and responding to the shifting priorities of voters. There is much that is unknown about how the future elections in Brexitland will be won and lost, and by whom. But we know two things for sure: the latent potential for electoral disruption from identity politics will continue, and the choices parties make will influence how this potential is harnessed, and to what effect.

11 CONCLUSION: THE NEW POLITICS OF BREXITLAND

The road to Brexitland

Many natural processes involve pressures steadily accumulated, then suddenly released. Snow drifts build slowly on a mountain for months before a backfiring engine sends them racing down into the valley below in an avalanche. Vast polar ice sheets hollow out for decades, until a tipping point is reached, pitching hundreds of square miles of ice into the sea. Ecosystems facing increasing strains seem to maintain themselves under rising pressure until, suddenly, they collapse. The fuel for a wildfire gathers on the forest floor for season after season before the transformational spark arrives.

Political change can also involve such processes of accumulated pressure and sudden release. How Britain became Brexitland is one such story. The transformational processes of university expansion and rising ethnic diversity driven by mass immigration that we discussed in Chapter 2 have produced a steady accumulation of demographic pressure in the electoral system, as the composition of the electorate has changed and new fault lines have emerged. These demographic changes opened up new divides between 'identity conservatives' – white school leavers with an ethnocentric 'us against them' worldview – and 'identity liberals' – university graduates and ethnic minorities for whom anti-racism is a central social and political value (Chapter 3). The first wave of mass immigration in the 1960s began the process of ethnic change and triggered the first mass political mobilisation of these identity conflicts (Chapter 4).

Then, decades later, a second wave of immigration interacted with a political system where old loyalties were decaying, mobilising identity conflicts which have been working their way through the political system ever since (Chapter 5). There was growing evidence in the 2000s and early 2010s that the great tectonic plates of traditional party politics were beginning to shudder and creak under the accumulated pressures: New Labour's persistent troubles with immigration; the backfiring Conservative pledge on migration control; the emergence of UKIP, all were symptoms of a system under strain (see Chapters 6 and 7). The 2016 EU Referendum triggered the earthquake that released decades of built-up pressure, mobilising the identity divides which had been building for many years and forging them into new Leave and Remain political identities (Chapter 8).

While the ethnocentric impulse to see politics as an 'us against them' battle is fundamental, the nature of the identity conflicts which activate such impulses depends on the political context. In England and Wales, ethnocentric voters have come to see first immigrants, and then the EU, as the primary threat, the 'them' that 'we' must control. In Scotland, the same voters see England and Westminster as 'them', and often see immigrants and the EU as allies against this primary threat. Identity liberals are also sensitive to political context. Such voters regarded the immigration-focused mobilisation of ethnocentric sentiments in England and Wales as a violation of anti-racism social norms, and therefore strongly rejected both UKIP and the Leave campaign as agents of intolerance. In Scotland, by contrast, though the SNP and Yes campaigns mobilised ethnocentric sentiments against England and Westminster, they also framed their political goal of independence in terms of progressive values, enabling a campaign which at root involved an 'us against them' battle palatable to voters on the liberal side of the identity politics divide (see Chapter 9).

The forces unleashed by the referendums have reshaped British political competition, changing both main parties. The David Cameron-led Conservative Party that called the referendum in

2016 was one where (grudging) acceptance of EU membership as being in Britain's national interest was the norm. The Boris Johnson-led Conservative Party, which won a massive election mandate three years later, is one where British EU membership is anathema, and even close post-Brexit alignment with the EU is regarded with suspicion. The Labour Party of 2016 was one that sought to balance the interests of the large cohort of Labour MPs from the most strongly Remain constituencies with those of an equally large cohort of Labour MPs from the most strongly Leave seats. The Labour Party of 2020 is now dominated by MPs from identity liberal Remain-voting areas, but also reeling from a wave of historic defeats in longstanding, but Leave-voting, strongholds (see Chapter 10).

While both traditional governing parties have been shaken internally by the mobilisation of new identity politics conflicts, other parties have sought at various points to capitalise on the new divisions. UKIP and its rebranded successor the Brexit Party both caused turmoil by mobilising ethnocentric voters with an extreme 'us against them' message focused on assertive nationalism and opposition to the threats from Europe and immigration. The Liberal Democrats and the Green Party experienced polling surges by seeking to mobilise cosmopolitan, Europhile and anti-racist voters on the identity liberal end of the spectrum. Thus far, new parties have failed to break the traditional two-party duopoly, but the summer 2019 polling surges for the Liberal Democrats and the Brexit Party highlight the fragility of the old order in a political context where new identity conflicts continue to reshape loyalties. The changes in Scottish politics since 2014 highlight how a polarising identity conflict – over Scottish independence in this instance – can upend the political order and replace it with an entirely new pattern of party competition.

The demographic changes producing this new instability are unstoppable. This process has not ended with Brexit, indeed it is likely to accelerate in decades to come as the cohorts who came of age before the advent of mass higher education and mass immigration fade away and are replaced by the most highly

educated and ethnically diverse generations Britain has ever
seen. Every year Britain's politicians will face an electorate that
is a little more diverse and a little more university educated.
Every year the ethnocentric electorate of white school leavers
will get a little smaller. Such electoral climate change is unstoppable, creating unavoidable dilemmas for political parties, but as
we have argued throughout this book, the parties are not spec-
tators in this process – the choices they make in responding to
these changes inform the way voters understand the conflicts
they generate, framing how new and old divides are packaged
together, and structuring the choices available to voters.

Global Brexitland

While no other EU member state looks likely to repeat Britain's
EU exit adventure in the near future, the demographic trends
driving the emergence of identity conflicts – educational expansion and rising diversity through the twin influences of global-
isation and mass migration – are common to most wealthier
democracies. The effects of these demographic changes are
being felt everywhere – educational and ethnic divides are
becoming stronger predictors of political choices in many countries, with ethnocentric 'us against them' conflicts over issues
such as immigration, national identity and diversity pitting
identity conservative white school leavers against identity liberal
graduates and ethnic minorities.[1] The effects of these processes
are being felt in the emergence of new parties and in the greater
fragmentation of politics in most European countries, where
more proportional electoral systems make it easier for political
entrepreneurs to mobilise the new concerns generated by identity divides.[2] In the United States, which like the UK uses a first-
past-the-post electoral system, these new divides have reinforced

---

[1] For a review of these developments, see Ford and Jennings (2020).
[2] Kitschelt and McGann (1997).

and deepened longstanding party divisions on race and identity,[3] and accelerated the geographical polarisation of the parties' support.[4]

The most visible and debated manifestation of identity conflicts in Europe has been the rise of radical right parties, which mobilise ethnocentric sentiments by framing politics as a conflict between an embattled ethnic majority in-group and various threatening out-groups, in particular immigrants and Muslims.[5] Radical right parties were a fringe presence in just a handful of countries a generation ago, but today they are an established and electorally powerful force in practically every Western European society. Their core electorate everywhere is very similar: white school leavers with low education levels and a strongly ethnocentric worldview.[6] The rise of Europe's radical right parties is testament to both the power and the limits of ethnocentrism as a political force. Their ubiquity is testament to the power of ethnocentric feelings of threat activated by mass migration and broader social change among identity conservative voters.

Yet the evolution of radical right support has also highlighted the limits to this form of politics. Radical right parties' contentious and polarising politics mean they are perceived outside their core electorate as violating widely held anti-racism social norms. This places a ceiling on the radical right's electoral support,[7] and as a result radical right parties have not been able to build a broad enough electoral coalition to govern alone or as senior coalition partners in diverse Western European democracies. While they have entered some governments as junior coalition partners, the same toxic reputation that puts limits on

---

[3] Carmines and Stimson (1989); Tesler and Sears (2010); Valentino and Brader (2011).

[4] Bishop (2008); Gimpel and Hui (2015); Pew Research Center (2014); Sussell (2013) – but see Mummolo and Nall (2017).

[5] Mudde (2007; 2019); Rydgren (2008); Norris and Inglehart (2019).

[6] See Stockemer, Lentz and Mayer (2018) for a more detailed overview of the existing studies.

[7] Ivarsflaten (2006).

radical right support also generates substantial risks for main-stream parties contemplating allying with them.[8] Radical right parties therefore tend to punch below their electoral weight across Western Europe – while they are reliably able to secure substantial vote shares, they struggle to translate these into power or influence. Radical right parties themselves increasingly recognise the obstacles posed by their reputational baggage, and many now seek legitimating arguments to improve their image with voters outside their ethnocentric core electorate, by giving them 'reputational shields' – effective counter-arguments to charges of racism and intolerance.[9] Radical right parties can use their political histories for this purpose: many of the most electorally successful parties in this family began their political lives focused on other issues, before turning to nationalism and immigration. Parties that have been radical right from the outset, such as the Front national (FN) in France, can also look to change their image in an effort to broaden their appeal. Under new leader Marine Le Pen, the FN has pursued a 'de-demonisation' strategy, seeking to jettison past contentious stances and offer a more moderate image, focused on populist economics as much as ethnocentric nationalism. The party even went so far as to change its name to 'National Rally' (Rassemblement national) in 2018 to help emphasise the break with its divisive past.[10] The changes have already delivered electoral gains for the party, which has secured its best results in regional, presidential and European Parliament elections, but it is not yet clear if they are sufficient to transform it into a party of government.

---

[8] A nice example of this unfolded when we were drafting this conclusion. The decision of the centre-right CDU to collaborate with the radical right AfD in the German state of Thuringia triggered an immediate national backlash, which led to the resignation of the CDU's national leader (and heir apparent to long-serving German CDU Chancellor Angela Merkel), and triggering a collapse in CDU support in the state.

[9] Ivarsflaten (2006); Berntzen, Bjånesøy and Ivarsflaten (2017).

[10] Ivaldi (2015).

With radical right parties now commonly securing double-digit vote shares in many countries, and pursuing new strategies to broaden their appeal beyond their identity conservative core electorate, the traditional governing parties in many European countries face deepening dilemmas. The rise of the radical right throughout Europe increases the temptations of ethnocentric and anti-immigration campaigns to mainstream parties seeking to appeal to identity conservative voters.[11] This is another parallel with the UK, where it has been the embrace of ethnocentric anti-immigration politics by the mainstream Conservatives in the late 1960s and again since 2010 which has done most to reshape British politics (see Chapter 4). This type of impact on mainstream, particularly right-wing, parties has been documented in many countries, including Denmark, Austria, Italy and the Netherlands[12] among others. Such initiatives can backfire, as mainstream parties hoping to poach votes from the radical right can end up increasing the appeal of the latter, by signalling to their own voters that the radical right agenda is a 'normal' and acceptable part of politics. Such mainstreaming of radical right ideas can also happen in countries such as Australia where the radical right itself is electorally marginal, if brief surges in support for radical right movements encourage the mainstream right to adopt similar ethnocentric arguments.[13]

While the radical right has been on the rise, and has exercised growing influence on the mainstream parties, on the other side of the identity divide, ethnic minority electorates have also been growing rapidly. Although the process of diversification started later in most Western European countries than in the UK, many now have substantial and rapidly growing migrant-origin non-white ethnic minority populations. European electorates are diversifying more slowly than the British one, however, because

---

[11] Mudde (2019).
[12] Akkerman, de Lange and Rooduijn (2016); Dahlström and Esaiasson (2013).
[13] Fleming and Mondon (2018).

these countries have more restrictive rules on electoral participation than applied in Britain to Commonwealth migrants,
requiring that migrants first gain citizenship. As a result, it is
only in the last couple of decades that migrant-origin ethnic
minorities have become a substantial electoral constituency in
most countries. Rapid population growth among younger ethnic
minority communities, naturalisation, and the rise of native-
born second and third generations with greater access to citizenship will all drive rapid growth in European ethnic minority
electorates in years to come. This, in turn, is likely to have
substantial political effects as European ethnic minorities, like
their British counterparts, show a strong tendency to align with
the centre-left.[14] As these populations become more electorally
significant, centre-left parties will have a growing incentive to
take stronger identity liberal stances on issues of importance to
ethnic minority voters, including policies to counter discrimination, open migration policies, and efforts to strengthen
multicultural accommodation and anti-racism social norms,
but it will become even trickier to do this while keeping
ethnocentric white school leavers happy.

The distinctive behaviour of migrant-origin ethnic minorities
has also impacted on politics outside Europe. The United States,
where race has long been a central dividing line in politics, has
experienced explosive growth in migrant-origin ethnic minority
voters following the abolition of ethnically discriminatory
migration quotas in the 1960s, and the sharp increase in
native-born or naturalised Hispanic American electorates with
ethnic links to Mexico and other South American countries.[15]
These new migrant-origin minority electorates have generally
shown the same centre-left leaning as their European counterparts, and have aligned themselves with African Americans and
white identity liberals in the Democratic Party electoral

---

[14] For a review of studies documenting this tendency in Europe, see Sobolewska
(2017) and Ford and Jennings (2020).
[15] Gutiérrez (2016).

coalition.[16] Meanwhile, the longstanding alignment of ethnocentric white school leavers with the Republican Party intensified during the presidency of Barack Obama, when race and racial attitudes became ever more closely aligned with party preference and even with support for policies ostensibly not linked to race at all, such as healthcare.[17] Donald Trump, who has run classic ethnocentric campaigns portraying immigrants, Muslim Americans and other minorities as threatening out-groups, has benefitted directly from this tendency, and the centrality of identity conflicts is one important parallel between Trump's 2016 victory and the EU Referendum in Britain, held just months earlier.[18] The Trump Republican Party, with its intensive focus on assertive and ethnically exclusive nationalism, and hostility to migrants and minorities, increasingly resembles the radical right parties of Western Europe.[19]

White university graduates are also becoming a distinctive political constituency in many developed democracies,[20] particularly among younger generations where mass university expansion has made graduates a larger share of the cohort. University graduates everywhere in the developed world shun radical right parties and politics,[21] and their intense antipathy to parties perceived to violate anti-racism norms is one factor which discourages other parties in more pluralistic systems from working with the radical right or embracing their policies. Graduates also show a stronger willingness to back various kinds of 'new left' parties who make identity liberal appeals to multiculturalism, anti-racism and open immigration policies a prominent part of their electoral platform. Such stances are widely found packed together with environmentalism among Europe's Green parties, who everywhere tend to do better among younger university graduates.[22] Other countries have seen the growing support for

[16] Morín, Macías Mejía and Sanchez (2020).
[17] Tesler and Sears (2010); Tesler (2016).
[18] Curtice (2016); Sobolewska (2016); Sobolewska and Ford (2019).
[19] Inglehart and Norris (2016).
[20] Van der Waal, Achterberg and Houtman (2007); Stubager (2009; 2010).
[21] Guth and Nelsen (2019).   [22] Dolezal (2010).

parties that, like the British Liberal Democrats, offer a package of socially liberal, cosmopolitan and pro-EU positions, such as France's En Marche or the Netherlands' Democrats '66. In the United States, the growing importance of socially liberal white graduates has shifted the balance of power within the Democratic Party, leading to much stronger liberal stances on race and migration issues, a phenomenon some have dubbed 'the Great Awokening',[23] and to growing Democratic strength in the wealthy suburban areas where such liberal graduates congregate. Everywhere, the distinctive value alignments of graduate conviction liberals are encouraging stronger identity liberal stances from traditional and new parties of the progressive left. Such positions include the rejection of ethnic and national group attachments, the embrace of strong anti-racist social norms, and the embrace of cosmopolitan preferences for open borders and multicultural preferences for minority rights. Yet as parties on the left increasingly embrace such stances to appeal to growing graduate electorates, they also increase the risk of alienating the declining but still large identity conservative electorate, by raising the salience of issues where such voters are at odds with the left. The dilemmas faced by Britain's left are also found in many other developed democracies as they seek to come to terms with the emergence of new identity divides. Brexit may be made in Britain, but the identity conflicts which made Brexitland are a global phenomenon.

Identity conflicts beyond party politics

We have focused on how identity conflicts become mobilised into party competition. But the divides between identity conservatives and identity liberals can also impact on other aspects of politics. The activation of ethnocentric sentiments among identity conservatives and of anti-racism norms among identity liberals can transform policy debates, reframing the arguments for

---

[23] See at: www.vox.com/2019/3/22/18259865/great-awokening-white-liberals-race-polling-trump-2020.

and against policies and the groups willing to back them. Given that most policies involve decisions about the distribution of resources between differently defined groups, they lend themselves to arguments about in-groups' and out-groups' rights; the conditions under which groups access resources; the boundaries between groups with and without access; and how these boundaries are policed. Policy debates that have typically been focused on cost-effectiveness and efficiency as the main criteria for success can be transformed by identity conflicts, where very different concerns apply. Welfare policy provides a prominent example of this. Making the ethnic difference or foreign birth of welfare recipients salient can dramatically reduce public support for welfare provision, as ethnocentric white voters become more opposed to welfare provision when they think it benefits out-groups they dislike.[24] This process, known as racialisation, has long played a role in US welfare politics, where many of the poor white Americans who would benefit from more generous welfare provisions oppose welfare, as they see it as primarily benefitting African Americans and not their own group. Thus, economic self-interest is eclipsed by these voters' ethnocentric hostility to an out-group: African Americans.[25] A fast-growing body of research indicates that a similar racialisation mechanism can have a dramatic impact on views of welfare recipients in the UK,[26] and may in future come to change perceptions of welfare policies more generally. Welfare, including pensions, is one of the largest items on the government's spending bill,[27] and so the potential impact of racially motivated identity conservative mobilisation on government activity is very large. Right-wing governments have long employed negative stereotypes of

---

[24] Ford (2016); Ford and Kootstra (2017).   [25] Gilens (1999).

[26] Ford (2016); Kootstra (2016); Ford and Kootstra (2017).

[27] The government's own estimates for 2017, 2018 and 2019 put welfare spending at almost a third of overall government spending, see at: www.gov .uk/government/publications/benefit-expenditure-and-caseload-tables-information-and-guidance/benefit-expenditure-and-caseload-tables-information-and-guidance.

welfare recipients to argue for spending reductions.[28] Racially coding such stereotypes to make them more powerful with ethno-centric white voters in diverse societies is a logical next step, and one radical right parties, at least, are likely to attempt in future.

Welfare is a policy with the potential to be racialised, but is not inherently focused on group conflict. Identity conflicts are therefore even more likely in discussion of a policy field more directly related to race: equal opportunity and anti-discrimination policies. This area has seen much less research in the UK, but given that attitudes towards these policies were strongly linked to vote choice in the EU Referendum,[29] even controlling for anti-immigrant attitudes, it is an area that warrants further research. While the term 'culture wars' in America embraces many issues which are not relevant in this area (such as abortion and access to firearms), the rights of ethnic minorities is an area where the pattern of identity-based political polarisation shows many of the same characteristics, suggesting that such issues may form the focus of future British 'culture wars'.[30] Political arguments in this area are very likely to increase as the population of British-born ethnic minorities is set to continue rising rapidly, meaning growing policymaker attention to discrimination and persistent disadvantage, and increasing the potency among identity liberals of charges of racism made against opponents of policies designed to address such disadvantage. We showed in Chapter 3 how powerful this charge is, and how identity liberals and identity conservatives employ different social norms to negotiate this divisive area. We can see examples of this playing out in politics today, with polarised debates over ethnic minority scholarships for elite universities playing out in a similar way to the longstanding and heated debate over affirmative action in the United States.[31]

---

[28] Katz (1989); Romano (2015).
[29] Hobolt (2016); Sobolewska and Ford (2018). See also Chapter 8.
[30] Sobolewska and Ford (2019).
[31] See at: www.telegraph.co.uk/news/2019/12/30/race-row-leading-private-schools-turn-donors-1m-offer-help-poor.

Another policy area that lends itself to both racialisation and polarisation is immigration. As we have seen in earlier chapters, immigration is a debate inherently prone to activating identity politics divides. It is about defining the borders between 'us' and 'them', who gets to cross these borders, and on what terms. The influence of identity attachments and identity conflicts has long been evident on immigration policy, both in terms of public demands and the policies elected politicians have enacted in response to them. Although Britain's departure from the EU provides an opportunity to rethink and redesign British immigration policy without the constraints of EU free movement rights, the challenges to any cool-headed policymaking in this area are already evident. The government's proposals to introduce a uniform 'points-based' system have already been attacked by anti-immigration lobbying groups as enabling mass immigration to continue, and by pro-migration groups as appeasing xenophobia.[32] The 'hostile environment' policy framework developed by David Cameron and Theresa May in the 2010–15 Coalition government continues to generate polarising controversies, with identity liberals attacking it as a discriminatory system that causes harm and distress to migrants who through no fault of their own are unable to prove their status, while identity conservatives defend it as a system to prevent illegal immigrants coming to Britain. An escalation of such arguments is likely within the next couple of years, as millions of EU citizens, often resident in Britain for decades, fall under the remit of the system. Substantial numbers are likely to be either unaware of the need to prove their status or unable to do so.[33]

As we have shown throughout the book, identity conflicts over immigration are not limited to the narrow remit of immigration policy but are prone to spill over and generate broader disruption. In the 2000s and 2010s, conflicts over immigration

---

[32] See at: www.theguardian.com/commentisfree/2020/feb/19/immigration-proposal-english-language; https://www.migrationwatchuk.org/media-reports.

[33] Migration Observatory (2018).

reshaped British voters' views of EU membership, and hostility to immigration prevented Labour from reconnecting with identity conservative voters opposed to the Conservative governments' austerity economic policies. Such spill-overs are likely to happen again when identity conflicts are activated. When voters focus on identity-based arguments about a policy, it can disrupt the patterns of support for that policy. If debates about welfare or university access policies take on a racial aspect, the mix of supporters and opponents is changed. The mobilisation of identity conflicts can also shift the political agenda, displacing other issues as the focus of voter and politician concern. This was the problem Labour faced in the 2010s, when it was unable to fully capitalise on unpopular austerity policies because many voters' attention was focused instead on identity conflicts over immigration and Brexit. But such agenda shifts may also happen in reverse. The dominant electoral position of the Conservative Party at the time of writing (March 2020) would be rapidly destabilised if identity conservative voters' attention returned to economic issues following the resolution of Brexit and the introduction of new controls on immigration.

The future study of identity politics

The impact of identity politics on policy is not the only area of study that we hope will be taken up by future research. Although we have done our best to present a broad perspective on the identity conflicts that have torn Brexitland apart, there are many issues that we did not have the space to cover in detail. Two of the biggest are the role of geography and economics. Although we do mention geography as a factor exacerbating educational divides between urban cosmopolitan centres that attract graduates from smaller towns and rural areas that increases the value divide between them (in Chapter 2), we did not consider this issue systematically. Geography is likely to be a critical factor in generating voters' social identities, in causing and sustaining the conflicts between 'us' and 'them' which form the heart of identity conflicts, and in structuring the political impact of such conflicts in an electoral system that gives a disproportionate role to geographically structured divides.[34]

Another area where further work is needed is the interaction between the new identity divides we examine and the older class–economic cleavages which long structured British politics. As we show in Chapters 8 and 10, the influence of economics in the EU Referendum was uniquely weak, even if economic perceptions and ideology continued to exercise a powerful influence on general election votes: both before and after the referendum. Yet this does not mean that objective economic circumstances played no role, even in the EU Referendum itself. Economic conflicts and identity conflicts interact in complex ways, and more work is needed to unpack how economic forces influence group alignments, and vice versa. For example, researchers examining longer-term trends in the areas which voted for Brexit in 2016 have already shown how ethnocentric and xenophobic attitudes can develop as a defensive reaction to economic decline, and how these 'cultural grievances' in turn drove support for Brexit. Such research highlights how economics and identity are often not competing explanations for political outcomes, but complementary parts of a broader story.[35]

A better understanding of how new identity conflicts and old economic conflicts interact will therefore require further thinking about the distinctions we draw between these. A lot of research on the 'left behind' voters seen as a central factor in recent radical right and populist political movements has focused heavily on economic factors, yet it is often identity factors which most set these voters apart. While economic divisions and resentments also exist among such voters, qualitative research makes abundantly clear that such voters' accounts of their grievances constantly mix economic concerns together with identity attachments and cultural arguments.[36]

---

[34] Jennings and Stoker (2016); McKay (2019); Jump and Michell (2019).
[35] Carreras, Carreras and Bowler (2019).
[36] Gest (2016); Cramer (2016); Hochschild (2018).

It is age, ethnicity and levels of education that are the dominant demographic predictors of identity conservatism and are the dominant drivers of mobilisation behind UKIP, behind the Leave campaign, and, more recently, behind the success of the Conservative Party in places that have rejected it for generations. The moniker of 'working class' to describe the identity conservatives driving these changes is a distraction, which is misleading in its foregrounding of economic factors as the primary motive defining and driving these voters. Yet one of the problems in studying identity conservatives, which we identified throughout, is that they are harder to define consistently than economic groups. We have few stable over-time measures of their most distinctive attitudinal characteristic: a tendency towards an ethnocentric worldview that divides the safe and familiar 'us' from the dangerous and strange 'them'. In times where identity conflicts are low in political salience, measures of these attitudes disappear from surveys and studies, rendering identity conservatives and identity liberals invisible to researchers. Even in times when identity conflicts are high on the agenda, the measures used to examine them are inconsistent, and often focus on short-term conflicts rather than long-term identity and value attachments. The lack of consistent measures hampers our ability to trace the impact of ethnocentrism on political behaviour, yet such tendencies are not limited to just national politics and fights over issues such as migration. We can see similar conflicts igniting in earlier eras, as, for example, internal migration for jobs in neighbouring towns and counties triggers feelings of threat and defensive mobilisation from ethnocentric voters, as shown by Margaret Stacey in her study of Banbury in 1930.

What next for Brexitland?

The process of demographic change that produced the political earthquakes of 2016 and 2019 is not over. New electoral pressures will soon begin to build again as the composition and outlook of the electorate continues its relentless process of change. Both traditional governing parties continue to face deep dilemmas in attempting to respond to the electoral tensions produced by identity conflicts. In the wake of its worst defeat in eighty-five years, the Labour Party faces strong pressure to renew its appeal to the Leave-supporting identity conservatives whose abandonment of the party cost it so many seats in 2019. Yet this group has been drifting away from the party for many years, and undoing decades of accumulated disaffection and distrust will be very difficult. The kind of ethnocentric appeals to nationalism, nativism and Euroscepticism – to 'us against them' – which would stand the best chance of succeeding with such voters would put Labour politicians at odds with the rapidly growing, vocal and highly organised identity liberal electorate for whom such ethnocentrism is anathema. The Labour Party cannot, in the short term at least, hope to win power without being able to appeal to both identity liberal and identity conservative people and places. Yet as long as polarising identity conflicts remain salient, it is not obvious how the party can appeal to one of these groups without antagonising the other. The party's long, bitter and ultimately failed effort to bridge such divides on Brexit is a worrying precedent.

Although the Conservatives won their biggest majority in a generation in 2019, the price of victory was a deepening of the long-term demographic dilemmas facing the party. The party's mobilisation of ethnocentric white school leavers behind Brexit has intensified the hostility it faces from identity liberal groups – graduates, younger voters, ethnic minorities. The Conservatives' embrace of the hardest Brexit may also generate lingering hostility among Remain partisans. If Brexit proves economically and socially disruptive, then these costs could be held against the Conservatives by tribal Remainers in future elections, including many whose comfortable economic circumstances and liberal economic views might otherwise incline them to the party. Demographic change will steadily intensify the risks posed by alienating identity liberals and Remainers. When the Conservatives seek a fifth election win in a row around 2024, they will face an electorate with more identity liberals, and fewer identity conservatives, than the ones which handed them their past mandates. The oldest cohorts where the party won overwhelming majorities in 2017 and 2019 will inevitably shrink over time. Conversely, the youngest generation of voters, who have known nothing but Conservative governments presiding over austerity and Brexit, and overwhelmingly backed Labour in both 2017 and 2019, will inevitably grow.

Demographic change thus presents ongoing long-run challenges for both traditional parties, but shorter-run political and social changes could also alter the environment in which they operate. We can sketch out different broad scenarios for future change, though we can never be sure how things will play out in practice. One major source of change could be a shift in the political agenda, with identity conflicts no longer a high priority. The Johnson government's large majority reduces the legislative uncertainties in the Brexit process and increases the chances that the high-stakes elements of the negotiation, at least, are resolved relatively soon. Conflicts over immigration, too, may fall down the political agenda for the first time in two decades, as the first comprehensive reforms to the immigration system since the Thatcher government better satisfy public demands for control over the entry process and a stronger focus on migrants with skills and economic resources. The fading of both identity conflicts could lead to a renewed focus on traditional conflicts over redistribution, investment and public services – all issues which have slowly been rising up the agenda with voters over the course of a decade of spending restraint and stagnant incomes.

A shift back to traditional economic conflicts could swiftly destabilise the parties' new electoral coalitions: the identity conservatives won over by the Conservative Party since 2015 often hold relatively left-wing views on redistribution and public services, while the identity liberals who make up a growing part of the Labour coalition include many prosperous graduate professionals with an interest in lower taxes and higher house prices. A return to economic debates will also bring new challenges, in particular growing generational conflicts between older voters, who disproportionately depend on the state for their incomes and health but have taken an ever-larger share of public spending, and younger voters, who for the first time are experiencing less security and prosperity than their parents, and will make growing demands to see this addressed. The fading of identity conflicts could be just as disruptive as their rise.

The resolution of disputes over Brexit and immigration, even if it comes, need not mean an end to identity politics. New identity conflicts could rise up the agenda as these issues fade away. The most obvious short-term candidate is Scottish independence. At the time of writing (March 2020) the demands of the resurgent SNP, which secured another domin-ant victory in the 2019 general election, look set to put it on a collision course with the Westminster Conservative govern-ment. The SNP, buoyed by evidence of rising public support for independence, are determined to have another referendum on leaving the UK while Boris Johnson and the Conservatives are equally determined to stop them. As we saw in Chapter 9, the SNP have prospered electorally by blurring together the Conservatives, Westminster and England as a hostile out-group frustrating Scotland's interests, and a new referendum fight would play straight into this narrative. The wild card this time, though, may be English nationalism. English voters' resentments at Scotland's privileged position in the existing constitutional and fiscal settlement have been growing and are concentrated among the ethnocentric identity conservative voters whose attention was previously focused on the battle with Brussels. A fight over independence could provide the Conservative Party with a new way to mobilise ethnocentric English voters against Scotland, just as it has enabled the SNP to mobilise ethnocentric Scottish voters against Westminster. Once mobilised, such English nationalism could be a very disruptive force: England is so numerically dominant within the United Kingdom – making up 85 per cent of the popula-tion – that any effort to accommodate English sentiment in separate institutions will be destabilising for the whole UK constitutional system.[37]

Constitutional conflict is not the only issue that could generate new tensions. In much of Western Europe, the dominant identity conflicts in recent decades have been over Muslim minorities. Muslim communities and Muslim migrants are the main target of most of the European radical right parties, who portray them as unwilling to assimilate, as a threat to majority cultural identities and liberal values, and as a source of Islamist extremism that poses a security risk.[38] This is classic ethnocentric activation – Muslims are a visible and distinctive out-group, a threatening and dangerous 'them' – and radical right parties mobilise ethnocentric majority voters by demanding that the in-group be protected from the alleged threat. Such mobilisation has not been so evident since the early/mid-2000s, when the BNP played upon fears of Islamic extremism, but negative views of Muslims as an out-group remain widespread in Britain,[39] which has experienced a number of serious terror atrocities committed by Islamist extremists. Efforts to mobilise ethnocentric anti-Muslim sentiments were evident in the EU Referendum Leave campaign, hostility to Muslims became a more prominent theme in UKIP campaigning as the party sought a new focus after the Brexit vote, and even the current prime minister has deployed negative stereotypes of Muslims in his journalism. The evidence from Europe suggests that tensions over Islam and Muslim minorities could provide fertile terrain for radical right actors looking for a new threat to mobilise ethnocentric voters and may therefore become a new focus for identity conflict as Brexit and immigration fade from the agenda.

While Europe's many radical right parties highlight one potential new identity politics fault line, developments in the

---

[37] For more on the disruptive potential of English nationalism, see Henderson and Wyn-Jones (2020).

[38] Rydgren (2008); Norris and Inglehart (2019).

[39] Storm, Sobolewska and Ford (2017).

United States in recent years highlight another. Identity liberal Americans have reacted to the election of Donald Trump as president by intensifying their commitment to strong anti-prejudice norms and liberal stances on race, gender and migration issues, a development some American commentators have dubbed 'the Great Awokening'.[40] There has been a dramatic acceleration in the rise of strongly liberal stances among white university graduates in the United States since 2016, with younger white graduates in particular now firmly of the view that the intolerance of ethnocentric identity conservative Americans is a primary source of their country's social problems. Younger white graduates in America now overwhelmingly agree that prejudice against African Americans and other minorities is a major social problem, hold positive views of immigrants and support liberal immigration reforms, and adopt strongly liberal stances on LGBT issues.[41]

America's recent political experience suggests that identity liberals, too, can mobilise politically in response to the emergence of a salient threat – in this case the threat identity liberals perceive from President Trump and his supporters. A similar 'awokening' process could occur in Britain if younger white graduates react to Brexit-related disruptions, or the emergence of new English nationalist or anti-Muslim political movements, by coming to see white identity conservatives as a threatening out-group, and intensifying their commitment to anti-prejudice norms and the defence of minorities in response to this threat. We have shown that the mobilisation of ethnocentrism is a powerful political weapon. Yet the political power of identity conservatives also reflected the weakness of their antagonists, who did not mobilise to the same extent in the years prior to the EU Referendum. Now that Brexit has given identity liberal voters a common political identity, a set of power grievances regarding

---

[40] 'Woke' is a term applied in recent years to strongly identity liberal white voters. Its existence and spread as a label is in itself an illustration of the growing salience and mobilisation of identity liberal politics.

[41] Bolzendahl and Myers (2004); Maxwell and Schulte (2018).

the political status quo, and a belief that political opponents pose a threat to their core values, politicians on the liberal left may have an opportunity to mobilise their side of the identity politics divide more effectively. The past decade has belonged to those who activated and mobilised identity conservatives. The next decades may belong to those who learn to do the same with identity liberals.

BIBLIOGRAPHY

Abou-Chadi, T. and Wagner, M. (2019). 'The Electoral Appeal of Party Strategies in Post-Industrial Democracies: When Can the Mainstream Left Succeed?', *Journal of Politics* 81(4), 1405–19.

Abrams, M. and Rose, R. (1960). *Must Labour Lose?* London: Penguin.

Adams, J., Green, J. and Milazzo, C. (2012). 'Has the British Public Depolarized Along with Political Elites? An American Perspective on British Public Opinion', *Comparative Political Studies* 45(4), 507–30.

Adelman, P. (1995). *The Decline of the Liberal Party 1910–1935*, London: Routledge.

Adorno, T., Frenkel-Brunswick, E., Levinson, D. and Sanford, N. (1950). *The Authoritarian Personality*, New York: Harper.

Akkerman, T., de Lange, S. L. and Rooduijn, M. (2016). 'Inclusion and Mainstreaming? Radical Right-wing Populist Parties in the New Millennium', in T. Akkerman, S. L. de Lange and M. Rooduijn (eds), *Radical Right-Wing Populist Parties in Western Europe: Into the Mainstream?*, Abingdon: Routledge, 19–46.

Akkerman, T., de Lange, S. L. and Rooduijn, M. (eds) (2016). *Radical Right-Wing Populist Parties in Western Europe: Into the Mainstream?*, Abingdon: Routledge.

Alba, R. and Foner, N. (2015). *Strangers No More: Immigration and the Challenges of Integration*, Princeton: Princeton University Press.

Alba, R. and Nee, V. (2003). *Remaking the American Mainstream: Assimilation and Contemporary Immigration*, Cambridge, MA: Harvard University Press.

Allen, P. (2013). 'Linking Pre-Parliamentary Political Experience and the Career Trajectories of the 1997 General Election Cohort', *Parliamentary Affairs* 66(4), 685–707.

(2018). *The Political Class: Why It Matters Who Our Politicians Are*, Oxford: Oxford University Press.

Altemeyer, R. (1981). *Right Wing Authoritarianism*, Manitoba: University of Manitoba Press.

(2007). *The Authoritarians*, Manitoba: University of Manitoba Press.

Alford, J., Funk, C. and Hibbing, J. (2005). 'Are Political Orientations Genetically Transmitted?' *American Political Science Review* 99(2), 154–67.

Altbach, P., Reisberg, L. and Rumbley, L. (2009). 'Trends in Global Higher Education: Tracking an Academic Revolution', UNESCO, available at: http://iie.fing.edu.uy/~geirea/adfi/unesco_tendenciasedusuperior.pdf, last accessed 23 April 2019.

Alwin, D. F. and Krosnick, J. A. (1991). 'Aging, Cohorts and the Stability of Sociopolitical Orientations over the Life Span', *American Journal of Sociology* 97(1), 169–95.

Alwyn, D. and McCammon, R. (2003). 'Generations, Cohorts and Social Change', in J. Mortimer and M. Shanahan (eds), *Handbook of the Lifecourse*, New York: Kluwer Academic, 23–49.

Ashcroft, M. (2012a). 'Degrees of Separation: Ethnic Minority Voters and the Conservative Party', available at: https://lordashcroftpolls .com/wp-content/uploads/2012/04/DEGREES-OF-SEPARATION.pdf, last accessed 21 May 2019.

   (2012b). '"They're Thinking What We're Thinking": Understanding the UKIP Temptation', available at: https://lordashcroftpolls.com/ wp-content/uploads/2012/12/THEYRE-THINKING-WHAT-WERE-THINKING.pdf, last accessed 30 August 2019.

Audickas, L., Dempsey, N. and Loft, P. (2019). 'Membership of UK Political Parties', House of Commons Library Briefing Paper No. SN05125, available at: https://researchbriefings.parliament.uk/ResearchBrief ing/Summary/SN05125#fullreport, last accessed 24 October 2019.

Ausburg, K., Schnek, A. and Hinz, T. (2019). 'Closed Doors Everywhere? A Meta-Analysis of Field Experiments on Ethnic Discrimination in Rental Housing Markets', *Journal of Ethnic and Migration Studies* 45(1), 95–114.

Awan-Scully, R. (2018). 'Devolutionist Unionist? Brexit Won't Ease the Complexities of Welsh Politics', LSE Brexit blog.

Ayres, S. (2014). 'Demographic Differences and Voting Patterns in Scotland's Independence Referendum', House of Commons Library, available at: https://commonslibrary.parliament.uk/parliament-and-elections/ elections-elections/demographic-differences-and-voting-patterns-in-scotlands-independence-referendum, last accessed 25 April 2020.

Bale, T. (2003). 'Cinderella and Her Ugly Sisters: The Mainstream and Extreme Right in Europe's Bipolarising Party Systems', *West European Politics* 26(3), 67–90.

(2010). *The Conservative Party: From Thatcher to Cameron*, London: Polity Press.

(2015). *Five Year Mission: The Labour Party Under Ed Miliband*, Oxford: Oxford University Press.

(2018). 'Who Leads and Who Follows? The Symbiotic Relationship between UKIP and the Conservatives – and Populism and Euroscepticism', *Politics* 38(3), 263–77.

Bale, T., Webb, P. and Pelotti, M. (2019). *Footsoldiers*, Basingstoke: Routledge.

Bale, T., Green-Pedersen, C., Krouwel, A.. Luther, K. R. and Sitter, N. (2010). 'If You Can't Beat Them, Join Them? Explaining Social Democratic Responses to the Challenge from the Populist Radical Right in Western Europe', *Political Studies* 58(3), 410–26.

Barclay, A., Ford, R. and Sobolewska, M. (2019). 'Political Realignment of British Jews: Testing Competing Explanations', *Electoral Studies* 61, 102063.

Barnett, D. (2018). 'Is Flying a George Cross Flag an Act of Patriotism or a Symbol of All That Is Bad about England?' available at: www.independent.co.uk/sport/football/world-cup/st-georges-flag-patriot-england-world-cup-cars-racism-jingosim-brexit-a8398376.html, last accessed 5 August 2019.

Barrett, M. (2000). 'The Development of National Identity in Childhood and Adolescence', University of Surrey Inaugural Lecture.

Barry, B. (2000). *Culture and Equality*, Cambridge: Polity Press.

Bartels, L. and Jackman, S. (2014). 'A Generational Model of Political Learning', *Electoral Studies* 33, 7–18.

Bartolini, S. and Mair, P. (1990). *Identity, Competition, and Electoral Availability: The Stabilization of European Electorates 1885–1985*, Cambridge: Cambridge University Press.

Bawdon, F. (2014). *Chasing Status: The 'Surprised Brits' Who Find They Are Living with Irregular Migration Status*, London: Legal Action Group, available at: www.lag.org.uk/about-us/policy/campaigns/chasing-status, last accessed 23 October 2019.

BBC (2006). 'Profile: Nigel Farage', available at: http://news.bbc.co.uk/1/hi/uk_politics/5338364.stm, last accessed 6 August 2019.

(2013). 'David Cameron Promises In/Out Referendum on EU', available at: www.bbc.co.uk/news/uk-politics-21148282, last accessed 7 August 2019.

(2014). 'Farage Defends Romanian Comments amid Racism Claims', available at: www.bbc.co.uk/news/uk-politics-27474099.

(2016). 'Poland Overtakes India as Country of Origin, UK Migration Statistics Show', available at: www.bbc.co.uk/news/uk-politics-37183733, last accessed 9 May 2019.

Beech, M. and Lee, S. (eds) (2015). *The Conservative–Liberal Democrat Coalition: Examining the Cameron–Clegg Government*, Basingstoke: Palgrave Macmillan.

Begum, N. (2018). 'Minority Ethnic Attitudes and the 2016 EU Referendum', available at: https://ukandeu.ac.uk/minority-ethnic-attitudes-and-the-2016-eu-referendum, last accessed 5 September 2019.

(2019). '"The Eastern Europeans Are Taking All the Asian Jobs": Ethnic Minority Support for Brexit', in P. Cowley and R. Ford (eds), *Sex, Lies and Politics: The Secret Influences that Drive Our Political Choices*, London: Biteback, ch. 42.

Béland, D. and Lecours, A. (2016). 'The 2014 Scottish Referendum and the Nationalism–Social Policy Nexus', *Canadian Political Science Review* 10(1), 1–30.

Belanger, E. (2004). 'Antipartyism and Third Party Vote Choice: A Comparison of Canada, Britain and Australia', *Comparative Political Studies* 37(9), 1054–1078.

Belanger, E. and Godbout, J.-F. (2010). 'Why Do Parties Merge? The Case of the Conservative Party in Canada', *Parliamentary Affairs* 63(1), 41–65.

Benedetto, G., Hix, S. and Mastrorocco, N. (2019). 'The Rise and Fall of Social Democracy 1918–2017', paper presented at the American Political Science Association annual conference, August 2019, Washington DC.

Bergh, J. and Bjørklund, T. (2011). 'The Revival of Group Voting: Explaining the Voting Preferences of Immigrants in Norway', *Political Studies* 59(2), 308–27.

Berntzen, L. E., Bjånesøy, L. and Ivarsflaten, E. (2017). 'Patterns of Legitimacy on the Far Right', paper presented at ECPR general conference, March.

Best, H. and Cotta, M. (eds) (2000). *Parliamentary Representatives in Europe 1848–2000*, Oxford: Oxford University Press.

Betz, H. (2016). 'Against the "Green Totalitarianism": Anti-Islamic Nativism in Contemporary Radical Right Populism in Western Europe', in C. Liang (ed.), *Europe for the Europeans: The Foreign and Security Policy of the Radical Right*, Abingdon: Routledge, 33–54.

Bishop, B. (2008). *The Big Sort: Why the Clustering of Like-Minded America Is Tearing Us Apart*, New York: Houghton Mifflin.

Blair, T. (2005). 'Speech on Asylum and Immigration', available at: www .theguardian.com/politics/2005/apr/22/election2005 .immigrationandpublicservices, last accessed 6 August 2019.

Blais, A. and Carty, R. K. (1991). 'The Psychological Impact of Electoral Laws: Measuring Duverger's Elusive Factor', *British Journal of Political Science* 21(1), 79–93.

Blanden, J. and Macmillan, L. (2016). 'Educational Inequality, Educational Expansion and Intergenerational Mobility', *Journal of Social Policy* 45(4), 589–614.

Blanden, J. and Manchin, S. (2004). 'Educational Inequality and the Expansion of UK Higher Education', *Scottish Journal of Political Economy* 51(2), 230–49.

Bleich, E. (2003). *Race Politics in Britain and France: Ideas and Policymaking since the 1960s*, Cambridge: Cambridge University Press.

Blinder, S. (2015). 'Imagined Immigration: The Impact of Different Meanings of "Immigrants" in Public Opinion and Policy Debates in Britain', *Political Studies* 63(1), 80–100.

Blinder, S. and Fernandez-Reino, M. (2018). 'Non-European Student Migration to the UK', Migration Observatory briefing, available at: https://migrationobservatory.ox.ac.uk/resources/briefings/non-euro pean-student-migration-to-the-uk, last accessed 6 August 2019.

Blinder, S., Ford, R. and Ivarsflaten, E. (2013). 'The Better Angels of Our Nature: How the Antiprejudice Norm Affects Policy and Party Preferences in Great Britain and Germany', *American Journal of Political Science* 57(4), 841–57.

(2019). 'Discrimination, Anti-prejudice Norms and Public Support for Multicultural Policies in Europe: The Case of Religious Schools', *Comparative Political Studies* 52(8), 1232–55.

Blinder, S. and Richards, L. (2018). 'UK Public Opinion towards Immigration: Overall Attitudes and Levels of Concern', Migration Observatory briefing paper, available at: https://migrationobservatory.ox .ac.uk/resources/briefings/uk-public-opinion-toward-immigration-overall-attitudes-and-level-of-concern, last accessed 9 May 2019.

Boliver, V. (2011). 'Expansion, Differentiation, and the Persistence of Social Class Inequalities in British Higher Education', *Higher Education*, 61(3), 229–42.

(2013). 'How Fair Is Access to More Prestigious UK Universities?', *British Journal of Sociology* 64(2), 344–64.

(2016). 'Exploring Ethnic Inequalities in Admissions to Russell Group Universities', *Sociology* 50(2), 247–66.

Bolzendahl, C. and Myers, D. (2004). 'Feminist Attitudes and Support for Gender Equality: Opinion Change in Women and Men, 1974–1998', *Social Forces* 83, 759–89.

Bowling, B. and Philips, C. (2007). 'Disproportionate and Discriminatory: Reviewing the Evidence on Police Stop and Search', *Modern Law Review* 70(6), 936–61.

Brand, J., Mitchell, J. and Surridge, P. (1994). 'Social Constituency and Ideological Profile: Scottish Nationalism in the 1990s', *Political Studies* 42(4), 616–29.

Breen, R., Luijka, R., Müller, W. and Pollak, R. (2009). 'Non-persistent Inequality in Educational Attainment: Evidence from Eight European Countries', *American Journal of Sociology* 114, 1475–1525.

Brewer, M. (1999). 'The Psychology of Prejudice: Ingroup Love and Outgroup Hate?' *Journal of Social Issues* 55(3), 429–44.

British Future (2012). 'This Sceptred Isle: Pride Not Prejudice Across the Nations of Britain', available at: www.britishfuture.org/wp-content/uploads/2012/04/BritishFutureSceptredIsle.pdf, last accessed 7 August 2019.

Bulman, M. (2018). 'Home Office Accused of Using Children of Immigrants as a "Cash Cow" with Extortionate Citizenship Fees', available at: www.independent.co.uk/news/uk/home-news/child-immigrants-uk-home-office-citizenship-fees-immigration-amnesty-a8423491.html, last accessed 23 October 2019.

Burnham, A. (2016). 'Labour Needs to Take Back Control of the Immigration Debate', available at: www.theguardian.com/commentisfree/2016/dec/16/take-back-control-immigration-debate-labour, last accessed 5 August 2019.

Butler, C. (2019). 'The Liberal Democrats and Tuition Fees: Lessons for the Conservatives Today', available at: https://wonkhe.com/blogs/the-liberal-democrats-and-tuition-fees-lessons-for-the-conservatives-today, last accessed 21 August 2019.

Butler, D. and Kavanagh, D. (2005). *The British General Election of 2005*, Basingstoke: Palgrave Macmillan.

Butler, D. and Stokes, D. (1974). *Political Change in Britain: Basis of Electoral Choice*, Basingstoke: Macmillan.

Cairney, P. (2007). 'The Professionalisation of MPs: Refining the "Politics-facilitating" Explanation', *Parliamentary Affairs* 60(2), 212–33.

Cameron, D. (2010). Interview on the Andrew Marr Show, 10 January, available at: www.theguardian.com/uk/2010/jan/11/david-cameron-limit-immigration, last accessed 26 June 2019.

Campbell, R. and Heath, O. (n.d.). 'Fuelling the Populist Divide: Nativist and Cosmopolitan Preferences for Representation at the Elite and Mass Level', unpublished paper.

Cannadine, D. (2017). *Victorious Century*, London: Penguin.

Carella, L. (2019). 'Bloc Politics: A Split Remain Vote May Not Equal a Large Conservative Majority', UK in a Changing Europe, available at: https://ukandeu.ac.uk/bloc-politics-a-split-remain-vote-may-not-equal-a-large-conservative-majority, last accessed 17 October 2019.

Carey, S. (2002). 'Undivided Loyalties: Is National Identity an Obstacle to European Integration? *European Union Politics* 3, 387–413.

Carl, N., Dennison, J. and Evans, G. (2018). 'European but not European Enough: An Explanation for Brexit', *European Union Politics* 20(2), 282–304.

Carlson, M. and Eriksson, S. (2015). 'Ethnic Discrimination in the London Market for Shared Housing', *Journal of Ethnic and Migration Studies* 41(8), 1276–301.

Carmines, E. G. and Stimson, J. A. (1989). *Issue Evolution: Race and the Transformation of American Politics*, Princeton: Princeton University Press.

Carreras, M., Irepoglu Carreras, Y. and Bowler, S. (2019). 'Long-term Economic Distress, Cultural Backlash, and Support for Brexit', *Comparative Political Studies* 52(9), 1396–424.

Carter, H. and Wainwright, M. (2010). 'Gillian Duffy: A Lifelong Labour Voter Who May Bring Down the PM', available at: www.theguardian.com/politics/2010/apr/28/gillian-duffy-gordon-brown-general-election-2010, last accessed 18 June 2019.

Charney, E. and English, W. (2012). 'Candidate Genes and Political Behaviour', *American Political Science Review* 106(1), 1–34.

Choonara, J. (2016). 'After the Leave Vote: We Can Beat Back Racism and Austerity', available at: http://socialistreview.org.uk/415/after-leave-vote-we-can-beat-back-racism-and-austerity, last accessed 8 April 2020.

Citrin, J., Reingold, B. and Green, D. (1990). 'American Identity and the Politics of Ethnic Change', *Journal of Politics* 52(4), 1124–54.

Citrin, J. and Sears, D. (2014). *American Identity and the Politics of Multiculturalism*, Cambridge: Cambridge University Press.

Clarke, H., Goodwin, M. and Whiteley, P. (2017). *Brexit: Why Britain Voted to Leave the European Union*, Cambridge: Cambridge University Press.

Clarke, H. and Kornberg, A. (1996). 'Partisan Dealignment, Electoral Choice and Party-System Change in Canada', *Party Politics* 2, 455–78.

Clarke, H., Sanders, D., Stewart, M. and Whiteley, P. (2003). *Political Choice in Britain*, Oxford: Oxford University Press.

(2009). *Performance Politics and the British Voter*, Cambridge: Cambridge University Press.

Clegg, N. (2017). *Politics between the Extremes*, London: Vintage.

Clements, B. (2015). *Religion and Public Opinion in Britain: Continuity and Change*, Basingstoke: Palgrave Macmillan.

Colley, L. (1992). *Britons: Forging the Nation*, New Haven, CT: Yale University Press.

Consterdine, E. (2017). *Labour's Immigration Policy: The Making of the Migration State*, Basingstoke: Palgrave Macmillan.

Cooper, A. (2018). 'On Diversity: Conservatives Are Losing the Generation Game', in S. Ballinger (ed.), *Many Rivers Crossed: Britain's Attitudes to Race and Immigration 50 Years after 'Rivers of Blood'*, London: British Future, 46–7.

Copeland, P. and Copsey, N. (2017). 'Rethinking Britain and the European Union: Politicians, the Media and Public Opinion Reconsidered', *Journal of Common Market Studies* 55(4), 709–26.

Copsey, N. and Macklin, G. (eds) (2011). *The British National Party: Contemporary Perspectives*, Abingdon: Routledge.

Cowley, P. (2012). 'Arise, Novice Leader! The Continuing Rise of the Career Politician in Britain', *Politics* 30, 31–8.

Cowley, P. and Kavanagh, D. (2016). *The British General Election of 2015*, Basingstoke: Palgrave Macmillan.

Cowley, P. and Norton, P. (1999). 'Rebels and Rebellions: Conservative MPs in the 1992 Parliament', *British Journal of Politics and International Relations* 1, 84–105.

Cowley, P. and Stuart, M. (2013). 'Cambo Chained: Or, Dissension amongst the Coalition's Parliamentary Parties, 2012–13: A Data Handbook', University of Nottingham, available at: http://nottspolitics.org/wp-content/uploads/2013/05/Cambo-Chained.pdf, last accessed 25 October 2019.

Cramer, K. (2016). *The Politics of Resentment: Rural Consciousness in Wisconsin and the Rise of Scott Walker*, Chicago: University of Chicago Press.

Criddle, B. (2010). 'More Diverse Yet More Uniform: MPs and Candidates', in D. Kavanagh and P. Cowley (eds), *The British General Election of 2010*, Basingstoke: Palgrave Macmillan, 306–29.

(2015). 'Variable Diversity: MPs and Candidates'. in P. Cowley and D. Kavanagh, *The British General Election of 2015*, Basingstoke: Palgrave Macmillan, 336–60.

Cruddas, J., Pecorelli, N. and Rutherford, J. (2016). 'Labour's Future: Why Labour Lost in 2015 and How It Can Win Again', Report of the Independence Inquiry into Why Labour Lost in 2015, One Nation Register, London, available at: www.cultdyn.co.uk/ART067736u/313245238-Labour-s-Future-19-05-16.pdf, last accessed 29 August 2019.

Curtice, J. (2005). 'Turnout: Electors Stay Home – Again', *Parliamentary Affairs* 58(4), 776–85.

(2007). 'New Labour, New Protest? How the Liberal Democrats Profited from Blair's Mistakes', *Political Quarterly* 78(1), 117–26.

(2014). 'So How Many 16 and 17 Year Olds Voted?', available at: http://blog.whatscotlandthinks.org/2014/12/many-16-17-year-olds-voted, last accessed 8 August 2019.

(2015a). 'How Deeply Does Britain's Euroscepticism Run?' *British Social Attitudes: 33rd Report*, London: NatCen Social Research.

(2015b). 'A Return to Normality? How the Electoral System Operated', *Parliamentary Affairs* 68(1), 25–40.

(2016). 'US Election 2016: The Trump–Brexit Voter Revolt', available at: www.bbc.co.uk/news/election-us-2016-37943072, last accessed 4 May 2020.

Curtice, J., Devine, P. and Ormston, R. (2013). 'Trends in National Identity', in *British Social Attitudes: 30th Report*, London: NatCen Social Research.

Curtice, J., Fisher, S., Ford, R. and English, P. (2018). 'Appendix 1: The Results Analysed', in P. Cowley and D. Kavanagh (eds), The British General Election of 2017, Basingstoke: Palgrave Macmillan.

Curtice, J., Fisher, S. and Ford, R. (2016). 'Appendix 2: The Results Analysed', in P. Cowley and D. Kavanagh (eds), *The British General Election of 2015*, Basingstoke: Palgrave Macmillan, 387–431.

Curtice, J., Fisher, S. and Steed, M. (2006). 'Appendix 2: An Analysis of the Results', in D. Kavanagh, and D. Butler (eds), *The British General Election of 2005*, Basingstoke: Palgrave Macmillan, 235–9.

Curtice, J. and Ormston, R. (2011). 'Is Scotland More Left-wing than England?' available at: www.scotcen.org.uk/media/176048/2011-is-scotland-more-left-wing-than-england.pdf, last accessed 19 August 2019.

Curtice, J. and Steed, M. (2001). 'Appendix 2: The Results Analysed', in D. Butler and D. Kavanagh (eds), *The British General Election of 2001*, Basingstoke: Palgrave.

Cutts, D., Ford, R. and Goodwin, M. J. (2011). 'Anti-immigrant, Politically Disaffected or Still Racist After All? Examining the Attitudinal Drivers of Extreme Right Support in Britain in the 2009 European Elections', *European Journal of Political Research* 50(3), 418–40.

Daddow, O. (2012). 'The UK Media and "Europe": From Permissive Consensus to Destructive Dissent', *International Affairs* 88(6), 1219–36.

Dahlström, C. and Esaiasson, P. (2013). 'The Immigration Issue and Anti-immigrant Party Success in Sweden 1970–2006: A Deviant Case Analysis', *Party Politics* 19(2), 343–64.

Dalton, R. and Wattenberg, M. (eds) (2002). *Parties without Partisans: Political Change in Advanced Industrial Democracies*, Oxford: Oxford University Press.

Dancygier, R. and Saunders, E. (2006). 'A New Electorate? Comparing Preferences and Partisanship between Immigrants and Natives', *American Journal of Political Science* 50(4), 962–81.

Davis, R. (2011). *Tangled Up in Blue: Blue Labour and the Struggle for Labour's Soul*, London: Ruskin.

Davis, S. and Greenstein, T. (2009). 'Gender Ideology: Components, Predictors and Consequences', *Annual Review of Sociology* 35, 87–105.

Dawson, M. (1996). *Behind the Mule: Race and Class in African-American Politics*, Princeton: Princeton University Press.

De Vries, C. E. (2007). 'Sleeping Giant: Fact or Fairytale? How European Integration Affects National Elections,' *European Union Politics* 8(3), 363–85.

    (2018). *Euroscepticism and the Future of European Integration*, Oxford: Oxford University Press.

Denham, J. (2019). 'The Truth about "English nationalism"', available at: www.theoptimisticpatriot.co.uk/post/187029356313/the-truth-about-english-nationalism, last accessed 27 October 2019.

Dennison, J. (2015). 'The Loser Takes It All: The SNP after the Referendum', available at: https://blogs.lse.ac.uk/politicsandpolicy/the-loser-takes-it-all-the-snp-after-the-referendum, last accessed 15 July 2019.

Dennison, J. and Goodwin, M. (2015). 'Immigration, Issue Ownership, and the Rise of UKIP', *Parliamentary Affairs* 68(1), 168–87.

Denver, D. (2015). 'The Results: How Britain Voted', *Parliamentary Affairs* 68(1), 5–24.

Denver, D., Hands, G., Fisher, J. and MacAllister, I. (2003). 'Constituency Campaigning in Britain 1992–2001: Centralization and Modernization', *Party Politics* 9(5), 541–59.

Devereux, P. and Fan, W. (2011). 'Earning Returns to the British Education Expansion', *Economics of Education Review* 30(6), 1153–66.

Dolezal, M. (2010). 'Exploring the Stabilization of a Political Force: the Social and Attitudinal Basis of Green Parties in the Age of Globalization', *West European Politics* 33(3), 534–52.

Dorling, D. (2014). 'Mapping the Thatcherite Legacy', in S. Farrall and C. Hay (eds), *The Legacy of Thatcherism: Assessing and Exploring Thatcherite Economic and Social Policies*, Oxford: Oxford University Press, 240–72.

Dorling, D., Stuart, B. and Stubbs, J. (2016). 'Don't Mention This Around the Christmas Table: Brexit, Inequality and the Demographic Divide', LSE European Politics and Policy (EUROPP) blog.

Dorling, D. and Tomlinson, S. (2019). *Rule Britannia: Brexit and the End of Empire*, London: Biteback.

Du Bois, W. (1903). *The Souls of Black Folk*, New York: New American Library.

Duffy, B. (2013). 'Generations', IPSOS-MORI Social Research Institute, London.

Duffy, B., Hall, S., O'Leary, D. and Pope, S. (2013). *Generation Strains*, London: Demos.

Dustmann, C., Casanova, M., Fertig, M., Preston, I. and Schmidt, C. (2003). 'The Impact of EU Enlargement on Migration Flows', Home Office Online Report 25/03, available at: https://webarchive .nationalarchives.gov.uk/20110218141514/http://rds.homeoffice .gov.uk/rds/pdfs2/rdsolr2503.pdf, last accessed 15 April 2020.

Eatwell, R. and Goodwin, M. (2018). *National Populism: The Revolt against Liberal Democracy*, London: Pelican.

Edgerton, D. (2018). *The Rise and Fall of the British Nation*, London: Penguin.

Ermisch, J. and Richards, L. (2016). 'Trends in Educational Mobility in the UK', Centre for Social Investigation, Briefing paper 25, available at: http://csi.nuff.ox.ac.uk/wp-content/uploads/2016/07/CSI-25-Trends-in-educational-mobility.pdf, last accessed 23 April 2019.

Esteves, O. (2019). 'Wrathful Rememberers: Harnessing the Memory of World War II in Letters of Support to Powell', in O. Esteves and S. Poiron (eds), *The Lives and Afterlives of Enoch Powell: The Undying Political Animal*, Abingdon: Routledge, 32–46.

Evans, G. (1998). 'Euroscepticism and Conservative Electoral Support: How an Asset Became a Liability', *British Journal of Political Science* 28(4), 573–90.

Evans, G. and Chzhen, K. (2013). 'Explaining Voters' Defection from Labour in the 2005–10 Electoral Cycle: Leadership, Economics and the Rising Importance of Immigration', *Political Studies* 61(1), 138–57.

Evans, G. and Mellon, J. (2014). 'All Roads Lead to UKIP?', British Election Study blog, available at: www.britishelectionstudy.com/bes-resources/all-roads-lead-to-ukip-by-geoff-evans-and-jon-mellon-university-of-oxford/#.XRSQ3ehKiUk, last accessed 27 June 2019.

(2019). 'Immigration, Euroscepticism and the Rise and Fall of UKIP', *Party Politics* 25(1), 76–87.

Evans, G. and Menon, A. (2017). *Brexit and British Politics*, Chichester: John Wiley.

Evans, G. and Tilley, J. (2012a). 'The Depoliticization of Inequality and Redistribution: Explaining the Decline of Class Voting', *Journal of Politics* 74, 963–76.

(2012b). 'How Parties Shape Class Politics: Explaining the Decline in the Class Basis of Party Support', *British Journal of Political Science* 42, 137–61.

(2017). *The New Politics of Class: The Political Exclusion of the British Working Class*, Oxford: Oxford University Press.

Feldman, S. and Stenner, K. (1997). 'Perceived Threat and Authoritarianism', *Political Psychology* 18(4), 741–70.

Fetzer, T. (2019). 'Did Austerity Cause Brexit?', *American Economic Review* 109(11), 3849–86.

Fieldhouse, E. (2014). 'Thatcher's Legacy Still Looms: The North–South Divide in Britain's Electoral Support', available at: www.britishelectionstudy.com/bes-findings/thatchers-legacy-still-looms-large-the-north-south-divide-in-britains-electoral-support/#.XR8MJuhKiUk, last accessed 5 July 2019.

Fieldhouse, E., Green, J., Evans, G., Mellon, C., Prosser, C., Schmidt, H. and Van der Eijk, C. (2019). *Electoral Shocks: The Volatile Voter in a Turbulent World*, Oxford: Oxford University Press.

Fieldhouse, E. and Prosser, C. (2018). 'The Limits of Partisan Loyalty: How the Scottish Independence Referendum Cost Labour', *Electoral Studies* 52, 11–25.

Fieldhouse, E. and Russell, A. (2005). *Neither Left nor Right? The Liberal Democrats and the Electorate*, Manchester: Manchester University Press.

Fieldhouse, E., Russell, A. and Cutts, D. (2006). 'Neither North nor South: Liberal Democrat Performance in the 2005 General Election', *Journal of Elections, Public Opinion and Parties* 16(1), 77–92.

Finney, N. and Simpson, L. (2009a). *'Sleepwalking to Segregation?' Challenging Myths about Race and Migration*, Bristol: Policy Press.

(2009b). 'Population Dynamics: The Roles of Natural Change and Migration in Producing the Ethnic Mosaic', *Journal of Ethnic and Migration Studies* 35(9), 1479–96.

Fisher, J., Cutts, D. and Fieldhouse, E. (2011). 'The Electoral Effectiveness of Constituency Campaigning in the 2010 British General Election: The "Triumph" of Labour?', *Electoral Studies* 30(4), 816–28.

Fisher, J. and Denver, D. (2008). 'From Foot-slogging to Call Centres and Direct Mail: A Framework for Analysing the Development of District Level Campaigning', *European Journal of Political Research* 47(6), 794–826.

(2009). 'Evaluating the Electoral Effects of Traditional and Modern Modes of Constituency Campaigning in Britain 1992–2005', *Parliamentary Affairs* 62(2), 196–210.

Fisher, S. (2004). 'Definition and Measurement of Tactical Voting: The Role of Rational Choice', *British Journal of Political Science* 34, 152–66.

Fleming A. and Mondon A. (2018). 'The Radical Right in Australia', in J. Rydgren (ed.), *The Oxford Handbook of the Radical Right*, Oxford: Oxford University Press, 650–66.

Ford, R. (2008). 'Is Racial Prejudice Declining in Britain?' *British Journal of Sociology* 59(4), 609–36.

(2012). 'Acceptable and Unacceptable Migrants: How Opposition to Immigration in Britain Is Affected by Migrants' Regions of Origin', *Journal of Ethnic and Migration Studies* 37(7), 1017–37.

(2016). 'Who Should We Help? An Experimental Test of Discrimination in the Welfare State', *Political Studies* 64(3), 630–50.

(2018a). 'Why Voting Rights for EU Citizens Should Be on the Political Agenda', *Political Insight* 9(2), 26–8.

(2018b). 'How Have Attitudes to Immigration Changed since Brexit?', available at: https://ukandeu.ac.uk/how-have-attitudes-to-immigration-changed-since-brexit, last accessed 17 May 2019.

(2019a). 'Immigration: Is Public Opinion Changing?' in A. Menon (ed.), *Brexit and Public Opinion*, London: UK in a Changing Europe, 13–16.

(2019b). 'Powell and After: Race, Immigration and Politics in Britain 1964–1979', in O. Esteves and S. Poiron (eds), *The Lives and Afterlives of Enoch Powell*, Abingdon: Routledge.

Ford, R. and Goodwin, M. (2010). 'Angry White Men: Individual and Contextual Predictors of BNP Support', *Political Studies* 58, 1–25.

(2011). 'Labour, Fear UKIP', *The Guardian*, available at: www .theguardian.com/commentisfree/2011/apr/18/ukip-labour-british-electorate, accessed 5 July 2019.

(2014a). 'Understanding UKIP: Identity, Social Change and the Left Behind', *Political Quarterly* 85(3), 277–84.

(2014b). *Revolt on the Right: Explaining Support for the Radical Right in Britain*, Abingdon: Routledge.

(2014c). 'The 100 Most 'UKIP-friendly' Conservative Seats', available at: www.conservativehome.com/platform/2014/09/dr-robert-ford-and-dr-matthew-goodwin-the-top-100-most-ukip-friendly-conserva tive-seats.html, last accessed 27 October 2019.

Ford, R., Goodwin, M. and Cutts, D. (2012). 'Strategic Eurosceptics and Polite Xenophobes: Support for the United Kingdom Independence Party (UKIP) in the 2009 European Parliament Elections', *European Journal of Political Research* 51(2), 204–34.

Ford, R., Goodwin, M. and Sobolewska, M. (2017). 'British Politics', in A. Menon (ed.), *The EU Referendum: One Year On*, 16–17, available at: www.psa.ac.uk/sites/default/files/EU-referendum-one-year-on.pdf, last accessed 15 July 2019.

Ford, R. and Heath, A. (2014). 'Immigration: A Nation Divided', *British Social Attitudes: 31st Report*, London: NatCen Social Research.

Ford, R. and Jennings, W. (2020). 'The Changing Cleavage Politics of Western Europe', *Annual Review of Political Science* 23(1), 1–20.

Ford, R., Jennings, W. and Pickup, M. (2011). 'Polling Observatory #1: The Story So Far', available at: http://nottspolitics.org/2011/04/13/ polling-observatory1-the-story-so-far, last accessed 21 August 2019.

Ford, R., Jennings, W. and Somerville, W. (2015). 'Public Opinion, Responsiveness and Constraint: Britain's Three Immigration Policy Regimes', *Journal of Ethnic and Migration Studies* 41(9), 1391–411.

Ford, R., Jolley, R., Katwala, S. and Mehta, B. (2012). 'The Melting Pot Generation', British Future, available at: www.britishfuture.org/

wp-content/uploads/2012/12/The-melting-pot-generation.pdf, last accessed 10 May 2019.

Ford, R. and Kootstra, A. (2017). 'Do White Voters Support Welfare Policies Targeted at Ethnic Minorities? Experimental Evidence from Britain', *Journal of Ethnic and Migration Studies* 43(1), 80–101.

Ford, R. and Lymperopoulou, K. (2017). 'Immigration: How Attitudes in the UK Compare with Europe', in *British Social Attitudes: 34th Report*, London: NatCen Social Research, 1–30.

Ford, R., Morrell, G. and Heath, A. (2012). 'Fewer but Better? Public Views about Immigration', in A. Park, E. Clery, J. Curtice, M. Phillips and D. Utting (eds), *British Social Attitudes: 29th Report*, London: NatCen Social Research.

Forster, A. (2002). *Euroscepticism in Contemporary British Politics: Opposition to Europe in the British Conservative and Labour Parties since 1945*, London: Routledge.

Funk, C. L., Smith, K. B., Alford, J. R., Hibbing, M. V., Eaton, N. R., Krueger, R. F., Eaves, L. J. and Hibbing, J. R. (2013). 'Genetic and Environmental Transmission of Political Orientations', *Political Psychology* 34, 805–19.

Geary, I. and Pabst, A. (eds) (2015). *Blue Labour: Forging a New Politics*, London: I. B. Tauris.

Geddes, A. (2014). 'The EU, UKIP and the Politics of Immigration in Britain', *Political Quarterly* 85(3), 289–95.

Gentleman, A. (2018). 'The Week that Took Windrush from Low Profile Investigation to National Scandal', available at: www.theguardian.com/uk-news/2018/apr/20/the-week-that-took-windrush-from-low-profile-investigation-to-national-scandal, last accessed 15 May 2019.

(2019). *The Windrush Betrayal: Exposing the Hostile Environment*, London: Guardian Faber.

Gest, J. (2016). *The New Minority: White Working Class Americans in an Age of Immigration and Inequality*, Oxford: Oxford University Press.

Giddens, A. (1998). *The Third Way: The Renewal of Social Democracy*, London: Polity Press.

Gilens, M. (1999). *Why Americans Hate Welfare: Race, Media and the Politics of Antipoverty Policy*, Chicago: University of Chicago Press.

Glasman, M., Rutherford, J., Stears, M. and White, S. (eds) (2011). *The Labour Tradition and the Politics of Paradox: The Oxford–London Seminars 2010–11*, London: Lawrence & Wishart.

Golder, M. (2016). 'Far Right Parties in Europe', *Annual Review of Political Science* 19. 477–97.

Goodfellow, M. (2019). 'To Fix Its Problems Now, Labour Must Face the Racism of Its Past', available at: www.theguardian.com/commentisfree/2019/mar/08/labour-party-racism-truth-past, last accessed 8 April 2020.

Goodhart, D. (2017). *The Road to Somewhere: The Populist Revolt and the Future of Politics*, London: Hurst.

Goodwin, M. (2011). *New British Fascism: Rise of the British National Party*, Abingdon: Routledge.

Goodwin, M., Cutts, D. and Ford, R. (2012). 'Extreme Right Footsoldiers, Legacy Effects and Deprivation: A Contextual Analysis of the Leaked BNP Membership List', *Party Politics* 19(6), 897–906.

Goodwin, M. and Heath, O. (2016). 'The 2016 Referendum, Brexit and the Left Behind: An Aggregate-level Analysis of the Result', *Political Quarterly* 87(3), 323–32.

Goodwin, M. and Milazzo, C. (2015). *UKIP: Inside the Campaign to Redraw the Map of British Politics*, Oxford: Oxford University Press.

    (2017). 'Taking Back Control? Investigating the Role of Immigration in the 2016 Vote for Brexit', *British Journal of Politics and International Relations* 19(3), 450–64.

Gower, M. (2015). 'Immigration and Asylum: Changes Made by the Coalition Government 2010–15', House of Commons Library, available at: https://commonslibrary.parliament.uk/research-briefings/sn05829, last accessed 16 April 2020.

    (2018), 'The UK's Points Based System for Migration', House of Commons Library Briefing Paper, available at: https://commonslibrary.parliament.uk/research-briefings/cbp-7662, last accessed 15 April 2020.

Grasso, M., Farrall, S., Gray, E., Hay, C. and Jennings, W. (2017). 'Thatcher's Children, Blair's Babies, Political Socialization and Trickle-Down Value Change: An Age, Period, Cohort Analysis', *British Journal of Political Science* 49, 17–36.

Green, D., Palmquist, B. and Schinkler, E. (2004). *Partisan Hearts and Minds: Political Parties and the Social Identities of Voters*, New Haven, CT: Yale University Press.

Green, J. (2007). 'When Parties and Voters Agree: Valence Issues and Party Competition', *Political Studies* 55(3), 629–55.

Green, J. and Hobolt, S. (2008). 'Owning the Issue Agenda: Party Strategies and Vote Choices in British Elections', *Electoral Studies* 27(3), 460–76.

Green, J. and Jennings, W. (2012). "Valence as Macro-Competence: An Analysis of Mood in Party Competence Evaluations in Great Britain', *British Journal of Political Science* 42(2), 311–43.

Green, J. and Prosser, C. (2015). 'Learning the Right Lessons from Labour's 2015 Defeat', IPPR, London, available at: www.ippr.org/juncture/learning-the-right-lessons-from-labours-2015-defeat, last accessed 1 September 2019.

Guardian, The (2015). 'Diane Abbott: Labour's "Controls on Immigration" Mugs are Shameful', available at: www.theguardian.com/politics/2015/mar/29/diane-abbott-labour-immigration-controls-mugs-shameful, last accessed 8 April 2020.

Guth, J. L. and Nelsen, B. F. (2019). 'Party Choice in Europe: Social Cleavages and the Rise of Populist Parties', *Party Politics*, 1354068819853965.

Gutiérrez, D. G. (2016). 'A Historic Overview of Latino Immigration and the Demographic Transformation of the United States', in R. A. Gutiérrez and T. Almaguer (eds), *The New Latino Studies Reader: A Twenty-first-century Perspective*, Berkeley: California University Press, 108–25.

Hagendoorn, L. (1995). 'Intergroup Biases in Multiple Group Systems: the Perception of Ethnic Hierarchies', *European Review of Social Psychology* 6, 199–228.

Hakhverdian, A. (2015). 'Does it Matter That Most Representatives Are Higher Educated?', *Swiss Political Science Review* 21(2), 237–45.

Hakhverdian, A., Elsas, E., van der Brug, W. and Kuhn, T. (2013). 'Euroscepticism and Education: A Longitudinal Study of 12 Member States 1973–2010', *European Union Politics* 14(4), 522–41.

Hall, S. (2018). *Familiar Stranger: A Life between Two Islands*, London: Allen Lane.

Hampshire, J. and Bale, T. (2016). 'New Administration, New Immigration Regime: Do Parties Matter After All? A UK Case Study', *West European Politics* 38(1), 145–66.

Hansen, R. (2000). *Citizenship and Immigration in Postwar Britain*, Oxford: Oxford University Press.

Harris, G. (2012). 'The Rise and Fall of the BNP: The Demand for Extreme Right Politics in the UK', unpublished PhD thesis, University of Birkbeck.

Harrison, A. (2017). 'A Brief History of Britain's Racist Sitcoms', available at: www.vice.com/en_uk/article/mba49a/all-your-favourite-old-british-sitcoms-are-racist-as-hell, last accessed 17 May 2019.

Hasan, M. (2014), 'Five Questions for Anyone Who Says "It's Not Racist to Talk About Immigration"', available at: www.newstatesman.com/politics/2014/11/five-questions-anyone-who-says-its-not-racist-talk-about-immigration, last accessed 5 August 2019.

Hassan, G. (ed.) (2009). *The Making of the Modern SNP: From Protest to Power*, Edinburgh: Edinburgh University Press.

Hayton, R. (2012). *Reconstructing Conservatism? The Conservative Party in Opposition 1997–2010*, Manchester: Manchester University Press.

Heath, A. and Cheung, S. (eds) (2007). *Unequal Chances: Ethnic Minorities in Western Labour Markets*, Oxford: Oxford University Press.

Heath, A. and DiStasio, V. (2019). 'Racial Discrimination in Britain 1969–2017: A Meta-Analysis of Field Experiments on Racial Discrimination in the British Labour Market', *British Journal of Sociology* 70(5), 1774–98.

Heath, A., Fisher, S. D., Rosenblatt, G., Sanders, D. and Sobolewska, M. (2013). *The Political Integration of Ethnic Minorities in Britain*. Oxford: Oxford University Press.

Heath, A., Jowell, R., Curtice, J. and Taylor, B. (1994). *Labour's Last Chance? The 1992 Election and Beyond*, London: Dartmouth.

Heath, A. and Taylor, B. (1999). 'New Sources of Abstention?', in G. Evans and P. Norris (eds), *Critical Elections: British Parties and Voters in Long-term Perspective*, London: Sage, 164–78.

Heath, O. (2018). 'Policy Alienation, Social Alienation and Working Class Abstention in Britain 1964–2010', *British Journal of Political Science* 48, 1053–73.

Helbling, M. (2013). *Islamophobia in the West: Measuring and Explaining Individual Attitudes*, Basingstoke: Routledge.

Henderson, A. (2007). *Hierarchies of Belonging: National Identity and Political Culture in Scotland and Quebec*, Montreal: McGill-Queen's University Press.

(2014). 'Myth of Meritocratic Scotland', in P. Cowley and R. Ford (eds), *Sex, Lies and the Ballot Box*, London: Biteback, 103–8.

Henderson, A. and Wyn-Jones, R. (2020). *Englishness: The Political Force Transforming British Politics*, Oxford: Oxford University Press, in press.

Hobolt, S. B. (2009). *Europe in Question: Referendums on European Integration*, Oxford: Oxford University Press.

(2016). 'The Brexit Vote: A Divided Nation, a Divided Continent', *Journal of European Public Policy* 23(9), 1259–77.

Hobolt, S., Spoon, J. and Tilley, J. (2009). 'A Vote against Europe? Explaining Defection at the 1999 and 2004 European Parliament Elections', *British Journal of Political Science* 39(1), 93–115.

Hobolt, S., Leeper, T. and Tilley, J. (2018). 'Divided by the Vote: Affective Polarisation in the Wake of Brexit', paper presented to the American Political Science Association annual conference, available at: https://s3.us-east-2.amazonaws.com/tjl-sharing/assets/DividedByTheVote.pdf, last accessed 6 September 2019.

Hochschild, A. R. ([2016] 2018). *Strangers in Their Own Land: Anger and Mourning on the American Right*, New York: New Press.

Home Office (2019). 'Immigration Statistics, Year Ending September 2019', available at: www.gov.uk/government/statistics/immigration-statistics-year-ending-september-2019, last accessed 25 April 2020.

Hooghe, L. and Marks, G. (2017). 'Cleavage Theory Meets Europe's Crises: Lipset, Rokkan, and the Transnational Cleavage', *Journal of European Public Policy* 25(1), 109–35.

Hopkins, D. and Hainmueller, J. (2014). 'Public Attitudes toward Immigration', *Annual Review of Political Science* 17, 225–49.

Horowitz, D. (2000). *Ethnic Groups in Conflict*, Berkeley: University of California Press.

Hunt, T. (2016). 'Labour's Identity Crisis: England and the Politics of Patriotism', University of Winchester, Centre for English Identity and Politics.

Husbands, C. (1983). *Racial Exclusionism and the City: The Urban Support of the National Front*, London: Routledge.

Inglehart, R. (1971). 'The Silent Revolution in Europe: Intergenerational Change in Post-Industrial Societies', *American Political Science Review* 65(4), 991–1017.

(1977). *The Silent Revolution*, Princeton: Princeton University Press.

(1990). *Culture Shift in Advanced Industrial Society*, Princeton: Princeton University Press.

(1997). *Modernization and Postmodernization*, Princeton: Princeton University Press.

Inglehart, R. and Abramson, P. R. (1994). 'Economic Security and Value Change', *American Political Science Review* 88(2), 336–54.

Inglehart, R. and Norris, P. (2003). *Rising Tide: Gender Equality and Cultural Change Around the World*, Cambridge: Cambridge University Press.

(2004). *Sacred and Secular: Religion and Politics Worldwide*, Cambridge: Cambridge University Press.

(2016). 'Trump, Brexit, and the Rise of Populism: Economic Have-nots and Cultural Backlash', available at: https://www.hks.harvard.edu/publications/trump-brexit-and-rise-populism-economic-have-nots-and-cultural-backlash.

Inglehart, R. and Welzel, C. (2005). *Modernization, Cultural Change and Democracy: The Human Development Sequence*, Cambridge: Cambridge University Press.

Ivaldi, G. (2015). 'Towards the Median Economic Crisis Voter? The New Leftist Economic Agenda of the Front national in France', *French Politics* 13(4), 346–69.

Ivarsflaten, E. (2006). 'Reputational Shields: Why Most Anti-Immigrant Parties Failed in Western Europe 1980–2005', paper presented at the American Political Science Association conference, 2006, available at: www.nuffield.ox.ac.uk/politics/papers/2006/Ivarsflatenapsa2006.pdf, last accessed 21 June 2019.

(2008). 'What Unites Right Wing Populists in Western Europe? Re-examining Grievance Models in Seven Successful Cases', *Comparative Political Studies* 41(1), 3–23.

Ivarsflaten, E., Blinder, S. and Ford, R. (2010). 'The Anti-racism Norm in West European Politics: Why We Need to Consider It and How to Measure It', *Journal of Elections, Public Opinion and Parties* 20(4), 421–44.

Jardina, A. (2019). *White Identity Politics*, Cambridge: Cambridge University Press.

Jeffries, S. (2014). 'Britain's Most Racist Election: the Story of Smethwick, 50 Years On', *The Guardian*, 14 October 2014, available at: www.theguardian.com/world/2014/oct/15/britains-most-racist-election-smethwick-50-years-on, last accessed 17 April 2019.

Jennings, W. (2009). 'The Public Thermostat, Political Responsiveness and Error Correction: Border Control and Asylum in Britain 1994–2007', *British Journal of Political Science* 39(4), 847–70.

(2017). 'Cities, Towns and the General Election of 2017, Part 1, Cities and Towns: The 2017 General Election and the Social Divisions of Place, New Economics Foundation, London.

Jennings, W. and Stoker, G. (2016). 'The Bifurcation of Politics: Two Englands', *Political Quarterly* 87(3), 372–82.

(2017). 'Tilting Towards the Cosmopolitan Axis? Political Change in England and the 2017 Election', *Political Quarterly* 88(3), 359–69.

Jivraj, S. (2012). 'How Has Ethnic Diversity Grown 1991–2001–2011?', Centre on the Dynamics of Ethnicity 'Dynamic of Diversity' series, available at: http://hummedia.manchester.ac.uk/institutes/code/brief ings/dynamicsofdiversity/how-has-ethnic-diversity-grown-1991-2001-2011.pdf, last accessed 23 April 2019.

Jobson, R. (2018). *Nostalgia and the Postwar Labour Party: Prisoners of the Past*, Manchester: Manchester University Press.

John, P., Margetts, H., Rowlands, D. and Weir, S. (2006). 'The BNP: The Roots of Its Appeal', Democratic Audit, Human Rights Centre, University of Essex.

John, P. and Margetts, H. (2009). 'The Latent Support for the Extreme Right in British Politics', *West European Politics* 32(3), 496–513.

Johns, R., Henderson, A., Carmen, C. and Larner, J. (2020). 'Brexit or Independence? Scotland's General Election', *Political Insight* 11(1), 28–31.

Johns, R., Mitchell, J. and Denver, D. (2009). 'Valence Politics in Scotland: Towards an Explanation of the 2007 Election', *Political Studies* 77(1), 207–33.

Johns, R., Mitchell, J. and Carmen, C. (2013). 'Constitution or Competence? The SNP's Re-election in 2011', *Political Studies* 61(S1), 158–78.

(2014). *More Scottish Than British? The 2011 Scottish Parliament Election*, Basingstoke: Palgrave Macmillan.

Johns, R. and Mitchell, J. (2016). *Takeover: Explaining the Extraordinary Rise of the SNP*, London: Biteback.

Johnston, C., Lavine, H. and Federico, C. (2017). *Open versus Closed: Personality, Identity and the Politics of Redistribution*, Cambridge: Cambridge University Press.

Johnston, R. (2014). 'Withering Grassroots: The Problems of Constituency Campaigning', in P. Cowley and R. Ford (eds), *Sex, Lies and the Ballot Box*, London: Biteback, 219–24.

Johnston, R. and Pattie, C. (2006). *Putting Voters in Their Place: Geography and Elections in Great Britain*, Oxford: Oxford University Press.

Jump, R. C. and Michell, J. (2019). 'Education and the Geography of Brexit', 25 June, available at: SSRN: https://ssrn.com/abstract=3411493.

Kallis, A. (2018). 'The Radical Right and Islamophobia', in J. Rydgren (ed.), *The Oxford Handbook of the Radical Right*, Oxford: Oxford University Press, 42–60.

Katz, M. B. (1989). *The Undeserving Poor: From the War on Poverty to the War on Welfare*, New York: Pantheon.

Katz, R. S. and Mair, P. (1995). 'Changing Models of Party Organization and Party Democracy: The Emergence of the Cartel Party', *Party Politics* 1(1), 5–28.

Kaufmann, E. (2016). 'It's NOT the Economy, Stupid: Brexit as a Story of Personal Values', British Politics and Policy at LSE, available at http://eprints.lse.ac.uk/71585/, last accessed 24 June 2020.

(2017). 'Levels or Changes?: Ethnic Context, Immigration and the UK Independence Party Vote', *Electoral Studies* 48, 57–69.

(2018). *Whiteshift*, London: Pelican.

Kellner, P. (2012). 'The Perilous Politics of Immigration', available at: https://yougov.co.uk/topics/politics/articles-reports/2012/12/17/perilous-politics-immigration, last accessed 30 August 2019.

Kimber, C. (2014). 'Standing up to UKIP's Racism', *Socialist Review*, available at: http://socialistreview.org.uk/391/standing-ukips-racism, last accessed 8 April 2020.

Kinder, D. and Kam, C. (2009). *Us versus Them: Ethnocentric Foundations of American Opinion*, Chicago: University of Chicago Press.

Kinder, D. and Sanders, L. (1996). *Divided by Color: Racial Politics and Democratic Ideals*, Chicago: University of Chicago Press.

Kirchheimer, O. (1957). 'The Waning of Opposition in Parliamentary Regimes', *Social Research* 24, 127–56.

(1958). 'The Party in Mass Society', *World Politics* 2, 289–94.

Kirkup, J. (2014). 'UKIP Voters Will Make Ed Miliband Prime Minister, Labour Claims', available at: www.telegraph.co.uk/news/politics/ukip/10994493/Ukip-voters-will-make-Ed-Miliband-Prime-Minister-Labour-claims.html, last accessed 17 April 2020.

Kitschelt, H. (1990), *The Transformation of European Social Democracy*, Cambridge: Cambridge University Press.

Kitschelt, H. and McGann, A. J. (1997). *The Radical Right in Western Europe: A Comparative Analysis*, Ann Arbor, MI: University of Michigan Press.

Kootstra, A. (2016). 'Deserving and Undeserving Welfare Claimants in Britain and the Netherlands: Examining the Role of Race and Ethnicity Using a Vignette Experiment', *European Sociological Review* 32(3), 325–38.

Kriesi, H. et al. (2012). *Political Conflict in Western Europe*, Cambridge: Cambridge University Press.

Kutsov, A., Laaker, D. and Reller, R. (2019). 'The Stability of Immigration Attitudes: Evidence and Implications', available at: https://papers

.ssrn.com/sol3/papers.cfm?abstract_id=3322121, last accessed 11 June 2019.

Labour Party (2017). 'Negotiating Brexit', available at: https://labour .org.uk/manifesto/negotiating-brexit, last accessed 19 September 2019.

Lancee, B. and Sarrasin, O. (2015). 'Educated Preferences or Selection Effects? A Longitudinal Analysis of the Impact of Education on Attitudes Towards Immigrants', *European Sociological Review* 31(4), 490–501.

Laniyonu, A. (2019). 'A Comparative Analysis of Racial Group Consciousness in the United States and Britain', *Journal of Race, Ethnicity and Politics* 4(1), 117–47.

Laycock, D. (2002). *The New Right and Democracy in Canada: Understanding Reform and the Canadian Alliance*, Oxford: Oxford University Press.

Laycock, S., Renwick, A., Stevens, D. and Vowles, J. (2013). 'The UK's Electoral Reform Referendum of May 2011', *Electoral Studies* 32(2), 211–14.

Layton-Henry, Z. (1992). *The Politics of Immigration: Immigration, 'Race' and 'Race' Relations in Britain*, Oxford: Blackwell.

Lebo, M. and Young, E. (2009). 'The Comparative Dynamics of Party Support in Great Britain: Conservatives, Labour and the Liberal Democrats', *Journal of Elections, Public Opinion and Parties* 19(1), 73–103.

Levy, R. (1995). 'Finding a Place in the World Economy: Party Strategy and Party Vote: the Regionalization of SNP and Plaid Cymru Support, 1979–1992', *Political Geography* 14(3), 295–308.

Lewis, V. and Kayshap, R. (2013). 'Are Muslims a Distinctive Minority? An Empirical Analysis of Religion, Social Attitudes and Islam', *Journal for the Scientific Study of Religion* 52(3): 617–26.

Lymperopoulou, K. (2015). 'The Area Determinants of the Location Choices of New Immigrants in England', *Environment and Planning A* 45(3), 575–92.

Lynch, P. (2009). 'From Social Democracy Back to No Ideology? The Scottish National Party and Ideological Change in a Multi-Level Electoral Setting', *Regional and Federal Studies* 19(4/5), 619–37.

(2015). 'Conservative Modernisation and European Integration: From Silence to Salience and Schism', *British Politics* 10(2), 185–203.

Lynch, P. and Whittaker, R. (2013). 'Rivalry on the Right: The Conservatives, UKIP and the EU Issue', *British Politics* 8(3), 285–312.

Macpherson, W. (1999). 'The Stephen Lawrence Inquiry, Report of an Inquiry by Sir William Macpherson of Cluny', February 1999, Cm 4262-I.

Mannheim, K. (1928). 'The Problem of Generations', in *Essays on the Sociology of Knowledge*, London: Routledge, 276–320.

Martin, N. (2017). 'Are British Muslims Alienated from Mainstream Politics by British Foreign Policy?', *Ethnicities* 17(3), 350–70.

  (2019). 'Ethnic Minority Voters in the UK 2015 General Election: A Breakthrough for the Conservative Party?' *Electoral Studies* 57, 174–85.

Martin, N and Mellon, J (2020). 'The Puzzle of High Political Partisanship among Ethnic Minority Young People in Great Britain', *Journal of Ethnic and Migration Studies* 46(5), 936–56.

Martin, N. and Khan, O. (2019). 'Ethnic Minority Voters at the 2017 British Election', Runnymede Trust, available at: www .runnymedetrust.org/uploads/2017%20Election%20Briefing.pdf, last accessed 12 July 2019.

Martin, N., Sobolewska, M. and Begum, N. (2019). 'Left Out of the Left Behind: Ethnic Minority Support for Brexit', University of Manchester working paper.

Martin, N. G., Eaves, L. J., Heath, A. C., Jardine, R., Feingold, L. M. and Eysenck, H. J. (1986). 'Transmission of Social Attitudes', *Proceedings of the National Academy of Sciences* 83(12), 4364–8.

Mason, R. and Asthana, A. (2017). 'Labour Would End Free Movement but Not "Sever Ties" with EU, Starmer Says', available at: www .theguardian.com/politics/2017/apr/24/labour-vows-to-rip-up-and-rethink-brexit-white-paper, last accessed 19 September 2019.

Matthews, D. (2018). *Voices of the Windrush Generation: The Real Story Told by the People Themselves*, London: Blink Publishing.

Maxwell, A. and Schulte, S. R. (2018). 'Racial Resentment Attitudes among White Millennial Youth: The Influence of Parents and Media', *Social Science Quarterly* 99(3), 1183–99.

Maxwell, R. (2012). *Ethnic Minority Migrants in Britain and France: Integration Trade-offs*, Cambridge: Cambridge University Press.

  (2019). 'Cosmopolitan Immigration Attitudes in Large European Cities: Contextual or Compositional Effects?' *American Political Science Review* 113(2), 456–74.

May, T. (2018). 'Taking Back Control of Our Borders, Money and Laws While Protecting Our Economy, Security and Union', presented by

the Prime Minister to Parliament, available at: https://assets
.publishing.service.gov.uk/government/uploads/system/uploads/
attachment_data/file/759792/28_November_EU_Exit_-_Taking_
back_control_of_our_borders__money_and_laws_while_protect
ing_our_economy__security_and_Union__1_.pdf.

Mayne, Q. and Hakhverdian, A. (2017). 'Ideological Congruence and
Citizen Satisfaction: Evidence from 25 Advanced Democracies',
Comparative Political Studies 50(6), 822–49.

McAllister, L. and Awan-Scully, R. (2019). 'For Wales, Do Not
See England? An Analysis of the 2017 General Election', *Parliamentary Affairs*.

McAnulla, S. (2010). 'Heirs to Blair's Third Way? David Cameron's
Triangulating Conservatism', *British Politics* 5(3), 286–314.

McKay, L. (2019). 'Left Behind People or Places? The Role of Local
Economies in Perceived Community Representation', *Electoral Studies* 60, 102046.

McKay, L. and Bailey, J. (2019). 'Was Brexit Really Caused by Austerity?
Here's Why We Are Not Convinced', available at: https://
theconversation.com/was-brexit-really-caused-by-austerity-heres-
why-were-not-convinced-102124, last accessed 17 April 2020.

McKenzie, L. (2017). '"It's not Ideal": Reconsidering Anger and Apathy in
the Brexit Vote Among an Invisible Working Class', *Competition and
Change* 21(3), 199–210.

McKenzie, R. (1956). *British Political Parties*, London: Heinemann.

McLaren, L. (2002). 'Public Support for the European Union: Cost–Benefit
Analysis or Perceived Cultural Threat?' *Journal of Politics* 64(2), 551–66.

(2013). 'Immigration and Perceptions of the Political System in Britain', *Political Quarterly* 84(1), 90–100.

McLean, I. (1970). 'Rise and Fall of the Scottish National Party', *Political
Studies* 18(3), 357–72.

Meesen, C., Vroome, T. and Hooghe, M. (2013). 'How Does Education
Have an Impact on Ethnocentrism? A Structural Equation Analysis
of Cognitive, Occupational Status and Network Mechanisms', *International Journal of Intercultural Relations* 14, 23–30.

Mellon, J. (2017). 'Party Attachment in Great Britain: Five Decades of
Dealignment', available at: https://papers.ssrn.com/sol3/papers
.cfm?abstract_id=2745654, last accessed 29 August 2019.

Mellors, C. (1978). The British MP: A Socio-economic Study of the House
of Commons, Farnborough: Saxon House.

Merolla, J. and Zechmeister, E. (2009). *Democracy at Risk: How Terrorist Threats Affect the Public*, Chicago: University of Chicago Press.

Migration Observatory (2016). 'Pulling Power: Why Are EU Citizens Migrating to the UK?', available at: https://migrationobservatory.ox.ac.uk/resources/commentaries/pulling-power-eu-citizens-migrating-uk, last accessed 6 August 2019.

(2018). 'Unsettled Status? Which EU Citizens Are at Risk of Failing to Secure their Rights after Brexit?', available at: https://migrationobservatory.ox.ac.uk/resources/reports/unsettled-status-which-eu-citizens-are-at-risk-of-failing-to-secure-their-rights-after-brexit.

Mooney, G. and Scott, G. (2015). 'The 2014 Scottish Independence Debate: Questions of Social Welfare and Social Justice', *Journal of Poverty and Social Justice* 23(1), 5–16.

Moreno, L. (2006). 'Dual Identities and Stateless Nations (the "Moreno Question")', *Scottish Affairs* 54, 1–21.

Morín, J. L., Macías Mejía, Y. and Sanchez, G. R. (2020). 'Is the Bridge Broken? Increasing Ethnic Attachments and Declining Party Influence among Latino Voters', *Political Research Quarterly*, 1065912919888577.

MORI (2018), 'A Review of Survey Evidence on Muslims in Britain', available at: www.ipsos.com/sites/default/files/ct/publication/documents/2018-03/a-review-of-survey-research-on-muslims-in-great-britain-ipsos-mori_0.pdf, last accessed 22 October 2019.

Moss, S. (2017). 'Labour's Angela Rayner: "Ideology Never Put Food on My Table"', Guardian Saturday Interview, available at: www.theguardian.com/politics/2017/jul/28/angela-rayner-shadow-education-secretary-interview, last accessed 20 May 2019.

Mudde, C. (2007). *Populist Radical Right Parties in Europe*, Cambridge: Cambridge University Press.

(2019). *The Far Right Today*, Chichester: John Wiley.

Mummolo, J. and Nall, C. (2017). 'Why Partisans Do Not Sort: The Constraints on Political Segregation', *Journal of Politics* 79(1), 45–59.

Murphy, J. and Devine, D. (2018). 'Does Media Coverage Drive Public Support for UKIP or Does Public Support for UKIP Drive Media Coverage?', *British Journal of Political Science* 45(3), 707–23.

Murray, C. (2016). *Becoming One of Us: Reforming the UK's Citizenship System for a Competitive, post-Brexit World*, London: IPPR.

Muttarak, R. and Heath, A. (2010). 'Who Intermarries in Britain? Explaining Ethnic Diversity in Intermarriage Patterns', *British Journal of Sociology* 61, 275–305.

Myrdal, G. (1944). *An American Dilemma: The Negro Problem and Modern Democracy*, New York: Harper & Row.

Nandi, A. and Platt, L. (2015). 'Patterns of Minority and Majority Identification in a Multicultural Society', *Ethnic and Racial Studies* 38(15), 2615–34.

Nelson, F. (2018). '"I'll Eat You Alive" – Angela Rayner Interview', available at: www.spectator.co.uk/2018/01/why-isnt-angela-rayner-a-tory, last accessed 20 May 2019.

Newman, C. (2016). 'Teen Mum Turned Labour MP: Why Angela Rayner Should Have the Tories Running Scared', available at: www.telegraph.co.uk/women/politics/teen-mum-turned-labour-mp-why-angela-rayner-should-have-the-tori/, last accessed 24 June 2020.

Norris, P. (1997). *Passages to Power*, Cambridge: Cambridge University Press.

(2006). 'Did the Media Matter? Agenda-Setting, Persuasion and Mobilization Efforts in the British General Election Campaign', *British Politics* 1, 195–221.

Norris, P. and Inglehart, R. (2019). *Cultural Backlash: Trump, Brexit, and Authoritarian Populism*, Cambridge: Cambridge University Press.

Office for National Statistics (2017). 'What's Happening with International Student Migration?' available at: www.ons.gov.uk/people populationandcommunity/populationandmigration/international migration/articles/whatshappeningwithinternationalstudentmigra tion/2017-08-24, last accessed 6 August 2019.

Oliver, C. (2016). *Unleashing Demons: The Inside Story of Brexit*, London: Hodder & Stoughton.

Olusoga, D. (2017). *Black and British: A Forgotten History*, London: Pan.

O'Grady, T. (2019). 'Careerists versus Coal-Miners: Welfare Reforms and the Substantive Representation of Social Groups in the British Labour Party', *Comparative Political Studies* 54(4), 544–78.

O'Hara, K. (2007). *After Blair: David Cameron and the Conservative Tradition*, London: Icon Books.

O'Rourke, K. (2018). *A Short History of Brexit: From Brentry to Backstop*, London: Penguin.

O'Toole, F. (2018). *Heroic Failure: Brexit and the Politics of Pain*, New York: Apollo.

Ohlander, J., Batalova, J. and Treas, J. (2005). 'Explaining Educational Influences on Attitudes toward Homosexual Relations', *Social Science Research* 34, 781–99.

Oliver, J. and Smith, D. (2010). 'Nick Clegg Nearly as Popular as Churchill', *The Sunday Times*, available at: www.thetimes.co.uk/article/nick-clegg-is-nearly-as-popular-as-winston-churchill-t9gn20hnmbm, last accessed 6 August 2019.

Osmond, J. (2017). 'Welsh Politics after the EU Referendum, *Scottish Affairs* 26(2), 212–28.

Owen, D. (1995). 'Ethnic Minorities in Britain: Patterns of Population Change 1981–1991', University of Warwick Centre for Research in Ethnic Relations 1991 Census Statistical Paper No. 10, available at: https://warwick.ac.uk/fac/soc/crer/research/publications/nemda/nemda1991sp10.pdf, last accessed 23 April 2019.

Paldam, M. (1986). 'The Distribution of Election Results and the Two Explanations of the Cost of Ruling', *European Journal of Political Economy*, 2(1), 5–24.

Paterson, L. (2006). 'Sources of Support for the SNP', in C. Bromley et al. (eds), *Has Devolution Delivered?*, Edinburgh: Edinburgh University Press.

Pattie, C. and Johnston, R. (1998). 'Voter Turnout and Constituency Marginality: Geography and Rational Choice', *Area* 30, 38–48.

(2011). 'Tactical Voting at the 2010 British General Election: Rational Behaviour in Local Contexts?', *Environment and Planning A* 37, 1191–1206.

(2017). 'Sticking to the Union? Nationalism, Inequality and Political Disaffection and the Geography of Scotland's 2014 Independence Referendum', *Regional & Federal Studies* 27(1), 83–96.

Pattie, C., Hartman, T. and Johnston, R. (2017). 'Incumbent Parties, Incumbent MPs and the Effectiveness of Constituency Campaigns: Evidence from the 2015 UK General Election', *British Journal of Politics and International Relations* 19(4), 824–41.

Pecorelli, N. (2013). *The New Electorate: Why Understanding Values is the Key to Electoral Success*, London: IPPR.

Pew Research Center (2014). 'Political Polarization in American Public', available at: www.pewresearch.org/wp-content/uploads/sites/4/2014/06/6-12-2014-Political-Polarization-Release.pdf.

Philips, C. and Bowling, B. (2017). 'Ethnicities, Racism, Crime and Criminal Justice', in A. Liebling, S. Maruna and L. McAra (eds),

Oxford Handbook of Criminology, Oxford: Oxford University Press, 190–212.

Phillips, M. and Phillips, T. (2009). *Windrush: The Irresistible Rise of Multi-Racial Britain*, London: HarperCollins.

Platt, L. and Nandi, A. (2018). 'Ethnic Diversity in the UK: New Opportunities and Changing Constraints', *Journal of Ethnic and Migration Studies*, available at: www.tandfonline.com/doi/full/10.1080/1369183X.2018.1539229, last accessed 23 April 2019.

Powell, E. (1968). Speech to the Conservative Association meeting in Birmingham, 20 April 1968, available at: www.telegraph.co.uk/comment/3643823/Enoch-Powells-Rivers-of-Blood-speech.html, last accessed 17 May 2019.

Pratto, F. and Sidanius, J. (2001). *Social Dominance: An Intergroup Theory of Hierarchy and Oppression*, Cambridge: Cambridge University Press.

Przeworski, A. (1985). *Capitalism and Social Democracy*, Cambridge: Cambridge University Press.

Przeworski, A. and Sprague, J. (1986). *Paper Stones: A History of Electoral Socialism*, Chicago: University of Chicago Press.

Pulzer, P. (1972). *Political Representation and Elections in Britain*, London: Routledge.

Rendell, M. and Salt, J. (2005). 'The Foreign Born Population', available at: https://webarchive.nationalarchives.gov.uk/20100521053049/http://www.statistics.gov.uk/downloads/theme_compendia/fom2005/08_FOPM_ForeignBorn.pdf, last accessed 17 May 2019.

Renwick, A. (2017). 'Referendums', in K. Arzheimer, J. Evans and M. Lewis-Beck (eds), *Sage Handbook of Electoral Behaviour*, London: Sage, 433–58.

Riddell, S., Blackburn, L. and Minty, S. (2015). 'Widening Access to Higher Education: Scotland in UK Comparative Perspective', paper prepared for the Scottish Government Widening Access Commission, available at: www.docs.hss.ed.ac.uk/education/creid/NewsEvents/52_v_CoWA_Paper.pdf, last accessed 15 July 2019.

Roberts, M., Ford, R. and Warren, I. (2014). 'Revolt on the Left: Labour's UKIP Problem and How it Can be Overcome', Fabian Society, available at: https://fabians.org.uk/revolt-on-the-left-labours-ukip-problem-and-how-it-can-be-overcome, last accessed 1 May 2020.

Romano, S. (2015). 'Idle Paupers, Scroungers and Shirkers: Past and New Social Stereotypes of the Undeserving Welfare Claimant in the UK', in L. Foster et al. (eds), *In Defence of Welfare*, Bristol: Policy Press, 65–8.

Rose, R. and McAllister, I. (1983). *Voters Begin to Choose: From Closed Class to Open Elections in Britain*, London: Sage.

Rutter, J. and Carter, R. (2018). 'The National Conversation on Immigration: Final Report', London: British Future and Hope Not Hate, available at: www.britishfuture.org/wp-content/uploads/2018/09/Final-report.National-Conversation.17.9.18.pdf, last accessed 1 May 2020.

Rydgren, J. (2008). 'Immigration Sceptics, Xenophobes or Racists? Radical Right-wing Voting in Six West European Countries', *European Journal of Political Research* 47(6), 737–65.

Rydgren, J. (ed.) (2018). *Oxford Handbook of the Radical Right*, Oxford: Oxford University Press.

Sabater, A. (2015). 'Between Flows and Places: Using Geodemographics to Explore EU Migration Across Neighbourhoods in Britain', *European Journal of Population* 31(2), 207–30.

Saggar, S. (1992). *Race and Politics in Britain*, London: Harvester Wheatsheaf.

(2000). *Race and Representation: Electoral Politics and Ethnic Pluralism*, Manchester: Manchester University Press.

(2001). 'The Race Card and Party Strategy: The 2001 General Election', in P. Norris (ed.), *Britain Votes 2001*, Oxford: Oxford University Press, 195–210.

(2004). *Race and Politics in Britain*, Abingdon: Routledge.

Sanders, D. (2005). 'The Political Economy of UK Party Support, 1997–2004: Forecasts for the 2005 General Election', *Journal of Elections, Public Opinion & Parties*, 15, 47–71.

Sanders, D., Heath, A., Fisher, S. and Sobolewska, M. (2014). 'The Calculus of Ethnic Minority Voting in Britain', *Political Studies* 62(2), 230–51.

Sanders, D. and Shorrocks, R. (2019). 'All in This Together? Austerity and the Gender–Age Gap in the 2015 and 2017 British General Elections', *British Journal of Politics and International Relations* 21(4), 667–88.

Sapiro, V. (2004). 'Not Your Parents' Political Socialisation: Introduction for a New Generation', *Annual Review of Political Science* 7, 1–23.

Sassoon, D. (1996). *One Hundred Years of Socialism: The West European Left in the Twentieth Century*, New York: New York University Press.

Saunders, R. (2018). *Yes to Europe! The 1975 Referendum and Seventies Britain*, Cambridge: Cambridge University Press.

Scarrow, S. (1996). *Parties and Their Members: Organising for Victory in Britain and Germany*, Oxford: Oxford University Press.

Schattschneider, E. E. (1961). *The Semi-sovereign People: A Realist's View of Democracy in America*, New York: Holt, Rinehart & Winston.

Schoen, D. (1977). *Enoch Powell and the Powellites*, Basingstoke: Macmillan.

Schofer, E. and Meyer, J. (2005). 'The Worldwide Expansion of Higher Education in the Twentieth Century', *American Sociological Review* 70(6), 898–920.

Schofield, C. (2013). *Enoch Powell and the Making of Postcolonial Britain*, Cambridge: Cambridge University Press.

Schwartz, C., Simon, M., Hudson, D. and van-Heerde-Hudson, J. (2020). 'A Populist Paradox? How Brexit Softened Anti-immigration Attitudes', *British Journal of Political Science*, in press.

Scotsman, The (2016). 'Farage Defends Breaking Point Immigration Poster', available at: www.scotsman.com/news-2-15012/nigel-farage-defends-breaking-point-immigration-poster-1-4161545, last accessed 5 August 2019.

   (2019), 'Boris Johnson Defends Comments about Veiled Muslim Women at Launch', available at: www.scotsman.com/news/politics/boris-johnson-defends-comments-about-veiled-muslim-women-at-launch-1-4946001.

Scwartz, J. (2010). 'Investigating Differences in Public Support for Gay Rights Issues', *Journal of Homosexuality* 57(6), 748–59.

Sears, D. O. and Valentino, N. A. (1997). 'Politics Matters: Political Events as Catalysts for Preadult Socialization', *American Political Science Review* 91(1), 45–65.

Seyd, P., Whitely, P. and Parry, J. (1996). *Labour and Conservative Party Members 1990–1992: Social Characteristics, Political Attitudes and Activities*, London: Dartmouth.

Seyd, P. and Whiteley, P. (2004). 'British Party Members: An Overview', *Party Politics* 10(4), 355–66.

Shaw, M. (2019). 'Vote Leave Relied on Racism. Brexit: The Uncivil War Disguised that Ugly Truth', available at: www.theguardian.com/commentisfree/2019/jan/08/vote-leave-racism-brexit-uncivil-war-channel-4, last accessed 5 August 2019.

Sherif, M., Harvey, O. J., White, B. J., Hood, W. R. and Sherif, C. W. (1961). *Intergroup Conflict and Cooperation: The Robbers Cave Experiment, Vol. 10*, Norman, OK: University Book Exchange.

Shipman, T. (2017). *All Out War: The Full Story of Brexit*, London: Collins.
(2018). *Fall Out: A Year of Political Mayhem*, London: Collins.

Shorrocks, R. (2016). 'Modernisation and Government Socialisation: Considering Explanations for Gender Differences in Cohort Trends in British Political Behaviour', *Electoral Studies* 42, 237–48.

Sides, J., Tesler, M. and Vavreck, L. (2018). *Identity Crisis: The 2016 Presidential Campaign and the Battle for the Meaning of America*, Princeton: Princeton University Press.

Skinner, G. and Gottfried, G. (2016). 'How Britain Voted in the 2016 EU Referendum', available at: www.ipsos.com/ipsos-mori/en-uk/how-britain-voted-2016-eu-referendum, last accessed 8 August 2019.

Smith, M. (2019). 'Margaret Thatcher: The Public View 40 Years On', available at: https://yougov.co.uk/topics/politics/articles-reports/2019/05/03/margaret-thatcher-public-view-40-years, last accessed 17 April 2020.

Sniderman, P., Hagendoorn, L. and Prior, M. (2004). 'Predisposing Factors and Situational Triggers: Exclusionary Reactions to Immigrant Minorities', *American Political Science Review* 98(1), 45–59.

Sniderman, P. and Hagendoorn, L. (2007). *When Ways of Life Collide: Multiculturalism and its Discontents in the Netherlands*, Princeton: Princeton University Press.

Sniderman, P., Petersen, M., Slothuus, R. and Stubager, R. (2014). *Paradoxes of Liberal Democracy: Islam, Western Europe and the Danish Cartoon Crisis*, Princeton: Princeton University Press.

Sniderman, P. and Piazza, T. (1993). *The Scar of Race*, Oxford: Oxford University Press.

Snow, S. and Jones, E. (2011). 'Immigration and the National Health Service: Putting History to the Forefront', available at: www.historyandpolicy.org/policy-papers/papers/immigration-and-the-national-health-service-putting-history-to-the-forefron, last accessed 17 May 2019.

Sobolewska, M. (2005). 'Ethnic Agenda: Relevance of Political Attitudes to Party Choice', *Journal of Elections, Public Opinion and Parties* 15(2), 197–214.

(2013). 'Party Strategies and the Descriptive Representation of Ethnic Minorities: The 2010 British General Election', *West European Politics* 36(3), 615–63.

(2016). 'More Tolerant, Yet More Divided? UK–US Parallels in the Wake of Brexit and Trump', available at: https://blogs.lse.ac.uk/politicsandpolicy/more-tolerant-yet-more-divided-uk-us-parallels-in-the-wake-of-brexit-and-trump.

(2017). 'Race, Ethnicity and Elections: From Recognizable Patterns to Generalized Theories', in K. Arzheimer, J. Evans and M. S. Lewis-Beck (eds), *Sage Handbook of Electoral Behaviour*, London: Sage, 220–40.

Sobolewska, M. and Ford, R. (2018). 'UKIP, Brexit and the Disruptive Potential of English National Identity', in M. Kenny, I. McLean and A. Paun (eds), *Governing England: English Identity and Institutions in a Changing United Kingdom*, London: British Academy, 159–86.

(2019), 'British Culture Wars? Brexit and the Future Politics of Immigration and Ethnic Diversity', *Political Quarterly*, 90, 142–54.

Somerville, W. (2007). *Immigration under New Labour*, Bristol: Policy Press.

Spencer, M. (2019). Judgment: *R. (Joint Council for the Welfare of Immigrants) v. Secretary of State for the Home Department*, available at: www.bailii.org/ew/cases/EWHC/Admin/2019/452.html, last accessed 29 July 2019.

Stacey, M. (1960). *Tradition and Change: A Study of Banbury*, Oxford: Oxford University Press.

Stenner, K. (2005). *The Authoritarian Dynamic*, New York: Cambridge University Press.

Stenner, K. and Haidt, J. (2018). 'Authoritarianism is Not a Momentary Madness but an Eternal Dynamic within Liberal Democracies', in C. Sunstein (ed.), *Can It Happen Here? Authoritarianism in America*, New York: HarperCollins, 175–220.

Stewart, H., Mason, R. and Grierson, J. (2017). 'Theresa May under Fire as Student Visa Myth Exposed', *The Guardian*, available at: www.theguardian.com/education/2017/aug/24/pressure-grows-for-immigration-targets-to-exclude-foreign-students, last accessed 6 August 2019.

Stockemer, D., Lentz, T. and Mayer, D. (2018). 'Individual Predictors of the Radical Right-wing Vote in Europe: A Meta-analysis of Articles in Peer-reviewed Journals (1995–2016)', *Government and Opposition* 53(3), 569–93.

Storm, I., Sobolewska, M. and Ford, R. (2017). 'Is Ethnic Prejudice Declining in Britain? Change in Social Distance Attitudes among Ethnic Minority and Majority Britons', *British Journal of Sociology* 68(3), 410–34.

Stubager, R. (2009). 'Education-based Group Identity and Consciousness in the Authoritarian–Libertarian Value Conflict', *European Journal of Political Research* 48(2), 204–33.

(2010). 'The Development of the Education Cleavage: Denmark as a Critical Case', *West European Politics* 33(3), 505–33.

Studlar, D. (1978). 'Policy Voting in Britain: The Coloured Immigration Issue in the 1964, 1966 and 1970 Elections', *American Science Political Review* 72, 46–64.

(1986). 'Non-White Policy Preferences, Political Participation and the Political Agenda in Britain', in Z. Layton-Henry and P. Rich (eds), *Race, Government and Politics in Britain*, Basingstoke: Macmillan, 159–86.

Sumner, W. G. ([1906] 2006). *Folkways: A Study of the Sociological Importance of Usages, Manners, Customs, Mores and Morals*, Hong Kong: Hesperides Press.

Sunstein, C. (2002). 'The Law of Group Polarization', *Journal of Political Philosophy* 10(2), 175–95.

Surridge, P. (2016). 'Education and Liberalism: Pursuing the Link', *Oxford Review of Education* 42, 146–64.

Sussell, J. (2013). 'New Support for the Big Sort Hypothesis: An Assessment of Partisan Geographic Sorting in California, 1992–2010', *Political Science & Politics* 46(4), 768–73.

Swinney, P. and Williams, M. (2016). 'The Great British Brain Drain', Centre for Cities, available at: www.centreforcities.org/wp-con tent/uploads/2016/11/16-11-18-The-Great-British-Brain-Drain.pdf, last accessed 26 April 2019.

Tajfel, H. (1970). 'Experiments in Intergroup Discrimination,' *Scientific American* 223, 96–102.

(1981). *Human Groups and Social Categories*, Cambridge: Cambridge University Press.

Taylor, A. J. (2005). 'Stanley Baldwin, Heresthetics and the Realignment of British Politics', *British Journal of Political Science* 35(3), 429–63.

Tesler, M. (2016). *Post-Racial or Most Racial? Race and Politics in the Obama Era*, Chicago: University of Chicago Press.

Tesler. M. and Sears, D. (2010). *Obama's Race: The 2008 Election and the Dream of a Post-Racial America*, Chicago: University of Chicago Press.

Thatcher, M. (1978). TV Interview for Granada 'World in Action', full transcript available at: www.margaretthatcher.org/document/ 103485, last accessed 17 May 2019.

(1995). *The Path to Power*, London: HarperCollins, 405–6.

Thomas, J. M. (2013). 'Free Riding Foreigners: The Next NHS Scandal', *The Spectator*, available at: https://www.spectator.co.uk/article/free-riding-foreigners-the-next-nhs-scandal.

Thorburn, P. (1977). 'Political Generations: The Case of Class and Party in Britain', *European Journal of Political Research* 5, 135–48.

Tilley, J. (2002). 'Political Generations and Partisanship in the UK, 1964–1997', *Journal of the Royal Statistical Society, Series A (Statistics in Society)* 165(1), 121–35.

(2005). 'Libertarian–Authoritarian Value Change in Britain 1974–2001', *Political Studies* 53(2), 442–53.

(2015). '"We Don't Do God?" Religion and Party Choice in Britain', *British Journal of Political Science* 45(4), 907–27.

Uberoi, V. and Modood, T. (2013). 'Inclusive Britishness: A Multiculturalist Advance', *Political Studies* 61(1), 23–41.

Valentino, N. A. and Brader, T. (2011). 'The Sword's Other Edge: Perceptions of Discrimination and Racial Policy Opinion after Obama', *Public Opinion Quarterly* 75(2), 201–26.

Van der Eijk, C. and Franklin, M. (2004). 'Potential for Contestation on European Matters at National Elections in Europe', in G. Marks and M. Steenbergen (eds), *European Integration and Political Conflict: Themes in European Governance*, Cambridge: Cambridge University Press, 32–50.

Van der Waal, J., Achterberg, P. and Houtman, D. (2007). 'Class Is Not Dead – It Has Been Buried Alive: Class Voting and Cultural Voting in Postwar Western Societies (1956–1990)', *Politics & Society* 35(3), 403–26.

Vargas-Silva, C. and Sumption, M. (2018). 'Net Migration to the UK', Migration Observatory briefing paper, available at: https://migrationobservatory.ox.ac.uk/resources/briefings/long-term-international-migration-flows-to-and-from-the-uk, last accessed 9 May 2019.

Vasilopoulou, S. (2016). 'British Eurosceptic Voting in 2014: Anti-EU or Anti-Government?', in J. Nielsen, and M. Franklin (eds), *The Eurosceptic 2014 European Parliament Elections*, Abingdon: Routledge, 57–81.

Vertovec, S. (2007). 'Super-diversity and its Implications', *Ethnic and Racial Studies* 30(6), 1024–54.

Voas, D. and Ling, R. (2010). 'Religion in Britain and the United States', in A. Park et al. (eds), *British Social Attitudes: 26th Report*. British Social Attitudes Survey Series, London: Sage, 65–87.

Voas, D. and Fleischmann, F. (2012). 'Islam Moves West: Religious Change in the First and Second Generations', *Annual Review of Sociology* 38, 525–45.

Warren, I. (2018). 'The Ageing of Our Towns', Centre for Towns, available at: www.centrefortowns.org/reports/the-ageing-of-our-towns, last accessed 23 April 2019.

Weakliem, D. L. (2002). 'The Effects of Education on Political Opinions: An International Study', *International Journal of Public Opinion Research* 13, 141–57.

Weiler, J. and Hetherington, M. (2009). *Authoritarianism and Polarisation in American Politics*, Cambridge: Cambridge University Press.

Wheatcroft, G. (2005). *The Strange Death of Tory England*, London: Allen Lane.

Whiteley, P., Clarke, H., Sanders, D. and Stewart, M. (2013). *Affluence, Austerity and Electoral Change in Britain*, Cambridge: Cambridge University Press.

Wiggan, J. (2017). 'Contesting the Austerity and "Welfare Reform" Narrative of the UK Government: Forging a Social Democratic Imaginary in Scotland', *International Journal of Sociology and Social Policy* 37(11/12), 639–54.

Wight, J. (2015). 'Labour's Immigration Mug Will Be a Collector's Item For Racists Up and Down the Country', available at: www.huffingtonpost.co.uk/john-wight/labour-immigration-mug_b_6964734.html, last accessed 8 April 2020.

Wilks-Heeg, S. (2009). 'The Canary in the Coalmine? Exploring the Emergence of the BNP in English Local Politics', *Parliamentary Affairs* 62(2), 377–98.

Willetts, D. (2018). *A University Education*, Oxford: Oxford University Press.

Wills, C. (2018). *Love and Strangers: An Immigrant History of Postwar Britain*, London: Penguin.

Wilson, P. (2016). 'Corbyn Sabotaged Labour's Remain Campaign. He Must Resign', available at: www.theguardian.com/commentisfree/2016/jun/26/corbyn-must-resign-inadequate-leader-betrayal, last accessed 3 September 2019.

Wintour, P., Watt, N. and Carrell, S. (2014). 'UKIP Condemned by Cross-Party Group for Running "Racist" Campaign', available at: www.theguardian.com/politics/2014/apr/28/ukip-european-election-accused-of-racism, last accessed 18 June 2019.

Wyn-Jones, R. (2019). 'Why the Future of Welsh Politics Is Likely to Be Much More Fractured and Divided than its Past', Nation-Cymru, available at: https://nation.cymru/opinion/richard-wyn-jones-brexit-wales-identity, last accessed 7 February 2020.

INDEX